ROTHMAN
SNOOKER
1985-86

Editor: Janice Hale

Queen Anne Press

A **Queen Anne Press** BOOK

© **Rothmans Publications Ltd 1985**

First published in Great Britain in 1985 by
Queen Anne Press, a division of
Macdonald & Co (Publishers) Ltd,
Maxwell House, 74 Worship Street,
London EC2A 2EN

A BPCC plc Company

Front cover photograph: Dennis Taylor (David Muscroft)

Back cover photograph: The Hexagon, Reading, home of the Rothmans Grand Prix
(Rothmans UK Ltd)

British Library Cataloguing in Publication Data

Rothmans snooker yearbook.—1985–86–
1. Snooker—Periodicals
794.7'35'05   GV900.S6

ISBN 0-356-12022-8
ISBN 0-356-12023-6 Pbk

Typeset by Acorn Bookwork, Salisbury, Wilts.

Printed and bound in Great Britain by Hazell, Watson & Viney Limited,
Member of the BPCC Group, Aylesbury, Bucks.

CONTENTS

FOREWORD
FROM ROTHMANS PUBLICATIONS LTD

It is with great pleasure that Rothmans are able to bring to you the first edition of the *Rothmans Snooker Yearbook*.

We became involved with the game through sponsorship of the Rothmans Grand Prix snooker tournament, which on its inception in 1984 was the world's richest snooker tournament. In no time at all we came to admire the strength of administration within the sport and the friendship which exists among the participants.

In Janice Hale we have managed to secure one of the sport's most knowledgeable editorial contributors. We offer our thanks to Janice, to David Vine, who introduces the Yearbook, and to the many other people who have helped us to put this publication together.

ACKNOWLEDGEMENTS

The editor would like to thank the following for their assistance in compiling this book:
Clive Everton, editor of *Snooker Scene* magazine
Julie Kane, whose statistical research has been invaluable

FOREWORD FROM DAVID VINE

The game of snooker and the people who play it at championship level have given us over the last few years some of the most compelling and the most honest moments of excitement and emotion that sport is capable of producing.

'Sporting Theatre' is a phrase now widely used when you discuss the fascination of the coloured balls moving around the famous green baize, coupled with the contrast between the two contestants: in play – the aggressor, planning his next shot, commanding the stage; in the wings, in that chair in the corner that can become the loneliest place in the world – the defender, unable to do anything but sit and stare, waiting for the mistake that lets him in. Spellbinding if you are watching it all unfold on television – and snooker does attract television's biggest and most consistent audience – but heartbreaking if you are still sitting in that chair as the last black rolls slowly into the pocket a few inches from your eyes.

Only a few years ago, this drama was going on only a few times a year in front of tiny audiences with no television cameras anywhere near. I remember conducting some street interviews as we attempted to compile a list of 'the top ten sportsmen you most like to watch'. Not one snooker player was mentioned. If I did the same job today, I know that every person questioned would include at least one, if not several, in their list. The charisma of Dennis Taylor, the dedication of Steve Davis, the flair of Alex Higgins and Jimmy White, the generalship of Ray Reardon . . . the list goes on.

One journalist who, in little more than ten years, has seen the sport grow into one of television's biggest attractions is Janice Hale, snooker correspondent of the *Daily Telegraph* and the *Observer*. She is responsible for assembling the comprehensive career records and other facts and figures which will make this book a snooker 'Wisden'. *Rothmans Snooker Yearbook*, with which I am delighted to be associated, will provide, I am sure, not only a mass of argument-settling information but the definitive record of snooker's players and events.

THE RANKING LIST

As both the number of snooker professionals and the number of tournaments have expanded, the game's governing body, the World Professional Billiards and Snooker Association, have had to devise some form of ranking list, not only to quantify the standings of the players but also to enable them to seed tournaments. Without a seeding system, it would be possible for the best two players in the world to meet in the first round or even, highly provident as it would be, for all the best players to be in one half of the draw and all those of poorer standard in the other.

The ranking list which will be in operation for the whole of next season is based on performances in all the professional tournaments and/or championships which are open to all professionals. Where an event has been in existence with that qualification for three years or more, then the last three years count. Where the tournament is new, or comparatively new, only the previous one or two years count.

For five of the six ranking tournaments (the Jameson International, Rothmans Grand Prix, Coral UK Open, Mercantile Credit Classic and Dulux British Open), five points are awarded to the winner, four to the runner-up, three to losing semi-finalists, two to losing quarter-finalists and one to losers in the last 16. The Embassy World Championship, the sport's blue riband event, carries double points with ten for the champion down to two for losers in the last 16. Losers in the last 32 do not receive a point.

To separate players who tie on ranking points, merit points have also been introduced to the system for performances in earlier rounds, but these are taken into account only where there has been an equal opportunity to earn them.

Players ranked from 1–16, until last season, have been exempted in many tournaments from having to play until the last 32, but for the 1985–86 season, for all events except the World Championship, they will be exempted only until the last 64 where they will be joined by those ranked 17–32 and 32 qualifiers. The World Championship will remain in its present format, with the top 16 exempted until the last 32 – the first round at Sheffield's Crucible Theatre. After next year's World Championship, the world ranking list for the 1986–87 season will be compiled but will only include the previous *two* season's performances not *three* as it does now.

NB Number 13, Silvino Francisco, was fined 2 world ranking points for his part in incidents during the Dulux British Open final.

WORLD RANKING LIST 1985

	JAMESON			PPT/ROTHMANS			CORAL	LADA/MCC		DULUX	WORLD			TOTAL	MERIT POINTS
	1982	1983	1984	1982	1983	1984	1985	1984	1985	1985	1983	1984	1985		
1 S. Davis	2	5	5	–		3	5	5	3	3	10	10	8	59	1½
2 C. Thorburn	1	4	0	1	2	4	3	0	4	1	8	4	4	36	2
3 A. Knowles	5	1	4		5	2	2	2	0	1	6	0	6	34	2
4 Dennis Taylor	2	1	2	1	0	5	1	0	1	2	2	6	10	32	1½
5 K. Stevens	3	0	0	5	2	2	3	2	2	4	4	6	2	29	2
6 R. Reardon	1	1	2	4	1	1	2	0	1	0	2	4	6	26	2
7 J. White	1	0	1				2	1	1	0	0	8	4	23	2
8 T. Griffiths	2	3	1	2	1	0	0	2	2	0	2	4	4	23	1½
9 A. Higgins	1	0	2		0		4	1	1	3	6	0	2	20	1½
10 T. Meo	0	0	1	1	3	1	1	4	0	2	4	0	2	19	3
11 W. Thorne	0	2	2		3	1	2		5	0	2	2	2	19	3½
12 E. Charlton	0	3	0	3	1	1	1	2	0	0	4	2	0	19	1½
13 S. Francisco	–	2	3	–		1	0	1		5		2	2	15	7
14 David Taylor	4	0	1				1	0	0	0	2	2	2	13	1½
15 D. Mountjoy	0	2	0	0	0	2	1	0	0	0	2	4	2	13	½
16 J. Johnson	0	–	1	2	4		0		3	0	0		0	11	6
17 B. Werbeniuk	1	0	0	2		0		0	0	0	4	2	2	11	1
18 J. Parrott	–	–	0	–			0	3	0		–	2	4	9	4½
19 J. Virgo	3	0	1	3		0	0	0	2	0	0	0	0	9	4½
20 J. Spencer	1	2	0	1		0		1	0	2	2	2	0	9	1½
21 E. Hughes	–	–	3	0	2		1		1	0		0	0	8	6
22 C. Wilson	2	0	0	1	1		0	0	1			0	0	6	4½
23 N. Foulds	–	–		–	0	3	0		0		–	2	0	5	3½
24 D. Reynolds	1	–		2		2	0		0			0	0	5	6
25 M. Wildman	–	–	0	1	1		0	3	0			0	0	5	4½

	...	5
26 M. Macleod		5
27 R. Williams		7
28 M. Hallett		6½
29 D. Martin		3½
30 P. Mans		½
31 J. Campbell		4½
32 D. O'Kane		2
33 P. Fagan		2
34 S. Newbury		1
35 W. King		2
36 G. Miles		4
37 S. Longworth		1
38 E. Sinclair		3½
39 M. Gauvreau		2½
40 M. Bradley		½
41 G. Scott		2
42 M. Watterson		2
43 M. Morra		1½
44 R. Chaperon		½
45 C. Roscoe		1
46 J. Donnelly		½
47 I. Williamson		½

Remaining rankings based on merit points and/or World Championship performance:
48 J. Meadowcroft (3); 49 W. Jones (2); 50 T. Jones (2); 51 R. Edmonds (2); 52 J. Wych (2); 53 L. Dodd (2); 54 M. Fisher (2); 55 D. Fowler (1½); 56 F. Davis (1); 57 I. Black (1); 58 T. Murphy (1); 59 P. Francisco (½); 60 P. Medati (½); 61 P. Browne (½); 62 R. Foldvari (½); 63 E. McLaughlin (½); 64 J. Dunning (½); 65 V. Harris (½); 66 B. Harris (½); 67 John Rea (½); 68 T. Chappel (½); 69 J. McLaughlin (½); 70 S. Duggan (½); 71 B. Kelly (½); 72 F. Jonik (½); 73 C. Everton (½); 74 J. Fitzmaurice (½); 75 P. Morgan (½); 76 Jack Rea (½); 77 G. Rigitano; 78 G. Foulds; 79 D. Chalmers; 80 J. Van Rensberg; 81 M. Gibson; 82 B. Mikkelsen; 83 M. Hines; 84 I. Anderson; 85 B. Oliver; 86 P. Burke; 87 J. Caggianello; 88 D. Hughes; 89 G. Cripsey; 90 A. Kearney; 91 M. Parkin; 92 B. Demarco; 93 P. Watchorn; 94 B. Bennett; 95 D. Mienie; 96 D. Greaves; 97 M. Darrington; 98 L. Heywood; 99 D. Sheehan; 100 R. Bales; 101 J. Giannaros; 102 J. Hargreaves.

MONEY LIST

		Langs	Jameson	Rothmans	Coral	Hofmeister	Mercantile
1	S. Davis	10,000	30,000	15,000	20,000	5,625	12,800
2	Dennis Taylor	–	4,300	45,000	2,000	1,500	2,000
3	C. Thorburn	1,500	1,350	27,000	6,750	9,375	24,000
4	A. Higgins	3,000	4,300	2,000	12,000	17,250	3,750
5	A. Knowles	3,000	18,000	6,500	3,000	5,625	2,000
6	J. White	6,000	4,300	2,000	3,000	17,250	3,750
7	W. Thorne	–	4,300	3,500	3,000	9,375	40,000
8	S. Francisco	–	10,125	3,500	1,000	1,500	2,000
9	K. Stevens	1,500	1,350	6,500	6,750	2,812	3,750
10	R. Reardon	–	3,000	3,500	3,000	2,812	6,000
11	T. Meo	–	3,000	3,500	2,000	5,625	2,000
12	T. Griffiths	1,500	3,000	1,000	1,000	2,812	6,000
13	D. Mountjoy	–	1,350	6,500	2,000	1,500	2,000
14	E. Hughes	–	10,125	1,000	1,000	750	3,750
15	J. Spencer	–	1,350	1,000	1,000	5,625	2,000
16	E. Charlton	–	1,350	3,500	2,000	1,500	2,000
17	David Taylor	–	3,000	3,500	2,000	2,812	2,000
18	J. Johnson	–	3,000	2,000	2,000	750	12,800
19	N. Foulds	–	1,350	15,000	500	750	1,000
20	M. Macleod	1,500	1,350	2,000	1,000	–	3,750
21	J. Virgo	–	3,000	2,000	500	2,812	6,000
22	J. Parrott	–	675	2,000	1,000	2,812	1,000
23	B. Werbeniuk	–	1,350	1,000	1,000	1,500	2,000
24	D. O'Kane	–	1,350	1,000	150	1,500	–
25	D. Reynolds	–	1,350	6,500	500	1,500	1,000
26	M. Hallett	–	675	3,500	1,000	2,812	2,000
27	R. Williams	–	1,350	2,000	2,000	1,500	3,750
28	C. Wilson	–	675	2,000	2,000	750	3,750
29	W. King	–	–	1,000	1,000	750	6,000
30	G. Miles	–	675	2,000	500	1,500	1,000
	D. Martin	–	675	2,000	500	750	1,000
32	S. Newbury	–	3,000	1,000	150	750	1,000
33	J. Campbell	–	1,350	2,000	1,000	750	1,000
34	S. Longworth	–	–	–	150	–	3,750
35	M. Gauvreau	–	3,000	1,000	1,000	750	2,000
36	M. Wildman	–	675	2,000	500	1,500	1,000
37	T. Jones	–	150	2,000	1,000	1,500	1,000
38	E. Sinclair	–	1,350	–	500	–	1,000
39	D. Fowler	–	1,350	1,000	1,000	750	1,000
40	P. Fagan	–	–	–	–	–	2,000
41	M. Bradley	–	150	1,000	500	750	–
42	W. Jones	–	1,350	1,000	–	1,500	150
43	J. Donnelly	–	–	1,000	500	750	1,000
44	P. Medati	–	–	1,000	–	750	2,000
45	R. Chaperon	–	–	1,000	–	–	–
46	T. Murphy	–	–	1,000	1,000	2,812	–
47	P. Francisco	–	–	2,000	150	1,500	–
48	R. Bales	–	675	1,000	150	1,500	1,000
49	R. Edmonds	–	–	–	–	750	1,000
50	D. Chalmers	–	150	1,000	–	750	–

B & H Masters	National Championship	Dulux British Open	Guinness World Cup	B & H Irish Masters	World	Total £
3,843	17,500	17,500	8,333	6,900	35,000	182,501
3,843	7,500	9,000	13,333	2,400	60,000	150,876
37,500	–	4,625	2,500	4,100	10,000	128,700
8,250	4,500	17,500	13,333	10,000	5,250	101,133
3,843	9,375	4,625	8,333	6,900	20,000	91,201
12,000	2,750	2,000	4,166	17,250	10,000	84,466
3,843	1,500	2,000	4,166	–	2,500	74,184
–	–	50,000	2,500	–	2,500	73,125
3,843	–	30,000	2,500	4,100	5,250	68,356
8,250	1,500	2,000	4,166	2,400	20,000	56,628
8,250	5,625	9,000	8,333	2,400	5,250	54,983
12,000	6,000	2,000	4,166	2,400	10,000	51,878
21,000	3,750	750	4,166	–	5,250	48,266
–	2,000	9,000	13,333	4,100	2,500	47,558
8,250	750	2,000	4,166	–	2,500	28,641
3,843	–	750	2,500	4,100	5,250	26,793
3,843	2,750	750	–	–	5,250	25,906
–	1,500	750	–	–	2,500	25,300
–	1,500	2,000	–	–	2,500	24,600
–	3,000	4,625	2,500	–	2,500	22,225
–	2,750	2,000	–	–	2,500	21,562
–	1,500	2,000	–	–	10,000	20,987
3,843	–	750	2,500	–	5,250	19,193
–	–	9,000	2,500	–	2,500	18,500
–	2,750	2,000	–	–	2,500	18,100
–	1,500	2,000	–	–	2,500	15,987
–	1,500	750	–	–	2,500	15,350
–	1,500	750	–	–	1,500	12,925
–	–	750	2,500	–	750	12,750
–	750	4,625	–	–	1,500	12,550
–	1,500	4,625	–	–	1,500	12,550
–	375	4,625	–	–	1,500	12,400
–	–	750	2,500	–	2,500	11,850
–	5,625	2,000	–	–	150	11,675
–	–	750	–	–	1,500	10,000
–	750	2,000	–	–	1,500	9,925
–	750	750	–	–	2,500	9,650
–	2,000	750	2,500	–	1,500	9,600
–	750	2,000	–	–	1,500	9,350
–	2,000	–	–	–	5,250	9,250
–	750	4,625	–	–	750	8,525
–	–	2,000	–	–	2,500	8,500
–	750	–	2,500	–	750	7,250
–	1,500	–	–	–	1,500	6,750
–	–	4,625	–	–	750	6,375
–	750	750	–	–	–	6,312
–	–	750	–	–	1,500	5,900
–	–	750	–	–	–	5,075
–	–	750	–	–	2,500	5,000
–	750	750	–	–	1,500	4,900

		Langs	Jameson	Rothmans	Coral	Hofmeister	Mercantile
51	G. Foulds	–	675	–	150	750	1,000
52	G. Scott	–	–	–	500	–	2,000
53	M. Morra	–	675	1,000	500	750	250
54	L. Dodd	–	1,350	–	500	750	250
55	John Rea	–	–	2,000	500	–	–
56	P. Browne	–	150	–	150	750	2,000
57	I. Williamson	–	150	3,500	–	–	250
58	T. Chappel	–	–	1,000	1,000	750	–
59	R. Foldvari	–	150	–	150	–	2,000
	C. Roscoe	–	675	1,000	–	750	250
61	M. Fisher	–	–	–	500	1,500	250
	V. Harris	–	–	1,000	–	750	–
63	B. Oliver	–	150	1,000	–	1,500	–
64	J. McLaughlin	–	150	1,000	1,000	750	250
65	G. Rigitano	–	–	1,000	–	–	–
66	F. Davis	–	675	–	–	750	250
67	P. Watchorn	–	–	1,000	150	750	250
68	J. Fitzmaurice	–	–	–	500	750	250
69	M. Gibson	–	150	–	150	–	–
70	E. McLaughlin	–	–	1,000	–	–	1,000
71	J. Rempe	–	–	–	–	–	–
72	J. Meadowcroft	–	675	–	–	750	250
73	I. Black	–	675	–	–	–	–
	P. Mans	–	675	1,000	500	–	–
75	S. Duggan	–	150	1,000	–	–	250
	J. Dunning	–	150	2,000	–	–	–
77	B. Harris	–	–	–	–	–	–
78	P. Burke	–	150	1,000	–	–	–
	D. Sheehan	–	–	1,000	–	750	150
80	G. Cripsey	–	150	–	150	750	–
	A. Kearney	–	–	–	–	750	150
82	M. Watterson	–	–	–	–	750	250
	B. Demarco	–	–	1,000	–	–	–
88	D. Hughes	–	–	–	–	750	–
85	J. Wych	–	–	–	–	–	–
86	B. Bennett	–	675	–	–	–	–
	B. Kelly	–	675	–	–	–	–
88	C. Everton	–	–	1,000	–	–	–
89	J. Hargreaves	–	150	–	150	–	150
90	B. Mikkelsen	–	150	–	–	–	150
91	J. Giannaros	–	–	–	–	–	250
92	F. Jonik	–	150	–	–	–	–
93	M. Darrington	–	–	–	–	–	–
	D. French	–	–	–	–	–	–
	Jack Rea	–	–	–	–	–	–
	J. Van Rensberg	–	–	–	–	–	–
97	I. Anderson	–	–	–	–	–	–
	Mike Hines	–	–	–	–	–	–

B & H Masters	National Championship	Dulux British Open	Guinness World Cup	B & H Irish Masters	World	Total £
–	750	–	–	–	1,500	4,825
–	750	750	–	–	750	4,750
–	–	–	–	–	1,500	4,675
–	750	–	–	–	750	4,350
–	1,000	750	–	–	–	4,250
–	150	–	–	–	750	3,950
–	–	–	–	–	–	3,900
–	375	750	–	–	–	3,875
–	–	750	–	–	750	3,800
–	375	–	–	–	750	3,800
–	750	–	–	–	750	3,750
–	–	2,000	–	–	–	3,750
–	–	750	–	–	–	3,400
–	150	–	–	–	–	3,300
–	–	750	–	–	1,500	3,250
–	–	–	–	–	1,500	3,175
–	150	750	–	–	–	3,050
–	750	–	–	–	750	3,000
–	1,000	750	–	–	750	2,800
–	750	–	–	–	–	2,750
–	–	–	2,500	–	–	2,500
–	–	–	–	–	750	2,425
–	750	–	–	–	750	2,175
–	–	–	–	–	–	2,175
–	750	–	–	–	–	2,150
–	–	–	–	–	–	2,150
–	–	2,000	–	–	–	2,000
–	750	–	–	–	–	1,900
–	–	–	–	–	–	1,900
–	750	–	–	–	–	1,800
–	150	750	–	–	–	1,800
–	–	–	–	–	750	1,750
–	750	–	–	–	–	1,750
–	750	–	–	–	150	1,650
–	–	–	–	–	1,500	1,500
–	–	750	–	–	–	1,425
–	750	–	–	–	–	1,425
–	375	–	–	–	–	1,375
–	–	750	–	–	–	1,200
–	–	750	–	–	–	1,050
–	–	750	–	–	–	1,000
–	–	750	–	–	–	900
–	750	–	–	–	–	750
–	–	750	–	–	–	750
–	750	–	–	–	–	750
–	–	–	–	–	750	750
–	–	–	–	–	150	150
–	–	–	–	–	150	150

THE GROWTH OF SNOOKER 1976 TO 1985

Total network television hours UK
1976–1984 BBC/ITV

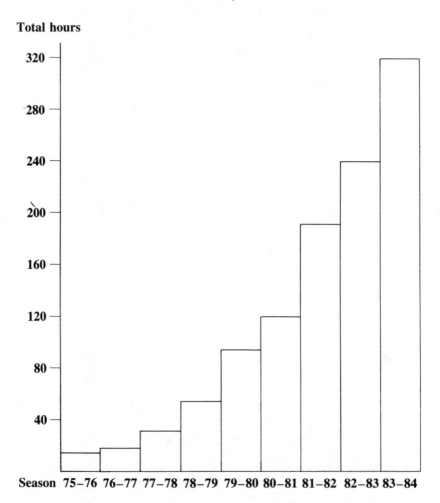

Total hours

Season 75–76 76–77 77–78 78–79 79–80 80–81 81–82 82–83 83–84

Figures supplied by BBC & ITV

Highest audience to date: BBC TV – Embassy World Championship at midnight on 28.4.85 18.5 million viewers. These are the highest viewing figures for any sporting event, the largest audience recorded after midnight by any British TV company, and a record audience for BBC2.

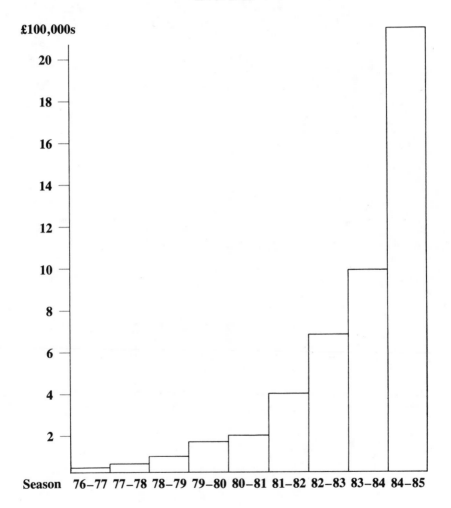

**Tournament prize funds
1976–1985**

Figures supplied by Snooker Scene

THE PLAYERS

THE PLAYERS

IAN ANDERSON (Australia)

Born 2.4.46
Turned professional 1974
World ranking 84

Although he regularly travels to Britain to compete in the Embassy World Professional Championship, Anderson has never qualified for the later stages although his voice is heard from Sheffield as he frequently summarises for the BBC. He also appeared on television when he was a member of Australia's State Express World Team Classic trio in 1980, 1981 and 1982.

1974	v Mans	1-8	1st round	World Professional Championship
1975	v Condo	15-8	1st round	World Professional Championship
	v Williams	4-15	2nd round	World Professional Championship
1976	v Jack Rea	5-8	Qualifying	Embassy World Professional Championship
1979	v S. Davis	1-9	Prelim	Embassy World Professional Championship
1981	v Martin	3-9	Qualifying	Embassy World Professional Championship
1982	v Houlihan	5-9	Qualifying	Embassy World Professional Championship
	v Sinclair	2-5	Qualifying	Jameson International
	v David Taylor	1-5	1st round	Professional Players Tournament
1983	v King	6-10	Qualifying	Embassy World Professional Championship
	v Oliver	9-1	Qualifying	Coral UK Championship
	v Dunning	2-9	Qualifying	Coral UK Championship
1984	v Watson	10-4	Qualifying	Embassy World Professional Championship
	v Donnelly	6-10	Qualifying	Embassy World Professional Championship
1985	v Kearney	10-8	Qualifying	Embassy World Professional Championship
	v Browne	5-10	Qualifying	Embassy World Professional Championship

ROGER BALES (England)

Born 15.8.48
Turned professional 1984
World ranking 100

A Birmingham casino manager, Bales twice reached the first round of a major tournament in his first professional season but in both the Rothmans Grand Prix and the Dulux British Open he lost to Alex Higgins.

1984	v Sheehan	5-2	Qualifying	Jameson International
	v Murphy	5-4	Qualifying	Jameson International
	v Fisher	5-3	Qualifying	Jameson International
	v Reynolds	4-5	Qualifying	Jameson International
	v Higgins	1-5	1st round	Rothmans Grand Prix

	v Chalmers	9-2	Qualifying	Coral UK Open
	v E. McLaughlin	9-4	Qualifying	Coral UK Open
	v Gauvreau	8-9	Qualifying	Coral UK Open
	v Bennett	5-1	Qualifying	Mercantile Credit Classic
	v Kelly	5-3	Qualifying	Mercantile Credit Classic
	v Virgo	1-5	Qualifying	Mercantile Credit Classic
1985	v Dodd	3-9	Qualifying	Tolly Cobbold English Professional Championship
	v Black	6-4	Qualifying	Dulux British Open
	v Higgins	3-6	1st round	Dulux British Open
	v Chaperon	7-0	Qualifying	Embassy World Professional Championship

JOHN BEAR (Canada)

Born 8.8.50
Turned professional 1979
World ranking unranked

Bear's best performance as a professional was to reach the first round of the Embassy World Professional Championship in 1982 when he lost 10-7 to his fellow Canadian Bill Werbeniuk. He has not competed in a major tournament since he failed to survive his first world championship qualifying match in 1983.

1980	v Wych	5-9	Qualifying	Embassy World Professional Championship
1982	v Jonik	9-4	Qualifying	Embassy World Professional Championship
	v Wych	9-4	Qualifying	Embassy World Professional Championship
	v Werbeniuk	7-10	1st round	Embassy World Professional Championship
1983	v Medati	7-10	Qualifying	Embassy World Professional Championship

BERNARD BENNETT (England)

Born 31.8.31
Turned professional 1968
World ranking 94

Bennett is a Southampton businessman who owns three Snooker centres.

1969	v Williams	11-38	Quarter-final	World Professional Championship
1970	v David Taylor	8-11	1st round	World Professional Championship
1972	v Miles	6-15	Qualifying	World Professional Championship
1973	v Greaves	8-9	1st round	World Professional Championship
1974	v Simpson	8-2	1st round	World Professional Championship
	v Higgins	4-15	2nd round	World Professional Championship
1976	v Jack Rea	5-8	Qualifying	Embassy World Professional Championship
1977	v Thorne	4-11	Qualifying	Embassy World Professional Championship
	v Thorne	1-5	1st round	Super Crystalate Championship

1978	v Parkin	4-9	Prelim	World Professional Championship
	v Thorne	4-9	Qualifying	Coral UK Championship
1979	v Griffiths	2-9	Prelim	Embassy World Professional Championship
	v Jack Rea	8-9	1st round	Coral UK Championship
1980	v Hallett	4-9	Qualifying	Coral UK Championship
1981	v Wildman	3-9	Qualifying	John Courage English Professional Championship
	v Dunning	6-9	Qualifying	Embassy World Professional Championship
	v Fitzmaurice	1-5	Qualifying	Jameson International
	v Watterson	4-9	Qualifying	Coral UK Championship
1982	v French	3-9	Qualifying	Embassy World Professional Championship
	v M. Owen	5-2	Qualifying	Jameson International
	v Wych	0-5	Qualifying	Jameson International
	v Meadowcroft	4-5	1st round	Professional Players Tournament
	v Medati	1-9	Qualifying	Coral UK Championship
1983	v Meadowcroft	3-10	Qualifying	Embassy World Professional Championship
	v Donnelly	1-5	Qualifying	Jameson International
	v Demarco	5-4	Qualifying	Jameson International
	v Wilson	1-5	1st round	Professional Players Tournament
	v Macleod	0-9	Qualifying	Coral UK Championship
1984	v Watterson	5-10	Qualifying	Embassy World Professional Championship
	v Demarco	5-1	Qualifying	Jameson International
	v N. Foulds	0-5	Qualifying	Jameson International
	v Oliver	3-5	Qualifying	Rothmans Grand Prix
	v John Rea	5-9	Qualifying	Coral UK Open
	v Bales	1-5	Qualifying	Mercantile Credit Classic
1985	v Cripsey	0-9	Qualifying	Tolly Cobbold English Professional Championship
	v Martin	0-6	1st round	Dulux British Open
	v Medati	4-10	Qualifying	Embassy World Professional Championship

IAN BLACK (Scotland)

Born 11.12.54
Turned professional 1981
World ranking 57

Scottish professional champion in 1981 and runner-up the following year, Black was a regular member of Scotland's World Cup team in 1982 and 1983.

1981	v Macleod	5-4	Quarter-final	Scottish Professional Championship
	v E. McLaughlin	6-3	Semi-final	Scottish Professional Championship
	v Gibson	**11-7**	**Final**	**Scottish Professional Championship**
	v E. McLaughlin	5-3	Qualifying	Jameson International
	v Houlihan	4-9	Qualifying	Coral UK Championship
1982	v Parkin	9-6	Qualifying	Embassy World Professional Championship
	v Williams	2-9	Qualifying	Embassy World Professional Championship
	v Macleod	6-0	Quarter-final	Scottish Professional Championship
	v Ross	6-4	Semi-final	Scottish Professional Championship

	v Sinclair	7-11	Final	Scottish Professional Championship
	v Fitzmaurice	3-5	Qualifying	Jameson International
	v Virgo	2-5	1st round	Professional Players Tournament
	v Fisher	3-9	Qualifying	Coral UK Championship
1983	v Morra	10-9	Qualifying	Embassy World Professional Championship
	v Medati	10-4	Qualifying	Embassy World Professional Championship
	v Mans	3-10	1st round	Embassy World Professional Championship
	v E. McLaughlin	6-4	1st round	Scottish Professional Championship
	v Macleod	2-6	Semi-final	Scottish Professional Championship
	v King	3-5	Qualifying	Jameson International
	v Spencer	2-5	1st round	Professional Players Tournament
	v Williamson	9-6	Qualifying	Coral UK Championship
	v White	1-9	1st round	Coral UK Championship
1984	v Hines	5-10	Qualifying	Embassy World Professional Championship
	v Browne	5-4	Qualifying	Jameson International
	v Watterson	5-3	Qualifying	Jameson International
	v Macleod	3-5	Qualifying	Jameson International
	v P. Francisco	4-5	Qualifying	Rothmans Grand Prix
	v Chappel	3-9	Qualifying	Coral UK Open
	v J. McLaughlin	0-5	Qualifying	Mercantile Credit Classic
1985	v Bales	4-6	Qualifying	Dulux British Open
	v Chalmers	4-10	Qualifying	Embassy World Professional Championship

MALCOLM BRADLEY (England)

Born 8.7.48
Turned professional 1984
World ranking 40

Formerly co-proprietor of the North Midland Snooker Centre in Worksop, Bradley sold out his share on turning professional and had an encouraging first season, picking up one world ranking point for reaching the last 16 of the Dulux British Open.

He also reached the first round of the Rothmans Grand Prix and the Tolly Cobbold English Professional Championship.

	v Darrington	5-3	Qualifying	Jameson International
	v Jack Rea	5-2	Qualifying	Jameson International
	v Morra	3-5	Qualifying	Jameson International
	v Jonik	5-1	Qualifying	Rothmans Grand Prix
	v Virgo	0-5	1st round	Rothmans Grand Prix
	v V. Harris	9-8	Qualifying	Coral UK Open
	v Kelly	9-6	Qualifying	Coral UK Open
	v Meadowcroft	9-7	Qualifying	Coral UK Open
	v Hallett	8-9	Qualifying	Coral UK Open
	v Browne	3-5	Qualifying	Mercantile Credit Classic
1985	v Williamson	9-8	Qualifying	Tolly Cobbold English Professional Championship
	v Knowles	8-9	Qualifying	Tolly Cobbold English Professional Championship

v Morra	6-2	Qualifying	Dulux British Open
v David Taylor	6-3	1st round	Dulux British Open
v Fowler	5-4	2nd round	Dulux British Open
v S. Davis	2-5	3rd round	Dulux British Open
v Mienie	10-4	Qualifying	Embassy World Professional Championship
v Mikkelsen	10-9	Qualifying	Embassy World Professional Championship
v Wych	7-10	Qualifying	Embassy World Professional Championship

PADDY BROWNE (Republic of Ireland)

Born 1.4.65
Turned professional 1983
World ranking 61

Republic of Ireland amateur champion in 1982, Browne beat Graham Miles, then ranked 32nd in the world, to reach the first round of the Mercantile Credit Classic – his best tournament performance to date.

1983 v Murphy	2-5	Qualifying	Professional Players Tournament
1984 v Duggan	10-9	Qualifying	Embassy World Professional Championship
v Roscoe	10-4	Qualifying	Embassy World Professional Championship
v Sinclair	1-10	Qualifying	Embassy World Professional Championship
v John Rea	5-2	Qualifying	Jameson International
v Black	4-5	Qualifying	Jameson International
v Duggan	2-5	Qualifying	Rothmans Grand Prix
v G. Foulds	9-5	Qualifying	Coral UK Open
v King	5-9	Qualifying	Coral UK Open
v Bradley	5-3	Qualifying	Mercantile Credit Classic
v Everton	5-0	Qualifying	Mercantile Credit Classic
v Miles	5-3	Qualifying	Mercantile Credit Classic
v White	2-5	1st round	Mercantile Credit Classic
1985 v Newbury	0-6	Qualifying	Dulux British Open
v Murphy	3-6	Qualifying	Irish Professional Championship
v Anderson	10-5	Qualifying	Embassy World Professional Championship
v Morra	6-10	Qualifying	Embassy World Professional Championship

PASCAL BURKE (Republic of Ireland)

Born 19.6.32
Turned professional 1982
World ranking 86

Burke was twice Republic of Ireland amateur champion and a world amateur semi-finalist in 1974 before turning professional.

1983 v E. Hughes	2-6	Quarter-final	Irish Professional Championship
v Meo	0-5	1st round	Benson & Hedges Irish Masters
v Morgan	9-10	Qualifying	Embassy World Professional Championship
v G. Foulds	2-5	Qualifying	Jameson International
v G. Foulds	5-4	Qualifying	Professional Players Tournament

	v Johnson	3-5	1st round	Professional Players Tournament
1984	v Kelly	10-7	Qualifying	Embassy World Professional Championship
	v B. Harris	10-4	Qualifying	Embassy World Professional Championship
	v Hallett	5-10	Qualifying	Embassy World Professional Championship
	v Kearney	5-4	Qualifying	Jameson International
	v Newbury	0-5	Qualifying	Jameson International
	v Darrington	5-3	Qualifying	Rothmans Grand Prix
	v Meo	1-5	1st round	Rothmans Grand Prix
	v Longworth	4-9	Qualifying	Coral UK Open
	v Newbury	1-5	Qualifying	Mercantile Credit Classic
1985	v Chalmers	5-6	Qualifying	Dulux British Open
	v Kearney	6-4	Qualifying	Irish Professional Championship
	v Higgins	0-6	Quarter-final	Irish Professional Championship
	v Newbury	3-10	Qualifying	Embassy World Professional Championship

JOE CAGGIANELLO (Canada)

Born 16.5.55
Turned professional 1983
World ranking 87

	v Darrington	10-7	Qualifying	Embassy World Professional Championship
1984	v Oliver	7-10	Qualifying	Embassy World Professional Championship

JOHN CAMPBELL (Australia)

Born 10.4.53
Turned professional 1982
World ranking 31

Campbell is a former Australian amateur champion, whose most successful tournament so far has been the 1983 Professional Players Tournament, in which he beat Doug Mountjoy, Graham Miles and Dave Martin to reach the quarter-finals where he lost 5-3 to Tony Knowles, the eventual winner.

For the past two seasons, he has been a member of Australia's World Cup team but lost to his captain, Eddie Charlton, in the first round of the 1985 Embassy World Championship.

	v Watterson	10-6	Qualifying	Embassy World Professional Championship
1983	v Donnelly	10-2	Qualifying	Embassy World Professional Championship
	v Thorburn	5-10	1st round	Embassy World Professional Championship
	v E. McLaughlin	2-5	Qualifying	Jameson International
	v Mountjoy	5-3	1st round	Professional Players Tournament
	v Miles	5-2	2nd round	Professional Players Tournament
	v Martin	5-0	3rd round	Professional Players Tournament
	v Knowles	3-5	Quarter-final	Professional Players Tournament

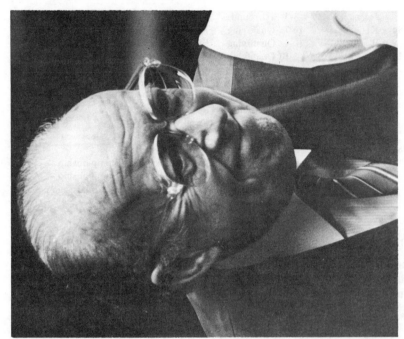

Fred Davis (David Muscroft)

John Campbell

1984	v White	1-5	Qualifying	Lada Classic
	v Gauvreau	7-10	Qualifying	Embassy World Professional Championship
	v G. Foulds	5-3	Qualifying	Jameson International
	v S. Davis	1-5	1st round	Jameson International
	v W. Jones	5-4	1st round	Rothmans Grand Prix
	v Thorburn	1-5	2nd round	Rothmans Grand Prix
	v Donnelly	9-6	Qualifying	Coral UK Open
	v White	7-9	1st round	Coral UK Open
	v Scott	4-5	Qualifying	Mercantile Credit Classic
1985	v O'Kane	4-6	1st round	Dulux British Open
	v Morra	10-9	Qualifying	Embassy World Professional Championship
	v Charlton	3-10	1st round	Embassy World Professional Championship

DAVE CHALMERS (England)

Born 14.7.48
Turned professional 1984
World ranking 79

After surviving three qualifying rounds, Chalmers fell at the final hurdle to Mike Hallett in the 1985 Embassy World Championship. He was English amateur champion in 1982.

1984	Chalmers wo Condo scr		Qualifying	Jameson International
	v Oliver	5-4	Qualifying	Jameson International
	v Meadowcroft	1-5	Qualifying	Jameson International
	v Andrewartha	5-2	Qualifying	Rothmans Grand Prix
	v Williams	0-5	1st round	Rothmans Grand Prix
	v Bales	2-9	Qualifying	Coral UK Open
	v Mikkelsen	1-5	Prelim	Mercantile Credit Classic
1985	v Meadowcroft	9-3	Qualifying	Tolly Cobbold English Professional Championship
	v White	5-9	Qualifying	Tolly Cobbold English Professional Championship
	v Burke	6-5	Qualifying	Dulux British Open
	v Griffiths	0-6	1st round	Dulux British Open
	v Greaves	10-3	Qualifying	Embassy World Professional Championship
	v E. McLaughlin	10-9	Qualifying	Embassy World Professional Championship
	v Black	10-4	Qualifying	Embassy World Professional Championship
	v Hallett	1-10	Qualifying	Embassy World Professional Championship

ROBERT CHAPERON (Canada)

Born –
Turned professional 1983
World ranking 44

Having qualified for the final stages of a professional tournament for the first time, Chaperon reached the third round of the Dulux British Open

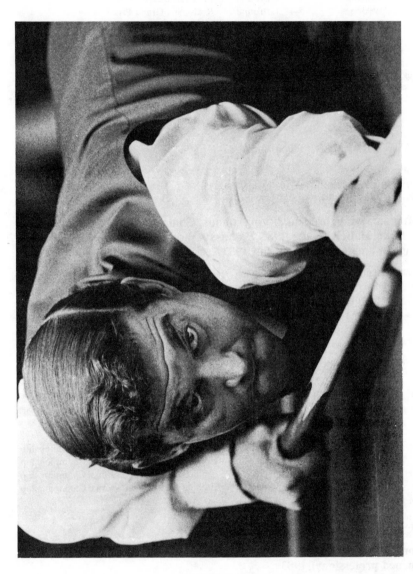

Eddie Charlton (George Herringshaw)

with wins over Patsy Fagan, Bill Werbeniuk and Wayne Jones before losing to Silvino Francisco, who went on to take the title.

1984	v Fowler	0-5	Qualifying	Jameson International
	v Kearney	5-1	Qualifying	Rothmans Grand Prix
	v Gibson	5-4	Qualifying	Rothmans Grand Prix
	v Martin	4-5	Qualifying	Rothmans Grand Prix
	v T. Jones	1-9	Qualifying	Coral UK Open
	v G. Foulds	3-5	Qualifying	Mercantile Credit Classic
1985	v Fagan	6-5	Qualifying	Dulux British Open
	v Werbeniuk	6-1	1st round	Dulux British Open
	v W. Jones	5-2	2nd round	Dulux British Open
	v S. Francisco	2-5	3rd round	Dulux British Open
	v Bales	10-7	Qualifying	Embassy World Professional Championship
	v Heywood	10-1	Qualifying	Embassy World Professional Championship
	v Morgan	10-3	Qualifying	Embassy World Professional Championship
	v F. Davis	9-10	Qualifying	Embassy World Professional Championship

TONY CHAPPEL (Wales)

Born 28.5.60
Turned professional 1984
World ranking 68

A Terry Griffiths protégé, Chappel took Steve Davis to a deciding 11th frame in the first round of the Dulux British Open, his best performance of his first professional season.

1984	v Mikkelsen	4-5	Qualifying	Jameson International
	v Scott	5-1	Qualifying	Rothmans Grand Prix
	v Stevens	3-5	1st round	Rothmans Grand Prix
	v Houlihan	9-3	Qualifying	Coral UK Open
	v Black	9-3	Qualifying	Coral UK Open
	v Reynolds	9-6	Qualifying	Coral UK Open
	v Stevens	7-9	1st round	Coral UK Open
	v Giannaros	2-5	Qualifying	Mercantile Credit Classic
	v Williamson	6-5	Qualifying	Dulux British Open
	v S. Davis	5-6	1st round	Dulux British Open
	v Hines	8-10	Qualifying	Embassy World Professional Championship
	v M. Owen	6-0	1st round	BCE Welsh Professional Championship
	v Griffiths	0-6	Quarter-final	BCE Welsh Professional Championship

EDDIE CHARLTON (Australia)

Born 31.10.29
Turned professional 1960
World ranking 12

By his own high standards, Charlton has had a very inconsistent season and for the first time since rankings were instituted is not among the top eight players in the world. In his 25-year professional career, Charlton has previously reached two world finals and six world semi-finals but has not actually won the title itself.

Although his steady, riskless style of play always makes him a very difficult player to beat, Charlton has never won a major international title.

1970	v Simpson	22-27	Semi-final	World Professional Championship
1972	v David Taylor	31-25	Quarter-final	World Professional Championship
	v Spencer	32-37	Semi-final	World Professional Championship
1973	v Mans	16-8	2nd round	World Professional Championship
	v Miles	16-6	Quarter-final	World Professional Championship
	v Higgins	23-9	Semi-final	World Professional Championship
	v Reardon	32-38	Final	World Professional Championship
	v Pulman	3-8	Semi-final	Norwich Union Open
1974	v Dunning	13-15	2nd round	World Professional Championship
1975	v F. Davis	5-3	Quarter-final	Benson & Hedges Masters
	v Spencer	2-5	Semi-final	Benson & Hedges Masters
	v Werbeniuk	15-11	2nd round	World Professional Championship
	v Thorburn	19-12	Quarter-final	World Professional Championship
	v Dennis Taylor	19-12	Semi-final	World Professional Championship
	v Reardon	30-31	Final	World Professional Championship
1976	v Williams	4-1	2nd round	Benson & Hedges Masters
	v Reardon	4-5	Semi-final	Benson & Hedges Masters
	v Pulman	15-9	1st round	Embassy World Professional Championship
	v F. Davis	15-13	Quarter-final	Embassy World Professional Championship
	v Higgins	18-20	Semi-final	Embassy World Professional Championship
1977	v David Taylor	13-5	1st round	Embassy World Professional Championship
	v Thorburn	12-13	Quarter-final	Embassy World Professional Championship
1978	v Thorne	13-12	1st round	Embassy World Professional Championship
	v Thorburn	13-12	Quarter-final	Embassy World Professional Championship
	v Reardon	14-18	Semi-final	Embassy World Professional Championship
1979	v Higgins	2-5	Quarter-final	Benson & Hedges Masters
	v Mountjoy	13-6	1st round	Embassy World Professional Championship
	v F. Davis	13-4	Quarter-final	Embassy World Professional Championship
	v Griffiths	17-19	Semi-final	Embassy World Professional Championship
1980	v Spencer	2-5	Quarter-final	Benson & Hedges Masters
	v Virgo	13-12	2nd round	Embassy World Professional Championship
	v Stevens	7-13	Quarter-final	Embassy World Professional Championship
1981	v Mountjoy	0-5	1st round	Benson & Hedges Masters
	v Mountjoy	7-13	2nd round	Embassy World Professional Championship
	v Martin	2-5	3rd round	Jameson International
1982	v White	5-4	1st round	Benson & Hedges Masters
	v Higgins	1-5	Quarter-final	Benson & Hedges Masters
	v Wilson	10-5	1st round	Embassy World Professional Championship
	v Werbeniuk	13-5	2nd round	Embassy World Professional Championship
	v Knowles	13-11	Quarter-final	Embassy World Professional Championship
	v Reardon	11-16	Semi-final	Embassy World Professional Championship
	v Virgo	4-5	1st round	Jameson International
	v D. Hughes	5-2	1st round	Professional Players Tournament

v Williams	5-2	2nd round	Professional Players Tournament
v Meo	5-3	3rd round	Professional Players Tournament
v Reynolds	5-2	Quarter-final	Professional Players Tournament
v Reardon	7-10	Semi-final	Professional Players Tournament
1983 v Virgo	5-2	1st round	Lada Classic
v S. Davis	4-5	Quarter-final	Lada Classic
v Meo	5-3	1st round	Benson & Hedges Masters
v Werbeniuk	5-3	Quarter-final	Benson & Hedges Masters
v Thorburn	5-6	Semi-final	Benson & Hedges Masters
v David Taylor	5-4	1st round	Benson & Hedges Irish Masters
v S. Davis	1-5	Quarter-final	Benson & Hedges Irish Masters
v Dodd	10-7	1st round	Embassy World Professional Championship
v Spencer	13-11	2nd round	Embassy World Professional Championship
v S. Davis	5-13	Quarter-final	Embassy World Professional Championship
v Johnson	5-2	1st round	Jameson International
v Morra	5-3	2nd round	Jameson International
v Thorne	5-0	Quarter-final	Jameson International
v S. Davis	2-9	Semi-final	Jameson International
v E. McLaughlin	5-0	1st round	Professional Players Tournament
v Fisher	5-4	2nd round	Professional Players Tournament
v Johnson	0-5	3rd round	Professional Players Tournament
1984 v Wilson	5-0	Qualifying	Lada Classic
v White	5-3	1st round	Lada Classic
v Wildman	4-5	Quarter-final	Lada Classic
v White	2-5	1st round	Benson & Hedges Masters
v Higgins	2-5	1st round	Benson & Hedges Irish Masters
v Stevens	3-5	1st round	Tolly Cobbold Classic
v Andrewartha	10-4	1st round	Embassy World Professional Championship
v White	7-13	2nd round	Embassy World Professional Championship
v David Taylor	5-4	Quarter-final	Winfield Australian Masters
v Knowles	0-6	Semi-final	Winfield Australian Masters
v Johnson	1-5	1st round	Jameson International
v Everton	5-1	1st round	Rothmans Grand Prix
v Parrott	5-1	2nd round	Rothmans Grand Prix
v Mountjoy	4-5	3rd round	Rothmans Grand Prix
v S. Francisco	9-4	1st round	Coral UK Open
v Thorne	7-9	2nd round	Coral UK Open
v Macleod	1-5	1st round	Mercantile Credit Classic
1985 v Spencer	3-5	1st round	Benson & Hedges Masters
v B. Harris	3-6	1st round	Dulux British Open
v Dennis Taylor	5-4	1st round	Benson & Hedges Irish Masters
v Knowles	3-5	Quarter-final	Benson & Hedges Irish Masters
v Campbell	10-3	1st round	Embassy World Professional Championship
v Dennis Taylor	6-13	2nd round	Embassy World Professional Championship

LOU CONDO (Australia)

Born 21.8.48
Turned professional 1975
World ranking unranked

Condo allowed his membership to lapse and was re-instated in 1984.

1975	v Anderson	8-15	1st round	World Professional Championship
1976	v M. Owen	8-6	Qualifying	Embassy World Professional Championship
	v Thorne	3-8	Qualifying	Embassy World Professional Championship

GRAHAM CRIPSEY (England)

Born 8.12.54
Turned professional 1982
World ranking 89

A former wall-of-death rider from Skegness, Cripsey won the 1980 All England CIU Championship and is a former English amateur international.

1982	v French	1-5	Qualifying	Jameson International
	v B. Harris	6-9	Qualifying	Coral UK Championship
1983	v D. Hughes	10-2	Qualifying	Embassy World Professional Championship
	v Meadowcroft	6-10	Qualifying	Embassy World Professional Championship
	v Ganim	4-5	Qualifying	Professional Players Tournament
	v Darrington	3-9	Qualifying	Coral UK Championship
1984	v Parkin	10-4	Qualifying	Embassy World Professional Championship
	v Gauvreau	1-10	Qualifying	Embassy World Professional Championship
	v Thornley	5-3	Qualifying	Jameson International
	v Dunning	3-5	Qualifying	Jameson International
	v Morra	3-5	Qualifying	Rothmans Grand Prix
	v Foldvari	9-7	Qualifying	Coral UK Open
	v Fitzmaurice	8-9	Qualifying	Coral UK Open
	v Medati	4-5	Qualifying	Mercantile Credit Classic
1985	v Bennett	9-0	Qualifying	Tolly Cobbold English Professional Championship
	v David Taylor	5-9	1st round	Tolly Cobbold English Professional Championship
	v O'Kane	4-6	Qualifying	Dulux British Open
	v Longworth	8-10	Qualifying	Embassy World Professional Championship

MIKE DARRINGTON (England)

Born 13.9.31
Turned professional 1982
World ranking 97

1983	v Williams	0-10	Qualifying	Embassy World Professional Championship
	v Williamson	5-3	Qualifying	Jameson International
	v S. Francisco	2-5	Qualifying	Jameson International
	v Duggan	4-5	Qualifying	Professional Players Tournament
	v Cripsey	9-3	Qualifying	Coral UK Championship
	v Hallett	1-9	Qualifying	Coral UK Championship

1984	v Caggianello	7-10	Qualifying	Embassy World Professional Championship
	v Bradley	3-5	Qualifying	Jameson International
	v Burke	3-5	Qualifying	Rothmans Grand Prix
	v Longworth	5-9	Qualifying	Coral UK Open
	v Hargreaves	2-5	Qualifying	Mercantile Credit Classic
1985	v Virgo	0-9	1st round	Tolly Cobbold English Professional Championship
	v Scott	3-6	Qualifying	Dulux British Open
	v T. Jones	2-10	Qualifying	Embassy World Professional Championship

FRED DAVIS (England)

Born 14.8.13
Turned professional 1930
World ranking 56

Fred Davis is certainly professional snooker's oldest active player and is probably the oldest active professional sportsman in Britain. During the early part of his professional career he lived under the shadow of his elder brother, Joe, but then himself dominated the game in the late 1940s and 1950s, winning the world title eight times. When the game was revived in the late 1960s, Davis proved he was still a force to be reckoned with, reaching the 1969, 1974 and 1978 semi-finals.

In 1980, at the age of 67, Davis became only the second player – the first, of course, being Joe – to achieve the feat of winning both the World Professional Snooker and Billiards titles when he successfully challenged Rex Williams for the latter. He retained it when the event was staged later that same year in a tournament format and was runner-up to Rex Williams in 1983.

1969	v Reardon	25-24	Quarter-final	World Professional Championship
	v G. Owen	28-45	Semi-final	World Professional Championship
1970	v Reardon	26-31	Quarter-final	World Professional Championship
1972	v Spencer	21-31	Quarter-final	World Professional Championship
1973	v Greaves	16-1	2nd round	World Professional Championship
	v Higgins	14-16	Quarter-final	World Professional Championship
1974	v Werbeniuk	15-5	2nd round	World Professional Championship
	v Higgins	15-14	Quarter-final	World Professional Championship
	v Reardon	3-15	Semi-final	World Professional Championship
1974	v Thorburn	4-5	1st round	Norwich Union Open
1975	v Charlton	3-5	Quarter-final	Benson & Hedges Masters
	v Dennis Taylor	14-15	2nd round	World Professional Championship
1976	v Thorburn	4-2	1st round	Benson & Hedges Masters
	v Spencer	0-4	2nd round	Benson & Hedges Masters
	v Werbeniuk	15-12	1st round	Embassy World Professional Championship
	v Charlton	13-15	Quarter-final	Embassy World Professional Championship
1977	v Mountjoy	2-4	Quarter-final	Benson & Hedges Masters
	v Pulman	12-13	1st round	Embassy World Professional Championship
	v Fagan	0-5	2nd round	Super Crystalate UK Championship

1978	v Miles	3-4	1st round	Benson & Hedges Masters
	v Virgo	9-8	Qualifying	Embassy World Professional Championship
	v Dennis Taylor	13-9	1st round	Embassy World Professional Championship
	v Fagan	13-10	Quarter-final	Embassy World Professional Championship
	v Mans	16-18	Semi-final	Embassy World Professional Championship
	v Dunning	9-2	1st round	Coral UK Championship
	v Higgins	4-9	Quarter-final	Coral UK Championship
1979	v Mountjoy	2-5	1st round	Benson & Hedges Masters
	v Stevens	13-8	1st round	Embassy World Professional Championship
	v Charlton	4-13	Quarter-final	Embassy World Professional Championship
	v Edmonds	6-9	3rd round	Coral UK Championship
1980	v David Taylor	5-13	2nd round	Embassy World Professional Championship
	v Wildman	9-6	2nd round	Coral UK Championship
	v Higgins	6-9	Quarter-final	Coral UK Championship
1981	v Stevens	5-4	1st round	Benson & Hedges Masters
	v Griffiths	2-5	Quarter-final	Benson & Hedges Masters
	v Edmonds	6-9	1st round	John Courage English Professional
	v David Taylor	3-13	2nd round	Embassy World Professional Championship
	v Williams	0-5	2nd round	Jameson International
	v Knowles	6-9	2nd round	Coral UK Championship
1982	v Reynolds	7-10	1st round	Embassy World Professional Championship
	v Fisher	3-5	Qualifying	Jameson International
	v Sinclair	2-5	1st round	Professional Players Tournament
	v Hallett	7-9	1st round	Coral UK Open
1983	v Williams	1-10	Qualifying	Embassy World Professional Championship
	v Kelly	5-1	Qualifying	Jameson International
	v Morgan	3-5	Qualifying	Jameson International
	v Fisher	4-5	1st round	Professional Players Tournament
	v Watterson	6-9	Qualifying	Coral UK Championship
	v Donnelly	10-5	Qualifying	Embassy World Professional Championship
	v Werbeniuk	4-10	1st round	Embassy World Professional Championship
1984	v Dunning	5-4	Qualifying	Jameson International
	v Virgo	3-5	Qualifying	Jameson International
	v V. Harris	1-5	Qualifying	Rothmans Grand Prix
	v Fowler	4-9	Qualifying	Coral UK Open
	v E. McLaughlin	1-5	Qualifying	Mercantile Credit Classic
1985	v G. Foulds	2-9	Qualifying	Tolly Cobbold English Professional Championship
	v Longworth	1-6	Qualifying	Dulux British Open
	v Chaperon	10-9	Qualifying	Embassy World Professional Championship
	v Williams	6-10	Qualifying	Embassy World Professional Championship

STEVE DAVIS (England)

Born 22.8.57
Turned professional 1978
World ranking 1

Steve Davis turned professional in September 1978 with a good amateur record and in November 1980 captured the Coral UK Championship by beating Alex Higgins 16-6 in the final. From that point it seemed as if the Londoner would never stop winning, or at least reaching the finals of major tournaments. From then until the start of last season, he played 96 matches in major tournaments of the best of nine frames or more and lost only 11 of them.

Last season, although he started well enough by retaining the Langs Scottish Masters and the Jameson International, he lost to Cliff Thorburn in the semi-finals of the Rothmans Grand Prix and to Willie Thorne at the same stage of the Mercantile Credit Classic. Between times he beat Alex Higgins to regain the Coral but then lost to the Irishman in the first round of the Benson and Hedges Masters, a defeat he failed to avenge in the event's Irish counterpart.

Kirk Stevens beat him in the semi-finals of the Dulux but the Embassy World Championship appeared to be his for the fourth time in five years when he led Dennis Taylor 8-0 in the final. Taylor, though, came back to take the deciding frame on the black in one of the most memorable matches ever seen in the event, and Davis had to be content with just the Langs, Jameson, Coral UK and Tolly Cobbold English Professional titles.

1979	v Anderson	9-1	Prelim	Embassy World Professional Championship
	v Fagan	9-2	Qualifying	Embassy World Professional Championship
	v Dennis Taylor	11-13	1st round	Embassy World Professional Championship
	v Dunning	9-3	2nd round	Coral UK Championship
	v Mountjoy	9-5	3rd round	Coral UK Championship
	v Virgo	7-9	Quarter-final	Coral UK Championship
1980	v Morgan	9-0	Qualifying	Embassy World Professional Championship
	v Fagan	10-6	1st round	Embassy World Professional Championship
	v Griffiths	13-10	2nd round	Embassy World Professional Championship
	v Higgins	9-13	Quarter-final	Embassy World Professional Championship
	v Hallett	9-1	1st round	Coral UK Championship
	v Werbeniuk	9-3	2nd round	Coral UK Championship
	v Meo	9-5	Quarter-final	Coral UK Championship
	v Griffiths	9-0	Semi-final	Coral UK Championship
	v Higgins	**16-6**	**Final**	**Coral UK Championship**
1981	v Mans	3-5	1st round	Benson & Hedges Masters
	v Dennis Taylor	5-2	Semi-final	Yamaha International Masters
	v David Taylor	**9-6**	**Final**	**Yamaha International Masters**
	v Meadowcroft	9-2	1st round	John Courage English Professional
	v Spencer	9-7	2nd round	John Courage English Professional
	v Edmonds	9-0	Semi-final	John Courage English Professional
	v Meo	**9-3**	**Final**	**John Courage English Professional**
	v White	10-8	1st round	Embassy World Professional Championship
	v Higgins	13-8	2nd round	Embassy World Professional Championship
	v Griffiths	13-9	Quarter-final	Embassy World Professional Championship
	v Thorburn	16-10	Semi-final	Embassy World Professional Championship
	v Mountjoy	**18-12**	**Final**	**Embassy World Professional Championship**
	v Mountjoy	5-0	Quarter-final	Langs Scottish Masters
	v White	5-6	Semi-final	Langs Scottish Masters

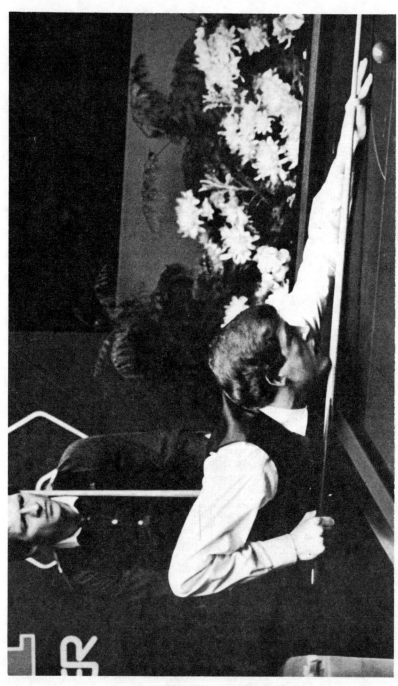

Steve Davis (Peter G. Reed)

v Mans	5-3	3rd round	Jameson International
v David Taylor	5-1	Quarter-final	Jameson International
v Higgins	9-8	Semi-final	Jameson International
v Dennis Taylor	**9-0**	**Final**	**Jameson International**
v Higgins	5-2	1st round	Northern Ireland Classic
v Griffiths	9-6	Semi-final	Northern Ireland Classic
v White	9-11	Final	Northern Ireland Classic
v Thorne	9-2	3rd round	Coral UK Championship
v Werbeniuk	9-5	Quarter-final	Coral UK Championship
v White	9-0	Semi-final	Coral UK Championship
v Griffiths	**16-3**	**Final**	**Coral UK Championship**
1982 v Spencer	5-2	1st round	Lada Classic
v Reardon	5-4	Semi-final	Lada Classic
v Griffiths	8-9	Final	Lada Classic
v Mountjoy	5-2	Quarter-final	Benson & Hedges Masters
v Meo	6-4	Semi-final	Benson & Hedges Masters
v Griffiths	**9-5**	**Final**	**Benson & Hedges Masters**
v Griffiths	**9-7**	**Final**	**Yamaha International Masters**
v Miles	5-2	Semi-final	Tolly Cobbold Classic
v Dennis Taylor	**8-3**	**Final**	**Tolly Cobbold Classic**
v Mountjoy	5-2	Quarter-final	Benson & Hedges Irish Masters
v Higgins	6-2	Semi-final	Benson & Hedges Irish Masters
v Griffiths	5-9	Final	Benson & Hedges Irish Masters
v Knowles	1-10	1st round	Embassy World Professional Championship
v Knowles	5-4	1st round	Langs Scottish Masters
v Dennis Taylor	6-1	Semi-final	Langs Scottish Masters
v Higgins	**9-4**	**Final**	**Langs Scottish Masters**
v Roscoe	5-0	1st round	Jameson International
v Reynolds	5-0	2nd round	Jameson International
v David Taylor	3-5	Quarter-final	Jameson International
v Williams	9-6	1st round	Coral UK Open
v Fagan	9-3	2nd round	Coral UK Open
v Griffiths	6-9	Quarter-final	Coral UK Open
1983 v Dennis Taylor	5-2	1st round	Lada Classic
v Charlton	5-4	Quarter-final	Lada Classic
v Spencer	5-4	Semi-final	Lada Classic
v Werbeniuk	**9-5**	**Final**	**Lada Classic**
v Wildman	5-2	1st round	Benson & Hedges Masters
v Mountjoy	4-5	Quarter-final	Benson & Hedges Masters
v Dennis Taylor	5-1	Semi-final	Tolly Cobbold Classic
v Griffiths	**7-5**	**Final**	**Tolly Cobbold Classic**
v Charlton	5-1	Quarter-final	Benson & Hedges Irish Masters
v Griffiths	6-2	Semi-final	Benson & Hedges Irish Masters
v Reardon	**9-2**	**Final**	**Benson & Hedges Irish Masters**
v Williams	10-4	1st round	Embassy World Professional Championship
v Dennis Taylor	13-11	2nd round	Embassy World Professional Championship
v Charlton	13-5	Quarter-final	Embassy World Professional Championship
v Higgins	16-5	Semi-final	Embassy World Professional Championship
v Thorburn	**18-6**	**Final**	**Embassy World Professional Championship**
v Macleod	5-1	1st round	Langs Scottish Masters

v Higgins	6-2	Semi-final	Langs Scottish Masters
v Knowles	**9-6**	**Final**	**Langs Scottish Masters**
v E. Hughes	5-1	1st round	Jameson International
v Watterson	5-0	2nd round	Jameson International
v S. Francisco	5-1	Quarter-final	Jameson International
v Charlton	9-2	Semi-final	Jameson International
v Thorburn	**9-4**	**Final**	**Jameson International**
v Donnelly	5-1	1st round	Professional Players Tournament
v Hallett	2-5	2nd round	Professional Players Tournament
v G. Foulds	9-1	1st round	Coral UK Championship
v Thorne	9-3	2nd round	Coral UK Championship
v Meo	9-4	Quarter-final	Coral UK Championship
v White	9-4	Semi-final	Coral UK Championship
v Higgins	15-16	Final	Coral UK Championship
1984 v Spencer	5-2	1st round	Lada Classic
v Griffiths	5-4	Quarter-final	Lada Classic
v Parrott	5-4	Semi-final	Lada Classic
v Meo	**9-8**	**Final**	**Lada Classic**
v Meo	5-0	1st round	Benson & Hedges Masters
v Stevens	3-5	Quarter-final	Benson & Hedges Masters
v Meo	5-4	Quarter-final	Benson & Hedges Irish Masters
v Higgins	6-4	Semi-final	Benson & Hedges Irish Masters
v Griffiths	**9-1**	**Final**	**Benson & Hedges Irish Masters**
v Thorne	5-2	1st round	Tolly Cobbold Classic
v Stevens	5-4	Semi-final	Tolly Cobbold Classic
v Knowles	**8-2**	**Final**	**Tolly Cobbold Classic**
v King	10-3	1st round	Embassy World Professional Championship
v Spencer	13-5	2nd round	Embassy World Professional Championship
v Griffiths	13-10	Quarter-final	Embassy World Professional Championship
v Dennis Taylor	16-9	Semi-final	Embassy World Professional Championship
v White	**18-16**	**Final**	**Embassy World Professional Championship**
v Thorburn	5-2	1st round	Langs Supreme Scottish Masters
v Higgins	6-4	Semi-final	Langs Supreme Scottish Masters
v White	**9-5**	**Final**	**Langs Supreme Scottish Masters**
v Campbell	5-1	1st round	Jameson International
v David Taylor	5-1	2nd round	Jameson International
v Higgins	5-1	Quarter-final	Jameson International
v E. Hughes	9-3	Semi-final	Jameson International
v Knowles	**9-2**	**Final**	**Jameson International**
v Morra	5-2	1st round	Rothmans Grand Prix
v Miles	5-0	2nd round	Rothmans Grand Prix
v David Taylor	5-1	3rd round	Rothmans Grand Prix
v Reynolds	5-0	Quarter-final	Rothmans Grand Prix
v Thorburn	7-9	Semi-final	Rothmans Grand Prix
v Murphy	9-1	1st round	Coral UK Open
v Meo	9-7	2nd round	Coral UK Open
v White	9-4	Quarter-final	Coral UK Open
v Stevens	9-2	Semi-final	Coral UK Open
v Higgins	**16-8**	**Final**	**Coral UK Open**
v S. Francisco	5-0	1st round	Mercantile Credit Classic

v Higgins	5-2	2nd round	Mercantile Credit Classic
v Reardon	5-1	Quarter-final	Mercantile Credit Classic
v Thorne	8-9	Semi-final	Mercantile Credit Classic
1985 v Higgins	4-5	1st round	Benson & Hedges Masters
v Fowler	9-3	1st round	Tolly Cobbold English Professional Championship
v Williams	9-2	2nd round	Tolly Cobbold English Professional Championship
v Virgo	9-2	Quarter-final	Tolly Cobbold English Professional Championship
v Meo	9-8	Semi-final	Tolly Cobbold English Professional Championship
v Knowles	**9-2**	**Final**	**Tolly Cobbold English Professional Championship**
v Chappel	6-5	1st round	Dulux British Open
v Virgo	5-2	2nd round	Dulux British Open
v Bradley	5-2	3rd round	Dulux British Open
v O'Kane	5-1	Quarter-final	Dulux British Open
v Stevens	7-9	Semi-final	Dulux British Open
v E. Hughes	5-4	Quarter-final	Benson & Hedges Irish Masters
v Higgins	2-6	Semi-finals	Benson & Hedges Irish Masters
v N. Foulds	10-8	1st round	Embassy World Professional Championship
v David Taylor	13-4	2nd round	Embassy World Professional Championship
v Griffiths	13-6	Quarter-final	Embassy World Professional Championship
v Reardon	16-5	Semi-final	Embassy World Professional Championship
v Dennis Taylor	17-18	Final	Embassy World Professional Championship

BERT DEMARCO (Scotland)

Born 9.6.24
Turned professional 1981
World ranking 92

Demarco won the Scottish Amateur Snooker Championship twice and the Scottish Billiards title once. He is now proprietor of snooker and squash clubs in Edinburgh.

1981 v D. Hughes	5-1	Qualifying	Jameson International
v Hallett	4-5	Qualifying	Jameson International
v Gibson	3-5	Quarter-final	Scottish Professional Championship
1982 v Watterson	6-9	Qualifying	Embassy World Professional Championship
v Ross	5-6	Quarter-final	Scottish Professional Championship
v Morra	2-5	Qualifying	Jameson International
v Thorne	3-5	1st round	Professional Players Tournament
v Hallett	1-9	Qualifying	Coral UK Championship
1983 v Kelly	4-10	Qualifying	Embassy World Professional Championship
v Donnelly	4-6	1st round	Scottish Professional Championship
v Watterson	3-5	Qualifying	Jameson International

	v Bennett	4-5	Qualifying	Professional Players Tournament
	v Murphy	4-9	Qualifying	Coral UK Open
1984	v Roscoe	7-10	Qualifying	Embassy World Professional Championship
	v Bennett	1-5	Qualifying	Jameson International
	v N. Foulds	2-5	1st round	Rothmans Grand Prix
	v Fowler	3-9	Qualifying	Coral UK Open
	v J. McLaughlin	1-5	Qualifying	Mercantile Credit Classic
1985	v Gibson	1-6	Qualifying	Dulux British Open
	v P. Francisco	4-10	Qualifying	Embassy World Professional Championship

LES DODD (England)

Born 11.2.54
Turned professional 1982
World ranking 53

A former Southport taxi driver, Dodd reached the first round of the 1983 Embassy World Professional Championship and the first round of the Jameson International the following year but last season slipped ten placings in the rankings as he failed to pick up either a ranking or merit point of any description.

1982	v Macleod	5-1	Qualifying	Jameson International
	v Fitzmaurice	5-3	Qualifying	Jameson International
	v Mans	3-5	1st round	Jameson International
	v Williamson	9-1	Qualifying	Coral UK Championship
	v French	9-7	Qualifying	Coral UK Championship
	v David Taylor	7-9	1st round	Coral UK Championship
1983	v Williamson	10-9	Qualifying	Embassy World Professional Championship
	v Charlton	7-10	1st round	Embassy World Professional Championship
	v Gibson	1-5	Qualifying	Jameson International
	v Griffiths	3-5	1st round	Professional Players Tournament
	v G. Foulds	7-9	Qualifying	Coral UK Championship
1984	v Giannaros	10-1	Qualifying	Embassy World Professional Championship
	v N. Foulds	4-10	Qualifying	Embassy World Professional Championship
	v Foldvari	5-3	Qualifying	Jameson International
	v Wilson	5-1	Qualifying	Jameson International
	v Reardon	4-5	1st round	Jameson International
	v Medati	4-5	Qualifying	Rothmans Grand Prix
	v Newbury	9-6	Qualifying	Coral UK Open
	v Wilson	8-9	Qualifying	Coral UK Open
	v T. Jones	1-5	Qualifying	Mercantile Credit Classic
1985	v Bales	9-5	Qualifying	Tolly Cobbold English Professional Championship
	v Thorne	1-9	1st round	Tolly Cobbold English Professional Championship
	v V. Harris	1-6	Qualifying	Dulux British Open
	v O'Kane	7-10	Qualifying	Embassy World Professional Championship

JIM DONNELLY (Scotland)

Born 13.6.46
Turned professional 1981
World ranking 46

Scottish amateur champion in 1978, Donnelly played for his country in the 1982 State Express World Team Classic and the 1985 Guinness World Cup.

1981	v Johnson	4-5	Qualifying	Jameson International
	v Sinclair	5-0	Quarter-final	Scottish Professional Championship
	v Gibson	4-6	Semi-final	Scottish Professional Championship
	v Medati	7-9	Qualifying	Coral UK Championship
1982	v Gibson	9-8	Qualifying	Embassy World Professional Championship
	v Sinclair	9-8	Qualifying	Embassy World Professional Championship
	v Reardon	5-10	1st round	Embassy World Professional Championship
	v Macleod	5-6	1st round	Scottish Professional Championship
	v Williamson	3-5	Qualifying	Jameson International
	v Watterson	4-5	1st round	Professional Players Tournament
	v Ross	9-5	Qualifying	Coral UK Championship
	v Knowles	6-9	1st round	Coral UK Championship
1983	v Sheehan	10-6	Qualifying	Embassy World Professional Championship
	v Campbell	2-10	Qualifying	Embassy World Professional Championship
	v Demarco	6-4	1st round	Scottish Professional Championship
	v Sinclair	5-6	Semi-final	Scottish Professional Championship
	v Bennett	5-1	Qualifying	Jameson International
	v Wilson	5-1	Qualifying	Jameson International
	v David Taylor	5-3	1st round	Jameson International
	v S. Francisco	1-5	2nd round	Jameson International
	v S. Davis	1-5	1st round	Professional Players Tournament
	v Murphy	4-9	Qualifying	Coral UK Championship
1984	v Watchorn	10-7	Qualifying	Embassy World Professional Championship
	v Anderson	10-6	Qualifying	Embassy World Professional Championship
	v F. Davis	5-10	Qualifying	Embassy World Professional Championship
	v G. Foulds	3-5	Qualifying	Jameson International
	v Hargreaves	5-4	Qualifying	Rothmans Grand Prix
	v Wilson	2-5	1st round	Rothmans Grand Prix
	v Gibson	9-6	Qualifying	Coral UK Open
	v Campbell	6-9	Qualifying	Coral UK Open
	v Watchorn	5-1	Qualifying	Mercantile Credit Classic
	v Williams	3-5	Qualifying	Mercantile Credit Classic
1985	v W. Jones	1-6	Qualifying	Dulux British Open
	v Fowler	0-10	Qualifying	Embassy World Professional Championship

STEVE DUGGAN (England)

Born 10.4.58
Turned professional 1983
World ranking 70

As an amateur, Duggan twice won the All England CIU Championship.

1983	v Darrington	5-4	Qualifying	Professional Players Tournament
	v Dunning	5-2	1st round	Professional Players Tournament
	v Reardon	2-5	2nd round	Professional Players Tournament
	v G. Foulds	8-9	Qualifying	Coral UK Championship
1984	v Browne	9-10	Qualifying	Embassy World Professional Championship
	v T. Jones	5-2	Qualifying	Jameson International
	v Sinclair	0-5	Qualifying	Jameson International
	v Browne	5-2	Qualifying	Rothmans Grand Prix
	v S. Francisco	3-5	1st round	Rothmans Grand Prix
	v O'Kane	6-9	Qualifying	Coral UK Open
	v W. Jones	5-0	Qualifying	Mercantile Credit Classic
	v King	4-5	Qualifying	Mercantile Credit Classic
1985	v B. Harris	9-8	Qualifying	Tolly Cobbold English Professional Championship
	v Hallett	4-9	1st round	Tolly Cobbold English Professional Championship
	v Foldvari	4-6	Qualifying	Dulux British Open
	v T. Jones	8-10	Qualifying	Embassy World Professional Championship

JOHN DUNNING (England)

Born 18.4.27
Turned professional 1970
World ranking 64

The best performance of Dunning's 15-year professional career was to reach the final group of the 1984 Yamaha International. During the qualifying section of last season's Rothmans Grand Prix, he suffered a heart attack and did not play again that season until the Embassy World Championship.

1972	v Houlihan	11-10	Qualifying	World Professional Championship
	v Miles	11-5	Qualifying	World Professional Championship
	v Pulman	7-19	1st round	World Professional Championship
1973	v David Taylor	4-9	1st round	World Professional Championship
1974	v David Taylor	8-6	1st round	World Professional Championship
	v Charlton	15-13	2nd round	World Professional Championship
	v Miles	13-15	Quarter-final	World Professional Championship
1975	v G. Owen	8-15	2nd round	World Professional Championship
1976	v Reardon	7-15	1st round	Embassy World Professional Championship
1977	v Virgo	6-11	Qualifying	Embassy World Professional Championship
	v Parkin	5-4	1st round	Super Crystalate UK Championship
	v Higgins	0-5	Quarter-final	Super Crystalate UK Championship
1978	v Fagan	5-9	Qualifying	Embassy World Professional Championship
	v Greaves	9-3	Qualifying	Coral UK Championship
	v F. Davis	2-9	1st round	Coral UK Championship
1979	v Jack Rea	9-5	Prelim	Embassy World Professional Championship

v David Taylor	8-9	Qualifying	Embassy World Professional Championship
v Greaves	9-8	1st round	Coral UK Championship
v S. Davis	3-9	2nd round	Coral UK Championship
1980 v Johnson	6-9	Qualifying	Coral UK Championship
1981 v Greaves	9-4	Qualifying	John Courage English Professional
v David Taylor	9-8	1st round	John Courage English Professional
v Thorne	0-9	2nd round	John Courage English Professional
v Bennett	9-6	Qualifying	Embassy World Professional Championship
v Fagan	9-7	Qualifying	Embassy World Professional Championship
v Stevens	4-10	1st round	Embassy World Professional Championship
v Gibson	5-3	Qualifying	Jameson International
v Martin	2-5	1st round	Jameson International
1982 v Macleod	9-4	Qualifying	Embassy World Professional Championship
v Spencer	4-10	1st round	Embassy World Professional Championship
v Roscoe	2-5	Qualifying	Jameson International
v Wildman	4-5	1st round	Professional Players Tournament
Houlihan *wo*		Qualifying	Coral UK Championship
Dunning *scr*			
1983 v B. Harris	3-5	Qualifying	Jameson International
v Duggan	2-5	1st round	Professional Players Tournament
v Andrewartha	9-2	Qualifying	Coral UK Championship
v Spencer	7-9	1st round	Coral UK Championship
1984 v Oliver	3-10	Qualifying	Embassy World Professional Championship
v Cripsey	5-3	Qualifying	Jameson International
v F. Davis	4-5	Qualifying	Jameson International
v D. Hughes	5-0	Qualifying	Rothmans Grand Prix
v Mans	5-4	1st round	Rothmans Grand Prix
v Knowles	1-5	2nd round	Rothmans Grand Prix
v John Rea	3-9	Qualifying	Coral UK Open
1985 v W. Jones	6-10	Qualifying	Embassy World Professional Championship

RAY EDMONDS (England)

Born 28.5.36
Turned professional 1978
World ranking 51

Twice World Amateur champion, Edmonds only achieved a measure of this success as a professional snooker player but gained some consolation in March 1985 when he won the Eurotherm World Professional Billiards Championship by beating the defending titleholder Mark Wildman in the semi-finals and Norman Dagley in the final. He is a regular member of ITV's commentary team.

1978 v Virgo	4-9	Qualifying	Coral UK Championship
1979 v Meadowcroft	9-3	2nd round	Coral UK Championship
v F. Davis	9-6	3rd round	Coral UK Championship
v Werbeniuk	8-9	Quarter-final	Coral UK Championship
1980 v Hood	9-6	Qualifying	Embassy World Professional Championship

	v David Taylor	3-10	1st round	Embassy World Professional Championship
	v Hallett	8-9	Qualifying	Coral UK Open
1981	v Hallett	9-3	Qualifying	John Courage English Professional
	v F. Davis	9-6	1st round	John Courage English Professional
	v Johnson	9-5	2nd round	John Courage English Professional
	v S. Davis	0-9	Semi-final	John Courage English Professional
	v Wildman	9-3	Qualifying	Embassy World Professional Championship
	v Williams	9-7	Qualifying	Embassy World Professional Championship
	v Spencer	9-10	1st round	Embassy World Professional Championship
	v E. Hughes	5-4	1st round	Jameson International
	v Spencer	3-5	2nd round	Jameson International
	v Thorne	4-9	2nd round	Coral UK Championship
1982	v Reynolds	6-9	Qualifying	Embassy World Professional Championship
	v D. Hughes	5-0	Qualifying	Jameson International
	v Miles	5-1	Qualifying	Jameson International
	v Spencer	2-5	1st round	Jameson International
	v Dennis Taylor	4-5	1st round	Professional Players Tournament
	v Fisher	8-9	Qualifying	Coral UK Championship
1983	v Jonik	10-4	Qualifying	Embassy World Professional Championship
	v Reynolds	6-10	Qualifying	Embassy World Professional Championship
	v Jack Rea	5-1	Qualifying	Jameson International
	v E. McLaughlin	5-1	Qualifying	Jameson International
	v Knowles	1-5	1st round	Jameson International
	v Stevens	1-5	1st round	Professional Players Tournament
	v Medati	7-9	Qualifying	Coral UK Championship
1984	v Greaves	10-0	Qualifying	Embassy World Professional Championship
	v Van Rensberg	9-10	Qualifying	Embassy World Professional Championship
	v Foldvari	1-5	Qualifying	Jameson International
	v Rigitano	3-5	Qualifying	Rothmans Grand Prix
	v John Rea	6-9	Qualifying	Coral UK Open
	v Hargreaves	5-2	Qualifying	Mercantile Credit Classic
	v Watterson	5-2	Qualifying	Mercantile Credit Classic
	v Johnson	4-5	Qualifying	Mercantile Credit Classic
1985	v Longworth	4-9	Qualifying	Tolly Cobbold English Professional Championship
	v Mienie	6-1	Qualifying	Dulux British Open
	v Miles	1-6	1st round	Dulux British Open
	v Foldvari	10-3	Qualifying	Embassy World Professional Championship
	v Wildman	10-7	Qualifying	Embassy World Professional Championship
	v Stevens	8-10	1st round	Embassy World Professional Championship

CLIVE EVERTON (Wales)

Born 7.9.37
Turned professional 1981
World ranking 73

Everton's playing commitments now take second place to his media
activities. Five times Welsh amateur billiards champion, he is snooker
correspondent of the *Guardian* and *The Sunday Times*, the editor/pro-

prietor of *Snooker Scene* magazine and a member of the BBC commentary team.

1981	v Gibson	9-7	Qualifying	Coral UK Championship
	v White	4-9	Qualifying	Coral UK Championship
1982	v Reardon	1-6	1st round	Woodpecker Welsh Professional Championship
	v D. Hughes	4-9	Qualifying	Embassy World Professional Championship
	v Watterson	1-5	Qualifying	Jameson International
	v Fagan	5-2	1st round	Professional Players Tournament
	v Thorburn	2-5	2nd round	Professional Players Tournament
	v Murphy	4-9	Qualifying	Coral UK Championship
1983	v Griffiths	1-6	Quarter-final	Woodpecker Welsh Professional Championship
	v Wilson	1-10	Qualifying	Embassy World Professional Championship
	v Andrewartha	1-5	Qualifying	Jameson International
	v Thorne	1-5	1st round	Professional Players Tournament
	v Watterson	6-9	Qualifying	Coral UK Championship
1984	v Mountjoy	1-6	1st round	Strongbow Welsh Professional Championship
	v Parrott	2-10	Qualifying	Embassy World Professional Championship
	v Mikkelsen	0-5	Qualifying	Jameson International
	v Houlihan	5-3	Qualifying	Rothmans Grand Prix
	v Charlton	1-5	1st round	Rothmans Grand Prix
	v Watchorn	6-9	Qualifying	Coral UK Open
	v Browne	0-5	Qualifying	Mercantile Credit Classic
1985	v Fowler	1-6	Qualifying	Dulux British Open
	v G. Foulds	2-10	Qualifying	Embassy World Professional Championship
	v Reardon	2-6	Quarter-final	BCE Welsh Professional Championship

PATSY FAGAN (Republic of Ireland)

Born 15.1.51
Turned professional 1976
World ranking 33

After Fagan had won the inaugural United Kingdom Championship in 1977 and reached the quarter-finals of the Embassy World Championship the following spring, his form deteriorated as he suffered a mental block which made him unable to use the rest. Miraculously, however, the problem ceased to trouble him last season and he reached the second round of the Embassy World Championship after a 10-6 victory over Willie Thorne.

1977	v Meadowcroft	11-9	Qualifying	Embassy World Professional Championship
	v Reardon	7-13	1st round	Embassy World Professional Championship
	v Jack Rea	5-1	1st round	Super Crystalate UK Championship
	v F. Davis	5-0	2nd round	Super Crystalate UK Championship
	v Meadowcroft	5-4	Quarter-final	Super Crystalate UK Championship

	v Virgo	9-8	Semi-final	Super Crystalate UK Championship
	v Mountjoy	**12-9**	**Final**	**Super Crystalate UK Championship**
1978	v Pulman	2-4	1st round	Benson & Hedges Masters
	v Dunning	9-5	Qualifying	Embassy World Professional Championship
	v Higgins	13-12	1st round	Embassy World Professional Championship
	v F. Davis	10-13	Quarter-final	Embassy World Professional Championship
	v David Taylor	7-9	1st round	Coral UK Championship
1979	v S. Davis	2-9	Qualifying	Embassy World Professional Championship
	v Hallett	9-4	2nd round	Coral UK Championship
	v Miles	9-5	3rd round	Coral UK Championship
	v Dennis Taylor	6-9	Quarter-final	Coral UK Championship
1980	v S. Davis	6-10	1st round	Embassy World Professional Championship
	v Johnson	9-4	1st round	Coral UK Championship
	v Griffiths	8-9	2nd round	Coral UK Championship
1981	v Dunning	7-9	Qualifying	Embassy World Professional Championship
	v Higgins	3-5	2nd round	Jameson International
	v Hallett	5-9	Qualifying	Coral UK Championship
1982	v Murphy	2-6	Quarter-final	Irish Professional Championship
	v French	9-6	Qualifying	Embassy World Professional Championship
	v David Taylor	10-9	1st round	Embassy World Professional Championship
	v Stevens	7-13	2nd round	Embassy World Professional Championship
	v Watterson	1-5	Qualifying	Jameson International
	v Everton	2-5	1st round	Professional Players Tournament
	v B. Harris	9-6	1st round	Coral UK Championship
	v S. Davis	3-9	2nd round	Coral UK Championship
1983	v Murphy	6-4	Quarter-final	Irish Professional Championship
	v Dennis Taylor	1-6	Semi-final	Irish Professional Championship
	v Fisher	8-10	Qualifying	Embassy World Professional Championship
	v Martin	0-5	Qualifying	Jameson International
	v Parrott	2-5	1st round	Professional Players Tournament
1984	v Higgins	3-5	Qualifying	Lada Classic
	v Wych	3-10	Qualifying	Embassy World Professional Championship
	v Newbury	0-5	Qualifying	Jameson International
	v T. Jones	2-9	Qualifying	Coral UK Open
	v Williamson	5-1	Qualifying	Mercantile Credit Classic
	v Wildman	5-3	Qualifying	Mercantile Credit Classic
	v Griffiths	0-5	1st round	Mercantile Credit Classic
1985	v Murphy	6-2	Quarter-final	Irish Professional Championship
	v Higgins	3-6	Semi-final	Irish Professional Championship
	v Gibson	10-8	Qualifying	Embassy World Professional Championship
	v Wilson	10-9	Qualifying	Embassy World Professional Championship
	v Thorne	10-6	1st round	Embassy World Professional Championship
	v Reardon	9-13	2nd round	Embassy World Professional Championship

MICK FISHER (England)

Born 12.7.44
Turned professional 1982
World ranking 54

Fisher is the proprietor of the successful Greyfriars Snooker Centre in Bedford.

1982 v Murphy	5-1	Qualifying	Jameson International
v F. Davis	5-3	Qualifying	Jameson International
v David Taylor	1-5	1st round	Jameson International
v Black	9-3	Qualifying	Coral UK Championship
v Edmonds	9-8	Qualifying	Coral UK Championship
v Reynolds	6-9	1st round	Coral UK Championship
1983 v Fagan	10-8	Qualifying	Embassy World Professional Championship
v E. McLaughlin	10-9	Qualifying	Embassy World Professional Championship
v Stevens	2-10	1st round	Embassy World Professional Championship
v E. Hughes	4-5	Qualifying	Jameson International
v F. Davis	5-4	1st round	Professional Players Tournament
v Charlton	4-5	2nd round	Professional Players Tournament
v Parrott	0-9	Qualifying	Coral UK Championship
1984 v Thornley	10-8	Qualifying	Embassy World Professional Championship
v Gibson	7-10	Qualifying	Embassy World Professional Championship
v Bales	3-5	Qualifying	Jameson International
v Newbury	0-5	Qualifying	Rothmans Grand Prix
v Watchorn	9-5	Qualifying	Coral UK Open
v Williams	8-9	Qualifying	Coral UK Open
v Longworth	1-5	Qualifying	Mercantile Credit Classic
1985 v French	9-8	Qualifying	Tolly Cobbold English Professional Championship
v Meo	3-9	1st round	Tolly Cobbold English Professional Championship
v John Rea	0-6	Qualifying	Dulux British Open
v Rigitano	2-10	Qualifying	Embassy World Professional Championship

JACK FITZMAURICE (England)

Born 25.4.28
Turned professional 1981
World ranking 74

Fitzmaurice won the All England CIU Championship in 1975 and was runner-up in the English Amateur Championship in 1958.

1981 v Bennett	5-1	Qualifying	Jameson International
v E. Hughes	3-5	Qualifying	Jameson International
v Gibson	6-9	Qualifying	Coral UK Championship
1982 v Morra	9-7	Qualifying	Embassy World Professional Championship
v Stevens	4-10	1st round	Embassy World Professional Championship
v Black	5-3	Qualifying	Jameson International
v Dodd	3-5	Qualifying	Jameson International
v Sheehan	5-1	1st round	Professional Players Tournament

	v Reynolds	0-5	2nd round	Professional Players Tournament
	v Kelly	0-8	Qualifying	Coral UK Championship
1983	v E. Hughes	7-10	Qualifying	Embassy World Professional Championship
	v Morgan	4-5	Qualifying	Jameson International
	v Martin	0-5	1st round	Professional Players Tournament
	v B. Harris	3-9	Qualifying	Coral UK Championship
1984	v Murphy	8-10	Qualifying	Embassy World Professional Championship
	v O'Kane	4-5	Qualifying	Jameson International
	v John Rea	2-5	Qualifying	Rothmans Grand Prix
	v Cripsey	9-8	Qualifying	Coral UK Open
	v Parrott	6-9	Qualifying	Coral UK Open
	v G. Foulds	1-5	Qualifying	Mercantile Credit Classic
1985	v Greaves	9-3	Qualifying	Tolly Cobbold English Professional Championship
	v Reynolds	2-9	1st round	Tolly Cobbold English Professional Championship
	v Watterson	1-6	Qualifying	Dulux British Open
	v T. Jones	4-10	Qualifying	Embassy World Professional Championship

ROBBIE FOLDVARI (Australia)

Born 2.6.60
Turned professional 1984
World ranking 62

A former Australian amateur billiards champion, Foldvari reached the semi-finals of the World Professional Billiards Championship at his first attempt last season.

1984	v Rigitano	5-2	Qualifying	Jameson International
	v Edmonds	5-1	Qualifying	Jameson International
	v Dodd	3-5	Qualifying	Jameson International
	v Gauvreau	2-5	Qualifying	Rothmans Grand Prix
	v Greaves	9-5	Qualifying	Coral UK Open
	v Cripsey	7-9	Qualifying	Coral UK Open
	v Houlihan	5-1	Qualifying	Mercantile Credit Classic
	v Jack Rea	5-4	Qualifying	Mercantile Credit Classic
	v Martin	5-2	Qualifying	Mercantile Credit Classic
	v Thorne	2-5	1st round	Mercantile Credit Classic
1985	v Duggan	6-4	Qualifying	Dulux British Open
	v Meo	0-6	1st round	Dulux British Open
	v Oliver	10-3	Qualifying	Embassy World Professional Championship
	v Edmonds	3-10	Qualifying	Embassy World Professional Championship

GEOFF FOULDS (England)

Born 20.11.39
Turned professional 1981
World ranking 78

The senior of the London father-and-son combination, Foulds is resident professional at Ealing Snooker Club and has recently made a speciality of acting as technical adviser to film and television dramas with snooker backgrounds.

1981	v French	2-5	Qualifying	Jameson International
	v Kelly	9-7	Qualifying	Coral UK Championship
	v Knowles	1-9	Qualifying	Coral UK Championship
1982	v Wildman	8-9	Qualifying	Embassy World Professional Championship
	v Kelly	4-5	Qualifying	Jameson International
	v Spencer	1-5	1st round	Professional Players Tournament
	v Gibson	9-3	Qualifying	Coral UK Championship
	v Williams	7-9	Qualifying	Coral UK Championship
1983	v Gibson	10-6	Qualifying	Embassy World Professional Championship
	v Meo	4-10	Qualifying	Embassy World Professional Championship
	v Burke	5-2	Qualifying	Jameson International
	v E. Hughes	1-5	Qualifying	Jameson International
	v Burke	4-5	Qualifying	Professional Players Tournament
	v Duggan	9-8	Qualifying	Coral UK Championship
	v Dodd	9-7	Qualifying	Coral UK Championship
	v S. Davis	1-9	1st round	Coral UK Championship
1984	v Morra	2-10	Qualifying	Embassy World Professional Championship
	v P. Francisco	5-4	Qualifying	Jameson International
	v Williamson	5-4	Qualifying	Jameson International
	v Donnelly	5-3	Qualifying	Jameson International
	v Campbell	3-5	Qualifying	Jameson International
	v Murphy	1-5	Qualifying	Rothmans Grand Prix
	v D. Hughes	9-7	Qualifying	Coral UK Open
	v Browne	5-9	Qualifying	Coral UK Open
	v Chaperon	5-3	Qualifying	Mercantile Credit Classic
	v Jonik	5-2	Qualifying	Mercantile Credit Classic
	v Fitzmaurice	5-1	Qualifying	Mercantile Credit Classic
	v Hallett	4-5	Qualifying	Mercantile Credit Classic
1985	v F. Davis	9-2	Qualifying	Tolly Cobbold English Professional Championship
	v Parrott	4-9	1st round	Tolly Cobbold English Professional Championship
	v T. Jones	0-6	Qualifying	Dulux British Open
	v Parkin	10-6	Qualifying	Embassy World Professional Championship
	v Everton	10-2	Qualifying	Embassy World Professional Championship
	v Roscoe	10-7	Qualifying	Embassy World Professional Championship
	v Johnson	6-10	Qualifying	Embassy World Professional Championship

NEAL FOULDS (England)

Born 13.7.63
Turned professional 1983
World ranking 23

Neal Foulds (David Muscroft)

Mike Hallet (David Muscroft)

Playing at the Crucible Theatre for the first time in 1984, Foulds achieved the distinction of beating Alex Higgins 10-9 in the first round of the Embassy World Professional Championship. Later that year, he beat Willie Thorne and Tony Knowles to reach the semi-finals of the Rothmans Grand Prix where he lost to the eventual winner, Dennis Taylor. It was this success that was mainly responsible for his rise of three places in the rankings.

1983	v French	2-5	Qualifying	Professional Players Tournament
	v Roscoe	9-2	Qualifying	Coral UK Championship
	v Meadowcroft	9-2	Qualifying	Coral UK Championship
	v David Taylor	4-9	1st round	Coral UK Championship
1984	v French	10-5	Qualifying	Embassy World Professional Championship
	v Dodd	10-4	Qualifying	Embassy World Professional Championship
	v Meadowcroft	10-2	Qualifying	Embassy World Professional Championship
	v Higgins	10-9	1st round	Embassy World Professional Championship
	v Mountjoy	6-13	2nd round	Embassy World Professional Championship
	v Bennett	5-0	Qualifying	Jameson International
	v Griffiths	3-5	1st round	Jameson International
	v Demarco	5-2	1st round	Rothmans Grand Prix
	v T. Jones	5-0	2nd round	Rothmans Grand Prix
	v Thorne	5-1	3rd round	Rothmans Grand Prix
	v Knowles	5-2	Quarter-final	Rothmans Grand Prix
	v Dennis Taylor	9-3	Semi-final	Rothmans Grand Prix
	v Fowler	6-9	Qualifying	Coral UK Open
	v Longworth	3-5	Qualifying	Mercantile Credit Classic
1985	v D. Hughes	9-3	1st round	Tolly Cobbold English Professional Championship
	v White	7-9	2nd round	Tolly Cobbold English Professional Championship
	v Hargreaves	6-1	1st round	Dulux British Open
	v Higgins	1-5	2nd round	Dulux British Open
	v Rigitano	10-8	Qualifying	Embassy World Professional Championship
	v S. Davis	8-10	1st round	Embassy World Professional Championship

DANNY FOWLER (England)

Born 30.7.56
Turned professional 1984
World ranking 55

A prolific winner of amateur tournaments, Fowler made a sound start to his professional career, qualifying for the first round of the Jameson International and reaching the second round of the Dulux British Open with a 6-4 win over Rex Williams.

1984	v Chaperon	5-0	Qualifying	Jameson International
	v Andrewartha	5-0	Qualifying	Jameson International
	v Martin	5-0	Qualifying	Jameson International
	v Dennis Taylor	0-5	1st round	Jameson International
	v Reynolds	2-5	1st round	Rothmans Grand Prix
	v Demarco	9-3	Qualifying	Coral UK Open
	v Oliver	9-3	Qualifying	Coral UK Open
	v F. Davis	9-4	Qualifying	Coral UK Open
	v N. Foulds	9-6	Qualifying	Coral UK Open
	v Reardon	2-9	1st round	Coral UK Open
	v Rigitano	5-0	Qualifying	Mercantile Credit Classic
	v Murphy	5-0	Qualifying	Mercantile Credit Classic
	v Meadowcroft	5-2	Qualifying	Mercantile Credit Classic
	v Wilson	4-5	Qualifying	Mercantile Credit Classic
1985	v Oliver	9-7	Qualifying	Tolly Cobbold English Professional Championship
	v S. Davis	3-9	1st round	Tolly Cobbold English Professional Championship
	v Everton	6-1	Qualifying	Dulux British Open
	v Williams	6-4	1st round	Dulux British Open
	v Bradley	4-5	2nd round	Dulux British Open
	v Hargreaves	10-0	Qualifying	Embassy World Professional Championship
	v Donnelly	10-0	Qualifying	Embassy World Professional Championship
	v Parrott	2-10	Qualifying	Embassy World Professional Championship

MANNIE FRANCISCO (South Africa)

Born –
Turned professional 1978
World ranking unranked

Runner-up in both the World Amateur Billiards Championship of 1971 and the World Amateur Snooker Championship in 1972, Francisco has never played in a major professional tournament. He is the elder brother of Silvino and the father of Peter, who both play full-time on the professional circuit.

PETER FRANCISCO (South Africa)

Born 14.2.62
Turned professional 1984
World ranking 59

Son of Mannie and nephew of Silvino, Peter Francisco played full-time on the British circuit with a 5-2 win over John Spencer in the first round of the Rothmans Grand Prix his best result.

1984	v G. Foulds	4-5	Qualifying	Jameson International
	v Black	5-4	Qualifying	Rothmans Grand Prix
	v Spencer	5-2	1st round	Rothmans Grand Prix
	v Reynolds	4-5	2nd round	Rothmans Grand Prix
	v Sheehan	9-5	Qualifying	Coral UK Open
	v Williamson	9-2	Qualifying	Coral UK Open
	v Sinclair	8-9	Qualifying	Coral UK Open
	v Longworth	4-5	Qualifying	Mercantile Credit Classic
1985	v Kelly	6-3	Qualifying	Dulux British Open
	v Virgo	2-6	1st round	Dulux British Open
	v Demarco	10-4	Qualifying	Embassy World Professional Championship
	v Murphy	10-4	Qualifying	Embassy World Professional Championship
	v Meadowcroft	10-5	Qualifying	Embassy World Professional Championship
	v Macleod	7-10	Qualifying	Embassy World Professional Championship

SILVINO FRANCISCO (South Africa)

Born 3.5.46
Turned professional 1978
World ranking 13

Uncle of Peter and younger brother of Mannie, who are also professional players, Silvino Francisco is the circuit's leading South African at 13th place in the world rankings. He has accumulated ranking points steadily in the last two seasons, notably through reaching the semi-finals of the Jameson International and through winning the £50,000 first prize in the Dulux Open.

1982	v Ross	9-0	Qualifying	Embassy World Professional Championship
	v Morgan	9-1	Qualifying	Embassy World Professional Championship
	v Dennis Taylor	10-7	1st round	Embassy World Professional Championship
	v Reynolds	13-8	2nd round	Embassy World Professional Championship
	v Reardon	8-13	Quarter-final	Embassy World Professional Championship
1983	v Kelly	10-5	Qualifying	Embassy World Professional Championship
	v Dennis Taylor	9-10	1st round	Embassy World Professional Championship
	v Darrington	5-2	Qualifying	Jameson International
	v Donnelly	5-1	2nd round	Jameson International
	v S. Davis	1-5	Quarter-final	Jameson International
	v Morra	5-3	1st round	Professional Players Tournament
	v Scott	5-1	2nd round	Professional Players Tournament
	v Knowles	0-5	3rd round	Professional Players Tournament
1984	v Thorburn	5-1	Qualifying	Lada Classic
	v Wildman	1-5	1st round	Lada Classic
	v Van Rensberg	10-3	Qualifying	Embassy World Professional Championship
	v Meo	10-5	1st round	Embassy World Professional Championship
	v Reardon	8-13	2nd round	Embassy World Professional Championship
	v Kelly	5-3	Qualifying	Jameson International
	v Spencer	5-2	1st round	Jameson International
	v Virgo	5-2	2nd round	Jameson International

Silvino Francisco (Adrian Murrell/All-Sport)

	v Knowles	6-9	Semi-final	Jameson International
	v Duggan	5-3	1st round	Rothmans Grand Prix
	v White	5-1	2nd round	Rothmans Grand Prix
	v Reynolds	1-5	3rd round	Rothmans Grand Prix
	v Sinclair	9-4	Qualifying	Coral UK Open
	v Charlton	4-9	1st round	Coral UK Open
	v T. Jones	5-1	Qualifying	Mercantile Credit Classic
	v S. Davis	0-5	1st round	Mercantile Credit Classic
1985	v Kearney	6-4	1st round	Dulux British Open
	v White	5-4	2nd round	Dulux British Open
	v Chaperon	5-2	3rd round	Dulux British Open
	v Meo	5-4	Quarter-final	Dulux British Open
	v Higgins	9-6	Semi-final	Dulux British Open
	v Stevens	**12-9**	**Final**	**Dulux British Open**
	v Medati	10-7	Qualifying	Embassy World Professional Championship
	v Dennis Taylor	2-10	1st round	Embassy World Professional Championship

DOUG FRENCH (England)

Born 26.1.35
Turned professional 1981
World ranking unranked

After four years as a professional, French resigned his membership of the WPBSA in April 1985 and was reinstated as an amateur.

1981	v G. Foulds	5-2	Qualifying	Jameson International
	v Houlihan	5-3	Qualifying	Jameson International
	v Williams	0-5	Qualifying	Jameson International
	v Williams	3-9	Qualifying	Coral UK Championship
1982	v Bennett	9-3	Qualifying	Embassy World Professional Championship
	v Fagan	6-9	Qualifying	Embassy World Professional Championship
	v Cripsey	5-1	Qualifying	Jameson International
	v Roscoe	2-5	Qualifying	Jameson International
	v Higgins	3-5	1st round	Professional Players Tournament
	v Dodd	7-9	Qualifying	Coral UK Championship
1983	v Williamson	8-10	Qualifying	Embassy World Professional Championship
	v Williams	1-5	Qualifying	Jameson International
	v N. Foulds	5-2	Qualifying	Professional Players Tournament
	v Virgo	4-5	1st round	Professional Players Tournament
	v Jack Rea	9-5	Qualifying	Coral UK Championship
	v Martin	3-9	Qualifying	Coral UK Championship
1984	v N. Foulds	5-10	Qualifying	Embassy World Professional Championship
	v T. Jones	1-5	Qualifying	Jameson International
	v Roscoe	0-5	Qualifying	Rothmans Grand Prix
	v J. McLaughlin	3-9	Qualifying	Coral UK Open
	v Kearney	1-5	Qualifying	Mercantile Credit Classic
1985	v Fisher	8-9	Qualifying	Tolly Cobbold English Professional Championship

v E. McLaughlin	6-0	Qualifying	Dulux British Open
v Knowles	2-6	1st round	Dulux British Open
v D. Hughes	5-10	Qualifying	Embassy World Professional Championship

GEORGE GANIM (Australia)

Born 20.3.48
Turned professional 1983
World ranking unranked

Six times Australian amateur billiards champion, Ganim did not compete on the circuit last season.

1983	v Cripsey	5-4	Qualifying	Professional Players Tournament
	v Reardon	4-5	1st round	Professional Players Tournament
1984	v Wych	1-10	Qualifying	Embassy World Professional Championship

MARCEL GAUVREAU (Canada)

Born 9.1.55
Turned professional 1983
World ranking 39

A win over Kirk Stevens in the 1984 Jameson International was Gauvreau's best performance last season following an appearance in the televised stage of the Embassy World Championship the previous spring.

1983	v Miles	3-5	1st round	Professional Players Tournament
1984	v Campbell	10-7	Qualifying	Embassy World Professional Championship
	v Cripsey	10-1	Qualifying	Embassy World Professional Championship
	v Macleod	10-6	Qualifying	Embassy World Professional Championship
	v David Taylor	5-10	1st round	Embassy World Professional Championship
	v Jonik	5-1	Qualifying	Jameson International
	v Parrott	5-4	Qualifying	Jameson International
	v Stevens	5-1	1st round	Jameson International
	v Thorne	3-5	2nd round	Jameson International
	v Foldvari	5-2	Qualifying	Rothmans Grand Prix
	v Parrott	3-5	1st round	Rothmans Grand Prix
	v Bales	9-8	Qualifying	Coral UK Open
	v Mans	9-6	Qualifying	Coral UK Open
	v Knowles	5-9	1st round	Coral UK Open
	v Giannaros	5-3	Qualifying	Mercantile Credit Classic
	v Sinclair	5-1	Qualifying	Mercantile Credit Classic
	v Higgins	3-5	1st round	Mercantile Credit Classic
1985	v Greaves	6-3	Qualifying	Dulux British Open
	v Stevens	3-6	1st round	Dulux British Open
	v Van Rensberg	10-9	Qualifying	Embassy World Professional Championship
	v Reynolds	1-10	Qualifying	Embassy World Professional Championship

JAMES GIANNAROS (Australia)

Born 25.7.52
Turned professional 1983
World ranking 101

Giannaros won the Australian Amateur Championship in 1982.

1984	v Dodd	1-10 Qualifying	Embassy World Professional Championship
	v Chappel	5-2 Qualifying	Mercantile Credit Classic
	v Gauvreau	3-5 Qualifying	Mercantile Credit Classic
1985	v Roscoe	6-1 Qualifying	Dulux British Open
	v Reynolds	3-6 1st round	Dulux British Open
	v Longworth	1-10 Qualifying	Embassy World Professional Championship

MATT GIBSON (Scotland)

Born 7.5.53
Turned professional 1981
World ranking 81

Gibson won the Scottish Amateur Snooker Championship in 1980.

1981	v Hood	5-3 Qualifying	Jameson International
	v Parkin	5-3 Qualifying	Jameson International
	v Dunning	3-5 Qualifying	Jameson International
	v Demarco	5-3 Quarter-final	Scottish Professional Championship
	v Donnelly	6-4 Semi-final	Scottish Professional Championship
	v Black	7-11 Final	Scottish Professional Championship
	v Fitzmaurice	9-6 Qualifying	Coral UK Championship
	v Everton	7-9 Qualifying	Coral UK Championship
1982	v Donnelly	8-9 Qualifying	Embassy World Professional Championship
	v E. McLaughlin	6-3 Quarter-final	Scottish Professional Championship
	v Sinclair	2-6 Semi-final	Scottish Professional Championship
	v Wildman	1-5 Qualifying	Jameson International
	v Martin	2-5 1st round	Professional Players Tournament
	v G. Foulds	3-9 Qualifying	Coral UK Championship
1983	v G. Foulds	6-10 Qualifying	Embassy World Professional Championship
	v Macleod	5-6 1st round	Scottish Professional Championship
	v Dodd	5-1 Qualifying	Jameson International
	v. Scott	3-5 Qualifying	Jameson International
	v Morgan	4-5 Qualifying	Professional Players Tournament
	v Johnson	6-9 Qualifying	Coral UK Championship
1984	v Rigitano	10-7 Qualifying	Embassy World Professional Championship
	v Fisher	10-7 Qualifying	Embassy World Professional Championship
	v Johnson	3-10 Qualifying	Embassy World Professional Championship
	v Medati	5-3 Qualifying	Jameson International
	v W. Jones	2-5 Qualifying	Jameson International
	v Chaperon	4-5 Qualifying	Rothmans Grand Prix
	v Hargreaves	9-8 Qualifying	Coral UK Open

	v Donnelly	6-9	Qualifying	Coral UK Open
	v T. Jones	0-5	Qualifying	Mercantile Credit Classic
1985	v Demarco	6-1	Qualifying	Dulux British Open
	v Wildman	1-6	1st round	Dulux British Open
	v Hines	10-7	Qualifying	Embassy World Professional Championship
	v Fagan	8-10	Qualifying	Embassy World Professional Championship

DAVID GREAVES (England)

Born 1.9.46
Turned professional 1973
World ranking 96

Year	Opponent	Score	Round	Event
1973	v Bennett	9-8	1st round	World Professional Championship
	v F. Davis	1-16	2nd round	World Professional Championship
1975	v G. Owen	3-15	1st round	World Professional Championship
1976	v Charlton	8-5	Qualifying	Embassy World Professional Championship
	v David Taylor	1-8	Qualifying	Embassy World Professional Championship
1977	v David Taylor	0-11	Qualifying	Embassy World Professional Championship
	v David Taylor	4-5	1st round	Super Crystalate UK Championship
1978	v Barrie	3-9	Prelim	Embassy World Professional Championship
	v Dunning	3-9	Qualifying	Coral UK Championship
1979	v Williams	2-9	Prelim	Embassy World Professional Championship
	v Dunning	8-9	1st round	Coral UK Championship
1980	v Meadowcroft	1-9	Qualifying	Coral UK Championship
1981	v Dunning	4-9	Qualifying	John Courage English Professional
	v Parkin	9-5	Qualifying	Embassy World Professional Championship
	v Thorne	3-9	Qualifying	Embassy World Professional Championship
	v E. McLaughlin	1-5	Qualifying	Jameson International
1982	v Morgan	2-9	Qualifying	Embassy World Professional Championship
1983	v E. McLaughlin	7-10	Qualifying	Embassy World Professional Championship
	v Martin	1-5	Qualifying	Jameson International
	v Andrewartha	5-2	Qualifying	Professional Players Tournament
	v Reynolds	1-5	1st round	Professional Players Tournament
	v Wildman	5-9	Qualifying	Coral UK Championship
1984	v Edmonds	0-10	Qualifying	Embassy World Professional Championship
	v J. McLaughlin	3-5	Qualifying	Jameson International
	v King	0-5	Qualifying	Rothmans Grand Prix
	v Foldvari	5-9	Qualifying	Coral UK Open
	v T. Jones	2-5	Qualifying	Mercantile Credit Classic
1985	v Fitzmaurice	3-9	Qualifying	Tolly Cobbold English Professional Championship
	v Gauvreau	3-6	Qualifying	Dulux British Open
	v Chalmers	3-10	Qualifying	Embassy World Professional Championship

TERRY GRIFFITHS (Wales)

Born 16.10.47
Turned professional 1978
World ranking 8

Embassy world champion at his first attempt in 1979, Benson and Hedges winner in 1980, three times winner of the Benson and Hedges Irish Masters, 1982 Coral UK champion and winner of the 1982 Lada Classic, Griffiths has not in the last couple of seasons reproduced quite this level of excellence.

He has continued to play well in fits and starts, even if an attempt to make a radical change in his technique late in his career was probably misguided. He has now reverted to his original style and at the end of the season won the BCE Welsh Professional Championship for the first time.

1978	v Williams	8-9	Qualifying	Coral UK Championship
1979	v Bennett	9-2	Prelim	Embassy World Professional Championship
	v Meadowcroft	9-6	Qualifying	Embassy World Professional Championship
	v Mans	13-8	1st round	Embassy World Professional Championship
	v Higgins	13-12	Quarter-final	Embassy World Professional Championship
	v Charlton	19-17	Semi-final	Embassy World Professional Championship
	v Dennis Taylor	**24-16**	**Final**	**Embassy World Professional Championship**
	v Wilson	9-4	3rd round	Coral UK Championship
	v Higgins	9-7	Quarter-final	Coral UK Championship
	v Werbeniuk	9-3	Semi-final	Coral UK Championship
	v Virgo	13-14	Final	Coral UK Championship
1980	v Thorburn	5-3	Quarter-final	Benson & Hedges Masters
	v Spencer	5-0	Semi-final	Benson & Hedges Masters
	v Higgins	**9-5**	**Final**	**Benson & Hedges Masters**
	v Mountjoy	**9-8**	**Final**	**Benson & Hedges Irish Masters**
	v S. Davis	10-13	2nd round	Embassy World Professional Championship
	v Fagan	9-8	2nd round	Coral UK Championship
	v Dennis Taylor	9-7	Quarter-final	Coral UK Championship
	v S. Davis	0-9	Semi-final	Coral UK Championship
1981	v F. Davis	5-2	Quarter-final	Benson & Hedges Masters
	v Spencer	6-5	Semi-final	Benson & Hedges Masters
	v Higgins	6-9	Final	Benson & Hedges Masters
	v Reardon	6-9	Semi-final	Woodpecker Welsh Professional Championship
	v Meo	13-6	2nd round	Embassy World Professional Championship
	v S. Davis	9-13	Quarter-final	Embassy World Professional Championship
	v Spencer	5-2	3rd round	Jameson International
	v Higgins	2-5	Quarter-final	Jameson International
	v Stevens	5-0	1st round	Northern Ireland Classic
	v S. Davis	6-9	Semi-final	Northern Ireland Classic
	v Miles	9-4	3rd round	Coral UK Championship
	v Knowles	9-5	Quarter-final	Coral UK Championship
	v Meo	9-3	Semi-final	Coral UK Championship

	v S. Davis	3-16	Final	Coral UK Championship
1982	v Thorburn	5-1	1st round	Lada Classic
	v Higgins	5-1	Semi-final	Lada Classic
	v S. Davis	**9-8**	**Final**	**Lada Classic**
	v Reardon	5-3	Quarter-final	Benson & Hedges Masters
	v Higgins	6-4	Semi-final	Benson & Hedges Masters
	v S. Davis	5-9	Final	Benson & Hedges Masters
	v S. Davis	7-9	Final	Yamaha International Masters
	v Roscoe	6-2	1st round	Woodpecker Welsh Professional Championship
	v Wilson	9-6	Semi-final	Woodpecker Welsh Professional Championship
	v Mountjoy	8-9	Final	Woodpecker Welsh Professional Championship
	v Meo	5-3	Quarter-final	Benson & Hedges Irish Masters
	v Reardon	6-3	Semi-final	Benson & Hedges Irish Masters
	v S. Davis	**9-5**	**Final**	**Benson & Hedges Irish Masters**
	v Thorne	6-10	1st round	Embassy World Professional Championship
	v Reardon	5-3	1st round	Langs Scottish Masters
	v Higgins	5-6	Semi-final	Langs Scottish Masters
	v Williams	5-2	1st round	Jameson International
	v Higgins	5-2	2nd round	Jameson International
	v Stevens	3-5	Quarter-final	Jameson International
	v Roscoe	5-1	1st round	Professional Players Tournament
	v Watterson	5-2	2nd round	Professional Players Tournament
	v Sinclair	5-3	3rd round	Professional Players Tournament
	v White	2-5	Quarter-final	Professional Players Tournament
	v Johnson	9-1	1st round	Coral UK Championship
	v Dennis Taylor	9-7	2nd round	Coral UK Championship
	v S. Davis	9-6	Quarter-final	Coral UK Championship
	v Meo	9-7	Semi-final	Coral UK Championship
	v Higgins	**16-15**	**Final**	**Coral UK Championship**
1983	v Mountjoy	1-5	1st round	Lada Classic
	v Stevens	5-3	1st round	Benson & Hedges Masters
	v Thorburn	3-5	Quarter-final	Benson & Hedges Masters
	v Everton	6-1	Quarter-final	Woodpecker Welsh Professional Championship
	v Reardon	4-9	Semi-final	Woodpecker Welsh Professional Championship
	v Werbeniuk	5-3	Semi-final	Tolly Cobbold Classic
	v S. Davis	5-7	Final	Tolly Cobbold Classic
	v Mountjoy	5-4	Quarter-final	Benson & Hedges Irish Masters
	v S. Davis	2-6	Semi-final	Benson & Hedges Irish Masters
	v Wildman	10-8	1st round	Embassy World Professional Championship
	v Thorburn	12-13	2nd round	Embassy World Professional Championship
	v Thorburn	1-5	1st round	Langs Scottish Masters
	v Miles	5-2	1st round	Jameson International
	v Scott	5-0	2nd round	Jameson International
	v Spencer	5-4	Quarter-final	Jameson International
	v Thorburn	8-9	Semi-final	Jameson International

v Dodd	5-3	1st round	Professional Players Tournament
v Parrott	5-1	2nd round	Professional Players Tournament
v E. Hughes	2-5	3rd round	Professional Players Tournament
v Martin	9-4	1st round	Coral UK Championship
v Hallett	9-5	2nd round	Coral UK Championship
v Johnson	9-2	Quarter-final	Coral UK Championship
v Higgins	4-9	Semi-final	Coral UK Championship
1984 v Reynolds	5-2	Qualifying	Lada Classic
v Roscoe	5-2	1st round	Lada Classic
v S. Davis	4-5	Quarter-final	Lada Classic
v Werbeniuk	5-1	1st round	Benson & Hedges Masters
v Spencer	5-4	Quarter-final	Benson & Hedges Masters
v Knowles	6-4	Semi-final	Benson & Hedges Masters
v White	5-9	Final	Benson & Hedges Masters
v Andrewartha	6-1	1st round	Strongbow Welsh Professional Championship
v Mountjoy	5-9	Semi-final	Strongbow Welsh Professional Championship
v Werbeniuk	5-2	1st round	Benson & Hedges Irish Masters
v Knowles	5-0	Quarter-final	Benson & Hedges Irish Masters
v Dennis Taylor	5-4	Semi-final	Benson & Hedges Irish Masters
v S. Davis	1-9	Final	Benson & Hedges Irish Masters
v Mifsud	10-2	1st round	Embassy World Professional Championship
v Werbeniuk	10-5	2nd round	Embassy World Professional Championship
v S. Davis	10-13	Quarter-final	Embassy World Professional Championship
v Knowles	3-5	1st round	Langs Scottish Masters
v N. Foulds	5-3	1st round	Jameson International
v Higgins	4-5	2nd round	Jameson International
v T. Jones	3-5	1st round	Rothmans Grand Prix
v Wilson	6-9	1st round	Coral UK Open
v Fagan	5-0	1st round	Mercantile Credit Classic
v Williams	5-3	2nd round	Mercantile Credit Classic
v Thorburn	4-5	Quarter-final	Mercantile Credit Classic
1985 v Werbeniuk	5-2	1st round	Benson & Hedges Masters
v Higgins	5-1	Quarter-final	Benson & Hedges Masters
v Mountjoy	2-6	Semi-final	Benson & Hedges Masters
v Chalmers	6-0	1st round	Dulux British Open
v Newbury	3-5	2nd round	Dulux British Open
v Higgins	2-5	1st round	Benson & Hedges Irish Masters
v Williams	10-3	1st round	Embassy World Professional Championship
v Higgins	13-7	2nd round	Embassy World Professional Championship
v S. Davis	6-13	Quarter-final	Embassy World Professional Championship
v Chappel	6-0	Quarter-final	BCE Welsh Professional Championship
v Reardon	9-3	Semi-final	BCE Welsh Professional Championship
v Mountjoy	**9-4**	**Final**	**BCE Welsh Professional Championship**

MIKE HALLETT (England)

Born 6.7.59
Turned professional 1979
World ranking 28

In his six years as a professional, Hallett has scored some fine wins, notably over Steve Davis in the 1983 Professional Players Tournament and Alex Higgins in the 1983 Rothmans Grand Prix, without ever quite managing to knit a series of such wins together.

Year	Opponent	Score	Round	Tournament
1979	v Parkin	9-1	1st round	Coral UK Championship
	v Fagan	4-9	2nd round	Coral UK Championship
1980	v Stevens	3-9	Qualifying	Embassy World Professional Championship
	v Bennett	9-4	Qualifying	Coral UK Championship
	v Edmonds	9-8	Qualifying	Coral UK Championship
	v S. Davis	1-9	1st round	Coral UK Championship
1981	v Edmonds	3-9	Qualifying	John Courage English Professional
	v Jonik	9-1	Qualifying	Embassy World Professional Championship
	v Meo	4-9	Qualifying	Embassy World Professional Championship
	v Demarco	5-4	Qualifying	Jameson International
	v Knowles	2-5	1st round	Jameson International
	v V. Harris	9-4	Qualifying	Coral UK Championship
	v D. Hughes	9-6	Qualifying	Coral UK Championship
	v Fagan	9-5	Qualifying	Coral UK Championship
	v Stevens	4-9	2nd round	Coral UK Championship
1982	v Johnson	9-8	Qualifying	Embassy World Professional Championship
	v Virgo	4-10	1st round	Embassy World Professional Championship
	v Jonik	5-2	Qualifying	Jameson International
	v Wildman	2-5	Qualifying	Jameson International
	v V. Harris	5-3	1st round	Professional Players Tournament
	v Virgo	2-5	2nd round	Professional Players Tournament
	v Demarco	9-1	Qualifying	Coral UK Championship
	v F. Davis	9-7	1st round	Coral UK Championship
	v Reardon	8-9	2nd round	Coral UK Championship
1983	v Andrewartha	10-7	Qualifying	Embassy World Professional Championship
	v King	10-6	Qualifying	Embassy World Professional Championship
	v Spencer	7-10	1st round	Embassy World Professional Championship
	v Roscoe	5-2	Qualifying	Jameson International
	v Morra	3-5	Qualifying	Jameson International
	v Kelly	5-0	1st round	Professional Players Tournament
	v S. Davis	5-2	2nd round	Professional Players Tournament
	v Meo	3-5	3rd round	Professional Players Tournament
	v Darrington	9-1	Qualifying	Coral UK Championship
	v Miles	9-4	1st round	Coral UK Championship
	v Griffiths	5-9	2nd round	Coral UK Championship
1984	v Dennis Taylor	5-4	Qualifying	Lada Classic
	v Knowles	3-5	1st round	Lada Classic
	v Burke	10-5	Qualifying	Embassy World Professional Championship
	v Mountjoy	4-10	1st round	Embassy World Professional Championship
	v O'Kane	4-5	Qualifying	Jameson International

	v Sheehan	5-1	1st round	Rothmans Grand Prix
	v Higgins	5-3	2nd round	Rothmans Grand Prix
	v Stevens	3-5	3rd round	Rothmans Grand Prix
	v Bradley	9-8	Qualifying	Coral UK Open
	v Mountjoy	2-9	1st round	Coral UK Open
	v G. Foulds	5-4	Qualifying	Mercantile Credit Classic
	v Reardon	3-5	1st round	Mercantile Credit Classic
1985	v Duggan	9-4	1st round	Tolly Cobbold English Professional Championship
	v Meo	4-9	2nd round	Tolly Cobbold English Professional Championship
	v Meo	4-5	2nd round	Dulux British Open
	v Chalmers	10-1	Qualifying	Embassy World Professional Championship
	v Thorburn	8-10	1st round	Embassy World Professional Championship

JOHN HARGREAVES (England)

Born 2.12.45
Turned professional 1983
World ranking 102

	v Morra	0-5	Qualifying	Professional Players Tournament
1983	v Williamson	4-9	Qualifying	Coral UK Championship
1984	v E. McLaughlin	5-10	Qualifying	Embassy World Professional Championship
	v Houlihan	5-2	Qualifying	Jameson International
	v Kelly	2-5	Qualifying	Jameson International
	v Donnelly	4-5	Qualifying	Rothmans Grand Prix
	v Medati	9-6	Qualifying	Coral UK Open
	v Gibson	8-9	Qualifying	Coral UK Open
	v Darrington	5-2	Qualifying	Mercantile Credit Classic
	v Edmonds	2-5	Qualifying	Mercantile Credit Classic
1985	v Medati	8-9	Qualifying	Tolly Cobbold English Professional Championship
	v N. Foulds	1-6	1st round	Dulux British Open
	v Fowler	0-10	Qualifying	Embassy World Professional Championship

BOB HARRIS (England)

Born 12.3.56
Turned professional 1982
World ranking 66

Harris's best victory in his three-year professional career came last season when he beat Eddie Charlton 6-3 in the first round of the Dulux British Open.

	Scott	4-5	Qualifying	Jameson International
1982	v Cripsey	9-6	Qualifying	Coral UK Championship
	v Watterson	9-3	Qualifying	Coral UK Championship
	v Fagan	6-9	1st round	Coral UK Championship
1983	v Wildman	7-10	Qualifying	Embassy World Professional Championship

	v Dunning	5-3	Qualifying	Jameson International
	v Wildman	2-5	Qualifying	Jameson International
	v King	3-5	Qualifying	Professional Players Tournament
	v E. McLaughlin	9-8	Qualifying	Coral UK Championship
	v Fitzmaurice	9-3	Qualifying	Coral UK Championship
	v Reardon	7-9	1st round	Coral UK Championship
1984	v Sheehan	10-3	Qualifying	Embassy World Professional Championship
	v Burke	4-10	Qualifying	Embassy World Professional Championship
	v Watchorn	7-9	Qualifying	Coral UK Open
1985	v Duggan	8-9	Qualifying	Tolly Cobbold English Professional Championship
	v Meadowcroft	6-1	Qualifying	Dulux British Open
	v Charlton	6-3	1st round	Dulux British Open
	v E. Hughes	4-5	2nd round	Dulux British Open
	v Rigitano	4-10	Qualifying	Embassy World Professional Championship

VIC HARRIS (England)

Born 16.8.45
Turned professional 1981
World ranking 65

English amateur champion in 1981, Harris achieved his best professional win in the 1984 Dulux British Open when he beat Doug Mountjoy 6-5 to reach the second round.

1981	v Sheehan	1-5	Qualifying	Jameson International
	v Higgins	3-5	Quarter-final	Langs Scottish Masters
	v Hallett	4-9	Qualifying	Coral UK Championship
	v Johnson	4-9	Qualifying	Embassy World Professional Championship
1982	v Hallett	3-5	1st round	Professional Players Tournament
	v M. Owen	9-4	Qualifying	Coral UK Championship
	v Johnson	8-9	Qualifying	Coral UK Championship
	v Sheehan	5-3	Qualifying	Jameson International
	v Virgo	2-5	Qualifying	Jameson International
1983	v Meo	0-10	Qualifying	Embassy World Professional Championship
	v Medati	0-5	Qualifying	Jameson International
	Harris *wo* Mifsud *scr*		Qualifying	Professional Players Tournament
	v Thorburn	1-5	1st round	Professional Players Tournament
	v Houlihan	9-6	Qualifying	Coral UK Championship
	v Williams	6-9	Qualifying	Coral UK Championship
1984	v Van Rensberg	7-10	Qualifying	Embassy World Professional Championship
	v Williamson	0-5	Qualifying	Jameson International
	v F. Davis	5-1	Qualifying	Rothmans Grand Prix
	v Knowles	1-5	1st round	Rothmans Grand Prix
	v Bradley	8-9	Qualifying	Coral UK Open
	v Newbury	3-5	Qualifying	Mercantile Credit Classic
1985	v Scott	7-9	Qualifying	Tolly Cobbold English Professional Champions..ip
	v Dodd	6-1	Qualifying	Dulux British Open

v Mountjoy	6-5	1st round	Dulux British Open
v O'Kane	3-5	2nd round	Dulux British Open
v O'Kane	5-10	Qualifying	Embassy World Professional Championship

LEON HEYWOOD (Australia)

Born 26.5.52
Turned professional 1983
World ranking 98

1984 v Scott	7-10	Qualifying	Embassy World Professional Championship
1985 v Chaperon	1-10	Qualifying	Embassy World Professional Championship

ALEX HIGGINS (Northern Ireland)

Born 18.3.49
Turned professional 1971
World ranking 9

World champion in 1972 and 1982, Higgins has also won the Benson and Hedges Masters twice, in 1978 and 1981, as well as being runner-up in the two intervening years. He made an epic recovery from 0-7 to beat Steve Davis 16-15 in the 1983 Coral UK final and last season won both the Hofmeister World Doubles with Jimmy White and the Guinness World Cup for Ireland with Dennis Taylor and Eugene Hughes.

Higgins lost his Irish title to Dennis Taylor just before his fellow Ulsterman won the world title.

1972 v Gross	15-6	Qualifying	World Professional Championship
v Parkin	11-3	Qualifying	World Professional Championship
v Jack Rea	19-11	1st round	World Professional Championship
v Pulman	31-23	Quarter-final	World Professional Championship
v Williams	31-30	Semi-final	World Professional Championship
v Spencer	**37-32**	**Final**	**World Professional Championship**
1973 v Houlihan	16-3	2nd round	World Professional Championship
v Davis	16-14	Quarter-final	World Professional Championship
v Charlton	9-23	Semi-final	World Professional Championship
v Spencer	2-8	Semi-final	Norwich Union Open
1974 v Bennett	15-4	2nd round	World Professional Championship
v F. Davis	14-15	Quarter-final	World Professional Championship
1974 v Dennis Taylor	5-1	1st round	Norwich Union Open
-75 v Werbeniuk	5-4	Quarter-final	Norwich Union Open
v Reardon	8-9	Semi-final	Norwich Union Open
1975 v Werbeniuk	5-0	1st round	Benson & Hedges Masters
v Williams	3-5	Quarter-final	Benson & Hedges Masters
v David Taylor	15-2	2nd round	World Professional Championship
v Williams	19-12	Quarter-final	World Professional Championship
v Reardon	14-19	Semi-final	World Professional Championship
1976 v Miles	1-4	2nd round	Benson & Hedges Masters
v Thorburn	15-14	1st round	Embassy World Professional Championship

	v Spencer	15-14	Quarter-final	Embassy World Professional Championship
	v Charlton	20-18	Semi-final	Embassy World Professional Championship
	v Reardon	16-27	Final	Embassy World Professional Championship
1977	v Mans	4-2	Quarter-final	Benson & Hedges Masters
	v Mountjoy	3-5	Semi-final	Benson & Hedges Masters
	v Mountjoy	12-13	1st round	Embassy World Professional Championship
	v David Taylor	5-4	2nd round	Super Crystalate UK Championship
	v Dunning	5-0	Quarter-final	Super Crystalate UK Championship
	v Mountjoy	2-9	Semi-final	Super Crystalate UK Championship
1978	v Dennis Taylor	4-3	Quarter-final	Benson & Hedges Masters
	v Reardon	5-1	Semi-final	Benson & Hedges Masters
	v Thorburn	**7-5**	**Final**	**Benson & Hedges Masters**
	v Fagan	12-13	1st round	Embassy World Professional Championship
	v Meadowcroft	9-6	1st round	Coral UK Championship
	v F. Davis	9-4	Quarter-final	Coral UK Championship
	v David Taylor	5-9	Semi-final	Coral UK Championship
1979	v Miles	3-6	Semi-final	Holsten Lager International
	v Charlton	5-2	Quarter-final	Benson & Hedges Masters
	v Mountjoy	5-1	Semi-final	Benson & Hedges Masters
	v Mans	4-8	Final	Benson & Hedges Masters
	v David Taylor	13-5	1st round	Embassy World Professional Championship
	v Griffiths	12-13	Quarter-final	Embassy World Professional Championship
	v Houlihan	9-3	3rd round	Coral UK Championship
	v Griffiths	7-9	Quarter-final	Coral UK Championship
1980	v F. Davis	5-1	1st round	Benson & Hedges Masters
	v Mans	5-1	Quarter-final	Benson & Hedges Masters
	v Reardon	5-2	Semi-final	Benson & Hedges Masters
	v Griffiths	5-9	Final	Benson & Hedges Masters
	v Meo	4-0	Semi-final	British Gold Cup
	v Reardon	**5-1**	**Final**	**British Gold Cup**
	v Meo	10-9	1st round	Embassy World Professional Championship
	v Mans	13-6	2nd round	Embassy World Professional Championship
	v S. Davis	13-9	Quarter-final	Embassy World Professional Championship
	v Stevens	16-13	Semi-final	Embassy World Professional Championship
	v Thorburn	16-18	Final	Embassy World Professional Championship
	v Thorne	9-7	2nd round	Coral UK Championship
	v F. Davis	9-6	Quarter-final	Coral UK Championship
	v Reardon	9-7	Semi-final	Coral UK Championship
	v S. Davis	6-16	Final	Coral UK Championship
1981	v Mountjoy	5-1	Quarter-final	Benson & Hedges Masters
	v Thorburn	6-5	Semi-final	Benson & Hedges Masters
	v Griffiths	**9-6**	**Final**	**Benson & Hedges Masters**
	v S. Davis	8-13	2nd round	Embassy World Professional Championship
	v V. Harris	5-3	Quarter-final	Langs Scottish Masters
	v Thorburn	2-6	Semi-final	Langs Scottish Masters
	v Fagan	5-3	2nd round	Jameson International
	v Mountjoy	5-1	3rd round	Jameson International
	v Griffiths	5-2	Quarter-final	Jameson International
	v S. Davis	8-9	Semi-final	Jameson International
	v S. Davis	2-5	1st round	Northern Ireland Classic

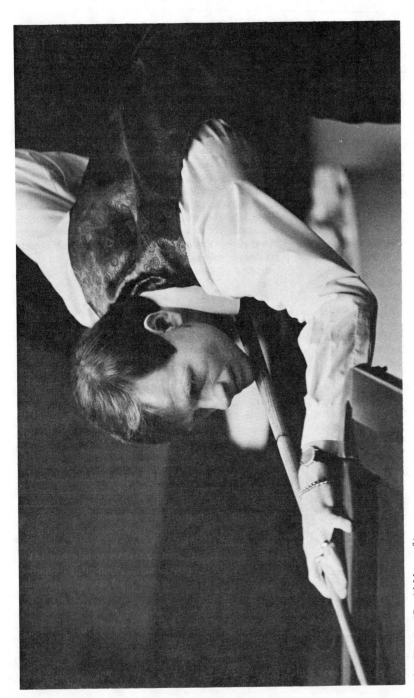

Alex Higgins (David Muscroft)

	v Martin	9-7	2nd round	Coral UK Championship
	v David Taylor	9-5	3rd round	Coral UK Championship
	v Meo	4-9	Quarter-final	Coral UK Championship
1982	v Dennis Taylor	5-1	1st round	Lada Classic
	v Griffiths	1-5	Semi-final	Lada Classic
	v Charlton	5-1	Quarter-final	Benson & Hedges Masters
	v Griffiths	4-6	Semi-final	Benson & Hedges Masters
	v D. Hughes	6-2	Semi-final	Irish Professional Championship
	v Dennis Taylor	13-16	Final	Irish Professional Championship
	v Wych	5-3	1st round	Benson & Hedges Irish Masters
	v Thorburn	5-4	Quarter-final	Benson & Hedges Irish Masters
	v S. Davis	2-6	Semi-final	Benson & Hedges Irish Masters
	v Meadowcroft	10-5	1st round	Embassy World Professional Championship
	v Mountjoy	13-12	2nd round	Embassy World Professional Championship
	v Thorne	13-10	Quarter-final	Embassy World Professional Championship
	v White	16-15	Semi-final	Embassy World Professional Championship
	v Reardon	**18-15**	**Final**	**Embassy World Professional Championship**
	v Sinclair	5-1	1st round	Langs Scottish Masters
	v Griffiths	6-5	Semi-final	Langs Scottish Masters
	v S. Davis	4-9	Final	Langs Scottish Masters
	v Kelly	5-3	1st round	Jameson International
	v Griffiths	2-5	2nd round	Jameson International
	v French	5-3	1st round	Professional Players Tournament
	v Reardon	2-5	2nd round	Professional Players Tournament
	v Martin	9-7	1st round	Coral UK Championship
	v Reynolds	9-8	2nd round	Coral UK Championship
	v Spencer	9-5	Quarter-final	Coral UK Championship
	v Reardon	9-6	Semi-final	Coral UK Championship
	v Griffiths	15-16	Final	Coral UK Championship
1983	v Werbeniuk	4-5	1st round	Lada Classic
	v Werbeniuk	4-5	1st round	Benson & Hedges Masters
	v Dennis Taylor	2-4	1st round	Tolly Cobbold Classic
	v Jack Rea	6-3	Quarter-final	Irish Professional Championship
	v E. Hughes	6-2	Semi-final	Irish Professional Championship
	v Dennis Taylor	**16-11**	**Final**	**Irish Professional Championship**
	v White	5-2	Quarter-final	Benson & Hedges Irish Masters
	v Reardon	3-6	Semi-final	Benson & Hedges Irish Masters
	v Reynolds	10-4	1st round	Embassy World Professional Championship
	v Thorne	13-8	2nd round	Embassy World Professional Championship
	v Werbeniuk	13-11	Quarter-final	Embassy World Professional Championship
	v S. Davis	5-16	Semi-final	Embassy World Professional Championship
	v White	5-3	1st round	Langs Supreme Scottish Masters
	v S. Davis	2-6	Semi-final	Langs Supreme Scottish Masters
	v Martin	2-5	1st round	Jameson International
	v Watterson	2-5	1st round	Professional Players Tournament
	v Macleod	9-6	1st round	Coral UK Championship
	v Medati	9-1	2nd round	Coral UK Championship
	v Knowles	9-5	Quarter-final	Coral UK Championship
	v Griffiths	9-4	Semi-final	Coral UK Championship
	v S. Davis	**16-15**	**Final**	**Coral UK Championship**

1984 v Fagan	5-3	Qualifying	Lada Classic
v Parrott	2-5	1st round	Lada Classic
v Mountjoy	5-2	1st round	Benson & Hedges Masters
v Knowles	1-5	Quarter-final	Benson & Hedges Masters
v Charlton	5-2	1st round	Benson & Hedges Irish Masters
v Reardon	5-2	Quarter-final	Benson & Hedges Irish Masters
v S. Davis	4-6	Semi-final	Benson & Hedges Irish Masters
v N. Foulds	9-10	1st round	Embassy World Professional Championship
v Stevens	5-2	1st round	Langs Supreme Scottish Masters
v S. Davis	4-6	Semi-final	Langs Supreme Scottish Masters
v Sinclair	5-1	1st round	Jameson International
v Griffiths	5-4	2nd round	Jameson International
v S. Davis	1-5	Quarter-final	Jameson International
v Bales	5-1	1st round	Rothmans Grand Prix
v Hallett	3-5	2nd round	Rothmans Grand Prix
v T. Jones	9-7	1st round	Coral UK Open
v Williams	9-7	2nd round	Coral UK Open
v Thorne	9-5	Quarter-final	Coral UK Open
v Thorburn	9-7	Semi-finals	Coral UK Open
v S. Davis	8-16	Final	Coral UK Open
v Gauvreau	5-3	1st round	Mercantile Credit Classic
v S. Davis	2-5	2nd round	Mercantile Credit Classic
1985 v S. Davis	5-4	1st round	Benson & Hedges Masters
v Griffiths	1-5	Quarter-final	Benson & Hedges Masters
v Bales	6-3	1st round	Dulux British Open
v N. Foulds	5-1	2nd round	Dulux British Open
v Thorburn	5-2	3rd round	Dulux British Open
v E. Hughes	5-2	Quarter-final	Dulux British Open
v S. Francisco	6-9	Semi-final	Dulux British Open
v Griffiths	5-2	1st round	Benson & Hedges Irish Masters
v Stevens	5-3	Quarter-final	Benson & Hedges Irish Masters
v S. Davis	6-2	Semi-final	Benson & Hedges Irish Masters
v White	5-9	Final	Benson & Hedges Irish Masters
v Burke	6-0	Quarter-final	Irish Professional Championship
v Fagan	6-3	Semi-final	Irish Professional Championship
v Dennis Taylor	5-10	Final	Irish Professional Championship
v Reynolds	10-4	1st round	Embassy World Professional Championship
v Griffiths	7-13	2nd round	Embassy World Professional Championship

MIKE HINES (South Africa)

Born 21.3.45
Turned professional 1983
World ranking 83

1984 v Black	10-5	Qualifying	Embassy World Professional Championship
v Williamson	6-10	Qualifying	Embassy World Professional Championship
1985 v Chappel	10-8	Qualifying	Embassy World Professional Championship
v Watchorn	10-4	Qualifying	Embassy World Professional Championship
v Gibson	7-10	Qualifying	Embassy World Professional Championship

PAT HOULIHAN (England)

Born 7.11.29
Turned professional 1969
World ranking unranked

English amateur champion in 1965, Houlihan achieved his best performance in a professional event in the 1978 Embassy World Professional
Championship when he qualified for the televised first round – his only
television appearance to date.

1972	v Dunning	10-11 Qualifying	World Professional Championship
1973	v Jack Rea	9-2 1st round	World Professional Championship
	v Higgins	3-16 2nd round	World Professional Championship
1977	v Meadowcroft	1-5 1st round	Super Crystalate UK
1978	v Ross	9-1 Prelim	Embassy World Professional Championship
	v Meadowcroft	9-6 Qualifying	Embassy World Professional Championship
	v Thorburn	8-13 1st round	Embassy World Professional Championship
	v Andrewartha	3-9 Qualifying	Coral UK Championship
1979	v Barrie	9-5 Prelim	Embassy World Professional Championship
	v Mountjoy	6-9 Qualifying	Embassy World Professional Championship
	v Jack Rea	9-3 2nd round	Coral UK Championship
	v Higgins	3-9 3rd round	Coral UK Championship
1980	v Meo	1-9 Qualifying	Embassy World Professional Championship
	v Meo	1-9 1st round	Coral UK Championship
1981	v Spencer	1-9 1st round	John Courage English Professional
	v French	3-5 Qualifying	Jameson International
	v Kennerley	9-1 Qualifying	Coral UK Championship
	v Black	9-4 Qualifying	Coral UK Championship
	Meadowcroft	9-4 Qualifying	Coral UK Championship
	v Miles	3-9 2nd round	Coral UK Championship
1982	v Anderson	9-5 Qualifying	Embassy World Professional Championship
	v Martin	3-9 Qualifying	Embassy World Professional Championship
	v E. McLaughlin	2-5 Qualifying	Jameson International
	v Knowles	4-5 1st round	Professional Players Tournament
	v Mountjoy	3-9 1st round	Coral UK Championship
1983	v Murphy	9-10 Qualifying	Embassy World Professional Championship
	v Scott	0-5 Qualifying	Jameson International
	v Sheehan	2-5 Qualifying	Professional Players Tournament
	v V. Harris	6-9 Qualifying	Coral UK Championship
1984	v Williamson	5-10 Qualifying	Embassy World Professional Championship
	v Hargreaves	2-5 Qualifying	Jameson International
	v Everton	3-5 Qualifying	Rothmans Grand Prix
	v Chappel	3-9 Qualifying	Coral UK Open
	v Foldvari	1-5 Qualifying	Mercantile Credit Classic
1985	v T. Jones	1-9 Qualifying	Tolly Cobbold English Professional Championship

DENNIS HUGHES (England)

Born 30.1.37
Turned professional 1981
World ranking 88

1981	v Jack Rea	5-4	Qualifying	Jameson International
	v Demarco	1-5	Qualifying	Jameson International
	v Hallett	6-9	Qualifying	Coral UK Championship
1982	v Higgins	2-6	Semi-final	Irish Professional Championship
	v Everton	9-4	Qualifying	Embassy World Professional Championship
	v Meo	4-9	Qualifying	Embassy World Professional Championship
	v Edmonds	0-5	Qualifying	Jameson International
	v Charlton	2-5	1st round	Professional Players Tournament
	v Meadowcroft	8-9	Qualifying	Coral UK Championship
1983	v Parkin	5-0	Qualifying	Jameson International
	v Johnson	1-5	Qualifying	Jameson International
	v Medati	1-5	Qualifying	Professional Players Tournament
	v Medati	2-9	Qualifying	Coral UK Championship
1984	v Parrott	3-10	Qualifying	Embassy World Professional Championship
	v Oliver	4-5	Qualifying	Jameson International
	v Dunning	0-5	Qualifying	Rothmans Grand Prix
	v G. Foulds	7-9	Qualifying	Coral UK Open
1984	v Watchorn	0-5	Prelim	Mercantile Credit Classic
1985	v Watterson	9-5	Qualifying	Tolly Cobbold English Professional Championship
	v N. Foulds	3-9	1st round	Tolly Cobbold English Professional Championship
	v Mikkelsen	0-6	Qualifying	Dulux British Open
	v French	10-5	Qualifying	Embassy World Professional Championship
	v Newbury	9-10	Qualifying	Embassy World Professional Championship

EUGENE HUGHES (Republic of Ireland)

Born 4.11.55
Turned professional 1981
World ranking 21

After he had been twice Republic of Ireland champion at both billiards and snooker, Hughes' professional breakthrough came last season through reaching the semi-finals of the Jameson International in a season which saw him advance from 28th to 21st.

1981	v M. Owen	5-1	Qualifying	Jameson International
	v Fitzmaurice	5-3	Qualifying	Jameson International
	v Sinclair	5-2	Qualifying	Jameson International
	v Edmonds	4-5	1st round	Jameson International
1982	v Mountjoy	4-5	1st round	Benson & Hedges Irish Masters
	v Jack Rea	6-1	Quarter-final	Irish Professional Championship
	v Higgins	2-6	Semi-final	Irish Professional Championship

	v Knowles	7-9	Qualifying	Embassy World Professional Championship
	v Parkin	5-2	Qualifying	Jameson International
	v Martin	5-4	Qualifying	Jameson International
	v Reardon	3-5	1st round	Jameson International
	v Stevens	2-5	1st round	Professional Players Tournament
1983	v Burke	6-2	Quarter-final	Irish Professional Championship
	v Higgins	2-6	Semi-final	Irish Professional Championship
	v Fitzmaurice	10-7	Qualifying	Embassy World Professional Championship
	v Sinclair	10-8	Qualifying	Embassy World Professional Championship
	v Reardon	7-10	1st round	Embassy World Professional Championship
	v Fisher	5-4	Qualifying	Jameson International
	v G. Foulds	5-1	Qualifying	Jameson International
	v S. Davis	1-5	1st round	Jameson International
	v Sinclair	5-4	1st round	Professional Players Tournament
	v Werbeniuk	5-0	2nd round	Professional Players Tournament
	v Griffiths	5-2	3rd round	Professional Players Tournament
	v Thorne	1-5	Quarter-final	Professional Players Tournament
1984	v Knowles	1-5	Qualifying	Lada Classic
	v Dennis Taylor	1-5	1st round	Benson & Hedges Irish Masters
	v Mifsud	5-10	Qualifying	Embassy World Professional Championship
	v Roscoe	5-1	Qualifying	Jameson International
	v Mountjoy	5-1	1st round	Jameson International
	v Reardon	5-1	2nd round	Jameson International
	v Thorne	5-2	Quarter-final	Jameson International
	v S. Davis	3-9	Semi-final	Jameson International
	v John Rea	4-5	1st round	Rothmans Grand Prix
	v Morra	9-8	Qualifying	Coral UK Open
	v Meo	4-9	1st round	Coral UK Open
	v Newbury	5-3	Qualifying	Mercantile Credit Classic
	v Meo	5-4	1st round	Mercantile Credit Classic
	v Reardon	1-5	2nd round	Mercantile Credit Classic
1985	v Watchorn	6-4	1st round	Dulux British Open
	v B. Harris	5-4	2nd round	Dulux British Open
	v Macleod	5-2	3rd round	Dulux British Open
	v Higgins	2-5	Quarter-final	Dulux British Open
	v Reardon	5-0	1st round	Benson & Hedges Irish Masters
	v S. Davis	4-5	Quarter-final	Benson & Hedges Irish Masters
	v Kelly	6-2	Quarter-final	Irish Professional Championship
	v Dennis Taylor	5-6	Semi-final	Irish Professional Championship
	v Newbury	10-6	Qualifying	Embassy World Professional Championship
	v Reardon	9-10	1st round	Embassy World Professional Championship

JOE JOHNSON (England)

Born 29.7.52
Turned professional 1979
World ranking 16

Uniquely, Joe Johnson has obtained a place in the top 16 of the world rankings without winning a single match in the televised phase of the

Eugene Hughes (David Muscroft)

Joe Johnson (Adrian Murrell/All-Sport)

Embassy World Championship. His chief earners of ranking points have been the 1983 Professional Players Tournament, when he reached the final, and the 1985 Mercantile Credit Classic, in which he reached the semi-finals.

1979	v Werbeniuk	3-9	2nd round	Coral UK Championship
1980	v Dunning	9-6	Qualifying	Coral UK Championship
	v Fagan	4-9	1st round	Coral UK Championship
1981	v Knowles	9-2	Qualifying	John Courage English Professional
	Johnson *wo*		1st round	John Courage English Professional
	v Edmonds	5-9	2nd round	John Courage English Professional
	v Meo	8-9	Qualifying	Embassy World Professional Championship
	v Donnelly	5-4	Qualifying	Jameson International
	v Macleod	5-1	Qualifying	Jameson International
	v Wych	5-2	1st round	Jameson International
	v Miles	3-5	2nd round	Jameson International
	v Murphy	9-1	Qualifying	Coral UK Championship
	v Watterson	9-3	Qualifying	Coral UK Championship
	v Wilson	9-5	Qualifying	Coral UK Championship
	v Spencer	9-5	2nd round	Coral UK Championship
	v Reardon	7-9	3rd round	Coral UK Championship
1982	v Harris	9-4	Qualifying	Embassy World Professional Championship
	v Hallett	8-9	Qualifying	Embassy World Professional Championship
	v Wilson	4-5	Qualifying	Jameson International
	v Miles	5-1	1st round	Professional Players Tournament
	v Stevens	5-1	2nd round	Professional Players Tournament
	v Wildman	5-4	3rd round	Professional Players Tournament
	v Virgo	1-5	Quarter-final	Professional Players Tournament
	v V. Harris	9-8	Qualifying	Coral UK Championship
	v Griffiths	1-9	1st round	Coral UK Championship
	v W. Jones	5-6	1st round	Dulux British Open
	v G. Foulds	10-6	Qualifying	Embassy World Professional Championship
	v Werbeniuk	8-10	1st round	Embassy World Professional Championship
1983	v Thorburn	2-5	1st round	Benson & Hedges Masters
	v Watchorn	10-0	Qualifying	Embassy World Professional Championship
	v Wilson	8-10	Qualifying	Embassy World Professional Championship
	v D. Hughes	5-1	Qualifying	Jameson International
	v Charlton	2-5	1st round	Jameson International
	v Burke	5-3	1st round	Professional Players Tournament
	v White	5-3	2nd round	Professional Players Tournament
	v Charlton	5-0	3rd round	Professional Players Tournament
	v Thorburn	5-1	Quarter-final	Professional Players Tournament
	v Meo	9-6	Semi-final	Professional Players Tournament
	v Knowles	8-9	Final	Professional Players Tournament
	v Gibson	9-6	Qualifying	Coral UK Championship
	v Virgo	9-6	1st round	Coral UK Championship
	v David Taylor	9-3	2nd round	Coral UK Championship
	v Griffiths	2-9	Quarter-final	Coral UK Championship
1984	v Spencer	4-5	Qualifying	Lada Classic
	v Gibson	10-3	Qualifying	Embassy World Professional Championship

v Dennis Taylor	1-10	1st round	Embassy World Professional Championship
v Morra	5-0	Qualifying	Jameson International
v Charlton	5-1	1st round	Jameson International
v Dennis Taylor	2-5	2nd round	Jameson International
v Medati	5-1	1st round	Rothmans Grand Prix
v Williamson	4-5	2nd round	Rothmans Grand Prix
v John Rea	9-6	Qualifying	Coral UK Open
v Spencer	9-6	1st round	Coral UK Open
v Stevens	2-9	2nd round	Coral UK Open
v Edmonds	5-4	Qualifying	Mercantile Credit Classic
v Knowles	5-1	1st round	Mercantile Credit Classic
v Wilson	5-0	2nd round	Mercantile Credit Classic
v King	5-3	Quarter-final	Mercantile Credit Classic
v Thorburn	2-9	Semi-finals	Mercantile Credit Classic
1985 v Scott	9-1	1st round	Tolly Cobbold English Professional Championship
v Virgo	4-9	2nd round	Tolly Cobbold English Professional Championship

TONY JONES (England)

Born 15.4.60
Turned professional 1983
World ranking 50

Jones, the 1983 English amateur champion, pressed Tony Knowles to a 10-8 decision on his television debut in the Embassy World Professional Championship.

1983 v Oliver	5-2	Qualifying	Professional Players Tournament
v Werbeniuk	4-5	1st round	Professional Players Tournament
v Sinclair	9-3	Qualifying	Coral UK Championship
v Knowles	5-9	1st round	Coral UK Championship
1984 v King	9-10	Qualifying	Embassy World Professional Championship
v French	5-1	Qualifying	Jameson International
v Duggan	2-5	Qualifying	Jameson International
v Sinclair	5-4	Qualifying	Rothmans Grand Prix
v Griffiths	5-3	1st round	Rothmans Grand Prix
v N. Foulds	0-5	2nd round	Rothmans Grand Prix
v Chaperon	9-1	Qualifying	Coral UK Open
v Fagan	9-2	Qualifying	Coral UK Open
v Wildman	9-2	Qualifying	Coral UK Open
v Higgins	7-9	1st round	Coral UK Open
v Greaves	5-2	Qualifying	Mercantile Credit Classic
v Gibson	5-0	Qualifying	Mercantile Credit Classic
v Dodd	5-1	Qualifying	Mercantile Credit Classic
v S. Francisco	1-5	Qualifying	Mercantile Credit Classic
1985 v Houlihan	9-1	Qualifying	Tolly Cobbold English Professional Championship

v Williams	6-9	1st round	Tolly Cobbold English Professional Championship
v G. Foulds	6-0	Qualifying	Dulux British Open
v White	5-6	1st round	Dulux British Open
v Darrington	10-2	Qualifying	Embassy World Professional Championship
v Duggan	10-8	Qualifying	Embassy World Professional Championship
v Fitzmaurice	10-4	Qualifying	Embassy World Professional Championship
v Sinclair	10-2	Qualifying	Embassy World Professional Championship
v Knowles	8-10	1st round	Embassy World Professional Championship

WAYNE JONES (Wales)

Born 24.12.59
Turned professional 1984
World ranking 49

Welsh amateur champion in 1983, Jones obtained 49th place in the world rankings at the end of his first professional season with the aid of an appearance in the first round of the Embassy World Championship's televised phase.

1984	v Watchorn	5-0	Qualifying	Jameson International
	v Gibson	5-2	Qualifying	Jameson International
	v Scott	5-0	Qualifying	Jameson International
	v Wildman	5-0	Qualifying	Jameson International
	v David Taylor	4-5	1st round	Jameson International
	v Watterson	5-3	Qualifying	Rothmans Grand Prix
	v Campbell	4-5	1st round	Rothmans Grand Prix
	v O'Kane	7-9	Qualifying	Coral UK Open
	v O'Kane	5-0	Qualifying	Mercantile Credit Classic
	v Duggan	0-5	Qualifying	Mercantile Credit Classic
1985	v Donnelly	6-1	Qualifying	Dulux British Open
	v Johnson	6-5	1st round	Dulux British Open
	v Chaperon	2-5	2nd round	Dulux British Open
	v Jack Rea	10-3	Qualifying	Embassy World Professional Championship
	v Dunning	10-6	Qualifying	Embassy World Professional Championship
	v Watterson	10-5	Qualifying	Embassy World Professional Championship
	v Miles	10-8	Qualifying	Embassy World Professional Championship
	v White	4-10	1st round	Embassy World Professional Championship
	v Newbury	2-6	1st round	BCE Welsh Professional Championship

FRANK JONIK (Canada)

Born 2.12.57
Turned professional 1979
World ranking 72

In his six-year professional career, Jonik's most notable win was beating

Doug Mountjoy in the first round of the Professional Players Tournament in 1982.

1980	v Wildman	9-7	Qualifying	Embassy World Professional Championship
	v Wilson	6-9	Qualifying	Embassy World Professional Championship
1981	v Hallett	1-9	Qualifying	Embassy World Professional Championship
1982	v Bear	4-9	Qualifying	Embassy World Professional Championship
	v Hallett	2-5	Qualifying	Jameson International
	v Mountjoy	5-3	1st round	Professional Players Tournament
	v Meo	0-5	2nd round	Professional Players Tournament
1983	v Edmonds	4-10	Qualifying	Embassy World Professional Championship
	v Wildman	4-5	1st round	Professional Players Tournament
1984	v Mikkelsen	9-10	Qualifying	Embassy World Professional Championship
	v J. McLaughlin	5-2	Qualifying	Jameson International
	v Gauvreau	1-5	Qualifying	Jameson International
	v Bradley	1-5	Qualifying	Rothmans Grand Prix
	v Newbury	3-9	Qualifying	Coral UK Open
	v G. Foulds	2-5	Qualifying	Mercantile Credit Classic
1985	v J. McLaughlin	6-2	Qualifying	Dulux British Open
	v Spencer	0-6	1st round	Dulux British Open
	v O'Kane	5-10	Qualifying	Embassy World Professional Championship

JACK KARNEHM (England)

Born 18.6.17
Turned professional 1971
World ranking unranked
see Billiards section

1977	v Dennis Taylor	0-11	Qualifying	Embassy World Professional Championship
	v Ross	4-5	1st round	Super Crystalate UK Championship
1978	v Andrewartha	0-9	Prelim	Embassy World Professional Championship

TONY KEARNEY (Republic of Ireland)

Born 24.6.54
Turned professional 1984
World ranking 90

Kearney was Republic of Ireland amateur champion in 1980.

1984	v Burke	4-5	Qualifying	Jameson International
	v Chaperon	1-5	Qualifying	Rothmans Grand Prix
	v Murphy	2-9	Qualifying	Coral UK Open
	v French	5-1	Qualifying	Mercantile Credit Classic
	v Williamson	3-5	Qualifying	Mercantile Credit Classic
1985	v Watterson	6-4	Qualifying	Dulux British Open
	v S. Francisco	4-6	1st round	Dulux British Open
	v Burke	4-6	Qualifying	Irish Professional Championship
	v Anderson	8-10	Qualifying	Embassy World Professional Championship

BILLY KELLY (Republic of Ireland)

Born 1.5.45
Turned professional 1981
World ranking 71

1981 v Macleod	1-5	Qualifying	Jameson International
v G. Foulds	7-9	Qualifying	Coral UK Championship
1982 v Sinclair	8-9	Qualifying	Embassy World Professional Championship
v G. Foulds	5-4	Qualifying	Jameson International
v Williamson	5-1	Qualifying	Jameson International
v Higgins	3-5	1st round	Jameson International
v Wych	0-5	1st round	Professional Players Tournament
v Fitzmaurice (retd)	8-0	Qualifying	Coral UK Championship
v Virgo	2-9	1st round	Coral UK Championship
1983 v Dennis Taylor	0-6	Quarter-final	Irish Professional Championship
v Demarco	10-4	Qualifying	Embassy World Professional Championship
v S. Francisco	5-10	Qualifying	Embassy World Professional Championship
v F. Davis	1-5	Qualifying	Jameson International
v Hallett	0-5	1st round	Professional Players Tournament
1984 v Burke	7-10	Qualifying	Embassy World Professional Championship
v Hargreaves	5-2	Qualifying	Jameson International
v King	5-4	Qualifying	Jameson International
v S. Francisco	3-5	Qualifying	Jameson International
v O'Kane	4-5	Qualifying	Rothmans Grand Prix
v Bradley	6-9	Qualifying	Coral UK Open
v Bales	3-5	Qualifying	Mercantile Credit Classic
v P. Francisco	3-6	Qualifying	Dulux British Open
v Watchorn	6-2	Qualifying	Irish Professional Championship
v E. Hughes	2-6	Quarter-final	Irish Professional Championship
v Rigitano	6-10	Qualifying	Embassy World Professional Championship
1985 v P. Francisco	3-6	Qualifying	Dulux British Open
v Watchorn	6-2	Qualifying	Irish Professional Championship
v E. Hughes	2-6	Quarter-final	Irish Professional Championship
v Rigitano	6-10	Qualifying	Embassy World Professional Championship

WARREN KING (Australia)

Born 1.4.55
Turned professional 1982
World ranking 35

Twice Australian amateur champion, King rose from 48th to 35th in the world rankings during the 1984-85 season with the aid of a quarter-final finish in the Mercantile Credit Classic. He has twice been a member of Australia's World Cup trio.

1983 v Anderson	10-6	Qualifying	Embassy World Professional Championship
v Hallett	6-10	Qualifying	Embassy World Professional Championship
v Black	5-3	Qualifying	Jameson International

v Miles	3-5	Qualifying	Jameson International
v B. Harris	5-3	Qualifying	Professional Players Tournament
v Meo	2-5	1st round	Professional Players Tournament
1984 v Jones	10-9	Qualifying	Embassy World Professional Championship
v Watterson	10-8	Qualifying	Embassy World Professional Championship
v Martin	10-8	Qualifying	Embassy World Professional Championship
v S. Davis	3-10	1st round	Embassy World Professional Championship
v Kelly	4-5	Qualifying	Jameson International
v Greaves	5-0	Qualifying	Rothmans Grand Prix
v Macleod	4-5	1st round	Rothmans Grand Prix
v Browne	9-5	Qualifying	Coral UK Open
v Virgo	9-4	Qualifying	Coral UK Open
v Dennis Taylor	5-9	1st round	Coral UK Open
v Duggan	5-4	Qualifying	Mercantile Credit Classic
v Reynolds	5-2	Qualifying	Mercantile Credit Classic
v Spencer	5-2	1st round	Mercantile Credit Classic
1985 v White	5-2	2nd round	Mercantile Credit Classic
v Johnson	3-5	Quarter-final	Mercantile Credit Classic
v Medati	6-4	Qualifying	Dulux British Open
v Reardon	5-6	1st round	Dulux British Open
v Medati	9-10	Qualifying	Embassy World Professional Championship

TONY KNOWLES (England)

Born 13.6.55
Turned professional 1980
World ranking 3

Knowles reached second place in the world rankings with the help of first prizes in the 1982 Jameson International and the 1983 Professional Players Tournament.

In 1984 he won the Winfield Australian Masters but an inconsistent 1984–85 season saw him drop to third place in the world list. Nevertheless, defeats in two finals, the Jameson International and the Tolly Cobbold English Professional Championship, both by Steve Davis, and a run to the semi-final of the Embassy World Championship, halted by Dennis Taylor, showed that his season was far from a write-off.

1980 v Andrewartha	8-9	Qualifying	Coral UK Championship
1981 v Johnson	2-9	Qualifying	John Courage English Professional
v Ross	7-0	Qualifying	Embassy World Professional Championship
v Wych	9-3	Qualifying	Embassy World Professional Championship
v Miles	8-10	1st round	Embassy World Professional Championship
v Hallett	5-2	1st round	Jameson International
v Virgo	2-5	2nd round	Jameson International
v G. Foulds	9-1	Qualifying	Coral UK Championship
v F. Davis	9-6	2nd round	Coral UK Championship
v Mountjoy	9-6	3rd round	Coral UK Championship
v Griffiths	5-9	Quarter-final	Coral UK Championship
1982 v Dennis Taylor	2-5	Semi-final	Tolly Cobbold Classic

Tony Knowles (David Muscroft)

v E. Hughes	9-7	Qualifying	Embassy World Professional Championship
v S. Davis	10-1	1st round	Embassy World Professional Championship
v Miles	13-7	2nd round	Embassy World Professional Championship
v Charlton	11-13	Quarter-final	Embassy World Professional Championship
v S. Davis	4-5	1st round	Langs Scottish Masters
v Sinclair	5-2	1st round	Jameson International
v Reardon	5-2	2nd round	Jameson International
v Wilson	5-4	Quarter-final	Jameson International
v Stevens	9-8	Semi-final	Jameson International
v David Taylor	**9-6**	**Final**	**Jameson International**
v Houlihan	5-4	1st round	Professional Players Tournament
v Wilson	4-5	2nd round	Professional Players Tournament
v Donnelly	9-6	1st round	Coral UK Championship
v Spencer	6-9	2nd round	Coral UK Championship
1983 v Stevens	0-5	1st round	Lada Classic
v Mountjoy	1-5	1st round	Benson & Hedges Irish Masters
v Miles	10-3	1st round	Embassy World Professional Championship
v Reardon	13-12	2nd round	Embassy World Professional Championship
v Meo	13-9	Quarter-final	Embassy World Professional Championship
v Thorburn	15-16	Semi-final	Embassy World Professional Championship
v Werbeniuk	0-5	Semi-final	Winfield Masters
v Meo	5-4	1st round	Langs Scottish Masters
v Thorburn	6-2	Semi-final	Langs Scottish Masters
v S. Davis	6-9	Final	Langs Scottish Masters
v Edmonds	5-1	1st round	Jameson International
v Spencer	4-5	2nd round	Jameson International
v Medati	5-1	1st round	Professional Players Tournament
v Williams	5-4	2nd round	Professional Players Tournament
v S. Francisco	5-0	3rd round	Professional Players Tournament
v Campbell	5-3	Quarter-final	Professional Players Tournament
v Thorne	9-7	Semi-final	Professional Players Tournament
v Johnson	**9-8**	**Final**	**Professional Players Tournament**
v T. Jones	9-5	1st round	Coral UK Championship
v Mountjoy	9-5	2nd round	Coral UK Championship
v Higgins	5-9	Quarter-final	Coral UK Championship
1984 v E. Hughes	5-1	Qualifying	Lada Classic
v Hallett	5-3	1st round	Lada Classic
v Parrott	1-5	Quarter-final	Lada Classic
v Dennis Taylor	5-2	1st round	Benson & Hedges Masters
v Higgins	5-1	Quarter-final	Benson & Hedges Masters
v Griffiths	4-6	Semi-final	Benson & Hedges Masters
v Griffiths	0-5	Quarter-final	Benson & Hedges Irish Masters
v White	5-1	1st round	Tolly Cobbold Classic
v Thorburn	5-3	Semi-final	Tolly Cobbold Classic
v S. Davis	2-8	Final	Tolly Cobbold Classic
v Parrott	7-10	1st round	Embassy World Professional Championship
v White	5-3	Quarter-final	Winfield Australian Masters
v Charlton	6-0	Semi-final	Winfield Australian Masters
v Virgo	**7-3**	**Final**	**Winfield Australian Masters**
v Griffiths	5-3	1st round	Langs Scottish Masters
v White	5-6	Semi-final	Langs Scottish Masters

v Reynolds	5-1	1st round	Jameson International
v Newbury	5-4	2nd round	Jameson International
v White	5-4	Quarter-final	Jameson International
v S. Francisco	9-6	Semi-final	Jameson International
v S. Davis	2-9	Final	Jameson International
v V. Harris	5-1	1st round	Rothmans Grand Prix
v Dunning	5-1	2nd round	Rothmans Grand Prix
v Williamson	5-2	3rd round	Rothmans Grand Prix
v N. Foulds	2-5	Quarter-final	Rothmans Grand Prix
v Gauvreau	9-5	1st round	Coral UK Open
v Dennis Taylor	9-2	2nd round	Coral UK Open
v Stevens	7-9	Quarter-final	Coral UK Open
v Johnson	1-5	1st round	Mercantile Credit Classic
1985 v Mountjoy	3-5	1st round	Benson & Hedges Masters
v Bradley	9-8	1st round	Tolly Cobbold English Professional Championship
v Martin	9-3	2nd round	Tolly Cobbold English Professional Championship
v David Taylor	9-2	Quarter-final	Tolly Cobbold English Professional Championship
v Longworth	9-6	Semi-final	Tolly Cobbold English Professional Championship
S. Davis	2-9	Final	Tolly Cobbold English Professional Championship
v French	6-2	1st round	Dulux British Open
v Longworth	5-2	2nd round	Dulux British Open
v Meo	2-5	3rd round	Dulux British Open
v Charlton	5-3	Quarter-final	Benson & Hedges Irish Masters
v White	4-6	Semi-final	Benson & Hedges Irish Masters
v T. Jones	10-8	1st round	Embassy World Professional Championship
v Mountjoy	13-6	2nd round	Embassy World Professional Championship
v White	13-10	Quarter-final	Embassy World Professional Championship
v Dennis Taylor	5-16	Semi-final	Embassy World Professional Championship

STEVE LONGWORTH (England)

Born 27.7.48
Turned professional 1984
World ranking 37

English amateur champion in 1984, Steve Longworth reached 37th place in the rankings in his first professional season. His run to the last 16 of the Mercantile Credit Classic and his semi-final place in the Tolly Cobbold English Professional Championship were the highlights.

1984 v Newbury	4-5	Qualifying	Jameson International
v E. McLaughlin	2-5	Qualifying	Rothmans Grand Prix
v Darrington	9-5	Qualifying	Coral UK Open
v Burke	9-4	Qualifying	Coral UK Open
v Morra	1-9	Qualifying	Coral UK Open

v P. Francisco	5-4	Qualifying	Mercantile Credit Classic
v Oliver	5-1	Qualifying	Mercantile Credit Classic
v Fisher	5-1	Qualifying	Mercantile Credit Classic
v N. Foulds	5-3	Qualifying	Mercantile Credit Classic
v David Taylor	5-4	1st round	Mercantile Credit Classic
v Cliff Thorburn	3-5	2nd round	Mercantile Credit Classic
1985 v Edmonds	9-4	Qualifying	Tolly Cobbold English Professional Championship
v Wildman	9-3	1st round	Tolly Cobbold English Professional Championship
v Medati	9-7	2nd round	Tolly Cobbold English Professional Championship
v White	9-5	Quarter-final	Tolly Cobbold English Professional Championship
v Knowles	6-9	Semi-final	Tolly Cobbold English Professional Championship
v F. Davis	6-1	Qualifying	Dulux British Open
v Wilson	6-3	1st round	Dulux British Open
v Knowles	2-5	2nd round	Dulux British Open
v Giannaros	10-1	Qualifying	Embassy World Professional Championship
v Cripsey	10-8	Qualifying	Embassy World Professional Championship
v Van Rensberg	7-10	Qualifying	Embassy World Professional Championship

EDDIE McLAUGHLIN (Scotland)

Born 27.6.52
Turned professional 1981
World ranking 63

1981 v Black	5-3	Qualifying	Jameson International
v Wildman	5-3	Qualifying	Jameson International
v Greaves	5-1	Qualifying	Jameson International
v Ross	5-3	Quarter-final	Scottish Professional Championship
v Black	3-6	Semi-final	Scottish Professional Championship
v Meo	2-5	1st round	Jameson International
v Medati	5-9	Qualifying	Coral UK Championship
1982 v Macleod	8-9	Qualifying	Embassy World Professional Championship
v Gibson	3-6	Quarter-final	Scottish Professional Championship
v Houlihan	5-2	Qualifying	Jameson International
v Williams	1-5	Qualifying	Jameson International
v Mans	2-5	1st round	Professional Players Tournament
v Wilson	6-9	Qualifying	Coral UK Championship
1983 v Greaves	10-7	Qualifying	Embassy World Professional Championship
v Fisher	9-10	Qualifying	Embassy World Professional Championship
v Black	4-6	1st round	Scottish Professional Championship
v Campbell	5-2	Qualifying	Jameson International
v Edmonds	1-5	Qualifying	Jameson International
v Charlton	0-5	1st round	Professional Players Tournament
v B. Harris	8-9	Qualifying	Coral UK Championship

1984	v Stevens	4-5	Qualifying	Lada Classic
	v Hargreaves	10-5	Qualifying	Embassy World Professional Championship
	v Andrewartha	8-10	Qualifying	Embassy World Professional Championship
	v O'Kane	1-5	Qualifying	Jameson International
	v Longworth	5-2	Qualifying	Rothmans Grand Prix
	v Mountjoy	4-5	1st round	Rothmans Grand Prix
	v Bales	4-9	Qualifying	Coral UK Open
	v Sheehan	5-2	Qualifying	Mercantile Credit Classic
	v F. Davis	5-1	Qualifying	Mercantile Credit Classic
	v Macleod	4-5	Qualifying	Mercantile Credit Classic
1985	v French	0-6	Qualifying	Dulux British Open
	v Chalmers	9-10	Qualifying	Embassy World Professional Championship

JACK McLAUGHLIN (Northern Ireland)

Born 29.1.59
Turned professional 1984
World ranking 69

McLaughlin won the Northern Ireland Amateur Championship in both 1983 and 1984.

1984	v Greaves	5-3	Qualifying	Jameson International
	v Jonik	2-5	Qualifying	Jameson International
	v Meadowcroft	5-1	Qualifying	Rothmans Grand Prix
	v Wildman	3-5	1st round	Rothmans Grand Prix
	v French	9-3	Qualifying	Coral UK Open
	v Roscoe	9-8	Qualifying	Coral UK Open
	v Miles	9-8	Qualifying	Coral UK Open
	v Thorburn	4-9	1st round	Coral UK Open
	v Demarco	5-1	Qualifying	Mercantile Credit Classic
	v Black	5-0	Qualifying	Mercantile Credit Classic
	v Scott	4-5	Qualifying	Mercantile Credit Classic
1985	v Jonik	2-6	Qualifying	Dulux British Open
	v Sheehan	6-3	Qualifying	Irish Professional Championship

MURDO MACLEOD (Scotland)

Born 14.1.47
Turned professional 1981
World ranking 26

Twice Scottish professional champion, Macleod has acquired some notable scalps, including Willie Thorn (twice), David Taylor and Eddie Charlton, but he has never yet won a match in the televised phase of a competition.

Murdo Macleod

Perrie Mans (David Muscroft)

1981	v Kelly	5-1 Qualifying	Jameson International
	v Johnson	1-5 Qualifying	Jameson International
	v Black	4-5 Quarter-final	Scottish Professional Championship
	v Roscoe	7-9 Qualifying	Coral UK Championship
1982	v E. McLaughlin	9-8 Qualifying	Embassy World Professional Championship
	v Dunning	4-9 Qualifying	Embassy World Professional Championship
	v Donnelly	6-5 1st round	Scottish Professional Championship
	v Black	0-6 Quarter-final	Scottish Professional Championship
	v Dodd	1-5 Qualifying	Jameson International
	v Thorne	5-2 2nd round	Professional Players Tournament
	v Reardon	2-5 3rd round	Professional Players Tournament
	v Martin	6-9 Qualifying	Coral UK Championship
1983	v M. Owen	10-5 Qualifying	Embassy World Professional Championship
	v Martin	7-10 Qualifying	Embassy World Professional Championship
	v Gibson	6-5 1st round	Scottish Professional Championship
	v Black	6-2 Semi-final	Scottish Professional Championship
	v Sinclair	**11-9 Final**	**Scottish Professional Championship**
	v S. Davis	1-5 1st round	Langs Supreme Scottish Masters
	v Medati	5-3 Qualifying	Jameson International
	v Reardon	2-5 1st round	Jameson International
	v Murphy	0-5 1st round	Professional Players Tournament
	v Bennett	9-0 Qualifying	Coral UK Championship
	v Higgins	6-9 1st round	Coral UK Championship
1984	v David Taylor	5-4 Qualifying	Lada Classic
	v Stevens	1-5 1st round	Lada Classic
	v Gauvreau	6-10 Qualifying	Embassy World Professional Championship
	v White	0-5 1st round	Langs Supreme Scottish Masters
	v Black	5-3 Qualifying	Jameson International
	v Meo	1-5 1st round	Jameson International
	v King	5-4 1st round	Rothmans Grand Prix
	v Thorne	3-5 2nd round	Rothmans Grand Prix
	v Scott	9-5 Qualifying	Coral UK Open
	v David Taylor	6-9 1st round	Coral UK Open
	v E. McLaughlin	5-4 Qualifying	Mercantile Credit Classic
	v Charlton	5-1 1st round	Mercantile Credit Classic
	v Virgo	0-5 2nd round	Mercantile Credit Classic
1985	v Murphy	6-5 1st round	Dulux British Open
	v Thorne	5-0 2nd round	Dulux British Open
	v E. Hughes	2-5 3rd round	Dulux British Open
	v P. Francisco	10-7 Qualifying	Embassy World Professional Championship
	v Mountjoy	5-10 1st round	Embassy World Professional Championship

PERRIE MANS (South Africa)

Born 14.10.40
Turned professional 1961
World ranking 30

Since winning the Benson and Hedges Masters in 1979, having reached the world final the previous year, Mans has slipped steadily down the rankings and has not visited England since November 1984, when he failed to qualify for the Coral UK Open.

1973	v Gross	9-2 1st round	World Professional Championship
	v Charlton	8-16 2nd round	World Professional Championship
1974	v Anderson	8-1 1st round	World Professional Championship
	v Spencer	15-13 2nd round	World Professional Championship
	v Williams	4-15 Quarter-final	World Professional Championship
1975	v Dennis Taylor	12-15 1st round	World Professional Championship
1976	v Miles	15-10 1st round	Embassy World Professional Championship
	v Meadowcroft	15-8 Quarter-final	Embassy World Professional Championship
	v Reardon	10-20 Semi-final	Embassy World Professional Championship
1977	v Dennis Taylor	11-13 1st round	Embassy World Professional Championship
1978	v Barrie	9-6 Qualifying	Embassy World Professional Championship
	v Spencer	13-8 1st round	Embassy World Professional Championship
	v Miles	13-7 Quarter-final	Embassy World Professional Championship
	v F. Davis	18-16 Semi-final	Embassy World Professional Championship
	v Reardon	18-25 Final	Embassy World Professional Championship
1979	v Thorburn	5-4 Quarter-final	Benson & Hedges Masters
	v Reardon	5-3 Semi-final	Benson & Hedges Masters
	v Higgins	**8-4 Final**	**Benson & Hedges Masters**
	v Griffiths	8-13 1st round	Embassy World Professional Championship
1980	v Higgins	1-5 Quarter-final	Benson & Hedges Masters
	v Higgins	6-13 2nd round	Embassy World Professional Championship
1981	v S. Davis	5-3 1st round	Benson & Hedges Masters
	v Thorburn	4-5 Quarter-final	Benson & Hedges Masters
	v Werbeniuk	5-13 2nd round	Embassy World Professional Championship
	v Meo	5-3 2nd round	Jameson International
	v S. Davis	3-5 3rd round	Jameson International
1982	v Meo	10-8 1st round	Embassy World Professional Championship
	v White	6-13 2nd round	Embassy World Professional Championship
	v Dodd	5-3 1st round	Jameson International
	v Stevens	2-5 2nd round	Jameson International
	v E. McLaughlin	5-2 1st round	Professional Players Tournament
	v Wildman	4-5 2nd round	Professional Players Tournament
1983	v Black	10-3 1st round	Embassy World Professional Championship
	v Stevens	3-13 2nd round	Embassy World Professional Championship
	v Watterson	4-5 Qualifying	Jameson International
1984	v Parrott	0-10 Qualifying	Embassy World Professional Championship
	v Sinclair	2-5 Qualifying	Jameson International
	v Dunning	4-5 1st round	Rothmans Grand Prix
	v Gauvreau	6-9 Qualifying	Coral UK Open

DAVE MARTIN (England)

Born 9.5.48
Turned professional 1981
World ranking 29

Strangely, Dave Martin's best professional performances have all been achieved at Derby Assembly Rooms where he was a semi-finalist in the 1981 Jameson International, runner-up in the 1984 Yamaha International Masters and a winner over Ray Reardon in reaching the last 16 of the Dulux British Open in 1985.

1981 v Anderson	9-3	Qualifying	Embassy World Professional Championship
v Pulman	9-2	Qualifying	Embassy World Professional Championship
v Werbeniuk	4-10	1st round	Embassy World Professional Championship
v Dunning	5-2	1st round	Jameson International
v Werbeniuk	5-2	2nd round	Jameson International
v Charlton	5-2	3rd round	Jameson International
v Miles	5-1	Quarter-final	Jameson International
v Dennis Taylor	1-9	Semi-final	Jameson International
v Sinclair	9-7	Qualifying	Coral UK Championship
v Higgins	7-9	2nd round	Coral UK Championship
1982 v Houlihan	9-3	Qualifying	Embassy World Professional Championship
v Miles	5-10	Qualifying	Embassy World Professional Championship
v E. Hughes	4-5	Qualifying	Jameson International
v Gibson	5-2	1st round	Professional Players Tournament
v Spencer	3-5	2nd round	Professional Players Tournament
v Macleod	9-6	Qualifying	Coral UK Championship
v Higgins	7-9	1st round	Coral UK Championship
1983 v Parkin	10-1	Qualifying	Embassy World Professional Championship
v Macleod	10-7	Qualifying	Embassy World Professional Championship
v Werbeniuk	4-10	Qualifying	Embassy World Professional Championship
v Greaves	5-1	Qualifying	Jameson International
v Fagan	5-0	Qualifying	Jameson International
v Higgins	5-2	1st round	Jameson International
v Mountjoy	0-5	2nd round	Jameson International
v Fitzmaurice	5-0	1st round	Professional Players Tournament
v Watterson	5-4	2nd round	Professional Players Tournament
v Campbell	0-5	3rd round	Professional Players Tournament
v French	9-3	Qualifying	Coral UK Championship
v Griffiths	4-9	Qualifying	Coral UK Championship
1984 v King	8-10	Qualifying	Embassy World Professional Championship
v Fowler	0-5	Qualifying	Jameson International
v Chaperon	5-4	1st round	Rothmans Grand Prix
v Meo	4-5	2nd round	Rothmans Grand Prix
v Murphy	8-9	Qualifying	Coral UK Open
v Foldvari	2-5	Qualifying	Mercantile Credit Classic
1985 v Miles	9-7	1st round	Tolly Cobbold English Professional Championship
v Knowles	3-9	2nd round	Tolly Cobbold English Professional Championship
v Bennett	6-0	1st round	Dulux British Open
v Reardon	5-4	2nd round	Dulux British Open
v O'Kane	4-5	3rd round	Dulux British Open
v O'Kane	8-10	Qualifying	Embassy World Professional Championship

JIM MEADOWCROFT (England)

Born 15.12.46
Turned professional 1971
World ranking 48

A quarter-finalist in the 1976 Embassy World Championship, Jim Meadowcroft also reached the last eight of the UK Championship the following year with a win over Ray Reardon but his subsequent record has been marked by several honourable defeats against top class players rather than by notable victories. In the last couple of years he has worked extensively as a summariser in the BBC's commentary team, as a coach and on the summer exhibition circuit of Butlins holiday camps.

Year	Opponent	Score	Round	Tournament
1973	v Reardon	10-16	2nd round	World Professional Championship
1974	v Kennerley	8-5	1st round	World Professional Championship
	v Reardon	3-15	2nd round	World Professional Championship
1975	v Werbeniuk	9-15	1st round	World Professional Championship
1976	v Wheelwright	8-1	Qualifying	Embassy World Professional Championship
	v Gross	8-4	Qualifying	Embassy World Professional Championship
	v Thorne	8-5	Qualifying	Embassy World Professional Championship
	v Williams	15-7	1st round	Embassy World Professional Championship
	v Mans	8-15	Quarter-final	Embassy World Professional Championship
1977	v Fagan	9-11	Qualifying	Embassy World Professional Championship
	v Houlihan	5-1	1st round	Super Crystalate UK Championship
	v Reardon	5-4	2nd round	Super Crystalate UK Championship
	v Fagan	4-5	Quarter-final	Super Crystalate UK Championship
1978	v Houlihan	6-9	Qualifying	Embassy World Professional Championship
	v Jack Rea	9-5	Qualifying	Coral UK Championship
	v Higgins	6-9	1st round	Coral UK Championship
1979	v Van Rensberg	9-7	Prelim	Embassy World Professional Championship
	v Griffiths	6-9	Qualifying	Embassy World Professional Championship
	v Edmonds	3-9	2nd round	Coral UK Championship
1980	v Sinclair	9-1	Qualifying	Embassy World Professional Championship
	v Virgo	2-10	1st round	Embassy World Professional Championship
	v Greaves	9-1	Qualifying	Coral UK Championship
	v Thorne	1-9	1st round	Coral UK Championship
1981	v Barrie	9-3	Qualifying	John Courage English Professional
	v S. Davis	2-9	1st round	John Courage English Professional
	v White	8-9	Qualifying	Embassy World Professional Championship
	v Roscoe	5-4	Qualifying	Jameson International
	v Wilson	5-4	1st round	Jameson International
	v Stevens	1-5	2nd round	Jameson International
	v Houlihan	4-9	Qualifying	Coral UK Championship
1982	v Watterson	9-7	Qualifying	Embassy World Professional Championship
	v Higgins	5-10	1st round	Embassy World Professional Championship
	v Ross	5-0	Qualifying	Jameson International
	v White	1-5	1st round	Jameson International
	v Bennett	5-4	1st round	Professional Players Tournament
	v Sinclair	3-5	2nd round	Professional Players Tournament

	v D. Hughes	9-8	Qualifying	Coral UK Championship
	v Dennis Taylor	7-9	1st round	Coral UK Championship
1983	v Bennett	10-3	Qualifying	Embassy World Professional Championship
	v Cripsey	10-6	Qualifying	Embassy World Professional Championship
	v David Taylor	2-10	1st round	Embassy World Professional Championship
	v Roscoe	5-4	1st round	Professional Players Tournament
	v Thorburn	1-5	2nd round	Professional Players Tournament
	v N. Foulds	2-9	Qualifying	Coral UK Championship
1984	v Meo	1-5	Qualifying	Lada Classic
	v N. Foulds	2-10	Qualifying	Embassy World Professional Championship
	v Chalmers	5-1	Qualifying	Jameson International
	v Williams	4-5	Qualifying	Jameson International
	v J. McLaughlin	1-5	Qualifying	Rothmans Grand Prix
	v Bradley	7-9	Qualifying	Coral UK Open
	v Fowler	2-5	Qualifying	Mercantile Credit Classic
1985	v Chalmers	3-9	Qualifying	Tolly Cobbold English Professional Championship
	v B. Harris	1-6	Qualifying	Dulux British Open
	v P. Francisco	5-10	Qualifying	Embassy World Professional Championship

PAUL MEDATI (England)

Born 14.11.44
Turned professional 1981
World ranking 60

1981	v E. McLaughlin	9-5	Qualifying	Coral UK Championship
	v Donnelly	9-7	Qualifying	Coral UK Championship
	v Thorne	6-9	Qualifying	Coral UK Championship
1982	v Phillips	9-3	Qualifying	Embassy World Professional Championship
	v Wilson	5-9	Qualifying	Embassy World Professional Championship
	v Williams	3-5	Qualifying	Jameson International
	v Thorburn	1-5	1st round	Professional Players Tournament
	v Bennett	9-1	Qualifying	Coral UK Championship
	v White	7-9	1st round	Coral UK Championship
1983	v Bear	10-7	Qualifying	Embassy World Professional Championship
	v Black	4-10	Qualifying	Embassy World Professional Championship
	v V. Harris	5-0	Qualifying	Jameson International
	v Macleod	3-5	Qualifying	Jameson International
	v D. Hughes	5-1	Qualifying	Professional Players Tournament
	v Knowles	1-5	1st round	Professional Players Tournament
	v D. Hughes	9-2	Qualifying	Coral UK Championship
	v Edmonds	9-7	Qualifying	Coral UK Championship
	v Reynolds	9-3	1st round	Coral UK Championship
	v Higgins	1-9	2nd round	Coral UK Championship
1984	v Mikkelsen	8-10	Qualifying	Embassy World Professional Championship
	v Gibson	3-5	Qualifying	Jameson International
	v Dodd	5-4	Qualifying	Rothmans Grand Prix
	v Johnson	1-5	1st round	Rothmans Grand Prix
	v Hargreaves	6-9	Qualifying	Coral UK Open

v Cripsey	5-4	Qualifying	Mercantile Credit Classic
v Roscoe	5-4	Qualifying	Mercantile Credit Classic
v Parrott	5-3	Qualifying	Mercantile Credit Classic
v Stevens	4-5	1st round	Mercantile Credit Classic
1985 v Hargreaves	9-8	Qualifying	Tolly Cobbold English Professional Championship
v Spencer	9-4	1st round	Tolly Cobbold English Professional Championship
v Longworth	7-9	2nd round	Tolly Cobbold English Professional Championship
v King	4-6	Qualifying	Dulux British Open
v Bennett	10-4	Qualifying	Embassy World Professional Championship
v Williamson	10-8	Qualifying	Embassy World Professional Championship
v King	10-9	Qualifying	Embassy World Professional Championship
v S. Francisco	7-10	Qualifying	Embassy World Professional Championship

TONY MEO (England)

Born 4.10.59
Turned professional 1979
World ranking 10

After rising from 24th to tenth by the end of the 1983–84 season, Meo held that place despite a relatively disappointing 1984–85 campaign. He was runner-up to Steve Davis in the 1984 Lada Classic and twice won the Hofmeister World Doubles title with Davis.

1979 v David Taylor	9-7	2nd round	Coral UK Championship
v Virgo	6-9	3rd round	Coral UK Championship
1980 v Van Rensberg	9-1	Qualifying	Embassy World Professional Championship
v Houlihan	9-1	Qualifying	Embassy World Professional Championship
v Higgins	9-10	1st round	Embassy World Professional Championship
v Hood	9-5	Qualifying	Coral UK Championship
v Houlihan	9-1	1st round	Coral UK Championship
v Virgo	9-1	2nd round	Coral UK Championship
v S. Davis	5-9	Quarter-final	Coral UK Championship
1981 v Virgo	9-6	1st round	John Courage English Professional
v Miles	9-7	2nd round	John Courage English Professional
v Thorne	9-8	Semi-final	John Courage English Professional
v S. Davis	3-9	Final	John Courage English Professional
v Johnson	9-8	Qualifying	Embassy World Professional Championship
v Hallett	9-4	Qualifying	Embassy World Professional Championship
v Virgo	10-6	1st round	Embassy World Professional Championship
v Griffiths	6-13	2nd round	Embassy World Professional Championship
v E. McLaughlin	5-2	1st round	Jameson International
v Mans	3-5	2nd round	Jameson International
v Williams	9-8	2nd round	Coral UK Championship
v Thorburn	9-6	3rd round	Coral UK Championship
v Higgins	9-4	Quarter-final	Coral UK Championship
v Griffiths	3-9	Semi-final	Coral UK Championship

Tony Meo (David Muscroft)

1982 v David Taylor	5-2	1st round	Benson & Hedges Masters
v Thorburn	5-0	Quarter-final	Benson & Hedges Masters
v S. Davis	4-6	Semi-final	Benson & Hedges Masters
v Spencer	5-3	1st round	Benson & Hedges Irish Masters
v Griffiths	3-5	Quarter-final	Benson & Hedges Irish Masters
v D. Hughes	9-4	Qualifying	Embassy World Professional Championship
v Mans	8-10	1st round	Embassy World Professional Championship
v Sinclair	3-5	Qualifying	Jameson International
v M. Owen	5-4	1st round	Professional Players Tournament
v Jonik	5-0	2nd round	Professional Players Tournament
v Charlton	3-5	3rd round	Professional Players Tournament
v Scott	9-5	Qualifying	Coral UK Championship
v Miles	9-4	1st round	Coral UK Championship
v David Taylor	9-6	2nd round	Coral UK Championship
v Virgo	9-6	Quarter-final	Coral UK Championship
v Griffiths	7-9	Semi-final	Coral UK Championship
1983 v Charlton	3-5	1st round	Benson & Hedges Masters
v Burke	5-0	1st round	Benson & Hedges Irish Masters
v Reardon	4-5	Quarter-final	Benson & Hedges Irish Masters
v V. Harris	10-0	Qualifying	Embassy World Professional Championship
v G. Foulds	10-4	Qualifying	Embassy World Professional Championship
v White	10-8	1st round	Embassy World Professional Championship
v Mountjoy	13-11	2nd round	Embassy World Professional Championship
v Knowles	9-13	Quarter-final	Embassy World Professional Championship
v Knowles	4-5	1st round	Langs Supreme Scottish Masters
v Watterson	3-5	1st round	Jameson International
v King	5-2	1st round	Professional Players Tournament
v Reynolds	5-0	2nd round	Professional Players Tournament
v Hallett	5-3	3rd round	Professional Players Tournament
v Stevens	5-3	Quarter-final	Professional Players Tournament
v Johnson	6-9	Semi-final	Professional Players Tournament
v Parrott	9-7	1st round	Coral UK Championship
v Spencer	9-5	2nd round	Coral UK Championship
v Davis	4-9	Quarter-final	Coral UK Championship
1984 v Meadowcroft	5-1	Qualifying	Lada Classic
v Williams	5-3	1st round	Lada Classic
v Stevens	5-2	Quarter-final	Lada Classic
v Wildman	5-3	Semi-final	Lada Classic
v S. Davis	8-9	Final	Lada Classic
v S. Davis	0-5	1st round	Benson & Hedges Masters
v White	5-4	1st round	Benson & Hedges Irish Masters
v S. Davis	4-5	Quarter-final	Benson & Hedges Irish Masters
v Thorburn	4-5	1st round	Tolly Cobbold Classic
v S. Francisco	5-10	1st round	Embassy World Professional Championship
v Stevens	5-1	Quarter-final	Winfield Australian Masters
v Virgo	2-6	Semi-final	Winfield Australian Masters
v Macleod	5-1	1st round	Jameson International
v White	1-5	2nd round	Jameson International
v Burke	5-1	1st round	Rothmans Grand Prix
v Martin	5-4	2nd round	Rothmans Grand Prix

	v Thorburn	4-5	3rd round	Rothmans Grand Prix
	v E. Hughes	9-4	1st round	Coral UK Open
	v S. Davis	7-9	2nd round	Coral UK Open
	v E. Hughes	4-5	1st round	Mercantile Credit Classic
1985	v Fisher	9-3	1st round	Tolly Cobbold English Professional Championship
	v Hallett	9-4	2nd round	Tolly Cobbold English Professional Championship
	v Reynolds	9-4	Quarter-final	Tolly Cobbold English Professional Championship
	S. Davis	8-9	Semi-final	Tolly Cobbold English Professional Championship
	v Foldvari	6-0	1st round	Dulux British Open
	v Hallett	5-4	2nd round	Dulux British Open
	v Knowles	5-2	3rd round	Dulux British Open
	v S. Francisco	4-5	Quarter-final	Dulux British Open
	v White	1-5	1st round	Benson & Hedges Irish Masters
	v Virgo	10-6	1st round	Embassy World Professional Championship
	v White	11-13	2nd round	Embassy World Professional Championship

DEREK MIENIE (South Africa)

Born –
Turned professional 1978
World ranking 95

Derek Mienie won the South African Professional Championship in 1979.

1979	v Mountjoy	1-9	Prelim	Embassy World Professional Championship
1985	v Edmonds	1-6	Qualifying	Dulux British Open
	v Bradley	4-10	Qualifying	Embassy World Professional Championship

BERNIE MIKKELSEN (Canada)

Born 11.4.50
Turned professional 1979
World ranking 81

1981	v White	4-9	Qualifying	Embassy World Professional Championship
1982	v Roscoe	6-9	Qualifying	Embassy World Professional Championship
1984	v Medati	10-8	Qualifying	Embassy World Professional Championship
	v Jonik	10-9	Qualifying	Embassy World Professional Championship
	v Thorne	3-10	Qualifying	Embassy World Professional Championship
	v Chappel	5-4	Qualifying	Jameson International
	v Everton	5-0	Qualifying	Jameson International
	v Roscoe	1-5	Qualifying	Jameson International
	v Sheehan	3-5	Qualifying	Rothmans Grand Prix
	v Chalmers	5-1	Prelim	Mercantile Credit Classic
	v Watchorn	1-5	Qualifying	Mercantile Credit Classic

| **1985** | v D. Hughes | 6-0 | Qualifying | Dulux British Open |
| | v Bradley | 9-10 | Qualifying | Embassy World Professional Championship |

GRAHAM MILES (England)

Born 11.5.41
Turned professional 1969
World ranking 36

After he was runner-up in the 1974 Park Drive World Professional Championship and the 1976 Benson and Hedges Masters, the underlying trend in Miles' career was downwards. Among his successes were a place in the semi-finals of the 1978 Coral UK Championship, in which his break of 139 set a tournament record (later equalled by Tony Meo), and second prize in the 1979 Holsten Lager International.

1972	v Bennett	15-6	Qualifying	World Professional Championship
	v Dunning	5-11	Qualifying	World Professional Championship
1973	v Thompson	9-5	1st round	World Professional Championship
	v Pulman	16-10	2nd round	World Professional Championship
	v Charlton	6-16	Quarter-final	World Professional Championship
1974	v Morgan	15-7	2nd round	World Professional Championship
	v Dunning	15-13	Quarter-final	World Professional Championship
	v Williams	15-7	Semi-final	World Professional Championship
	v Reardon	12-22	Final	World Professional Championship
1974	v Sinclair	5-0	1st round	Norwich Union Open
−75	v Spencer	2-5	Quarter-final	Norwich Union Open
1975	v Reardon	3-5	Quarter-final	Benson & Hedges Masters
	v Thorburn	2-15	2nd round	World Professional Championship
1976	v Spencer	5-4	Semi-final	Benson & Hedges Masters
	v Reardon	3-7	Final	Benson & Hedges Masters
	v Mans	10-15	1st round	Embassy World Professional Championship
1977	v Reardon	2-5	Semi-final	Benson & Hedges Masters
	v Thorne	13-4	1st round	Embassy World Professional Championship
	v Pulman	10-13	Quarter-final	Embassy World Professional Championship
	v Ross	5-1	2nd round	Super Crystalate UK Championship
	v Virgo	2-5	Quarter-final	Super Crystalate UK Championship
1978	v David Taylor	13-10	1st round	Embassy World Professional Championship
	v Mans	7-13	Quarter-final	Embassy World Professional Championship
	v Williams	9-8	1st round	Coral UK Championship
	v Thorne	9-1	Quarter-final	Coral UK Championship
	v Mountjoy	1-9	Semi-final	Coral UK Championship
1979	v Higgins	6-3	Semi-final	Holsten Lager International
	v Spencer	7-11	Final	Holsten Lager International
	v Williams	9-5	Qualifying	Embassy World Professional Championship
	v Reardon	8-13	1st round	Embassy World Professional Championship
	v Fagan	5-9	3rd round	Coral UK Championship

1980 v Stevens	3-10	1st round	Embassy World Professional Championship
v Sinclair	5-9	1st round	Coral UK Championship
1981 v Hood	9-1	1st round	John Courage English Professional
v Meo	7-9	2nd round	John Courage English Professional
v Knowles	10-8	1st round	Embassy World Professional Championship
v Thorburn	2-13	2nd round	Embassy World Professional Championship
v Johnson	5-3	2nd round	Jameson International
v Thorburn	5-0	3rd round	Jameson International
v Martin	1-5	Quarter-final	Jameson International
v Houlihan	9-5	2nd round	Coral UK Championship
v Griffiths	4-9	3rd round	Coral UK Championship
1982 v S. Davis	2-5	Semi-final	Tolly Cobbold Classic
v Martin	10-5	1st round	Embassy World Professional Championship
v Knowles	7-13	2nd round	Embassy World Professional Championship
v Edmonds	1-5	Qualifying	Jameson International
v Johnson	1-5	1st round	Professional Players Tournament
v Meo	4-9	1st round	Coral UK Championship
1983 v Morgan	10-6	Qualifying	Embassy World Professional Championship
v Knowles	3-10	1st round	Embassy World Professional Championship
v King	5-3	Qualifying	Jameson International
v Griffiths	2-5	1st round	Jameson International
v Gauvreau	5-3	1st round	Professional Players Tournament
v Campbell	2-5	2nd round	Professional Players Tournament
v Hallett	4-9	1st round	Coral UK Championship
1984 v Williamson	10-6	Qualifying	Embassy World Professional Championship
v Spencer	3-10	1st round	Embassy World Professional Championship
v Newbury	1-5	Qualifying	Jameson International
v Murphy	5-3	1st round	Rothmans Grand Prix
v S. Davis	0-5	2nd round	Rothmans Grand Prix
v J. McLaughlin	8-9	Qualifying	Coral UK Open
v Browne	3-5	Qualifying	Mercantile Credit Classic
1985 v Martin	7-9	1st round	Tolly Cobbold English Professional Championship
v Edmonds	6-1	1st round	Dulux British Open
v Spencer	2-5	2nd round	Dulux British Open
v Stevens	2-5	3rd round	Dulux British Open
v W. Jones	8-10	Qualifying	Embassy World Professional Championship

PADDY MORGAN (Australia)

Born 7.1.43
Turned professional 1970
World ranking 75

Born in Belfast, Morgan later represented the Republic of Ireland and after living for a while in Coventry emigrate. to Sydney. He was a member of the Australian trio in the first three World Cups.

1974	v Thorburn	8-4	1st round	World Professional Championship
	v Miles	7-15	2nd round	World Professional Championship
1975	v Thorburn	6-15	1st round	World Professional Championship
1978	v David Taylor	7-9	Qualifying	Embassy World Professional Championship
1980	v S. Davis	0-9	Qualifying	Embassy World Professional Championship
1981	v Sinclair	8-9	Qualifying	Embassy World Professional Championship
1982	v Greaves	9-2	Qualifying	Embassy World Professional Championship
	v S. Francisco	1-9	Qualifying	Embassy World Professional Championship
	v Werbeniuk	3-5	1st round	Professional Players Tournament
1983	v Burke	10-9	Qualifying	Embassy World Professional Championship
	v Miles	6-10	Qualifying	Embassy World Professional Championship
	v Fitzmaurice	5-4	Qualifying	Jameson International
	v F. Davis	5-3	Qualifying	Jameson International
	v Spencer	1-5	1st round	Jameson International
	v Gibson	5-4	Qualifying	Professional Players Tournament
	v David Taylor	3-5	1st round	Professional Players Tournament
1984	v Sanderson	8-10	Qualifying	Embassy World Professional Championship
1985	v Chaperon	3-10	Qualifying	Embassy World Professional Championship

MARIO MORRA (Canada)

Born 8.9.53
Turned professional 1979
World ranking 43

A diminutive Canadian with a deliberate, methodical style, Morra qualified for the televised stage of the 1984 Embassy World Championship and beat Jimmy White in the first round of the Jameson International the previous year.

1981	v Thorne	5-9	Qualifying	Embassy World Professional Championship
	v Wildman	3-5	Qualifying	Jameson International
1982	v Murphy	9-5	Qualifying	Embassy World Professional Championship
	v Fitzmaurice	7-9	Qualifying	Embassy World Professional Championship
	v Demarco	5-2	Qualifying	Jameson International
	v Reynolds	1-5	Qualifying	Jameson International
	v Wilson	2-5	1st round	Professional Players Tournament
1983	v Black	9-10	Qualifying	Embassy World Professional Championship
	v Watchorn	5-3	Qualifying	Jameson International
	v Hallett	5-3	Qualifying	Jameson International
	v White	5-3	1st round	Jameson International
	v Charlton	3-5	2nd round	Jameson International
	v Hargreaves	5-0	Qualifying	Professional Players Tournament
	v S. Francisco	3-5	1st round	Professional Players Tournament
	v Burke	5-2	Qualifying	Lada Classic
	v Everton	5-0	Qualifying	Lada Classic
	v S. Francisco	1-5	Qualifying	Lada Classic
1984	v G. Foulds	10-2	Qualifying	Embassy World Professional Championship
	v Murphy	10-5	Qualifying	Embassy World Professional Championship

v Reynolds	10-7	Qualifying	Embassy World Professional Championship
v Thorburn	3-10	1st round	Embassy World Professional Championship
v Bradley	5-3	Qualifying	Jameson International
v Johnson	0-5	Qualifying	Jameson International
v Cripsey	5-3	Qualifying	Rothmans Grand Prix
v S. Davis	2-5	1st round	Rothmans Grand Prix
v Longworth	9-1	Qualifying	Coral UK Open
v E. Hughes	8-9	Qualifying	Coral UK Open
v Newbury	2-5	Qualifying	Mercantile Credit Classic
1985 v Bradley	2-6	Qualifying	Dulux British Open
v Browne	10-6	Qualifying	Embassy World Professional Championship
v Campbell	9-10	Qualifying	Embassy World Professional Championship

DOUG MOUNTJOY (Wales)

Born 8.6.42
Turned professional 1976
World ranking 15

After winning the 1976 World Amateur title, Mountjoy started his professional career by winning the 1977 Benson and Hedges Masters. He won the Coral UK Championship in 1978, was runner-up to Steve Davis for the world title in 1981 and has won the Welsh Professional title three times since 1980. His break of 145 in the 1981 Embassy World Championship stands second only to Cliff Thorburn's maximum as the highest break made in the event.

A steady 1984–85 season was highlighted by victories over Tony Knowles, Tony Meo and Terry Griffiths in reaching the final of the Benson and Hedges Masters.

1977 v Higgins	5-3	Semi-final	Benson & Hedges Masters
v Reardon	**7-6**	**Final**	**Benson & Hedges Masters**
v Jack Rea	11-9	Qualifying	Embassy World Professional Championship
v Higgins	13-12	1st round	Embassy World Professional Championship
v Dennis Taylor	11-13	Quarter-final	Embassy World Professional Championship
v Andrewartha	5-2	1st round	Super Crystalate UK Championship
v Spencer	5-3	2nd round	Super Crystalate UK Championship
v Thorne	5-4	Quarter-final	Super Crystalate UK Championship
v Higgins	9-2	Semi-final	Super Crystalate UK Championship
v Fagan	9-12	Final	Super Crystalate UK Championship
1978 v Spencer	3-5	Final	Benson & Hedges Irish Masters
v Andrewartha	9-3	Qualifying	Embassy World Professional Championship
v Reardon	9-13	1st round	Embassy World Professional Championship
v Barrie	9-5	Qualifying	Coral UK Championship
v Dennis Taylor	9-4	1st round	Coral UK Championship
v Andrewartha	9-4	Quarter-final	Coral UK Championship
v Miles	9-1	Semi-final	Coral UK Championship
v David Taylor	**15-9**	**Final**	**Coral UK Championship**
1979 v F. Davis	5-2	1st round	Benson & Hedges Masters

Doug Mountjoy (David Muscroft)

Dave Martin (David Muscroft)

	v Spencer	5-0	Quarter-final	Benson & Hedges Masters
	v Higgins	1-5	Semi-final	Benson & Hedges Masters
	v Reardon	**6-5**	**Final**	**Benson & Hedges Irish Masters**
	v Mienie	9-1	Prelim	Embassy World Professional Championship
	v Houlihan	9-6	Qualifying	Embassy World Professional Championship
	v Charlton	6-13	1st round	Embassy World Professional Championship
	v S. Davis	5-9	3rd round	Coral UK Championship
1980	v Griffiths	8-9	Final	Benson & Hedges Irish Masters
	v Wilson	10-6	1st round	Embassy World Professional Championship
	v Thorburn	10-13	2nd round	Embassy World Professional Championship
	v Williams	8-9	1st round	Coral UK Championship
1981	v Charlton	5-0	1st round	Benson & Hedges Masters
	v Higgins	1-5	Quarter-final	Benson & Hedges Masters
	v Wilson	6-9	Semi-final	Woodpecker Welsh Professional Championship
	v Thorne	10-6	1st round	Embassy World Professional Championship
	v Charlton	13-7	2nd round	Embassy World Professional Championship
	v Dennis Taylor	13-8	Quarter-final	Embassy World Professional Championship
	v Reardon	16-10	Semi-final	Embassy World Professional Championship
	v S. Davis	12-18	Final	Embassy World Professional Championship
	v S. Davis	0-5	Quarter-final	Langs Supreme Scottish Masters
	v Higgins	1-5	3rd round	Jameson International
	v Dennis Taylor	5-4	1st round	Northern Ireland Classic
	v White	8-9	Semi-final	Northern Ireland Classic
	v Knowles	6-9	3rd round	Coral UK Championship
1982	v Spencer	5-4	1st round	Benson & Hedges Masters
	v S. Davis	2-5	Quarter-final	Benson & Hedges Masters
	v Andrewartha	6-3	1st round	Welsh Professional Championship
	v Reardon	9-7	Semi-final	Welsh Professional Championship
	v Griffiths	**9-8**	**Final**	**Welsh Professional Championship**
	v E. Hughes	5-4	1st round	Benson & Hedges Irish Masters
	v S. Davis	2-5	Quarter-final	Benson & Hedges Irish Masters
	v Williams	10-3	1st round	Embassy World Professional Championship
	v Higgins	12-13	2nd round	Embassy World Professional Championship
	v Wilson	4-5	1st round	Jameson International
	v Jonik	3-5	1st round	Professional Players Tournament
	v Houlihan	9-3	1st round	Coral UK Championship
	v Virgo	5-9	2nd round	Coral UK Championship
1983	v Griffiths	5-1	1st round	Lada Classic
	v Werbeniuk	2-5	Quarter-final	Lada Classic
	v Virgo	5-1	1st round	Benson & Hedges Masters
	v S. Davis	5-4	Quarter-final	Benson & Hedges Masters
	v Reardon	3-6	Semi-final	Benson & Hedges Masters
	v M. Owen	6-0	Quarter-final	Woodpecker Welsh Professional Championship
	v Wilson	9-3	Semi-final	Woodpecker Welsh Professional Championship
	v Reardon	1-9	Final	Woodpecker Welsh Professional Championship
	v Knowles	5-1	1st round	Benson & Hedges Irish Masters
	v Griffiths	4-5	Quarter-final	Benson & Hedges Irish Masters

v Wilson	10-2	1st round	Embassy World Professional Championship
v Meo	11-13	2nd round	Embassy World Professional Championship
v Wildman	5-4	1st round	Jameson International
v Martin	5-0	2nd round	Jameson International
v Thorburn	2-5	Quarter-final	Jameson International
v Campbell	3-5	1st round	Professional Players Tournament
v Watterson	9-2	1st round	Coral UK Championship
v Knowles	5-9	2nd round	Coral UK Championship
1984 v Parrott	4-5	Qualifying	Lada Classic
v Higgins	2-5	1st round	Benson & Hedges Masters
v Everton	6-1	1st round	Strongbow Welsh Professional Championship
v Griffiths	9-5	Semi-final	Strongbow Welsh Professional Championship
v Wilson	**9-3**	**Final**	**Strongbow Welsh Professional Championship**
v Hallett	10-4	1st round	Embassy World Professional Championship
v N. Foulds	13-6	2nd round	Embassy World Professional Championship
v Dennis Taylor	8-13	Quarter-final	Embassy World Professional Championship
v E. Hughes	1-5	1st round	Jameson International
v E. McLaughlin	5-4	1st round	Rothmans Grand Prix
v Wildman	5-0	2nd round	Rothmans Grand Prix
v Charlton	5-4	3rd round	Rothmans Grand Prix
v Thorburn	3-5	Quarter-final	Rothmans Grand Prix
v Hallett	9-2	1st round	Coral UK Open
v White	2-9	2nd round	Coral UK Open
v Wilson	4-5	1st round	Mercantile Credit Classic
1985 v Knowles	5-3	1st round	Benson & Hedges Masters
v Meo	5-4	Quarter-final	Benson & Hedges Masters
v Griffiths	6-2	Semi-final	Benson & Hedges Masters
v Thorburn	6-9	Final	Benson & Hedges Masters
v V. Harris	5-6	1st round	Dulux British Open
v Macleod	10-5	1st round	Embassy World Professional Championship
v Knowles	6-13	2nd round	Embassy World Professional Championship
v Newbury	6-5	Quarter-final	BCE Welsh Professional Championship
v Wilson	9-2	Semi-final	BCE Welsh Professional Championship
v Griffiths	4-9	Final	BCE Welsh Professional Championship

TOMMY MURPHY (Northern Ireland)

Born 8.1.62
Turned professional 1981
World ranking 58

Northern Ireland amateur champion in 1981, Murphy had played three times for Northern Ireland in the World Cup before an All Ireland team was entered in 1985.

1981 v Johnson	1-9	Qualifying	Coral UK Open
1982 v Fagan	6-2	Quarter-final	Irish Professional Championship

	v Dennis Taylor	0-6	Semi-final	Irish Professional Championship
	v Morra	5-9	Qualifying	Embassy World Professional Championship
	v Fisher	1-5	Qualifying	Jameson International
	v Reardon	0-5	1st round	Professional Players Tournament
	v Everton	9-4	Qualifying	Coral UK Open
	v Sinclair	5-9	Qualifying	Coral UK Open
1983	v Fagan	4-6	Quarter-final	Irish Professional Championship
	v Houlihan	10-9	Qualifying	Embassy World Professional Championship
	v Virgo	8-10	Qualifying	Embassy World Professional Championship
	v Sheehan	5-2	Qualifying	Jameson International
	v Thorne	2-5	Qualifying	Jameson International
	v Macleod	5-0	1st round	Professional Players Tournament
	v Stevens	1-5	2nd round	Professional Players Tournament
	v Demarco	9-4	Qualifying	Coral UK Championship
	v Donnelly	9-4	Qualifying	Coral UK Championship
	v Dennis Taylor	6-9	1st round	Coral UK Championship
1984	v Fitzmaurice	10-8	Qualifying	Embassy World Professional Championship
	v Morra	5-10	Qualifying	Embassy World Professional Championship
	v Bales	4-5	Qualifying	Jameson International
	v G. Foulds	5-1	Qualifying	Rothmans Grand Prix
	v Miles	3-5	1st round	Rothmans Grand Prix
	v Kearney	9-2	Qualifying	Coral UK Open
	v Watterson	9-4	Qualifying	Coral UK Open
	v Martin	9-8	Qualifying	Coral UK Open
	v S. Davis	1-9	1st round	Coral UK Open
	v Fowler	0-5	Qualifying	Mercantile Credit Classic
1985	v Sheehan	6-3	Qualifying	Dulux British Open
	v Macleod	5-6	1st round	Dulux British Open
	v Browne	6-3	Qualifying	Irish Professional Championship
	v Fagan	2-6	Quarter-final	Irish Professional Championship
	v P. Francisco	4-10	Qualifying	Embassy World Professional Championship

STEVE NEWBURY (Wales)

Born 21.4.56
Turned professional 1984
World ranking 34

Welsh amateur champion in 1980, Newbury rose to 34th in the rankings in his first professional season mainly through reaching the last 16 of the Jameson International and the Dulux British Open, the latter with a win over Terry Griffiths.

1984	v Longworth	5-4	Qualifying	Jameson International
	v Burke	5-0	Qualifying	Jameson International
	v Fagan	5-0	Qualifying	Jameson International
	v Miles	5-1	Qualifying	Jameson International
	v Werbeniuk	5-2	1st round	Jameson International
	v Knowles	4-5	2nd round	Jameson International

v Fisher	5-0	Qualifying	Rothmans Grand Prix
v Thorne	2-5	1st round	Rothmans Grand Prix
v Rigitano	9-6	Qualifying	Coral UK Open
v Jonik	9-3	Qualifying	Coral UK Open
v Dodd	6-9	Qualifying	Coral UK Open
v V. Harris	5-3	Qualifying	Mercantile Credit Classic
v Burke	5-1	Qualifying	Mercantile Credit Classic
v Morra	5-2	Qualifying	Mercantile Credit Classic
v E. Hughes	3-5	Qualifying	Mercantile Credit Classic
1985 v Browne	6-0	Qualifying	Dulux British Open
v Sinclair	6-3	1st round	Dulux British Open
v Griffiths	5-3	2nd round	Dulux British Open
v Dennis Taylor	3-5	3rd round	Dulux British Open
v D. Hughes	10-9	Qualifying	Embassy World Professional Championship
v Burke	10-3	Qualifying	Embassy World Professional Championship
v Scott	10-2	Qualifying	Embassy World Professional Championship
v E. Hughes	6-10	Qualifying	Embassy World Professional Championship
v W. Jones	6-2	1st round	BCE Welsh Professional Championship
v Mountjoy	5-6	Quarter-final	BCE Welsh Professional Championship

DENE O'KANE (New Zealand)

Born 24.2.63
Turned professional 1984
World ranking 32

New Zealand amateur champion at the age of 17 in 1980, O'Kane achieved the highest ranking – 32nd – of any of the new professionals last season. He picked up all his points by reaching the quarter-finals of the Dulux British Open although he amassed merit points by reaching the last 32 of the Jameson International, the Dulux and the Embassy World Championship.

1984 v Parkin	5-2	Qualifying	Jameson International
v E. McLaughlin	5-1	Qualifying	Jameson International
v Fitzmaurice	5-4	Qualifying	Jameson International
v Hallett	5-4	Qualifying	Jameson International
v Thorne	3-5	1st round	Jameson International
v Kelly	5-4	Qualifying	Rothmans Grand Prix
v David Taylor	1-5	1st round	Rothmans Grand Prix
v W. Jones	9-7	Qualifying	Coral UK Open
v Duggan	9-6	Qualifying	Coral UK Open
v Scott	7-9	Qualifying	Coral UK Open
v W. Jones	0-5	Qualifying	Mercantile Credit Classic
1985 v Cripsey	6-4	Qualifying	Dulux British Open
v Campbell	6-4	1st round	Dulux British Open
v V. Harris	5-3	2nd round	Dulux British Open
v Martin	5-4	3rd round	Dulux British Open
v S. Davis	1-5	Quarter-final	Dulux British Open

Dene O'Kane

John Parrott (David Muscroft)

wo J. McLaughlin	*scr*	Qualifying	Embassy World Professional Championship
v V. Harris	10-5	Qualifying	Embassy World Professional Championship
v Jonik	10-5	Qualifying	Embassy World Professional Championship
v Dodd	10-7	Qualifying	Embassy World Professional Championship
v Martin	10-8	Qualifying	Embassy World Professional Championship
v David Taylor	4-10	1st round	Embassy World Professional Championship

BILL OLIVER (England)

Born 3.12.48
Turned professional 1983
World ranking 85

1983	v T. Jones	2-5	Qualifying	Professional Players Tournament
	v Andrewartha	1-9	Qualifying	Coral UK Championship
1984	v Dunning	10-3	Qualifying	Embassy World Professional Championship
	v Caggianello	10-7	Qualifying	Embassy World Professional Championship
	v Williams	8-10	Qualifying	Embassy World Professional Championship
	v D. Hughes	5-4	Qualifying	Jameson International
	v Chalmers	4-5	Qualifying	Jameson International
	v Bennett	5-3	Qualifying	Rothmans Grand Prix
	v White	1-5	1st round	Rothmans Grand Prix
	v Fowler	3-9	Qualifying	Coral UK Open
	v Longworth	1-5	Qualifying	Mercantile Credit Classic
1985	v Fowler	7-9	Qualifying	Tolly Cobbold English Professional Championship
	v Thorne	3-6	1st round	Dulux British Open
	v Foldvari	3-10	Qualifying	Embassy World Professional Championship

MARCUS OWEN (Wales)

Born 4.4.35
Turned professional 1973
World ranking unranked

Four times English amateur champion and a world professional quarter-finalist in 1974, Owen has played comparatively little in recent years.

1974	v Parkin	8-5	1st round	World Professional Championship
	v G. Owen	15-8	2nd round	World Professional Championship
	v Reardon	11-15	Quarter-final	World Professional Championship
1976	v Conda	6-8	Qualifying	Embassy World Professional Championship
1981	v E. Hughes	1-5	Qualifying	Jameson International
1982	v Wilson	0-6	1st round	Welsh Professional Championship
	v Bennett	2-5	Qualifying	Jameson International
	v Meo	4-5	1st round	Professional Players Tournament

	v V. Harris	4-9	Qualifying	Coral UK Open
1983	v Mountjoy	0-6	Quarter-final	Woodpecker Welsh Professional Championship
	v Macleod	5-10	Qualifying	Embassy World Professional Championship
1984	v Reardon	1-6	1st round	Strongbow Welsh Professional Championship
1985	v Chappel	0-6	1st round	BCE Welsh Professional Championship

MAURICE PARKIN (England)

Born –
Turned professional 1970
World ranking 91

Parkin won the English Amateur Championship in 1955 but has not played regularly on the professional circuit.

1972	v Thompson	11-10	Qualifying	World Professional Championship
	v Higgins	3-11	Qualifying	World Professional Championship
1973	v Simpson	3-9	1st round	World Professional Championship
1974	v M. Owen	5-8	1st round	World Professional Championship
1976	v Gross	5-8	Qualifying	Embassy World Professional Championship
1977	v Dunning	4-5	1st round	Super Crystalate UK Championship
1978	v Bennett	9-4	Prelim	Embassy World Professional Championship
	v Werbeniuk	2-9	Qualifying	Embassy World Professional Championship
	v David Taylor	2-9	Qualifying	Coral UK Championship
1979	v Virgo	0-9	Prelim	Embassy World Professional Championship
	v Hallett	1-9	1st round	Coral UK Championship
1981	v Gibson	3-5	Qualifying	Jameson International
	v Greaves	5-9	Qualifying	Embassy World Professional Championship
1982	v Black	6-9	Qualifying	Embassy World Professional Championship
	v E. Hughes	2-5	Qualifying	Jameson International
1983	v Martin	1-10	Qualifying	Embassy World Professional Championship
	v D. Hughes	0-5	Qualifying	Jameson International
1984	v Cripsey	4-10	Qualifying	Embassy World Professional Championship
	v O'Kane	2-5	Qualifying	Jameson International
1985	v G. Foulds	6-10	Qualifying	Embassy World Professional Championship

JOHN PARROTT (England)

Born 11.5.64
Turned professional 1983
World ranking 18

An exceptionally encouraging initial season in 1983–84 saw Parrott reach the semi-finals of the Lada Classic with wins over Doug Mountjoy, Alex Higgins and Tony Knowles and the last 16 of the Embassy World Championship with another win over Knowles. 1984–85 was disappointing initially but ended in a blaze of glory when he reached the quarter-finals of the Embassy World Championship by beating John Spencer and Kirk Stevens before losing an epic 13-12 battle with Ray Reardon.

1983	v Watchorn	5-0	Qualifying	Professional Players Tournament
	v Fagan	5-2	1st round	Professional Players Tournament
	v Griffiths	1-5	2nd round	Professional Players Tournament
	v Scott	9-7	Qualifying	Coral UK Championship
	v Fisher	9-0	Qualifying	Coral UK Championship
	v Meo	7-9	1st round	Coral UK Championship
1984	v Mountjoy	5-4	Qualifying	Lada Classic
	v Higgins	5-2	1st round	Lada Classic
	v Knowles	5-1	Quarter-final	Lada Classic
	v S. Davis	4-5	Semi-final	Lada Classic
	v D. Hughes	10-3	Qualifying	Embassy World Professional Championship
	v Everton	10-2	Qualifying	Embassy World Professional Championship
	v Mans	10-0	Qualifying	Embassy World Professional Championship
	v Knowles	10-7	1st round	Embassy World Professional Championship
	v Dennis Taylor	11-13	2nd round	Embassy World Professional Championship
	v Gauvreau	4-5	Qualifying	Jameson International
	v Gauvreau	5-3	1st round	Rothmans Grand Prix
	v Charlton	1-5	2nd round	Rothmans Grand Prix
	v Fitzmaurice	9-6	Qualifying	Coral UK Open
	v Thorne	7-9	1st round	Coral UK Open
	v Medati	3-5	Qualifying	Mercantile Credit Classic
1985	v G. Foulds	9-4	1st round	Tolly Cobbold English Professional Championship
	v David Taylor	6-9	2nd round	Tolly Cobbold English Professional Championship
	v John Rea	6-4	1st round	Dulux British Open
	v Dennis Taylor	2-5	2nd round	Dulux British Open
	v Fowler	10-2	Qualifying	Embassy World Professional Championship
	v Spencer	10-3	1st round	Embassy World Professional Championship
	v Stevens	13-6	2nd round	Embassy World Professional Championship
	v Reardon	12-13	Quarter-final	Embassy World Professional Championship

JACK REA (Northern Ireland)

Born –
Turned professional 1948
World ranking 76

For 20 years Irish professional champion until deposed by Alex Higgins in 1972, Rea made his name on the exhibition circuit with a unique mixture of jokes, patter, trick shots and straight snooker. His competitive appearances have been comparatively infrequent in recent years although it will always be on his record that he was runner-up for the world title in 1957.

1969	v G. Owen	17-25	Quarter-final	World Professional Championship
1970	v Spencer	15-31	Quarter-final	World Professional Championship
1972	v Higgins	11-19	1st round	World Professional Championship
1973	v Houlihan	2-9	1st round	World Professional Championship
1976	v Anderson	8-5	Qualifying	Embassy World Professional Championship
1977	v John Rea	9-11	Qualifying	Embassy World Professional Championship
	v Fagan	1-5	1st round	Super Crystalate UK Championship
1978	v Meadowcroft	5-9	Qualifying	Coral UK Championship
1979	v Dunning	5-9	Prelim	Embassy World Professional Championship
	v Bennett	9-8	1st round	Coral UK Championship
	v Houlihan	3-9	2nd round	Coral UK Championship
1980	v Thorne	1-9	Qualifying	Embassy World Professional Championship
1981	v D. Hughes	4-5	Qualifying	Jameson International
1982	v E. Hughes	1-6	Quarter-final	Irish Professional Championship
	v Bennett	8-5	Qualifying	Embassy World Professional Championship
	v Werbeniuk	2-5	2nd round	Professional Players Tournament
	v Roscoe	6-9	Qualifying	Coral UK Championship
1983	v Higgins	3-6	Quarter-final	Irish Professional Championship
	v David Taylor	7-8	Qualifying	Embassy World Professional Championship
	v Edmonds	1-5	Qualifying	Jameson International
	v French	5-9	Qualifying	Coral UK Championship
1984	v Bradley	2-5	Qualifying	Jameson International
	v Foldvari	4-5	Qualifying	Mercantile Credit Classic
1985	v Dennis Taylor	0-6	Quarter-final	Irish Professional Championship

JOHN REA (Scotland)

Born 5.12.51
Turned professional 1984
World ranking 67

1984	v Browne	2-5	Qualifying	Jameson International
	v Fitzmaurice	5-2	Qualifying	Rothmans Grand Prix
	v E. Hughes	5-4	1st round	Rothmans Grand Prix
	v David Taylor	1-5	2nd round	Rothmans Grand Prix
	v Bennett	9-5	Qualifying	Coral UK Open
	v Dunning	9-3	Qualifying	Coral UK Open
	v Edmonds	9-6	Qualifying	Coral UK Open
	v Johnson	6-9	Qualifying	Coral UK Open
	v Sheehan	2-5	Qualifying	Mercantile Credit Classic
1985	v Fisher	6-0	Qualifying	Dulux British Open
	v Parrott	4-6	1st round	Dulux British Open
	v W. Jones	3-10	Qualifying	Embassy World Professional Championship

RAY REARDON (Wales)

Born 8.10.32
Turned professional 1967
World ranking 6

Welsh amateur champion six times in succession, the first of these when he was only 17, Reardon was professional snooker's dominant player in the 1970s, during which he won six world titles. The highlights of his recent career have been first prizes in the 1982 Professional Players Tournament and the 1983 Yamaha International Masters and two Welsh titles.

His best performance of the 1984–85 season was to reach the semi-finals of the Embassy World Championship but his status and reputation in the game is so high that it is now only partially dependent upon results.

1969	v F. Davis	24-25 Quarter-final	World Professional Championship
1970	v F. Davis	31-26 Quarter-final	World Professional Championship (Apr)
	v Spencer	37-33 Semi-final	World Professional Championship (Apr)
	v Pulman	**39-34 Final**	**World Professional Championship (Apr)**
	v Spencer	15-34 Semi-final	World Professional Championship (Nov)
1972	v Williams	23-25 Quarter-final	World Professional Championship
1973	v Meadowcroft	16-10 2nd round	World Professional Championship
	v G. Owen	16-6 Quarter-final	World Professional Championship
	v Spencer	23-22 Semi-final	World Professional Championship
	v Charlton	**38-32 Final**	**World Professional Championship**
1974	v Meadowcroft	15-3 2nd round	World Professional Championship
	v M. Owen	15-11 Quarter-final	World Professional Championship
	v F. Davis	15-3 Semi-final	World Professional Championship
	v Miles	**22-12 Final**	**World Professional Championship**
1974	v Burke	5-2 1st round	Norwich Union Open
–75	v Williams	5-2 Quarter-final	Norwich Union Open
	v Higgins	9-8 Semi-final	Norwich Union Open
	v Spencer	9-10 Final	Norwich Union Open
1975	v Miles	5-3 Quarter-final	Benson & Hedges Masters
	v Williams	5-4 Semi-final	Benson & Hedges Masters
	v Spencer	8-9 Final	Benson & Hedges Masters
	v Simpson	15-11 2nd round	World Professional Championship
	v Spencer	19-17 Quarter-final	World Professional Championship
	v Higgins	19-14 Semi-final	World Professional Championship
	v Charlton	**31-30 Final**	**World Professional Championship**
1976	v Charlton	5-4 Semi-final	Benson & Hedges Masters
	v Miles	**7-3 Final**	**Benson & Hedges Masters**
	v Dunning	15-7 1st round	Embassy World Professional Championship
	v Dennis Taylor	15-2 Quarter-final	Embassy World Professional Championship
	v Mans	20-10 Semi-final	Embassy World Professional Championship
	v Higgins	**27-16 Final**	**Embassy World Professional Championship**
1977	v Miles	5-2 Semi-final	Benson & Hedges Masters
	v Mountjoy	6-7 Final	Benson & Hedges Masters
	v Fagan	13-7 1st round	Embassy World Professional Championship

Ray Reardon (Keith Hailey)

v Spencer	6-13	Quarter-final	Embassy World Professional Championship
v Meadowcroft	4-5	2nd round	Super Crystalate UK Championship
1978 v Higgins	1-5	Semi-final	Benson & Hedges Masters
v Mountjoy	13-9	1st round	Embassy World Professional Championship
v Werbeniuk	13-6	Quarter-final	Embassy World Professional Championship
v Charlton	18-14	Semi-final	Embassy World Professional Championship
v Mans	**25-18**	**Final**	**Embassy World Professional Championship**
v Thorne	6-9	1st round	Coral UK Championship
1979 v David Taylor	5-2	Quarter-final	Benson & Hedges Masters
v Mans	3-5	Semi-final	Benson & Hedges Masters
v Mountjoy	5-6	Final	Benson & Hedges Irish Masters
v Miles	13-8	1st round	Embassy World Professional Championship
v Dennis Taylor	8-13	Quarter-final	Embassy World Professional Championship
1980 v Dennis Taylor	5-3	Quarter-final	Benson & Hedges Masters
v Higgins	2-5	Semi-final	Benson & Hedges Masters
v Higgins	1-5	Final	British Gold Cup
v Werbeniuk	13-6	2nd round	Embassy World Professional Championship
v David Taylor	11-13	Quarter-final	Embassy World Professional Championship
v Andrewartha	9-3	2nd round	Coral UK Championship
v Williams	9-4	Quarter-final	Coral UK Championship
v Higgins	7-9	Semi-final	Coral UK Championship
1981 v Spencer	1-5	Quarter-final	Benson & Hedges Masters
v Griffiths	9-6	Semi-final	Woodpecker Welsh Professional Championship
v Wilson	**9-6**	**Final**	**Woodpecker Welsh Professional Championship**
v Spencer	13-11	2nd round	Embassy World Professional Championship
v Werbeniuk	13-10	Quarter-final	Embassy World Professional Championship
v Mountjoy	10-16	Semi-final	Embassy World Professional Championship
v White	4-5	Quarter-final	Langs Supreme Scottish Masters
v Virgo	3-5	3rd round	Jameson International
v Johnson	9-7	3rd round	Coral UK Championship
v White	8-9	Quarter-final	Coral UK Championship
1982 v David Taylor	5-1	1st round	Lada Classic
v S. Davis	4-5	Semi-final	Lada Classic
v Dennis Taylor	5-3	1st round	Benson & Hedges Masters
v Griffiths	3-5	Quarter-final	Benson & Hedges Masters
v Everton	6-1	1st round	Welsh Professional Championship
v Mountjoy	7-9	Semi-final	Welsh Professional Championship
v Dennis Taylor	5-4	Quarter-final	Benson & Hedges Irish Masters
v Griffiths	3-6	Semi-final	Benson & Hedges Irish Masters
v Donnelly	10-5	1st round	Embassy World Professional Championship
v Virgo	13-8	2nd round	Embassy World Professional Championship
v S. Francisco	13-8	Quarter-final	Embassy World Professional Championship
v Charlton	16-11	Semi-final	Embassy World Professional Championship
v Higgins	15-18	Final	Embassy World Professional Championship
v Griffiths	3-5	1st round	Langs Supreme Scottish Masters
v E. Hughes	5-3	1st round	Jameson International
v Knowles	2-5	2nd round	Jameson International
v Murphy	5-0	1st round	Professional Players Tournament
v Higgins	5-2	2nd round	Professional Players Tournament

v Macleod	5-2	3rd round	Professional Players Tournament
v Werbeniuk	5-3	Quarter-final	Professional Players Tournament
v Charlton	10-7	Semi-final	Professional Players Tournament
v White	**10-5**	**Final**	**Professional Players Tournament**
v Wildman	9-5	1st round	Coral UK Championship
v Hallett	9-8	2nd round	Coral UK Championship
v White	9-8	Quarter-final	Coral UK Championship
v Higgins	6-9	Semi-final	Coral UK Championship
1983 v Spencer	3-5	1st round	Lada Classic
v Reynolds	5-1	1st round	Benson & Hedges Masters
v White	5-2	Quarter-final	Benson & Hedges Masters
v Mountjoy	6-3	Semi-final	Benson & Hedges Masters
v Thorburn	7-9	Final	Benson & Hedges Masters
v White	**9-6**	**Final**	**Yamaha International Masters**
v Andrewartha	6-2	Quarter-final	Woodpecker Welsh Professional Championship
v Griffiths	9-4	Semi-final	Woodpecker Welsh Professional Championship
v Mountjoy	**9-1**	**Final**	**Woodpecker Welsh Professional Championship**
v Meo	5-4	Quarter-final	Benson & Hedges Irish Masters
v Higgins	6-3	Semi-final	Benson & Hedges Irish Masters
v S. Davis	2-9	Final	Benson & Hedges Irish Masters
v E. Hughes	10-7	1st round	Embassy World Professional Championship
v Knowles	12-13	2nd round	Embassy World Professional Championship
v Macleod	5-2	1st round	Jameson International
v Thorne	0-5	2nd round	Jameson International
v Ganim	5-4	1st round	Professional Players Tournament
v Duggan	5-2	2nd round	Professional Players Tournament
v Thorne	3-5	3rd round	Professional Players Tournament
v B. Harris	9-7	1st round	Coral UK Championship
v Wilson	9-4	2nd round	Coral UK Championship
v White	4-9	Quarter-final	Coral UK Championship
1984 v Williams	4-5	Qualifying	Lada Classic
v Virgo	5-3	1st round	Benson & Hedges Masters
v White	3-5	Quarter-final	Benson & Hedges Masters
v M. Owen	6-1	1st round	Strongbow Welsh Professional Championship
v Wilson	4-9	Semi-final	Strongbow Welsh Professional Championship
v Higgins	2-5	Quarter-final	Benson & Hedges Irish Masters
v Wych	10-7	1st round	Embassy World Professional Championship
v S. Francisco	13-8	2nd round	Embassy World Professional Championship
v Stevens	2-13	Quarter-final	Embassy World Professional Championship
v Dodd	5-4	1st round	Jameson International
v E. Hughes	1-5	2nd round	Jameson International
v Roscoe	5-1	1st round	Rothmans Grand Prix
v Wilson	5-4	2nd round	Rothmans Grand Prix
v Dennis Taylor	3-5	3rd round	Rothmans Grand Prix
v Fowler	9-2	1st round	Coral UK Open
v David Taylor	9-4	2nd round	Coral UK Open

	v Thorburn	8-9	Quarter-final	Coral UK Open
	v Hallett	5-3	1st round	Mercantile Credit Classic
	v E. Hughes	5-1	2nd round	Mercantile Credit Classic
	v S. Davis	1-5	Quarter-final	Mercantile Credit Classic
1985	v David Taylor	5-1	1st round	Benson & Hedges Masters
	v Thorburn	0-5	Quarter-final	Benson & Hedges Masters
	v King	6-5	1st round	Dulux British Open
	v Martin	4-5	2nd round	Dulux British Open
	v E. Hughes	0-5	1st round	Benson & Hedges Irish Masters
	v E. Hughes	10-9	1st round	Embassy World Professional Championship
	v Fagan	13-9	2nd round	Embassy World Professional Championship
	v Parrott	13-12	Quarter-final	Embassy World Professional Championship
	v S. Davis	5-16	Semi-final	Embassy World Professional Championship
	v Everton	6-2	Quarter-final	BCE Welsh Professional Championship
	v Griffiths	3-9	Semi-final	BCE Welsh Professional Championship

JIM REMPE (USA)

Born –
Turned professional 1980
World ranking unranked

One of the all-time greats of the American pool circuit, Rempe has appeared in two World Cups as a member of the Rest of the World trio but has yet to compete on the authentic tournament circuit.

DEAN REYNOLDS (England)

Born 11.1.63
Turned professional 1981
World ranking 24

Only 19 when he reached the last 16 of the Embassy World Championship at his first attempt in 1982, Reynolds did not really justify his initial promise until he beat Silvino Francisco to reach the quarter-finals of the 1984 Rothmans Grand Prix. His record also includes two wins over Willie Thorne.

	v Sheehan	9-5	Qualifying	Embassy World Professional Championship
1982	v Sheehan	9-5	Qualifying	Embassy World Professional Championship
	v Edmonds	9-6	Qualifying	Embassy World Professional Championship
	v F. Davis	10-7	1st round	Embassy World Professional Championship
	v S. Francisco	8-13	2nd round	Embassy World Professional Championship
	v Morra	5-1	Qualifying	Jameson International
	v Thorne	5-3	1st round	Jameson International
	v S. Davis	0-5	2nd round	Jameson International
	v Fitzmaurice	5-0	2nd round	Professional Players Tournament
	v Wilson	5-1	3rd round	Professional Players Tournament
	v Charlton	2-5	Quarter-final	Professional Players Tournament
	v Fisher	9-6	1st round	Coral UK Championship
	v Higgins	8-9	2nd round	Coral UK Championship

Dean Reynolds (Adrian Murrell/All-Sport)

John Spencer (David Muscroft)

1983	v Reardon	1-5	1st round	Benson & Hedges Masters
	v Edmonds	10-6	Qualifying	Embassy World Professional Championship
	v Higgins	4-10	1st round	Embassy World Professional Championship
	v Williams	5-3	Qualifying	Jameson International
	v Dennis Taylor	3-5	1st round	Jameson International
	v Greaves	5-1	1st round	Professional Players Tournament
	v Meo	0-5	2nd round	Professional Players Tournament
	v Medati	3-9	1st round	Coral UK Championship
1984	v Griffiths	2-5	Qualifying	Lada Classic
	v Morra	7-10	Qualifying	Embassy World Professional Championship
	v Bales	5-4	Qualifying	Jameson International
	v Knowles	1-5	1st round	Jameson International
	v Fowler	5-2	1st round	Rothmans Grand Prix
	v P. Francisco	5-4	2nd round	Rothmans Grand Prix
	v S. Francisco	5-1	3rd round	Rothmans Grand Prix
	v S. Davis	0-5	Quarter-final	Rothmans Grand Prix
	v Chappel	6-9	Qualifying	Coral UK Open
	v King	2-5	Qualifying	Mercantile Credit Classic
1985	v Fitzmaurice	9-2	1st round	Tolly Cobbold English Professional Championship
	v Thorne	9-6	2nd round	Tolly Cobbold English Professional Championship
	v Meo	4-9	Quarter-final	Tolly Cobbold English Professional Championship
	v Giannaros	6-3	1st round	Dulux British Open
	v Thorburn	3-5	2nd round	Dulux British Open
	v Gauvreau	10-1	Qualifying	Embassy World Professional Championship
	v Higgins	4-10	1st round	Embassy World Professional Championship

GINO RIGITANO (Canada)

Born 14.8.57
Turned professional 1983
World ranking 77

1984	v Gibson	7-10	Qualifying	Embassy World Professional Championship
	v Foldvari	2-5	Qualifying	Jameson International
	v Edmonds	5-3	Qualifying	Rothmans Grand Prix
	v Thorburn	4-5	1st round	Rothmans Grand Prix
	v Newbury	6-9	Qualifying	Coral UK Open
	v Fowler	0-5	Qualifying	Mercantile Credit Classic
1985	v Thorburn	3-6	1st round	Dulux British Open
	v Sheehan	10-9	Qualifying	Embassy World Professional Championship
	v B. Harris	10-4	Qualifying	Embassy World Professional Championship
	v Kelly	10-6	Qualifying	Embassy World Professional Championship
	v Fisher	10-2	Qualifying	Embassy World Professional Championship
	v N. Foulds	8-10	Qualifying	Embassy World Professional Championship

COLIN ROSCOE (Wales)

Born 30.6.45
Turned professional 1981
World ranking 45

Welsh amateur champion in 1981, Roscoe reached the last 16 of the 1984 Lada Classic with a win over Bill Werbeniuk, his best performance on the circuit.

1981	v Macleod	9-7	Qualifying	Coral UK Championship
	v Williams	4-9	Qualifying	Coral UK Championship
	v Andrewartha	5-2	Qualifying	Jameson International
	v Sheehan	5-1	Qualifying	Jameson International
	v Meadowcroft	4-5	Qualifying	Jameson International
1982	v Griffiths	2-6	1st round	Welsh Professional Championship
	v Mikkelsen	9-6	Qualifying	Embassy World Professional Championship
	v Thorne	1-9	Qualifying	Embassy World Professional Championship
	v Dunning	5-2	Qualifying	Jameson International
	v French	5-2	Qualifying	Jameson International
	v S. Davis	0-5	1st round	Jameson International
	v Griffiths	1-5	1st round	Professional Players Tournament
	v Jack Rea	9-6	Qualifying	Coral UK Championship
	v Wildman	4-9	Qualifying	Coral UK Championship
1983	v Wilson	4-6	Quarter-final	Woodpecker Welsh Professional Championship
	v Sinclair	2-10	Qualifying	Embassy World Professional Championship
	v Hallett	2-5	Qualifying	Jameson International
	v Meadowcroft	4-5	1st round	Professional Players Tournament
	v N. Foulds	2-9	Qualifying	Coral UK Championship
1984	v Ganim	5-3	Qualifying	Lada Classic
	v Miles	5-2	Qualifying	Lada Classic
	v Werbeniuk	5-4	1st round	Lada Classic
	v Griffiths	2-5	2nd round	Lada Classic
	v Wilson	2-6	1st round	Strongbow Welsh Professional Championship
	v Demarco	10-7	Qualifying	Embassy World Professional Championship
	v Browne	4-10	Qualifying	Embassy World Professional Championship
	v Mikkelsen	5-1	Qualifying	Jameson International
	v French	5-0	Qualifying	Rothmans Grand Prix
	v Reardon	1-5	1st round	Rothmans Grand Prix
	v J. McLaughlin	8-9	Qualifying	Coral UK Open
	v Medati	4-5	Qualifying	Mercantile Credit Classic
1985	v Giannaros	1-6	Qualifying	Dulux British Open
	v G. Foulds	7-10	Qualifying	Embassy World Professional Championship
	v Wilson	3-6	Quarter-final	BCE Welsh Professional Championship

WAYNE SANDERSON (Canada)

Born –
Turned professional 1982
World ranking unranked

1984	v Morgan	10-8	Qualifying	Embassy World Professional Championship
	v Mifsud	5-10	Qualifying	Embassy World Professional Championship

GEORGE SCOTT (England)

Born 16.9.29
Turned professional 1981
World ranking 41

Having turned professional at the age of 51 after being Liverpool's best amateur for as long as anyone could remember, Scott has recorded wins over Bill Werbeniuk and Dennis Taylor. He was one of the formative influences on the early career of John Parrott.

1982	v B. Harris	5-4	Qualifying	Jameson International
	v Thorburn	1-5	1st round	Jameson International
	v Meo	5-9	Qualifying	Coral UK Championship
1983	v Houlihan	5-0	Qualifying	Jameson International
	v Gibson	5-3	Qualifying	Jameson International
	v Werbeniuk	5-3	1st round	Jameson International
	v Griffiths	0-5	2nd round	Jameson International
	v Dennis Taylor	5-4	1st round	Professional Players Tournament
	v S. Francisco	1-5	2nd round	Professional Players Tournament
	v Parrott	7-9	Qualifying	Coral UK Championship
1984	v Heywood	10-7	Qualifying	Embassy World Professional Championship
	v Wych	6-10	Qualifying	Embassy World Professional Championship
	v W. Jones	0-5	Qualifying	Jameson International
	v Chappel	1-5	Qualifying	Rothmans Grand Prix
	v O'Kane	9-7	Qualifying	Coral UK Open
	v Macleod	5-9	Qualifying	Coral UK Open
	v J. McLaughlin	5-4	Qualifying	Mercantile Credit Classic
	v Campbell	5-4	Qualifying	Mercantile Credit Classic
	v Thorburn	1-5	1st round	Mercantile Credit Classic
1985	v V. Harris	9-7	Qualifying	Tolly Cobbold English Professional Championship
	v Johnson	1-9	1st round	Tolly Cobbold English Professional Championship
	v Darrington	6-3	Qualifying	Dulux British Open
	v Dennis Taylor	2-6	1st round	Dulux British Open
	v Newbury	2-10	Qualifying	Embassy World Professional Championship

DESSIE SHEEHAN (Republic of Ireland)

Born 3.9.49
Turned professional 1981
World ranking 99

1981	v V. Harris	5-1	Qualifying	Jameson International
	v Roscoe	1-5	Qualifying	Jameson International
1982	v E. Hughes	1-6	1st round	Irish Professional Championship
	v V. Harris	3-5	Qualifying	Jameson International
	v Dennis Taylor	3-5	1st round	Benson & Hedges Irish Masters
	v Reynolds	5-9	Qualifying	Embassy World Professional Championship
	v Fitzmaurice	1-5	1st round	Professional Players Tournament
1983	v Donnelly	6-10	Qualifying	Embassy World Professional Championship
	v Murphy	2-5	Qualifying	Jameson International
	v Houlihan	5-2	Qualifying	Professional Players Tournament
	v Williams	1-5	1st round	Professional Players Tournament
1984	v B. Harris	3-10	Qualifying	Embassy World Professional Championship
	v Bales	2-5	Qualifying	Jameson International
	v Mikkelsen	5-3	Qualifying	Rothmans Grand Prix
	v Hallett	1-5	1st round	Rothmans Grand Prix
	v P. Francisco	5-9	Qualifying	Coral UK Open
	v John Rea	5-2	Qualifying	Mercantile Credit Classic
	v E. McLaughlin	2-5	Qualifying	Mercantile Credit Classic
1985	v Murphy	3-6	Qualifying	Dulux British Open
	v J. McLaughlin	3-6	Qualifying	Irish Professional Championship
	v Rigitano	9-10	Qualifying	Embassy World Professional Championship

EDDIE SINCLAIR (Scotland)

Born 5.5.37
Turned professional 1979
World ranking 38

Seven times Scottish amateur champion and twice Scottish professional champion, Sinclair has been an ever-present member of Scotland's World Cup team.

1974 –75	v Miles	0-5	1st round	Norwich Union Open
1980	v Meadowcroft	1-9	Qualifying	Embassy World Professional Championship
	v Kennerley	9-1	Qualifying	Coral UK Championship
	v Miles	9-5	1st round	Coral UK Championship
	v Dennis Taylor	6-9	2nd round	Coral UK Championship
1981	v Donnelly	0-5	Quarter-final	Scottish Professional Championship
	v Morgan	9-8	Qualifying	Embassy World Professional Championship
	v Wilson	4-9	Qualifying	Embassy World Professional Championship
	v E. Hughes	2-5	Qualifying	Jameson International
	v Wildman	9-8	Qualifying	Coral UK Championship

	v Hood	9-0	Qualifying	Coral UK Championship
	v Martin	7-9	Qualifying	Coral UK Championship
1982	v Kelly	9-8	Qualifying	Embassy World Professional Championship
	v Donnelly	8-9	Qualifying	Embassy World Professional Championship
	v Phillips	6-3	Quarter-final	Scottish Professional Championship
	v Gibson	6-2	Semi-final	Scottish Professional Championship
	v Black	**11-7**	**Final**	**Scottish Professional Championship**
	v Higgins	1-5	1st round	Langs Supreme Scottish Masters
	v Anderson	5-2	Qualifying	Jameson International
	v Meo	5-3	Qualifying	Jameson International
	v Knowles	2-5	1st round	Jameson International
	v F. Davis	5-2	1st round	Professional Players Tournament
	v Meadowcroft	5-3	2nd round	Professional Players Tournament
	v Griffiths	3-5	3rd round	Professional Players Tournament
	v Murphy	9-5	Qualifying	Coral UK Championship
	v Spencer	8-9	1st round	Coral UK Championship
1983	v Roscoe	10-2	Qualifying	Embassy World Professional Championship
	v E. Hughes	8-10	Qualifying	Embassy World Professional Championship
	v Donnelly	6-5	Semi-final	Scottish Professional Championship
	v Macleod	9-11	Final	Scottish Professional Championship
	v Andrewartha	5-4	Qualifying	Jameson International
	v Thorburn	0-5	1st round	Jameson International
	v E. Hughes	4-5	1st round	Professional Players Tournament
	v T. Jones	3-9	Qualifying	Coral UK Championship
1984	v S. Davis	2-5	Qualifying	Lada Classic
	v Browne	10-1	Qualifying	Embassy World Professional Championship
	v Stevens	1-10	1st round	Embassy World Professional Championship
	v Duggan	5-0	Qualifying	Jameson International
	v Mans	5-2	Qualifying	Jameson International
	v Higgins	1-5	1st round	Jameson International
	v T. Jones	4-5	Qualifying	Rothmans Grand Prix
	v P. Francisco	9-8	Qualifying	Coral UK Open
	v S. Francisco	4-9	Qualifying	Coral UK Open
1985	v Newbury	3-6	1st round	Dulux British Open
	v T. Jones	2-10	Qualifying	Embassy World Professional Championship

JOHN SPENCER (England)

Born 18.9.35
Turned professional 1967
World ranking 20

English amateur champion in 1966, Spencer won the first of his three world professional titles three years later and with Ray Reardon, and to a slightly lesser extent, Alex Higgins, dominated the early 1970s. He won several first prizes in tournaments now defunct including the 1979 Holsten Lager International at Slough, in which his 147 was the first maximum in a televised event. Unfortunately, this was before the days when every frame was recorded and the television crew were on a meal break when history was made.

He slipped steadily down the rankings after his third world title in 1977 and in the summer of 1984 even the continuance of his career was threatened by persistent double vision which is now controlled only by a daily intake of steroids.

1969	v Pulman	30-19 Quarter-final	World Professional Championship
	v Williams	55-18 Semi-final	World Professional Championship
	v G. Owen	46-27 Final	World Professional Championship
1970	v Jack Rea	31-15 Quarter-final	World Professional Championship (Apr)
	v Reardon	33-37 Semi-final	World Professional Championship (Apr)
	v Reardon	34-15 Semi-final	World Professional Championship (Nov)
	v Simpson	**42-31 Final**	**World Professional Championship (Nov)**
1972	v F. Davis	31-21 Quarter-final	World Professional Championship
	v Charlton	37-32 Semi-final	World Professional Championship
	v Higgins	32-37 Final	World Professional Championship
1973	v David Taylor	16-5 2nd round	World Professional Championship
	v Williams	16-7 Quarter-final	World Professional Championship
	v Reardon	22-23 Semi-final	World Professional Championship
	v Higgins	8-2 Semi-final	Norwich Union Open
	v Pulman	**8-7 Final**	**Norwich Union Open**
1974	v Mans	13-15 2nd round	World Professional Championship
1974	v Edmonds	5-0 1st round	Norwich Union Open
-75	v Miles	5-2 Quarter-final	Norwich Union Open
	v Thorburn	9-7 Semi-final	Norwich Union Open
	v Reardon	**10-9 Final**	**Norwich Union Open**
1975	v Pulman	5-3 Quarter-final	Benson & Hedges Masters
	v Charlton	5-2 Semi-final	Benson & Hedges Masters
	v Reardon	**9-8 Final**	**Benson & Hedges Masters**
	v Pulman	15-10 2nd round	World Professional Championship
	v Reardon	17-19 Quarter-final	World Professional Championship
1976	v Miles	4-5 Semi-final	Benson & Hedges Masters
	v David Taylor	15-5 1st round	Embassy World Professional Championship
	v Higgins	14-15 Quarter-final	Embassy World Professional Championship
1977	v Virgo	13-9 1st round	Embassy World Professional Championship
	v Reardon	13-6 Quarter-final	Embassy World Professional Championship
	v Pulman	18-16 Semi-final	Embassy World Professional Championship
	v Thorburn	**25-21 Final**	**Embassy World Professional Championship**
	v Mountjoy	3-5 2nd round	Super Crystalate UK Championship
1978	v Thorburn	3-5 Semi-final	Benson & Hedges Masters
	v Mountjoy	**5-3 Final**	**Benson & Hedges Irish Masters**
	v Mans	8-13 1st round	Embassy World Professional Championship
	v Andrewartha	8-9 1st round	Coral UK Championship
1979	v Williams	6-2 Semi-final	Holsten Lager International
	v Miles	**11-7 Final**	**Holsten Lager International**
	v Mountjoy	0-5 Quarter-final	Benson & Hedges Masters
	v Werbeniuk	11-13 1st round	Embassy World Professional Championship
	v Werbeniuk	8-9 3rd round	Coral UK Championship
1980	v Charlton	5-2 Quarter-final	Benson & Hedges Masters

	v Griffiths	0-5	Semi-final	Benson & Hedges Masters
	v Stevens	8-13	2nd round	Embassy World Professional Championship
	v Wildman	7-9	1st round	Coral UK Championship
1981	v Dennis Taylor	5-2	1st round	Benson & Hedges Masters
	v Reardon	5-1	Quarter-final	Benson & Hedges Masters
	v Griffiths	5-6	Semi-final	Benson & Hedges Masters
	v Houlihan	9-1	1st round	John Courage English Professional
	v S. Davis	7-9	2nd round	John Courage English Professional
	v Edmonds	10-9	1st round	Embassy World Professional Championship
	v Reardon	11-13	2nd round	Embassy World Professional Championship
	v Edmonds	5-3	2nd round	Jameson International
	v Griffiths	2-5	3rd round	Jameson International
	v Johnson	5-9	2nd round	Coral UK Championship
1982	v S. Davis	2-5	1st round	Lada Classic
	v Mountjoy	4-5	1st round	Benson & Hedges Masters
	v Meo	3-5	1st round	Benson & Hedges Irish Masters
	v Dunning	10-4	1st round	Embassy World Professional Championship
	v Thorne	5-13	2nd round	Embassy World Professional Championship
	v Edmonds	5-2	1st round	Jameson International
	v Virgo	4-5	2nd round	Jameson International
	v G. Foulds	5-1	1st round	Professional Players Tournament
	v Martin	5-3	2nd round	Professional Players Tournament
	v Virgo	1-5	3rd round	Professional Players Tournament
	v Sinclair	9-8	1st round	Coral UK Championship
	v Knowles	9-6	2nd round	Coral UK Championship
	v Higgins	5-9	Quarter-final	Coral UK Championship
1983	v Reardon	5-3	1st round	Lada Classic
	v David Taylor	5-2	Quarter-final	Lada Classic
	v S. Davis	4-5	Semi-final	Lada Classic
	v Hallett	10-7	1st round	Embassy World Professional Championship
	v Charlton	11-13	2nd round	Embassy World Professional Championship
	v Higgins	2-3	1st round	Winfield Masters
	v Morgan	5-1	1st round	Jameson International
	v Knowles	5-4	2nd round	Jameson International
	Griffiths	4-5	Quarter-final	Jameson International
	v Black	5-2	1st round	Professional Players Tournament
	v Thorne	1-5	2nd round	Professional Players Tournament
	v Dunning	9-7	1st round	Coral UK Championship
	v Meo	5-9	2nd round	Coral UK Championship
1984	v Johnson	5-4	Qualifying	Lada Classic
	v S. Davis	1-5	1st round	Lada Classic
	v Thorburn	5-4	1st round	Benson & Hedges Masters
	v Griffiths	4-5	Quarter-final	Benson & Hedges Masters
	v Miles	10-3	1st round	Embassy World Professional Championship
	v S. Davis	5-13	2nd round	Embassy World Professional Championship
	v S. Francisco	2-5	1st round	Jameson International
	v P. Francisco	2-5	1st round	Rothmans Grand Prix
	v Johnson	6-9	1st round	Coral UK Open
	v King	2-5	1st round	Mercantile Credit Classic
1985	v Charlton	5-3	1st round	Benson & Hedges Masters

v White	2-5	Quarter-final	Benson & Hedges Masters
v Medati	4-9	1st round	Tolly Cobbold English Professional Championship
v Jonik	6-0	1st round	Dulux British Open
v Miles	3-5	2nd round	Dulux British Open
v Parrott	3-10	1st round	Embassy World Professional Championship

KIRK STEVENS (Canada)

Born 17.8.58
Turned professional 1978
World ranking 5

Despite reaching his first-ever major tournament final in the Dulux British Open, which he lost to Silvino Francisco, Stevens fell from fourth to fifth in the world rankings after an inconsistent 1984–85 season. In 1983–84, he beat Steve Davis in the quarter-finals of the Benson and Hedges Masters and made a 147 maximum in the semi-finals in losing to Jimmy White. He also lost narrowly 16-14 to White in the 1984 world semi-final, his second appearance at that stage of the event.

His Dulux semi-final victory over Steve Davis was the highlight of a season which overall saw him struggling to cope with the often intolerable non-playing pressures posed by a career on the circuit.

1979	v Amdor	9-1	Prelim	Embassy World Professional Championship
	v Pulman	9-0	Qualifying	Embassy World Professional Championship
	v F. Davis	8-13	1st round	Embassy World Professional Championship
1980	v Hallett	9-3	Qualifying	Embassy World Professional Championship
	v Miles	10-3	1st round	Embassy World Professional Championship
	v Spencer	13-8	2nd round	Embassy World Professional Championship
	v Charlton	13-7	Quarter-final	Embassy World Professional Championship
	v Higgins	13-16	Semi-final	Embassy World Professional Championship
1981	v F. Davis	4-5	1st round	Benson & Hedges Masters
	v David Taylor	3-5	Semi-final	Yamaha International Masters
	v Dunning	10-4	1st round	Embassy World Professional Championship
	v Dennis Taylor	11-13	2nd round	Embassy World Professional Championship
	v Thorburn	1-5	Quarter-final	Langs Supreme Scottish Masters
	v Meadowcroft	5-1	2nd round	Jameson International
	v David Taylor	0-5	3rd round	Jameson International
	v Griffiths	0-5	1st round	Northern Ireland Classic
	v Hallett	9-4	2nd round	Coral UK Championship
	v Werbeniuk	7-9	3rd round	Coral UK Championship
1982	v Fitzmaurice	10-4	1st round	Embassy World Professional Championship
	v Fagan	13-7	2nd round	Embassy World Professional Championship
	v White	9-13	Quarter-final	Embassy World Professional Championship
	v Watterson	5-3	1st round	Jameson International
	v Mans	5-2	2nd round	Jameson International
	v Griffiths	5-3	Quarter-final	Jameson International
	v Knowles	3-9	Semi-final	Jameson International
	v E. Hughes	5-2	1st round	Professional Players Tournament

Kirk Stevens (David Muscroft)

	v Johnson	1-5	2nd round	Professional Players Tournament
1983	v Knowles	5-0	1st round	Lada Classic
	v Thorburn	5-3	Quarter-final	Lada Classic
	v Werbeniuk	2-5	Semi-final	Lada Classic
	v Griffiths	3-5	1st round	Benson & Hedges Masters
	v Fisher	10-2	1st round	Embassy World Professional Championship
	v Mans	13-3	2nd round	Embassy World Professional Championship
	v Thorburn	12-13	Quarter-final	Embassy World Professional Championship
	v Thorburn	2-5	Semi-final	Winfield Masters
	v Edmonds	5-1	1st round	Professional Players Tournament
	v Murphy	5-1	2nd round	Professional Players Tournament
	v Wildman	5-0	3rd round	Professional Players Tournament
	v Meo	3-5	Quarter-final	Professional Players Tournament
1984	v E. McLaughlin	5-4	Qualifying	Lada Classic
	v Macleod	5-1	1st round	Lada Classic
	v Meo	2-5	Quarter-final	Lada Classic
	v David Taylor	5-1	1st round	Benson & Hedges Masters
	v S. Davis	5-3	Quarter-final	Benson & Hedges Masters
	v White	4-6	Semi-final	Benson & Hedges Masters
	v Charlton	5-3	1st round	Tolly Cobbold Classic
	v S. Davis	4-5	Semi-final	Tolly Cobbold Classic
	v Sinclair	10-1	1st round	Embassy World Professional Championship
	v David Taylor	13-10	2nd round	Embassy World Professional Championship
	v Reardon	13-2	Quarter-final	Embassy World Professional Championship
	v White	14-16	Semi-final	Embassy World Professional Championship
	v Meo	1-5	Quarter-final	Winfield Australian Masters
	v Higgins	2-5	1st round	Langs Supreme Scottish Masters
	v Gauvreau	1-5	1st round	Jameson International
	v Chappel	5-3	1st round	Rothmans Grand Prix
	v Williams	5-3	2nd round	Rothmans Grand Prix
	v Hallett	5-3	3rd round	Rothmans Grand Prix
	v Dennis Taylor	2-5	Quarter-final	Rothmans Grand Prix
	v Chappel	9-7	1st round	Coral UK Open
	v Johnson	9-2	2nd round	Coral UK Open
	v Knowles	9-7	Quarter-final	Coral UK Open
	v S. Davis	2-9	Semi-final	Coral UK Open
	v Medati	5-4	1st round	Mercantile Credit Classic
	v Thorne	1-5	2nd round	Mercantile Credit Classic
1985	v Meo	2-5	1st round	Benson & Hedges Masters
	v Gauvreau	6-3	1st round	Dulux British Open
	v Wildman	5-2	2nd round	Dulux British Open
	v Miles	5-2	3rd round	Dulux British Open
	v Dennis Taylor	5-2	Quarter-final	Dulux British Open
	v S. Davis	9-7	Semi-final	Dulux British Open
	v S. Francisco	9-12	Final	Dulux British Open
	v Higgins	3-5	Quarter-final	Benson & Hedges Irish Masters
	v Edmonds	10-8	1st round	Embassy World Professional Championship
	v Parrott	6-13	2nd round	Embassy World Professional Championship

DAVID TAYLOR (England)

Born 29.7.43
Turned professional 1968
World ranking 14

English and world amateur champion in 1968, Taylor took ten years to make a significant impact on the professional game by reaching the final of the 1978 Coral UK Championship. He has appeared in two other major finals, the 1981 Yamaha International Masters and the 1982 Jameson International, in which he beat Steve Davis in the quarter-finals, and was a world semi-finalist in 1980.

In the last few years he has done just enough to maintain his place in the top 16, though this itself is creditable since he spent much of the 1984–85 season struggling to adjust to playing in spectacles for the first time.

1970 v Bennett	11-8	1st round	World Professional Championship
v Pulman	22-39	Quarter-final	World Professional Championship
1972 v Charlton	25-31	Quarter-final	World Professional Championship
1973 v Dunning	9-4	1st round	World Professional Championship
v Spencer	5-16	2nd round	World Professional Championship
1974 v Dunning	6-8	1st round	World Professional Championship
1975 v King	15-8	1st round	World Professional Championship
v Higgins	2-15	2nd round	World Professional Championship
1976 v Greaves	8-1	Qualifying	Embassy World Professional Championship
v Jack Rea	8-7	Qualifying	Embassy World Professional Championship
v Spencer	5-15	1st round	Embassy World Professional Championship
1977 v Greaves	11-0	Qualifying	Embassy World Professional Championship
v Charlton	5-13	1st round	Embassy World Professional Championship
v Greaves	5-4	1st round	Super Crystalate UK Championship
v Higgins	4-5	2nd round	Super Crystalate UK Championship
1978 v Morgan	9-7	Qualifying	Embassy World Professional Championship
v Miles	10-13	1st round	Embassy World Professional Championship
v Parkin	9-2	Qualifying	Coral UK Championship
v Fagan	9-7	1st round	Coral UK Championship
v Virgo	9-2	Quarter-final	Coral UK Championship
v Higgins	9-5	Semi-final	Coral UK Championship
v Mountjoy	9-15	Final	Coral UK Championship
1979 v Fagan	5-4	1st round	Benson & Hedges Masters
v Reardon	2-5	Quarter-final	Benson & Hedges Masters
v Dunning	9-8	Qualifying	Embassy World Professional Championship
v Higgins	5-13	1st round	Embassy World Professional Championship
v Meo	7-9	2nd round	Coral UK Championship
1980 v Edmonds	10-3	1st round	Embassy World Professional Championship
v F. Davis	13-5	2nd round	Embassy World Professional Championship
v Reardon	13-11	Quarter-final	Embassy World Professional Championship
v Thorburn	7-16	Semi-final	Embassy World Professional Championship
v Williams	7-9	2nd round	Coral UK Championship
1981 v Stevens	5-3	Semi-final	Yamaha International Masters

	v S. Davis	6-9	Final	Yamaha International Masters
	v Dunning	8-9	1st round	John Courage English Professional
	v Wilson	10-6	1st round	Embassy World Professional Championship
	v F. Davis	13-3	2nd round	Embassy World Professional Championship
	v Thorburn	6-13	Quarter-final	Embassy World Professional Championship
	v Stevens	5-0	3rd round	Jameson International
	v S. Davis	1-5	Quarter-final	Jameson International
	v Higgins	5-9	3rd round	Coral UK Championship
1982	v Reardon	1-5	1st round	Lada Classic
	v Meo	2-5	1st round	Benson & Hedges Masters
	v Fagan	9-10	1st round	Embassy World Professional Championship
	v Fisher	5-1	1st round	Jameson International
	v Werbeniuk	5-2	2nd round	Jameson International
	v S. Davis	5-3	Quarter-final	Jameson International
	v Virgo	9-5	Semi-final	Jameson International
	v Knowles	6-9	Final	Jameson International
	v Anderson	5-1	1st round	Professional Players Tournament
	v Dennis Taylor	1-5	2nd round	Professional Players Tournament
	v Dodd	9-7	1st round	Coral UK Championship
	v Meo	6-9	2nd round	Coral UK Championship
1983	v White	5-3	1st round	Lada Classic
	v Spencer	2-5	Quarter-final	Lada Classic
	v White	2-5	1st round	Benson & Hedges Masters
	v Charlton	4-5	1st round	Benson & Hedges Irish Masters
	v Meadowcroft	10-2	1st round	Embassy World Professional Championship
	v Werbeniuk	10-13	2nd round	Embassy World Professional Championship
	v Donnelly	3-5	1st round	Jameson International
	v Morgan	5-3	1st round	Professional Players Tournament
	v Wildman	3-5	2nd round	Professional Players Tournament
	v N. Foulds	9-4	1st round	Coral UK Championship
	v Johnson	3-9	2nd round	Coral UK Championship
1984	v Macleod	4-5	Qualifying	Lada Classic
	v Stevens	1-5	1st round	Benson & Hedges Masters
	v Gauvreau	10-5	1st round	Embassy World Professional Championship
	v Stevens	10-13	2nd round	Embassy World Professional Championship
	v Charlton	4-5	Quarter-final	Winfield Australian Masters
	v W. Jones	5-4	1st round	Jameson International
	v S. Davis	1-5	2nd round	Jameson International
	v O'Kane	5-1	1st round	Rothmans Grand Prix
	v John Rea	5-1	2nd round	Rothmans Grand Prix
	v S. Davis	1-5	3rd round	Rothmans Grand Prix
	v Macleod	9-6	1st round	Coral UK Open
	v Reardon	4-9	2nd round	Coral UK Open
	v Longworth	4-5	1st round	Mercantile Credit Classic
1985	v Reardon	1-5	1st round	Benson & Hedges Masters
	v Cripsey	9-5	1st round	Tolly Cobbold English Professional Championship
	v Parrott	9-6	2nd round	Tolly Cobbold English Professional Championship
	v Knowles	2-9	Quarter-final	Tolly Cobbold English Professional Championship

v Bradley	3-6	1st round	Dulux British Open
v O'Kane	10-4	1st round	Embassy World Professional Championship
v S. Davis	4-13	2nd round	Embassy World Professional Championship

DENNIS TAYLOR (Northern Ireland)

Born 19.1.49
Turned professional 1971
World ranking 4

Although Taylor has always been regarded as a good player, it was not until last season – his 13th as a professional – that he proved himself a winner. It took a traumatic bereavement to give this transformation impetus. The sudden death of his mother in Coalisland, Co Tyrone, caused Taylor to withdraw from the quarter-finals of the Jameson International and it was only through family pressure that he competed in the next event on the circuit, the Rothmans Grand Prix. Carried by an emotional wave, he won that event by beating Cliff Thorburn 10-2 in the final and succeeded in uniting his family in joy and alleviating their grief.

As often happens after a first major victory, Taylor's form deteriorated for a while but, just prior to the Embassy World Championship, he regained the Irish Professional Championship and then proceeded steadily towards the world final without a close match. Once there, he lost the first eight frames to Steve Davis but pulled up to trail only 7-9 overnight and on the second day levelled the match at 15-15 before going two down with three to play at 15-17. He forced the match to a deciding frame, providing an unforgettable climax to one of the greatest matches ever seen. A record 18.5 million viewers watched on BBC2 as, well past midnight, Taylor needed the last four colours to win and Davis only one. Eventually, Taylor potted them all to take the world title at his twelfth attempt.

1973	v Thorburn	8-9	1st round	World Professional Championship
1974	v Higgins	1-5	1st round	Norwich Union Open
1975	v Mans	15-12	1st round	World Professional Championship
	v F. Davis	15-14	2nd round	World Professional Championship
	v G. Owen	19-9	Quarter-final	World Professional Championship
	v Charlton	12-19	Semi-final	World Professional Championship
1976	v G. Owen	15-9	1st round	Embassy World Professional Championship
	v Reardon	2-15	Quarter-final	Embassy World Professional Championship
1977	v Karnehm	11-0	Qualifying	Embassy World Professional Championship
	v Mans	13-11	1st round	Embassy World Professional Championship
	v Mountjoy	13-11	Quarter-final	Embassy World Professional Championship
	v Thorburn	16-18	Semi-final	Embassy World Professional Championship
1978	v F. Davis	9-13	1st round	Embassy World Professional Championship
	v Mountjoy	4-9	1st round	Coral UK Championship
1979	v S. Davis	13-11	1st round	Embassy World Professional Championship
	v Reardon	13-8	Quarter-final	Embassy World Professional Championship
	v Virgo	19-12	Semi-final	Embassy World Professional Championship

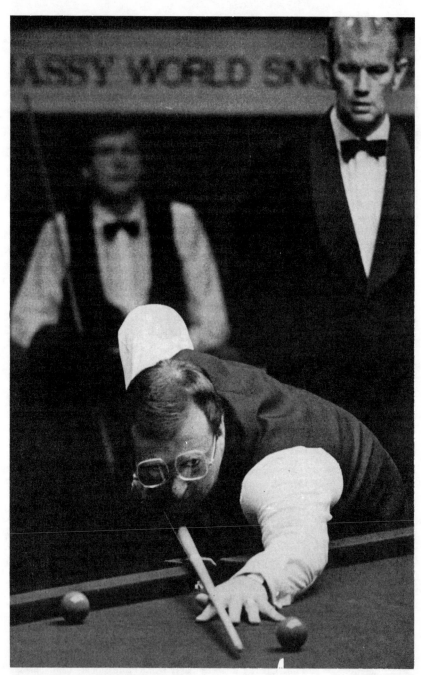

Dennis Taylor (Eric Whitehead/Scope)

	v Griffiths	16-24 Final	Embassy World Professional Championship
	v Thorne	9-8 3rd round	Coral UK Championship
	v Fagan	9-6 Quarter-final	Coral UK Championship
	v Virgo	4-9 Semi-final	Coral UK Championship
1980	v Reardon	3-5 Quarter-final	Benson & Hedges Masters
	v Wych	10-13 2nd round	Embassy World Professional Championship
	v Sinclair	9-6 2nd round	Coral UK Championship
	v Griffiths	2-9 Quarter-final	Coral UK Championship
1981	v Spencer	2-5 1st round	Benson & Hedges Masters
	v S. Davis	2-5 Semi-final	Yamaha International Masters
	v Stevens	13-11 2nd round	Embassy World Professional Championship
	v Mountjoy	8-13 Quarter-final	Embassy World Professional Championship
	v Williams	5-1 3rd round	Jameson International
	v Virgo	5-2 Quarter-final	Jameson International
	v Martin	9-1 Semi-final	Jameson International
	v S. Davis	0-9 Final	Jameson International
	v Mountjoy	4-5 1st round	Northern Ireland Classic
	v White	5-9 3rd round	Coral UK Championship
1982	v Higgins	1-5 1st round	Lada Classic
	v Reardon	3-5 1st round	Benson & Hedges Masters
	v Knowles	5-2 Semi-final	Tolly Cobbold Classic
	v S. Davis	3-8 Final	Tolly Cobbold Classic
	v Murphy	6-0 Semi-final	Irish Professional Championship
	v Higgins	**16-13 Final**	**Irish Professional Championship**
	v Sheehan	5-3 1st round	Benson & Hedges Irish Masters
	v Reardon	4-5 Quarter-final	Benson & Hedges Irish Masters
	v S. Francisco	7-10 1st round	Embassy World Professional Championship
	v White	5-4 1st round	Langs Supreme Scottish Masters
	v S. Davis	1-6 Semi-final	Langs Supreme Scottish Masters
	v Wildman	5-2 1st round	Jameson International
	v Thorburn	5-2 2nd round	Jameson International
	v Virgo	3-5 Quarter-final	Jameson International
	v Edmonds	5-4 1st round	Professional Players Tournament
	v David Taylor	5-1 2nd round	Professional Players Tournament
	v White	3-5 3rd round	Professional Players Tournament
	v Meadowcroft	9-7 1st round	Coral UK Championship
	v Griffiths	7-9 2nd round	Coral UK Championship
1983	v S. Davis	2-5 1st round	Lada Classic
	v S. Davis	1-5 Semi-final	Tolly Cobbold Classic
	v Kelly	6-0 Quarter-final	Irish Professional Championship
	v Fagan	6-1 Semi-final	Irish Professional Championship
	v Higgins	11-16 Final	Irish Professional Championship
	v White	4-5 1st round	Benson & Hedges Irish Masters
	v S. Francisco	10-9 1st round	Embassy World Professional Championship
	v S. Davis	11-13 2nd round	Embassy World Professional Championship
	v Reynolds	5-3 1st round	Jameson International
	v Thorburn	3-5 2nd round	Jameson International
	v Scott	4-5 1st round	Professional Players Tournament
	v Murphy	9-6 1st round	Coral UK Championship
	v White	4-9 2nd round	Coral UK Championship
1984	v Hallett	4-5 Qualifying	Lada Classic

	v Knowles	2-5	1st round	Benson & Hedges Masters
	v E. Hughes	5-1	1st round	Benson & Hedges Irish Masters
	v Thorburn	5-2	Quarter-final	Benson & Hedges Irish Masters
	v Griffiths	4-5	Semi-final	Benson & Hedges Irish Masters
	v Johnson	10-1	1st round	Embassy World Professional Championship
	v Parrott	13-11	2nd round	Embassy World Professional Championship
	v Mountjoy	13-8	Quarter-final	Embassy World Professional Championship
	v S. Davis	9-16	Semi-final	Embassy World Professional Championship
	v Fowler	5-0	1st round	Jameson International
	v Watchorn	5-1	1st round	Rothmans Grand Prix
	v Virgo	5-3	2nd round	Rothmans Grand Prix
	v Reardon	5-3	3rd round	Rothmans Grand Prix
	v Stevens	5-2	Quarter-final	Rothmans Grand Prix
	v N. Foulds	9-3	Semi-final	Rothmans Grand Prix
	v Thorburn	**10-2**	**Final**	**Rothmans Grand Prix**
	v King	9-5	1st round	Coral UK Open
	v Knowles	2-9	2nd round	Coral UK Open
	v Williams	3-5	1st round	Mercantile Credit Classic
1985	v Thorburn	3-5	1st round	Benson & Hedges Masters
	v Scott	6-2	1st round	Dulux British Open
	v Parrott	5-2	2nd round	Dulux British Open
	v Newbury	5-3	3rd round	Dulux British Open
	v Stevens	2-5	Quarter-final	Dulux British Open
	v Charlton	4-5	1st round	Benson & Hedges Irish Masters
	v Jack Rea	6-0	Quarter-final	Irish Professional Championship
	v E. Hughes	6-5	Semi-final	Irish Professional Championship
	v Higgins	**10-5**	**Final**	**Irish Professional Championship**
	v S. Francisco	10-2	1st round	Embassy World Professional Championship
	v Charlton	13-6	2nd round	Embassy World Professional Championship
	v Thorburn	13-5	Quarter-final	Embassy World Professional Championship
	v Knowles	16-5	Semi-final	Embassy World Professional Championship
	v S. Davis	**18-17**	**Final**	**Embassy World Professional Championship**

CLIFF THORBURN (Canada)

Born 16.1.48
Turned professional 1973
World ranking 2

Winner of the Benson and Hedges Masters twice in the last three years, Thorburn was also in the 1984–85 season runner-up in the Rothmans Grand Prix, the Mercantile Credit Classic and, with Willie Thorne, the Hofmeister World Doubles. His consistency enabled him to rise from third to second in the world rankings.

The first Canadian to win the world title, in 1980, and still the only overseas player to do so, Thorburn also reached the 1977 and 1983 world finals, the latter by winning a series of the epic battles which reveal his great virtues of concentration, patience and mental stamina at their best. It was also during this event that he became the first player to make a 147 maximum in the world championship.

1973	v Dennis Taylor	9-8	1st round	World Professional Championship
	v Williams	15-16	2nd round	World Professional Championship
1974	v Morgan	4-8	1st round	World Professional Championship
1974	v F. Davis	5-4	1st round	Norwich Union Open
-75	v Pulman	5-3	Quarter-final	Norwich Union Open
	v Spencer	7-9	Semi-final	Norwich Union Open
1975	v Pulman	3-5	1st round	Benson & Hedges Masters
	v Morgan	15-6	1st round	World Professional Championship
	v Miles	15-2	2nd round	World Professional Championship
	v Charlton	12-19	Quarter-final	World Professional Championship
1976	v Higgins	14-15	1st round	Embassy World Professional Championship
1977	v Ross	11-0	Qualifying	Embassy World Professional Championship
	v Williams	13-6	1st round	Embassy World Professional Championship
	v Charlton	13-12	Quarter-final	Embassy World Professional Championship
	v Dennis Taylor	18-16	Semi-final	Embassy World Professional Championship
	v Spencer	21-25	Final	Embassy World Professional Championship
1978	v Mountjoy	4-2	Quarter-final	Benson & Hedges Masters
	v Spencer	5-3	Semi-final	Benson & Hedges Masters
	v Higgins	5-7	Final	Benson & Hedges Masters
	v Houlihan	13-8	1st round	Embassy World Professional Championship
	v Charlton	12-13	Quarter-final	Embassy World Professional Championship
1979	v Mans	4-5	Quarter-final	Benson & Hedges Masters
	v Virgo	10-13	1st round	Embassy World Professional Championship
1980	v Virgo	5-3	1st round	Benson & Hedges Masters
	v Griffiths	3-5	Quarter-final	Benson & Hedges Masters
	v Mountjoy	13-10	2nd round	Embassy World Professional Championship
	v Wych	13-6	Quarter-final	Embassy World Professional Championship
	v David Taylor	16-7	Semi-final	Embassy World Professional Championship
	v Higgins	**18-16**	**Final**	**Embassy World Professional Championship**
1981	v Mans	5-4	Quarter-final	Benson & Hedges Masters
	v Higgins	5-6	Semi-final	Benson & Hedges Masters
	v Miles	13-2	2nd round	Embassy World Professional Championship
	v David Taylor	13-6	Quarter-final	Embassy World Professional Championship
	v S. Davis	10-16	Semi-final	Embassy World Professional Championship
	v Stevens	5-1	Quarter-final	Langs Supreme Scottish Masters
	v Higgins	6-2	Semi-final	Langs Supreme Scottish Masters
	v White	4-9	Final	Langs Supreme Scottish Masters
	v Miles	0-5	3rd round	Jameson International
	v White	2-5	1st round	Northern Ireland Classic
	v Meo	6-9	3rd round	Coral UK Championship
1982	v Griffiths	1-5	1st round	Lada Classic
	v Meo	0-5	Quarter-final	Benson & Hedges Masters
	v Higgins	4-5	Quarter-final	Benson & Hedges Irish Masters
	v White	4-10	1st round	Embassy World Professional Championship
	v Scott	5-1	1st round	Jameson International
	v Dennis Taylor	2-5	2nd round	Jameson International
	v Medati	5-1	1st round	Professional Players Tournament
	v Everton	5-2	2nd round	Professional Players Tournament
	v Werbeniuk	2-5	3rd round	Professional Players Tournament
1983	v Wilson	5-3	1st round	Lada Classic
	v Stevens	3-5	Quarter-final	Lada Classic

v Johnson	5-2	1st round	Benson & Hedges Masters
v Griffiths	5-3	Quarter-final	Benson & Hedges Masters
v Charlton	6-5	Semi-final	Benson & Hedges Masters
v Reardon	**9-7**	**Final**	**Benson & Hedges Masters**
v Campbell	10-5	1st round	Embassy World Professional Championship
v Griffiths	13-12	2nd round	Embassy World Professional Championship
v Stevens	13-12	Quarter-final	Embassy World Professional Championship
v Knowles	16-15	Semi-final	Embassy World Professional Championship
v S. Davis	6-18	Final	Embassy World Professional Championship
v Stevens	5-2	Semi-final	Winfield Masters
v Werbeniuk	**7-3**	**Final**	**Winfield Masters**
v Griffiths	5-1	1st round	Langs Supreme Scottish Masters
v Knowles	2-6	Semi-final	Langs Supreme Scottish Masters
v Sinclair	5-0	1st round	Jameson International
v Dennis Taylor	5-3	2nd round	Jameson International
v Mountjoy	5-2	Quarter-final	Jameson International
v Griffiths	9-8	Semi-final	Jameson International
v S. Davis	4-9	Final	Jameson International
v V. Harris	5-1	1st round	Professional Players Tournament
v Meadowcroft	5-1	2nd round	Professional Players Tournament
v Wilson	5-3	3rd round	Professional Players Tournament
v Johnson	1-5	Quarter-final	Professional Players Tournament
1984 v S. Francisco	1-5	Qualifying	Lada Classic
v Spencer	4-5	1st round	Benson & Hedges Masters
v Dennis Taylor	2-5	Quarter-final	Benson & Hedges Irish Masters
v Meo	5-4	1st round	Tolly Cobbold Classic
v Knowles	3-5	Semi-final	Tolly Cobbold Classic
v Morra	10-3	1st round	Embassy World Professional Championship
v Thorne	13-11	2nd round	Embassy World Professional Championship
v White	8-13	Quarter-final	Embassy World Professional Championship
v S. Davis	2-5	1st round	Langs Supreme Scottish Masters
v Virgo	0-5	1st round	Jameson International
v Rigitano	5-4	1st round	Rothmans Grand Prix
v Campbell	5-1	2nd round	Rothmans Grand Prix
v Meo	5-4	3rd round	Rothmans Grand Prix
v Mountjoy	5-3	Quarter-final	Rothmans Grand Prix
v S. Davis	9-7	Semi-final	Rothmans Grand Prix
v Dennis Taylor	2-10	Final	Rothmans Grand Prix
v J. McLaughlin	9-4	1st round	Coral UK Open
v Wilson	9-3	2nd round	Coral UK Open
v Reardon	9-8	Quarter-final	Coral UK Open
v Higgins	7-9	Semi-final	Coral UK Open
v Scott	5-1	1st round	Mercantile Credit Classic
v Longworth	5-3	2nd round	Mercantile Credit Classic
v Griffiths	5-4	Quarter-final	Mercantile Credit Classic
v Johnson	9-2	Semi-final	Mercantile Credit Classic
v Thorne	8-13	Final	Mercantile Credit Classic
1985 v Dennis Taylor	5-3	1st round	Benson & Hedges Masters
v Reardon	5-0	Quarter-final	Benson & Hedges Masters
v White	6-4	Semi-final	Benson & Hedges Masters

v Mountjoy	9-6	Final	Benson & Hedges Masters
v Rigitano	6-3	1st round	Dulux British Open
v Reynolds	5-3	2nd round	Dulux British Open
v Higgins	2-5	3rd round	Dulux British Open
v White	3-5	Quarter-final	Benson & Hedges Irish Masters
v Hallett	10-8	1st round	Embassy World Professional Championship
v Werbeniuk	13-3	2nd round	Embassy World Professional Championship
v Dennis Taylor	5-13	Quarter-final	Embassy World Professional Championship

WILLIE THORNE (England)

Born 4.3.54
Turned professional 1975
World ranking 11

The 1984–85 season brought Thorne his first major title, the Mercantile Credit Classic, but also a series of defeats by players ranked beneath him, which partly explains why he rose only one place in the rankings. With Cliff Thorburn, he reached the final of the Hofmeister World Doubles Championship. They were beaten by Alex Higgins and Jimmy White.

1976 v Condo	8-3	Qualifying	Embassy World Professional Championship
v Meadowcroft	5-8	Qualifying	Embassy World Professional Championship
1977 v Bennett	11-4	Qualifying	Embassy World Professional Championship
v Miles	4-13	1st round	Embassy World Professional Championship
v Bennett	5-1	1st round	Super Crystalate UK Championship
v Williams	5-4	2nd round	Super Crystalate UK Championship
v Mountjoy	4-5	Quarter-final	Super Crystalate UK Championship
1978 v Williams	9-3	Qualifying	Embassy World Professional Championship
v Charlton	12-13	1st round	Embassy World Professional Championship
v Bennett	9-4	Qualifying	Coral UK Championship
v Reardon	9-6	1st round	Coral UK Championship
v Miles	1-9	Quarter-final	Coral UK Championship
1979 v Jim Charlton	9-3	Prelim	Embassy World Professional Championship
v Virgo	8-9	Qualifying	Embassy World Professional Championship
v Andrewartha	9-4	2nd round	Coral UK Championship
v Dennis Taylor	8-9	3rd round	Coral UK Championship
1980 v Jack Rea	9-1	Qualifying	Embassy World Professional Championship
v Werbeniuk	9-10	1st round	Embassy World Professional Championship
v Meadowcroft	9-1	1st round	Coral UK Championship
v Higgins	7-9	2nd round	Coral UK Championship
1981 v Wildman	9-2	1st round	John Courage English Professional
v Dunning	9-0	2nd round	John Courage English Professional
v Meo	8-9	Semi-final	John Courage English Professional
v Morra	9-5	Qualifying	Embassy World Professional Championship
v Greaves	9-3	Qualifying	Embassy World Professional Championship
v Mountjoy	6-10	1st round	Embassy World Professional Championship

Willie Thorne (David Muscroft)

	v Medati	9-6	Qualifying	Coral UK Championship
	v Edmonds	9-4	2nd round	Coral UK Championship
	v S. Davis	2-9	3rd round	Coral UK Championship
1982	v Roscoe	9-1	Qualifying	Embassy World Professional Championship
	v Griffiths	10-6	1st round	Embassy World Professional Championship
	v Spencer	13-5	2nd round	Embassy World Professional Championship
	v Higgins	10-13	Quarter-final	Embassy World Professional Championship
	v Reynolds	3-5	1st round	Jameson International
	v Demarco	5-3	1st round	Professional Players Tournament
	v Macleod	4-5	2nd round	Professional Players Tournament
	v Wilson	7-9	1st round	Coral UK Championship
	v Virgo	10-3	1st round	Embassy World Professional Championship
	v Higgins	8-13	2nd round	Embassy World Professional Championship
1983	v Murphy	5-2	Qualifying	Jameson International
	v Virgo	5-2	1st round	Jameson International
	v Reardon	5-0	2nd round	Jameson International
	v Charlton	0-5	Quarter-final	Jameson International
	v Everton	5-1	1st round	Professional Players Tournament
	v Spencer	5-1	2nd round	Professional Players Tournament
	v Reardon	5-3	3rd round	Professional Players Tournament
	v E. Hughes	5-1	Quarter-final	Professional Players Tournament
	v Knowles	7-9	Semi-final	Professional Players Tournament
	v Wildman	9-5	1st round	Coral UK Championship
	v S. Davis	3-9	2nd round	Coral UK Championship
1984	v S. Davis	2-5	1st round	Tolly Cobbold Classic
	v Mikkelsen	10-3	Qualifying	Embassy World Professional Championship
	v Virgo	10-9	1st round	Embassy World Professional Championship
	v Thorburn	11-13	2nd round	Embassy World Professional Championship
	v Virgo	3-5	Quarter-final	Winfield Australian Masters
	v O'Kane	5-3	1st round	Jameson International
	v Gauvreau	5-3	2nd round	Jameson International
	v E. Hughes	2-5	Quarter-final	Jameson International
	v Newbury	5-2	1st round	Rothmans Grand Prix
	v Macleod	5-3	2nd round	Rothmans Grand Prix
	v N. Foulds	1-5	3rd round	Rothmans Grand Prix
	v Parrott	9-7	1st round	Coral UK Open
	v Charlton	9-7	2nd round	Coral UK Open
	v Higgins	5-9	Quarter-final	Coral UK Open
	v Foldvari	5-2	1st round	Mercantile Credit Classic
	v Stevens	5-1	2nd round	Mercantile Credit Classic
	v Virgo	5-1	Quarter-final	Mercantile Credit Classic
	v S. Davis	9-8	Semi-final	Mercantile Credit Classic
	v Thorburn	**13-8**	**Final**	**Mercantile Credit Classic**
1985	v White	2-5	1st round	Benson & Hedges Masters
	v Dodd	9-1	1st round	Tolly Cobbold English Professional Championship
	v Reynolds	6-9	2nd round	Tolly Cobbold English Professional Championship
	v Oliver	6-3	1st round	Dulux British Open
	v Macleod	0-5	2nd round	Dulux British Open
	v Fagan	6-10	1st round	Embassy World Professional Championship

PAUL THORNLEY (Canada)

Born –
Turned professional 1979
World ranking unranked

1984	v Fisher	8-10 Qualifying	Embassy World Professional Championship
	v Cripsey	3-5 Qualifying	Jameson International
	v Williamson	2-5 Qualifying	Rothmans Grand Prix

JIMMY VAN RENSBERG (South Africa)

Born 24.10.31
Turned professional 1978
World ranking 80

Van Rensberg was 11 times South African amateur champion.

1979	v Meadowcroft	7-9 Prelim	Embassy World Professional Championship
1980	v Meo	1-9 Qualifying	Embassy World Professional Championship
1984	v V. Harris	10-7 Qualifying	Embassy World Professional Championship
	v Edmonds	10-9 Qualifying	Embassy World Professional Championship
	v S. Francisco	3-10 Qualifying	Embassy World Professional Championship
1985	v Longworth	10-7 Qualifying	Embassy World Professional Championship
	v Gauvreau	9-10 Qualifying	Embassy World Professional Championship

JOHN VIRGO (England)

Born 3.4.46
Turned professional 1976
World ranking 19

Coral UK champion in 1979, a few months after reaching the world semi-finals, Virgo has never quite sustained what this promised. Even with the keen sense of humour which is revealed in the impressions of his fellow players with which he entertains exhibition crowds, he might find it difficult to appreciate that in the two tournaments in which he did shine, the Champion of Champions in 1980 in which he was runner-up and the Professional Snooker League in 1984 which he won, were both financial failures of sufficient magnitude to leave him without any prize-money.

1977	v Andrewartha	11-1 Prelim	Embassy World Professional Championship
	v Dunning	11-6 Qualifying	Embassy World Professional Championship
	v Spencer	9-13 1st round	Embassy World Professional Championship
	v Dennis Taylor	5-2 2nd round	Super Crystalate UK Championship
	v Miles	5-2 Quarter-final	Super Crystalate UK Championship
	v Fagan	8-9 Semi-final	Super Crystalate UK Championship

David Taylor (David Muscroft)

John Virgo (Eric Whitehead/Scope)

1978	v F. Davis	8-9	Qualifying	Embassy World Professional Championship
	v Edmonds	9-4	Qualifying	Coral UK Championship
	v Pulman	9-3	1st round	Coral UK Championship
	v David Taylor	2-9	Quarter-final	Coral UK Championship
1979	v Parkin	9-0	Prelim	Embassy World Professional Championship
	v Thorne	9-8	Qualifying	Embassy World Professional Championship
	v Thorburn	13-10	1st round	Embassy World Professional Championship
	v Werbeniuk	13-9	Quarter-final	Embassy World Professional Championship
	v Dennis Taylor	12-19	Semi-final	Embassy World Professional Championship
	v Meo	9-6	3rd round	Coral UK Championship
	v S. Davis	9-7	Quarter-final	Coral UK Championship
	v Dennis Taylor	9-4	Semi-final	Coral UK Championship
	v Griffiths	**14-13**	**Final**	**Coral UK Championship**
1980	v Thorburn	3-5	1st round	Benson & Hedges Masters
	v Meadowcroft	10-2	1st round	Embassy World Professional Championship
	v Charlton	12-13	2nd round	Embassy World Professional Championship
	v Meo	1-9	2nd round	Coral UK Championship
1981	v Meo	6-9	1st round	John Courage English Professional
	v Meo	6-10	1st round	Embassy World Professional Championship
	v Knowles	5-2	2nd round	Jameson International
	v Reardon	5-3	3rd round	Jameson International
	v Dennis Taylor	2-5	Quarter-final	Jameson International
	v White	6-9	2nd round	Coral UK Championship
1982	v Hallett	10-4	1st round	Embassy World Professional Championship
	v Reardon	8-13	2nd round	Embassy World Professional Championship
	v V. Harris	5-2	Qualifying	Jameson International
	v Charlton	5-4	1st round	Jameson International
	v Spencer	5-4	2nd round	Jameson International
	v Dennis Taylor	5-4	Quarter-final	Jameson International
	v David Taylor	5-9	Semi-final	Jameson International
	v Black	5-2	1st round	Professional Players Tournament
	v Hallett	5-2	2nd round	Professional Players Tournament
	v Spencer	5-1	3rd round	Professional Players Tournament
	v Johnson	5-1	Quarter-final	Professional Players Tournament
	v White	4-10	Semi-final	Professional Players Tournament
	v Kelly	9-2	1st round	Coral UK Championship
	v Mountjoy	9-5	2nd round	Coral UK Championship
	v Meo	6-9	Quarter-final	Coral UK Championship
1983	v Charlton	2-5	1st round	Lada Classic
	v Mountjoy	1-5	1st round	Benson & Hedges Masters
	v Murphy	10-8	Qualifying	Embassy World Professional Championship
	v Thorne	3-10	1st round	Embassy World Professional Championship
	v Thorne	2-5	1st round	Jameson International
	v French	5-4	1st round	Professional Players Tournament
	v Wilson	2-5	2nd round	Professional Players Tournament
	v Johnson	6-9	1st round	Coral UK Championship
1984	v Wildman	2-5	Qualifying	Lada Classic
	v Reardon	3-5	1st round	Benson & Hedges Masters
	v Thorburn	9-10	1st round	Embassy World Professional Championship
	v Thorne	5-3	Quarter-final	Winfield Australian Masters

v Meo	6-2	Semi-final	Winfield Australian Masters
v Knowles	3-7	Final	Winfield Australian Masters
v F. Davis	5-3	Qualifying	Jameson International
v Thorburn	5-0	1st round	Jameson International
v S. Francisco	2-5	2nd round	Jameson International
v Bradley	5-0	1st round	Rothmans Grand Prix
v Dennis Taylor	3-5	2nd round	Rothmans Grand Prix
v King	4-9	Qualifying	Coral UK Open
v Bales	5-1	Qualifying	Mercantile Credit Classic
v Werbeniuk	5-2	1st round	Mercantile Credit Classic
v Macleod	5-0	2nd round	Mercantile Credit Classic
v Thorne	1-5	Quarter-final	Mercantile Credit Classic
1985 v Darrington	9-0	1st round	Tolly Cobbold English Professional Championship
v Johnson	9-4	2nd round	Tolly Cobbold English Professional Championship
v S. Davis	2-9	Quarter-final	Tolly Cobbold English Professional Championship
v P. Francisco	6-2	1st round	Dulux British Open
v S. Davis	2-5	2nd round	Dulux British Open
v Wych	10-4	Qualifying	Embassy World Professional Championship
v Meo	6-10	1st round	Embassy World Professional Championship

PAUL WATCHORN (Republic of Ireland)

Born 19.7.58
Turned professional 1982
World ranking 93

1983 v Johnson	0-10	Qualifying	Embassy World Professional Championship
v Morra	3-5	Qualifying	Jameson International
v Parrott	0-5	Qualifying	Professional Players Tournament
1984 v Donnelly	7-10	Qualifying	Embassy World Professional Championship
v W. Jones	0-5	Qualifying	Jameson International
v Dennis Taylor	1-5	1st round	Rothmans Grand Prix
v B. Harris	9-7	Qualifying	Coral UK Open
v Everton	9-6	Qualifying	Coral UK Open
v Fisher	5-9	Qualifying	Coral UK Open
v D. Hughes	5-0	Prelim	Mercantile Credit Classic
v Mikkelsen	5-1	Qualifying	Mercantile Credit Classic
v Donnelly	1-5	Qualifying	Mercantile Credit Classic
1985 v Fitzmaurice	6-1	Qualifying	Dulux British Open
v E. Hughes	4-6	1st round	Dulux British Open
v Kelly	2-6	Qualifying	Irish Professional Championship
v Hines	4-10	Qualifying	Embassy World Professional Championship

GERRY WATSON (Canada)

Born 28.9.49
Turned professional 1983
World ranking unranked

| **1984** v Anderson | 4-10 Qualifying | Embassy World Professional Championship |

MIKE WATTERSON (England)

Born 26.8.42
Turned professional 1981
World ranking 42

Although he is a good enough player to have recorded wins over Tony Meo and Alex Higgins, Watterson's niche in snooker history will be his innovative role as a promoter. It was he who took the Embassy World Championship to the Crucible Theatre in 1977, a success which led to his instigating and promoting other events, notably the Coral UK Championship, the Jameson International, the Yamaha International Masters and the State Express (now Guinness) World Cup.

1981 v Bennett	9-4	Qualifying	Coral UK Championship
v Johnson	3-9	Qualifying	Coral UK Championship
1982 v Demarco	9-6	Qualifying	Embassy World Professional Championship
v Meadowcroft	7-9	Qualifying	Embassy World Professional Championship
v Everton	5-1	Qualifying	Jameson International
v Fagan	5-1	Qualifying	Jameson International
v Stevens	3-5	1st round	Jameson International
v Donnelly	5-4	1st round	Professional Players Tournament
v Griffiths	2-5	2nd round	Professional Players Tournament
v B. Harris	3-9	Qualifying	Coral UK Championship
1983 v Campbell	6-10	Qualifying	Embassy World Professional Championship
v Demarco	5-3	Qualifying	Jameson International
v Mans	5-4	Qualifying	Jameson International
v Meo	5-3	1st round	Jameson International
v S. Davis	0-5	2nd round	Jameson International
v Higgins	5-2	1st round	Professional Players Tournament
v Martin	4-5	2nd round	Professional Players Tournament
v Everton	9-6	Qualifying	Coral UK Championship
v F. Davis	9-6	Qualifying	Coral UK Championship
v Mountjoy	2-9	1st round	Coral UK Championship
1984 v Bennett	10-5	Qualifying	Embassy World Professional Championship
v King	8-10	Qualifying	Embassy World Professional Championship
v Black	3-5	Qualifying	Jameson International
v W. Jones	3-5	Qualifying	Rothmans Grand Prix
v Murphy	4-9	Qualifying	Coral UK Open
v Edmonds	2-5	Qualifying	Mercantile Credit Classic
1985 v Kearney	4-6	Qualifying	Dulux British Open
v W. Jones	5-10	Qualifying	Embassy World Professional Championship

BILL WERBENIUK (Canada)

Born 14.1.47
Turned professional 1973
World ranking 17

In two seasons, Werbeniuk has fallen from eighth to 17th in the world rankings and in 1984–85 won only one match. His massive girth is attributable in part to the huge intake of lager he uses as a medication to control a hereditary nervous disorder which causes his cue arm to tremble. In the 1985 Embassy World Championship he made a break of 143, the joint third-highest in the 57-year history of the event.

1974	v Thompson	8-3	1st round	World Professional Championship
	v F. Davis	5-15	2nd round	World Professional Championship
1974	v Dunning	5-1	1st round	Norwich Union Open
–75	v Higgins	4-5	Quarter-final	Norwich Union Open
1975	v Higgins	0-5	1st round	Benson & Hedges Masters
	v Meadowcroft	15-9	1st round	Embassy World Professional Championship
	v Charlton	11-15	2nd round	Embassy World Professional Championship
1976	v F. Davis	12-15	1st round	Embassy World Professional Championship
1978	v Parking	9-2	Qualifying	Embassy World Professional Championship
	v Pulman	13-4	1st round	World Professional Championship
	v Reardon	6-13	Quarter-final	World Professional Championship
1979	v Andrewartha	9-2	Qualifying	Embassy World Professional Championship
	v Spencer	13-11	1st round	Embassy World Professional Championship
	v Virgo	9-13	Quarter-final	Embassy World Professional Championship
	v Johnson	9-3	2nd round	Coral UK Championship
	v Spencer	9-8	3rd round	Coral UK Championship
	v Edmonds	9-8	Quarter-final	Coral UK Championship
	v Griffiths	3-9	Semi-final	Coral UK Championship
1980	v Thorne	10-9	1st round	Embassy World Professional Championship
	v Reardon	6-13	2nd round	Embassy World Professional Championship
	v S. Davis	3-9	2nd round	Coral UK Championship
1981	v Martin	10-4	1st round	Embassy World Professional Championship
	v Mans	13-5	2nd round	Embassy World Professional Championship
	v Reardon	10-13	Quarter-final	Embassy World Professional Championship
	v Martin	2-5	2nd round	Jameson International
	v Stevens	9-7	3rd round	Coral UK Championship
	v S. Davis	5-9	Quarter-final	Coral UK Championship
1982	v Bear	10-7	1st round	Embassy World Professional Championship
	v Charlton	5-13	2nd round	Embassy World Professional Championship
	v Wych	5-3	1st round	Jameson International
	v David Taylor	2-5	2nd round	Jameson International
	v Morgan	5-3	1st round	Professional Players Tournament
	v Jack Rea	5-2	2nd round	Professional Players Tournament
	v Thorburn	5-2	3rd round	Professional Players Tournament
	v Reardon	3-5	Quarter-final	Professional Players Tournament
1983	v Higgins	5-4	1st round	Lada Classic
	v Mountjoy	5-2	Quarter-final	Lada Classic
	v Stevens	5-2	Semi-final	Lada Classic

Bill Werbeniuk (Sportlines/Roy Peters)

Mark Wildman (David Muscroft)

v S. Davis	5-9	Final	Lada Classic
v Higgins	5-4	1st round	Benson & Hedges Masters
v Charlton	3-5	Quarter-final	Benson & Hedges Masters
v Griffiths	3-5	Semi-final	Tolly Cobbold Classic
v Martin	10-4	1st round	Embassy World Professional Championship
v David Taylor	13-10	2nd round	Embassy World Professional Championship
v Higgins	11-13	Quarter-final	Embassy World Professional Championship
v Knowles	5-0	Semi-final	Winfield Masters
v Thorburn	3-7	Final	Winfield Masters
v Scott	3-5	1st round	Jameson International
v T. Jones	5-4	1st round	Professional Players Tournament
v E. Hughes	0-5	2nd round	Professional Players Tournament
1984 v Roscoe	4-5	Qualifying	Lada Classic
v Griffiths	1-5	1st round	Benson & Hedges Masters
v Griffiths	2-5	1st round	Benson & Hedges Irish Masters
v F. Davis	10-4	1st round	Embassy World Professional Championship
v Griffiths	5-10	2nd round	Embassy World Professional Championship
v Williamson	2-5	1st round	Rothmans Grand Prix
v Williams	1-9	1st round	Coral UK Open
v Virgo	2-5	1st round	Mercantile Credit Classic
v Griffiths	2-5	1st round	Benson & Hedges Masters
1985 v Chaperon	1-6	1st round	Dulux British Open
v Johnson	10-8	1st round	Embassy World Professional Championship
v Thorburn	3-13	2nd round	Embassy World Professional Championship

JIMMY WHITE (England)

Born 2.5.62
Turned professional 1980
World ranking 7

The youngest-ever English amateur champion at the age of 16, the youngest-ever world amateur champion at 18 and the youngest-ever winner of a professional tournament, the Langs Scottish Masters, at 19, White came within two frames of becoming the youngest-ever world professional champion a few days after his 22nd birthday. Down 12-4 to Steve Davis overnight in the 1984 Embassy World Championship final, White lost only 18-16 after demonstrating yet again the greatest flair and natural talent the game has ever seen.

Winner of the Benson and Hedges Masters in 1984, White has taken first prize subsequently only in partnership with Alex Higgins in the 1984 Hofmeister World Doubles Championship as his 1984-85 season proved inconsistent overall.

1981 v Mikkelsen	9-4	Qualifying	Embassy World Professional Championship
v Meadowcroft	9-8	Qualifying	Embassy World Professional Championship
v S. Davis	8-10	1st round	Embassy World Professional Championship
v Reardon	5-4	Quarter-final	Langs Supreme Scottish Masters
v S. Davis	6-5	Semi-final	Langs Supreme Scottish Masters

v Thorburn	**9-4**	**Final**	**Langs Supreme Scottish Masters**
v Williams	1-5	1st round	Jameson International
v Thorburn	5-2	1st round	Northern Ireland Classic
v Mountjoy	9-8	Semi-final	Northern Ireland Classic
v S. Davis	**11-9**	**Final**	**Northern Ireland Classic**
v Everton	9-4	Qualifying	Coral UK Championship
v Virgo	9-6	2nd round	Coral UK Championship
v Dennis Taylor	9-5	3rd round	Coral UK Championship
v Reardon	9-8	Quarter-final	Coral UK Championship
v S. Davis	0-9	Semi-final	Coral UK Championship
1982 v Charlton	4-5	1st round	Benson & Hedges Masters
v Wildman	9-4	Qualifying	Embassy World Professional Championship
v Thorburn	10-4	1st round	Embassy World Professional Championship
v Mans	13-6	2nd round	Embassy World Professional Championship
v Stevens	13-9	Quarter-final	Embassy World Professional Championship
v Higgins	15-16	Semi-final	Embassy World Professional Championship
v Dennis Taylor	4-5	1st round	Langs Supreme Scottish Masters
v Meadowcroft	5-1	1st round	Jameson International
v Wilson	2-5	2nd round	Jameson International
v Wych	5-0	2nd round	Professional Players Tournament
v Dennis Taylor	5-3	3rd round	Professional Players Tournament
v Griffiths	5-2	Quarter-final	Professional Players Tournament
v Virgo	10-4	Semi-final	Professional Players Tournament
v Reardon	5-10	Final	Professional Players Tournament
v Medati	9-7	1st round	Coral UK Championship
v Wilson	9-5	2nd round	Coral UK Championship
v Reardon	8-9	Quarter-final	Coral UK Championship
1983 v David Taylor	3-5	1st round	Lada Classic
v David Taylor	5-2	1st round	Benson & Hedges Masters
v Reardon	2-5	Quarter-final	Benson & Hedges Masters
v Reardon	6-9	Final	Yamaha International Masters
v Dennis Taylor	5-4	1st round	Benson & Hedges Irish Masters
v Higgins	2-5	Quarter-final	Benson & Hedges Irish Masters
v Meo	8-10	1st round	Embassy World Professional Championship
v Higgins	3-5	1st round	Langs Supreme Scottish Masters
v Morra	3-5	1st round	Jameson International
v Williamson	5-2	1st round	Professional Players Tournament
v Johnson	3-5	2nd round	Professional Players Tournament
v Black	9-1	1st round	Coral UK Championship
v Dennis Taylor	9-4	2nd round	Coral UK Championship
v Reardon	9-4	Quarter-final	Coral UK Championship
v S. Davis	4-9	Semi-final	Coral UK Championship
1984 v Campbell	5-1	Qualifying	Lada Classic
v Charlton	3-5	1st round	Lada Classic
v Charlton	5-2	1st round	Benson & Hedges Masters
v Reardon	5-3	Quarter-final	Benson & Hedges Masters
v Stevens	6-4	Semi-final	Benson & Hedges Masters
v Griffiths	**9-5**	**Final**	**Benson & Hedges Masters**
v Meo	4-5	1st round	Benson & Hedges Irish Masters
v Knowles	1-5	1st round	Tolly Cobbold Classic
v Williams	10-6	1st round	Embassy World Professional Championship

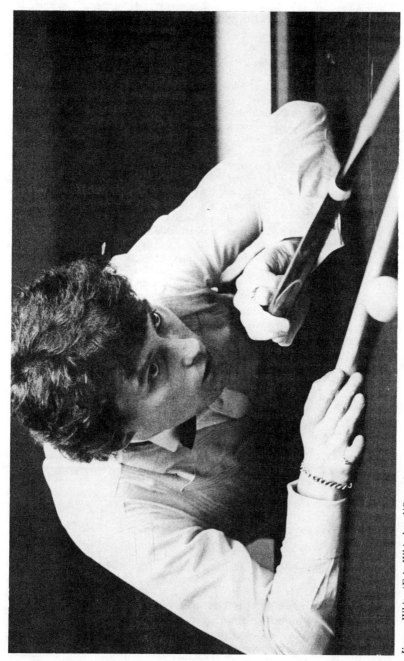

Jimmy White (Eric Whitehead/Scope)

	v Charlton	13-7	2nd round	Embassy World Professional Championship
	v Thorburn	13-8	Quarter-final	Embassy World Professional Championship
	v Stevens	16-14	Semi-final	Embassy World Professional Championship
	v S. Davis	16-18	Final	Embassy World Professional Championship
	v Knowles	3-5	Quarter-final	Winfield Australian Masters
	v Macleod	5-0	1st round	Langs Supreme Scottish Masters
	v Knowles	6-5	Semi-final	Langs Supreme Scottish Masters
	v S. Davis	4-9	Final	Langs Supreme Scottish Masters
	v Williams	5-3	1st round	Jameson International
	v Meo	5-1	2nd round	Jameson International
	v Knowles	4-5	Quarter-final	Jameson International
	v Oliver	5-1	1st round	Rothmans Grand Prix
	v S. Francisco	1-5	2nd round	Rothmans Grand Prix
	v Campbell	9-7	1st round	Coral UK Open
	v Mountjoy	9-2	2nd round	Coral UK Open
	v S. Davis	4-9	Quarter-final	Coral UK Open
	v Browne	5-2	1st round	Mercantile Credit Classic
	v King	2-5	2nd round	Mercantile Credit Classic
1985	v Thorne	5-2	1st round	Benson & Hedges Masters
	v Spencer	5-2	Quarter-final	Benson & Hedges Masters
	v Thorburn	4-6	Semi-final	Benson & Hedges Masters
	v Chalmers	9-5	1st round	Tolly Cobbold English Professional Championship
	v N. Foulds	9-7	2nd round	Tolly Cobbold English Professional Championship
	v Longworth	5-9	Quarter-final	Tolly Cobbold English Professional Championship
	v T. Jones	6-5	1st round	Dulux British Open
	v S. Francisco	4-5	2nd round	Dulux British Open
	v Meo	5-1	1st round	Benson & Hedges Irish Masters
	v Thorburn	5-3	Quarter-final	Benson & Hedges Irish Masters
	v Knowles	6-4	Semi-final	Benson & Hedges Irish Masters
	v Higgins	**9-5**	**Final**	**Benson & Hedges Irish Masters**
	v W. Jones	10-4	1st round	Embassy World Professional Championship
	v Meo	13-11	2nd round	Embassy World Professional Championship
	v Knowles	10-13	Quarter-final	Embassy World Professional Championship

MARK WILDMAN (England)

Born 25.1.36
Turned professional 1979
World ranking 25

Although he has made most impact as a billiards player, once winning and twice being runner-up for the world professional title, Wildman proved his quality as a snooker player by reaching the semi-finals of the 1984 Lada Classic with wins over John Virgo, Silvino Francisco and Eddie Charlton. He is a member of ITV's commentary team.

1980	v Jonik	7-9	Qualifying	Embassy World Professional Championship
	v Wilson	9-8	Qualifying	Coral UK Championship
	v Spencer	9-7	1st round	Coral UK Championship
	v F. Davis	6-9	2nd round	Coral UK Championship
1981	v Bennett	9-3	Qualifying	John Courage English Professional
	v Thorne	2-9	1st round	John Courage English Professional
	v Edmonds	3-9	Qualifying	Embassy World Professional Championship
	v Morra	5-3	Qualifying	Jameson International
	v E.McLaughlin	3-5	Qualifying	Jameson International
	v Sinclair	8-9	Qualifying	Coral UK Championship
1982	v G. Foulds	9-8	Qualifying	Embassy World Professional Championship
	v White	4-9	Qualifying	Embassy World Professional Championship
	v Gibson	5-1	Qualifying	Jameson International
	v Hallett	5-2	Qualifying	Jameson International
	v Dennis Taylor	2-5	1st round	Jameson International
	v Dunning	5-4	1st round	Professional Players Tournament
	v Mans	5-4	2nd round	Professional Players Tournament
	v Johnson	4-5	3rd round	Professional Players Tournament
	v Roscoe	9-4	Qualifying	Coral UK Championship
	v Reardon	5-9	1st round	Coral UK Championship
1983	v S. Davis	2-5	1st round	Benson & Hedges Masters
	v B. Harris	10-7	Qualifying	Embassy World Professional Championship
	v Griffiths	8-10	1st round	Embassy World Professional Championship
	v B. Harris	5-2	Qualifying	Jameson International
	v Mountjoy	4-5	1st round	Jameson International
	v Jonik	5-4	1st round	Professional Players Tournament
	v David Taylor	5-3	2nd round	Professional Players Tournament
	v Stevens	0-5	3rd round	Professional Players Tournament
	v Greaves	9-5	Qualifying	Coral UK Championship
	v Thorne	5-9	1st round	Coral UK Championship
1984	v Virgo	5-2	Qualifying	Lada Classic
	v S. Francisco	5-1	1st round	Lada Classic
	v Charlton	5-4	Quarter-final	Lada Classic
	v Meo	3-5	Semi-final	Lada Classic
	v Andrewartha	9-10	Qualifying	Embassy World Professional Championship
	v W. Jones	0-5	Qualifying	Jameson International
	v J. McLaughlin	5-3	1st round	Rothmans Grand Prix
	v Mountjoy	0-5	2nd round	Rothmans Grand Prix
	v T. Jones	2-9	Qualifying	Coral UK Open
	v Fagan	3-5	Qualifying	Mercantile Credit Classic
1985	v Longworth	3-9	1st round	Tolly Cobbold English Professional Championship
	v Gibson	6-1	1st round	Dulux British Open
	v Stevens	2-5	2nd round	Dulux British Open
	v Edmonds	7-10	Qualifying	Embassy World Professional Championship

REX WILLIAMS (England)

Born 20.7.33
Turned professional 1951
World ranking 27

Chairman of the World Professional Billiards and Snooker Association and an ITV commentator, Williams was world professional billiards champion on a challenge basis from 1968 until 1980 and twice won the event when it was restored to a tournament format in 1982 and 1983. He was a world professional snooker semi-finalist in 1972 and 1974 and, though diverted by his other interests in and around the game, remains more of a threat to the leading players than his comparatively low ranking suggests.

1969	v Bennett	38-11	Quarter-final	World Professional Championship
	v Spencer	18-55	Semi-final	World Professional Championship
1970	v G. Owen	11-31	Quarter-final	World Professional Championship (Apr)
1972	v Reardon	25-23	Quarter-final	World Professional Championship
	v Higgins	30-31	Semi-final	World Professional Championship
1973	v Thorburn	16-15	2nd round	World Professional Championship
	v Spencer	7-16	Quarter-final	World Professional Championship
1974	v Pulman	15-12	2nd round	World Professional Championship
	v Mans	15-4	Quarter-final	World Professional Championship
	v Miles	7-15	Semi-final	World Professional Championship
1974	v M. Owen	5-3	1st round	Norwich Union Open
–75	v Reardon	2-5	Quarter-final	Norwich Union Open
1975	v Higgins	5-3	Quarter-final	Benson & Hedges Masters
	v Reardon	4-5	Semi-final	Benson & Hedges Masters
	v Anderson	15-4	2nd round	World Professional Championship
	v Higgins	12-19	Quarter-final	World Professional Championship
1976	v Meadowcroft	7-15	1st round	Embassy World Professional Championship
1977	v Thorburn	6-13	1st round	Embassy World Professional Championship
1978	v Thorne	3-9	Qualifying	Embassy World Professional Championship
	v Griffiths	9-8	Qualifying	Coral UK Championship
	v Miles	8-9	1st round	Coral UK Championship
1979	v Spencer	2-6	Semi-final	Holsten Lager International
	v Greaves	9-2	Prelim	Embassy World Professional Championship
	v Miles	5-9	Qualifying	Embassy World Professional Championship
1980	v Wych	7-9	Qualifying	Embassy World Professional Championship
	v Barrie	9-1	Qualifying	Coral UK Championship
	v Mountjoy	9-8	1st round	Coral UK Championship
	v David Taylor	9-7	2nd round	Coral UK Championship
	v Reardon	4-9	Quarter-final	Coral UK Championship
1981	v Hood	9-4	Qualifying	Embassy World Professional Championship
	v Edmonds	7-9	Qualifying	Embassy World Professional Championship
	v French	5-0	Qualifying	Jameson International
	v White	5-1	1st round	Jameson International
	v F. Davis	5-0	2nd round	Jameson International
	v Dennis Taylor	1-5	3rd round	Jameson International

v French	9-3	Qualifying	Coral UK Championship
v Roscoe	9-4	Qualifying	Coral UK Championship
v Dunning	9-4	Qualifying	Coral UK Championship
v Meo	8-9	2nd round	Coral UK Championship
1982 v Black	9-2	Qualifying	Embassy World Professional Championship
v Mountjoy	3-10	1st round	Embassy World Professional Championship
v Medati	5-3	Qualifying	Jameson International
v E. McLaughlin	5-1	Qualifying	Jameson International
v Griffiths	2-5	1st round	Jameson International
v Ross	5-0	1st round	Professional Players Tournament
v Charlton	2-5	2nd round	Professional Players Tournament
v G. Foulds	9-7	Qualifying	Coral UK Championship
v S. Davis	6-9	1st round	Coral UK Championship
v Darrington	10-0	Qualifying	Embassy World Professional Championship
v F. Davis	10-1	Qualifying	Embassy World Professional Championship
v S. Davis	4-10	1st round	Embassy World Professional Championship
1983 v French	5-1	Qualifying	Jameson International
v Reynolds	3-5	Qualifying	Jameson International
v Sheehan	5-1	1st round	Professional Players Tournament
v Knowles	4-5	2nd round	Professional Players Tournament
v V. Harris	9-6	Qualifying	Coral UK Championship
v Wilson	4-9	1st round	Coral UK Championship
1984 v Reardon	5-4	Qualifying	Lada Classic
v Meo	3-5	1st round	Lada Classic
v Oliver	10-8	Qualifying	Embassy World Professional Championship
v White	6-10	1st round	Embassy World Professional Championship
v Meadowcroft	5-4	Qualifying	Jameson International
v White	3-5	Qualifying	Jameson International
v Chalmers	5-0	1st round	Rothmans Grand Prix
v Stevens	3-5	2nd round	Rothmans Grand Prix
v Fisher	9-8	Qualifying	Coral UK Open
v Werbeniuk	9-1	1st round	Coral UK Open
v Higgins	7-9	2nd round	Coral UK Open
v Donnelly	5-3	Qualifying	Mercantile Credit Classic
v Dennis Taylor	5-3	1st round	Mercantile Credit Classic
v Griffiths	3-5	2nd round	Mercantile Credit Classic
1985 v T. Jones	9-6	1st round	Tolly Cobbold English Professional Championship
v S. Davis	2-9	2nd round	Tolly Cobbold English Professional Championship
v Fowler	4-6	1st round	Dulux British Open
v F. Davis	10-6	Qualifying	Embassy World Professional Championship
v Griffiths	3-10	1st round	Embassy World Professional Championship

IAN WILLIAMSON (England)

Born 1.12.58
Turned professional 1982
World ranking 47

Williamson achieved his 47th place in the world rankings by virtue of beating Bill Werbeniuk and Joe Johnson to reach the third round of the Rothmans Grand Prix.

1982 v Donnelly	5-3	Qualifying	Jameson International
v Kelly	1-5	Qualifying	Jameson International
v Dodd	1-9	Qualifying	Coral UK Championship
1983 v French	10-8	Qualifying	Embassy World Professional Championship
v Dodd	9-10	Qualifying	Embassy World Professional Championship
v Darrington	3-5	Qualifying	Jameson International
v White	2-5	1st round	Professional Players Tournament
v Hargreaves	9-4	Qualifying	Coral UK Championship
v Black	6-9	Qualifying	Coral UK Championship
1984 v Houlihan	10-5	Qualifying	Embassy World Professional Championship
v Hines	10-6	Qualifying	Embassy World Professional Championship
v Miles	6-10	Qualifying	Embassy World Professional Championship
v V. Harris	5-0	Qualifying	Jameson International
v G. Foulds	4-5	Qualifying	Jameson International
v Thornley	5-2	Qualifying	Rothmans Grand Prix
v Werbeniuk	5-2	1st round	Rothmans Grand Prix
v Johnson	5-4	2nd round	Rothmans Grand Prix
v Knowles	2-5	3rd round	Rothmans Grand Prix
v P. Francisco	2-9	Qualifying	Coral UK Open
v Kearney	5-3	Qualifying	Mercantile Credit Classic
v Fagan	1-5	Qualifying	Mercantile Credit Classic
1985 v Bradley	8-9	Qualifying	Tolly Cobbold English Professional Championship
v Chappel	5-6	Qualifying	Dulux British Open
v Medati	8-10	Qualifying	Embassy World Professional Championship

CLIFF WILSON (Wales)

Born 10.5.34
Turned professional 1979
World ranking 22

Severe problems with his eyesight were the predominant cause of a 15-year retirement between the first phase of Wilson's career, in which he was a close and intense rival of Ray Reardon's in their native Tredegar, and the second, in which he recaptured the Welsh amateur title 21 years after he first won it and went on to win the World Amateur Championship in 1978. His professional career has been a thing of fits and starts but has included wins over three fellow Welshmen, Doug

Mountjoy, Terry Griffiths and Reardon, and also over Jimmy White, Tony Knowles and Willie Thorne.

1979	v Pulman	9-7	2nd round	Coral UK Championship
	v Griffiths	4-9	3rd round	Coral UK Championship
1980	v Jonik	9-6	Qualifying	Embassy World Professional Championship
	v Mountjoy	6-10	1st round	Embassy World Professional Championship
	v Wildman	8-9	Qualifying	Coral UK Championship
1981	v Andrewartha	6-5	Prelim	Woodpecker Welsh Professional Championship
	v Mountjoy	9-6	Semi-final	Woodpecker Welsh Professional Championship
	v Reardon	6-9	Final	Woodpecker Welsh Professional Championship
	v Andrewartha	9-4	Qualifying	Embassy World Professional Championship
	v Sinclair	9-4	Qualifying	Embassy World Professional Championship
	v David Taylor	6-10	1st round	Embassy World Professional Championship
	v Meadowcroft	4-5	1st round	Jameson International
	v Johnson	5-9	Qualifying	Coral UK Championship
1982	v M. Owen	6-0	1st round	Welsh Professional Championship
	v Griffiths	6-9	Semi-final	Welsh Professional Championship
	v Medati	9-5	Qualifying	Embassy World Professional Championship
	v Charlton	5-10	1st round	Embassy World Professional Championship
	v Johnson	5-4	Qualifying	Jameson International
	v Mountjoy	5-4	1st round	Jameson International
	v White	5-2	2nd round	Jameson International
	v Knowles	4-5	Quarter-final	Jameson International
	v Morra	5-2	1st round	Professional Players Tournament
	v Knowles	5-4	2nd round	Professional Players Tournament
	v Reynolds	1-5	3rd round	Professional Players Tournament
	v E. McLaughlin	9-6	Qualifying	Coral UK Championship
	v Thorne	9-7	1st round	Coral UK Championship
	v White	5-9	2nd round	Coral UK Championship
1983	v Thorburn	3-5	1st round	Lada Classic
	v Roscoe	6-4	Quarter-final	Woodpecker Welsh Professional Championship
	v Mountjoy	3-9	Semi-final	Woodpecker Welsh Professional Championship
	v Everton	10-1	Qualifying	Embassy World Professional Championship
	v Johnson	10-8	Qualifying	Embassy World Professional Championship
	v Mountjoy	2-10	1st round	Embassy World Professional Championship
	v Donnelly	1-5	Qualifying	Jameson International
	v Bennett	5-1	1st round	Professional Players Tournament
	v Virgo	5-2	2nd round	Professional Players Tournament
	v Thorburn	3-5	3rd round	Professional Players Tournament
	v Williams	9-4	1st round	Coral UK Championship
	v Reardon	4-9	2nd round	Coral UK Championship
1984	v Charlton	0-5	Qualifying	Lada Classic
	v Roscoe	6-2	1st round	Strongbow Welsh Professional Championship

Cliff Wilson

Rex Williams (David Muscroft)

v Reardon	9-4	Semi-final	Strongbow Welsh Professional Championship
v Mountjoy	3-9	Final	Strongbow Welsh Professional Championship
v Mifsud	8-10	Qualifying	Embassy World Professional Championship
v Dodd	1-5	Qualifying	Jameson International
v Donnelly	5-2	1st round	Rothmans Grand Prix
v Reardon	4-5	2nd round	Rothmans Grand Prix
v Dodd	9-8	Qualifying	Coral UK Open
v Griffiths	9-6	1st round	Coral UK Open
v Thorburn	3-9	2nd round	Coral UK Open
v Fowler	5-4	Qualifying	Mercantile Credit Classic
v Mountjoy	5-4	1st round	Mercantile Credit Classic
v Johnson	0-5	2nd round	Mercantile Credit Classic
1985 v Longworth	3-6	1st round	Dulux British Open
v Fagan	9-10	Qualifying	Embassy World Professional Championship
v Roscoe	6-3	Quarter-final	BCE Welsh Professional Championship
v Mountjoy	2-9	Semi-final	BCE Welsh Professional Championship

JIM WYCH (Canada)

Born 11.1.55
Turned professional 1979
World ranking 52

A quarter-finalist in the Embassy World Championship at his first attempt in 1980, Wych has not competed regularly on the circuit since and has thus not fulfilled his abundant early promise.

1980 v Bear	9-5	Qualifying	Embassy World Professional Championship
v Williams	9-7	Qualifying	Embassy World Professional Championship
v Pulman	10-5	1st round	Embassy World Professional Championship
v Dennis Taylor	13-10	2nd round	Embassy World Professional Championship
v Thorburn	6-13	Quarter-final	Embassy World Professional Championship
1981 v Knowles	3-9	Qualifying	Embassy World Professional Championship
v Johnson	2-5	1st round	Jameson International
1982 v Higgins	3-5	1st round	Benson & Hedges Irish Masters
v Bear	4-9	Qualifying	Embassy World Professional Championship
v Bennett	5-0	Qualifying	Jameson International
v Werbeniuk	3-5	1st round	Jameson International
v Kelly	5-0	1st round	Professional Players Tournament
v White	0-5	2nd round	Professional Players Tournament
1984 v Ganim	10-1	Qualifying	Embassy World Professional Championship
v Scott	10-6	Qualifying	Embassy World Professional Championship
v Fagan	10-3	Qualifying	Embassy World Professional Championship
v Reardon	7-10	1st round	Embassy World Professional Championship
1985 v Bradley	10-7	Qualifying	Embassy World Professional Championship
v Virgo	4-10	Qualifying	Embassy World Professional Championship

The following players have been granted professional status by the WPBSA and are eligible to compete in the 1985–86 circuit:

Dave Gilbert (England), Joe O'Boye (England), Martin Smith (England), Barry West (England), Tony Drago (Malta), François Ellis (South Africa), Robbie Grace (South Africa), Glen Wilkinson (Australia), Greg Jenkins (Australia), Gordon Robinson (Australia), Steve Mizerak (USA), Sakchai Sim-Ngarm (Thailand), Stephen Hendry (Scotland), Jim Bear (re-accepted) (Canada).

SNOOKER GREATS

JOE DAVIS O.B.E. (1901–1978)
Although only one of the 'Big Four' at billiards, Joe Davis was undoubtedly the number one at snooker. With his friend Bill Camkin, a Birmingham billiard trader, he promoted and won the first World Professional Snooker Championship in 1927. He went on to win the title every year until 1940. The Championship was suspended until 1946, at which point Davis beat Horace Lindrum 78-67 to take the title for the 15th time.

Davis then retired from Championship play. He continued to play in other tournaments and in the public's mind he was still the champion, whoever had won the World Championship in his absence.

His expertise at the three-ball game carried him to four World Professional Billiards titles but his name will always be synonymous with snooker. It was he who developed the modern break-making methods, using the black as the key colour, and it was he who brought the sport to the public's attention.

WALTER DONALDSON (1907–1973)
Consistent and steady, Walter Donaldson reached eight consecutive World Championship finals between 1948 and 1954. In 1947 and 1950 he beat Fred Davis to take the title.

As professional snooker's appeal dwindled in the mid-1950s, a disillusioned Donaldson turned his billiard room into a cowshed and broke up the slates of his table for crazy paving.

JOHN PULMAN (born 1926)
After winning the English Amateur Championship in 1946, John Pulman turned professional but was at his peak when the professional game was going through a period in the doldrums. He was never able to capitalise fully on his natural talent.

He won the world title in 1957 and then successfully withstood a series of challengers. When the influx of new professionals led to the Championship being restored to a tournament format, he once reached the final, losing to Ray Reardon.

An accident led to his retirement from playing in 1982 but he is still involved on the circuit as a member of ITV's commentary team.

The Derngate Centre, Northampton, home of the Hofmeister World Doubles Championship (Graham Trott)

THE BRITISH CIRCUIT

THE BRITISH CIRCUIT

LANGS SCOTTISH MASTERS

The inaugural Langs Scottish Masters was staged in 1981 at the massive Kelvin Hall, Glasgow. It failed to attract large crowds and suffered other teething problems before redeeming itself the following season when it moved to the Holiday Inn, Glasgow. For the last two years it has been staged at another Glasgow hotel, the Skean Dhu.

It is now firmly established as the first major event on the British circuit. Although it is restricted by invitation to eight players, it attracts most of the leading names and gives the Scottish public their only international tournament.

Jimmy White beat Cliff Thorburn to become the first titleholder but since then Steve Davis has completed a hat-trick of titles.

The event is televised by BBC Scotland and its prize-money has risen from £20,500 in 1981 to £28,500 last season.

1981
Preliminary round: V. Harris beat I. Black 4-0

First round: J. White beat R. Reardon 5-4; S. Davis beat D. Mountjoy 5-0; C. Thorburn beat K. Stevens 5-1; A. Higgins beat V. Harris 5-3

Semi-finals: White beat Davis 6-5; Thorburn beat Higgins 6-2

Final: White beat Thorburn 9-4

1982
First round: Dennis Taylor beat J. White 5-4; S. Davis beat A. Knowles 5-4; T. Griffiths beat R. Reardon 5-3; A. Higgins beat E. Sinclair 5-1

Semi-finals: S. Davis beat Dennis Taylor 6-1; Higgins beat Griffiths 6-5

Final: S. Davis beat Higgins 9-4

1983
First round: C. Thorburn beat T. Griffiths 5-1; S. Davis beat M. Macleod 5-1; A. Knowles beat T. Meo 5-4; A. Higgins beat J. White 5-3

Semi-finals: Knowles beat Thorburn 6-2; S. Davis beat Higgins 6-2

Final: S. Davis beat Knowles 9-6

1984

First round: A. Knowles beat T. Griffiths 5-3; J. White beat M. Macleod 5-0; S. Davis beat C. Thorburn 5-2; A. Higgins beat K. Stevens 5-2

Semi-finals: White beat Knowles 6-5; S. Davis beat Higgins 6-4

Final: S. Davis beat White 9-4

JAMESON INTERNATIONAL

When the tournament was instigated in 1981, the Jameson International achieved two firsts. It was the first tournament, other than the World Professional Championship, for which ranking points were awarded and it was the first event with which ITV was seriously to compete with the BBC with the same day transmission of pukka tournament play.

For its first two years, the closing stages of the event were held at Derby Assembly Rooms but in 1983 it transferred to Eldon Square Recreation Centre, Newcastle, giving the North-East of the country a major event for the first time.

Steve Davis captured the £20,000 first prize in 1981 by beating Dennis Taylor 9-0 in the final and last season, from a total prize fund of £150,000, he took the winner's cheque for £30,000.

1981

First round: J. Johnson beat J. Wych 5-2; D. Martin beat J. Dunning 5-2; R. Williams beat J. White 5-1; A. Knowles beat M. Hallett 5-2; R. Edmonds beat E. Hughes 5-4; J. Meadowcroft beat C. Wilson 5-4; T. Meo beat E. McLaughlin 5-2

Second round: G. Miles beat Johnson 5-3; Martin beat B. Werbeniuk 5-2; Williams beat F. Davis 5-0; A. Higgins beat P. Fagan 5-3; J. Spencer beat Edmonds 5-3; J. Virgo beat Knowles 5-2; K. Stevens beat Meadowcroft 5-1; P. Mans beat Meo 5-3

Third round: Miles beat C. Thorburn 5-0; Martin beat E. Charlton 5-2; Virgo beat R. Reardon 5-3; David Taylor beat Stevens 5-0; Dennis Taylor beat Williams 5-1; Higgins beat D. Mountjoy 5-1; T. Griffiths beat Spencer 5-2; S. Davis beat Mans 5-3

Quarter-finals: Martin beat Miles 5-1; Higgins beat Griffiths 5-2; Dennis Taylor beat Virgo 5-2; S. Davis beat David Taylor 5-1

Semi-finals: Dennis Taylor beat Martin 9-1; S. Davis beat Higgins 9-8

Final: S. Davis beat Dennis Taylor 9-0

1982

Qualifying groups

 1 R. Edmonds beat D. Hughes 5-0; Edmonds beat G. Miles 5-1
 2 V. Harris beat D. Sheehan 5-3; J. Virgo beat Harris 5-2
 3 M. Fisher beat T. Murphy 5-1; Fisher beat F. Davis 5-3
 4 B. Bennett beat M. Owen 5-2; J. Wych beat Bennett 5-0
 5 M. Morra beat B. Demarco 5-2; D. Reynolds beat Morra 5-1
 6 M. Watterson beat C. Everton 5-1; Watterson beat P. Fagan 5-1
 7 E. Sinclair beat I. Anderson 5-2; Sinclair beat T. Meo 5-3
 8 G. Scott beat B. Harris 5-4; Scott *wo* J. Bear *scr*
 9 J. Johnson *wo* J. Phillips *scr*; C. Wilson beat Johnson 5-4
10 E. Hughes beat M. Parkin 5-2; Hughes beat D. Martin 5-4
11 C. Ross *wo* D. Greaves *scr*; J. Meadowcroft beat Ross 5-0
12 I. Williamson beat J. Donnelly 5-3; B. Kelly beat G. Foulds 5-4; Kelly beat Williamson 5-1
13 C. Roscoe beat J. Dunning 5-2; D. French beat G. Cripsey 5-1; Roscoe beat French 5-2
14 M. Hallett beat F. Jonik 5-2; M. Wildman beat M. Gibson 5-1; Wildman beat Hallett 5-2
15 J. Fitzmaurice beat I. Black 5-3; L. Dodd beat M. Macleod 5-1; Dodd beat Fitzmaurice 5-3
16 R. Williams beat P. Medati 5-3; E. McLaughlin beat P. Houlihan 5-2; Williams beat McLaughlin 5-1

First round: A. Knowles beat Sinclair 5-2; Reynolds beat W. Thorne 5-3; S. Davis beat Roscoe 5-0; B. Werbeniuk beat Wych 5-3; David Taylor beat Fisher 5-1; K. Stevens beat Watterson 5-3; T. Griffiths beat Williams 5-2; J. Spencer beat Edmonds 5-2; Dennis Taylor beat Wildman 5-2; Virgo beat E. Charlton 5-4; P. Mans beat Dodd 5-3; J. White beat Meadowcroft 5-1; R. Reardon beat E. Hughes 5-3; C. Thorburn beat Scott 5-1; A. Higgins beat Kelly 5-3; Wilson beat D. Mountjoy 5-4

Second round: S. Davis beat Reynolds 5-0; David Taylor beat Werbeniuk 5-2; Stevens beat Mans 5-2; Griffiths beat Higgins 5-2; Dennis Taylor beat Thorburn 5-2; Wilson beat White 5-2; Virgo beat Spencer 5-4; Knowles beat Reardon 5-2

Quarter-finals: Virgo beat Dennis Taylor 5-3; David Taylor beat S. Davis 5-3; Knowles beat Wilson 5-4; Stevens beat Griffiths 5-3

Semi-finals: Knowles beat Stevens 9-3; David Taylor beat Virgo 9-5

Final: Knowles beat David Taylor 9-6

1983

Qualifying groups

 1 M. Watterson beat B. Demarco 5-3; Watterson beat P. Mans 5-4
 2 T. Murphy beat D. Sheehan 5-2; W. Thorne beat Murphy 5-2
 3 R. Williams beat D. French 5-1; D. Reynolds beat Williams 5-3
 4 J. Donnelly beat B. Bennett 5-1; Donnelly beat C. Wilson 5-1
 5 M. Darrington beat I. Williamson 5-3; S. Francisco beat Darrington 5-2

6   W. King beat I. Black 5-3; G. Miles beat King 5-3
7   D. Hughes beat M. Parkin 5-0; J. Johnson beat Hughes 5-1
8   B. Harris beat J. Dunning 5-3; M. Wildman beat Harris 5-2
9   D. Martin beat D. Greaves 5-1; Martin beat P. Fagan 5-0
10 R. Andrewartha beat C. Everton 5-1; E. Sinclair beat Andrewartha 5-4
11 P. Medati beat V. Harris 5-0; M. Macleod beat Medati 5-3
12 F. Davis beat B. Kelly 5-1; P. Morgan beat J. Fitzmaurice 5-4; Morgan
    beat Davis 5-3
13 M. Hallett beat C. Roscoe 5-2; M. Morra beat P. Watchorn 5-3; Morra
    beat Hallett 5-3
14 G. Foulds beat P. Burke 5-2; E. Hughes beat M. Fisher 5-4; Hughes beat
    Foulds 5-1
15 M. Gibson beat L. Dodd 5-1; G. Scott beat P. Houlihan 5-0; Scott beat
    Gibson 5-3
16 E. McLaughlin beat J. Campbell 5-2; R. Edmonds beat Jack Rea 5-1;
    Edmonds beat McLaughlin 5-1

First round: Dennis Taylor beat Reynolds 5-3; R. Reardon beat Macleod 5-2;
Thorne beat J. Virgo 5-2; Morra beat J. White 5-3; D. Mountjoy beat Wildman
5-4; Martin beat A. Higgins 5-2; Watterson beat T. Meo 5-3; Scott beat
B. Werbeniuk 5-3; T. Griffiths beat Miles 5-2; S. Davis beat Hughes 5-1;
Donnelly beat David Taylor 5-3; Francisco *wo* K. Stevens *scr*; E. Charlton
beat Johnson 5-2; C. Thorburn beat Sinclair 5-0; J. Spencer beat Morgan 5-1;
A. Knowles beat Edmonds 5-1

Second round: Griffiths beat Scott 5-0; Spencer beat Knowles 5-4; Thorburn
beat Dennis Taylor 5-3; Mountjoy beat Martin 5-0; Charlton beat Morra 5-3;
Thorne beat Reardon 5-0; S. Francisco beat Donnelly 5-1; S. Davis beat
Watterson 5-0

Quarter-finals: Griffiths beat Spencer 5-4; Thorburn beat Mountjoy 5-2;
Charlton beat Thorne 5-0; S. Davis beat S. Francisco 5-1

Semi-finals: Thorburn beat Griffiths 9-8; S. Davis beat Charlton 9-2

Final: S. Davis beat Thorburn 9-4

1984
Qualifying groups
1   G. Foulds beat P. Francisco 5-4; I. Williamson beat V. Harris 5-0; Foulds
    beat Williamson 5-4; Foulds beat J. Donnelly 5-3; J. Campbell beat Foulds
    5-3
2   W. Jones beat P. Watchorn 5-0; M. Gibson beat P. Medati 5-3; Jones beat
    Gibson 5-2; Jones beat G. Scott 5-0; Jones beat M. Wildman 5-0
3   T. Jones beat D. French 5-1; S. Duggan beat Jones 5-2; E. Sinclair beat
    Duggan 5-0; Sinclair beat P. Mans 5-2
4   B. Bennett beat B. Demarco 5-1; Bennett *wo* P. Morgan *scr*; Bennett *wo*
    J. Wych *scr*; N. Foulds beat Bennett 5-0
5   R. Foldvari beat G. Rigitano 5-2; Foldvari beat R. Edmonds 5-1; L. Dodd
    beat Foldvari 5-3; Dodd beat C. Wilson 5-1

 6   B. Mikkelsen beat T. Chappel 5-4; Mikkelsen beat C. Everton 5-0;
     C. Roscoe beat Mikkelsen 5-1; E. Hughes beat Roscoe 5-1
 7   D. O'Kane beat M. Parkin 5-2; O'Kane beat E. McLaughlin 5-1; O'Kane
     beat J. FitzMaurice 5-4; O'Kane beat M. Hallett 5-4
 8   J. McLaughlin beat D. Greaves 5-3; F. Jonik beat McLaughlin 5-2;
     M. Gauvreau beat Jonik 5-1; Gauvreau beat J. Parrott 5-4
 9   G. Cripsey beat P. Thornley 5-3; J. Dunning beat Cripsey 5-3; F. Davis
     beat Dunning 5-4; J. Virgo beat Davis 5-3
10   J. Hargreaves beat P. Houlihan 5-2; B. Kelly beat Hargreaves 5-2; Kelly
     beat W. King 5-4; S. Francisco beat Kelly 5-3
11   D. Fowler beat R. Chaperon 5-0; Fowler *wo* P. Mifsud *scr*; Fowler beat
     R. Andrewartha 5-0; Fowler beat D. Martin 5-0
12   M. Bradley beat M. Darrington 5-3; Bradley beat Jack Rea 5-2; M. Morra
     beat Bradley 5-3; J. Johnson beat Morra 5-0
13   D. Chalmers *wo* Condo *scr*; W. Oliver beat D. Hughes 5-4; Chalmers beat
     Oliver 5-4; J. Meadowcroft beat Chalmers 5-1; R. Williams beat
     Meadowcroft 5-4
14   P. Browne beat John Rea 5-2; I. Black beat Browne 5-4; Black beat
     M. Watterson 5-3; M. Macleod beat Black 5-3
15   S. Newbury beat S. Longworth 5-4; P. Burke beat A. Kearney 5-4;
     Newbury beat Burke 5-0; Newbury beat P. Fagan 5-0; Newbury beat
     G. Miles 5-1
16   R. Bales beat D. Sheehan 5-2; Bales beat T. Murphy 5-4; Bales beat
     M. Fisher 5-3; D. Reynolds beat Bales 5-4

First round: S. Davis beat Campbell 5-1; A. Higgins beat Sinclair 5-1;
T. Griffiths beat N. Foulds 5-3; R. Reardon beat Dodd 5-4; E. Hughes beat
D. Mountjoy 5-1; W. Thorne beat O'Kane 5-3; Gauvreau beat K. Stevens 5-1;
Virgo beat C. Thorburn 5-0; S. Francisco beat J. Spencer 5-2; Dennis Taylor
beat Fowler 5-0; Johnson beat E. Charlton 5-1; J. White beat Williams 5-3;
T. Meo beat Macleod 5-1; Newbury beat B. Werbeniuk 5-2; A. Knowles beat
Reynolds 5-1; David Taylor beat W. Jones 5-4

Second round: S. Davis beat David Taylor 5-1; Higgins beat Griffiths 5-4;
E. Hughes beat Reardon 5-1; Thorne beat Gauvreau 5-3; S. Francisco beat
Virgo 5-2; Dennis Taylor beat Johnson 5-2; White beat Meo 5-1; Knowles beat
Newbury 5-4

Quarter-finals: S. Davis beat Higgins 5-1; E. Hughes beat Thorne 5-2;
S. Francisco *wo* Dennis Taylor *scr*; Knowles beat White 5-4

Semi-finals: S. Davis beat E. Hughes 9-3; Knowles beat S. Francisco 9-6

Final: S. Davis beat Knowles 9-2

ROTHMANS GRAND PRIX

Rothmans entered snooker sponsorship for the first time last season, by taking over the Professional Players Tournament, and the television slot previously occupied by the State Express World Team Classic. The Professional Players Tournament had been first staged by the World Professional Billiards and Snooker Association in 1982 with the aim of distributing some of its funds (accumulated from television fees and prize-money levies) to its own members.

It was consequently untelevised and not commercially sponsored but proved so successful that it attracted the BBC and Rothmans. Coincidentally, State Express announced its withdrawal from all sponsorship and snooker's team event was re-scheduled later in the season with reduced television coverage.

After preliminary rounds, the Rothmans Grand Prix, a world ranking tournament, was staged at Redwood Lodge, Bristol before moving to its final televised phase at the former home of the team event, The Hexagon, Reading.

Although it was to be overtaken later in the season, the Grand Prix carried a then record first prize of £45,000.

1982 (*Professional Players Tournament*)
First round: E. Sinclair beat F. Davis 5-2; J. Meadowcroft beat B. Bennett 5-4; M. Watterson beat J. Donnelly 5-4; T. Griffiths beat C. Roscoe 5-1; A. Higgins beat D. French 5-3; R. Reardon beat T. Murphy 5-0; B. Werbeniuk beat P. Morgan 5-3; C. Everton beat P. Fagan 5-2; C. Thorburn beat P. Medati 5-1; David Taylor beat I. Anderson 5-1; Dennis Taylor beat R. Edmonds 5-4; J. Wych beat B. Kelly 5-0; R. Williams beat C. Ross 5-0; P. Mans beat E. McLaughlin 5-2; W. Thorne beat B. Demarco 5-3; M. Wildman beat J. Dunning 5-4; J. Johnson beat G. Miles 5-1; E. Charlton beat D. Hughes 5-2; F. Jonik beat D. Mountjoy 5-3; K. Stevens beat E. Hughes 5-2; T. Meo beat M. Owen 5-4; C. Wilson beat M. Morra 5-2; A. Knowles beat P. Houlihan 5-4; J. Virgo beat I. Black 5-2; M. Hallett beat V. Harris 5-3; D. Martin beat M. Gibson 5-2; J. Fitzmaurice beat D. Sheehan 5-1; J. Spencer beat G. Foulds 5-1

Second round: Werbeniuk beat Jack Rea 5-2; Sinclair beat Meadowcroft 5-3; Thorburn beat Everton 5-2; Griffiths beat Watterson 5-2; Reardon beat Higgins 5-2; Dennis Taylor beat David Taylor 5-1; Wildman beat Mans 5-4; Charlton beat Williams 5-2; M. Macleod beat Thorne 5-4; White beat Wych 5-0; Johnson beat Stevens 5-1; Meo beat Jonik 5-0; Wilson beat Knowles 5-4; Virgo beat Hallett 5-2; Spencer beat Martin 5-3; Reynolds beat Fitzmaurice 5-0

Third round: Werbeniuk beat Thorburn 5-2; Johnson beat Wildman 5-4; Reynolds beat Wilson 5-1; Virgo beat Spencer 5-1; Charlton beat Meo 5-3; White beat Dennis Taylor 5-3; Griffiths beat Sinclair 5-3; Reardon beat Macleod 5-2

Quarter-finals: White beat Griffiths 5-2; Virgo beat Johnson 5-1; Reardon beat Werbeniuk 5-3; Charlton beat Reynolds 5-1

Semi-finals: White beat Virgo 10-4; Reardon beat Charlton 10-7

Final: Reardon beat White 10-5

1983 (*Professional Players Tournament*)
Qualifying: G. Ganim Jr beat G. Cripsey 5-4; S. Duggan beat M. Darrington 5-4; T. Jones beat W. Oliver 5-2; D. French beat N. Foulds 5-2; B. Bennett beat B. Demarco 5-4; P. Burke beat G. Foulds 5-4; V. Harris *wo* P. Mifsud *scr*; P. Medati beat D. Hughes 5-1; T. Murphy beat P. Browne 5-2; J. Parrott beat P. Watchorn 5-0; D. Sheehan beat P. Houlihan 5-2; M. Morra beat J. Hargreaves 5-0; D. Greaves beat R. Andrewartha 5-2; W. King beat B. Harris 5-3; P. Morgan beat M. Gibson 5-4

First round: R. Reardon beat Ganim 5-4; C. Thorburn beat V. Harris 5-1; J. Meadowcroft beat C. Roscoe 5-4; Duggan beat J. Dunning 5-2; J. Virgo beat French 5-4; J. Spencer beat I. Black 5-2; W. Thorne beat C. Everton 5-1; C. Wilson beat Bennett 5-1; T. Griffiths beat L. Dodd 5-3; J. White beat I. Williamson 5-2; Parrott beat P. Fagan 5-2; J. Johnson beat Burke 5-3; E. Hughes beat E. Sinclair 5-4; M. Fisher beat F. Davis 5-4; B. Werbeniuk beat T. Jones 5-4; E. Charlton beat E. McLaughlin 5-0; M. Watterson beat A. Higgins 5-2; K. Stevens beat R. Edmonds 5-1; D. Martin beat J. Fitzmaurice 5-0; T. Murphy beat M. Macleod 5-0; J. Campbell beat D. Mountjoy 5-3; David Taylor beat P. Morgan 5-3; G. Miles beat M. Gauvreau 5-3; M. Wildman beat F. Jonik 5-4; G. Scott beat Dennis Taylor 5-4; T. Meo beat W. King 5-2; S. Francisco beat M. Morra 5-3; D. Reynolds beat D. Greaves 5-1; R. Williams beat D. Sheehan 5-1; M. Hallett beat B. Kelly 5-0; A. Knowles beat P. Medati 5-1; S. Davis beat J. Donnelly 5-1

Second round: Reardon beat Duggan 5-2; Thorburn beat Meadowcroft 5-1; Thorne beat Spencer 5-1; Wilson beat Virgo 5-2; Griffiths beat Parrot 5-1; Johnson beat White 5-3; E. Hughes beat Werbeniuk 5-0; Charlton beat Fisher 5-4; Stevens beat Murphy 5-1; Martin beat Watterson 5-4; Wildman beat David Taylor 5-3; Campbell beat Miles 5-2; Meo beat Reynolds 5-0; S. Francisco beat Scott 5-1; Knowles beat Williams 5-4; Hallett beat S. Davis 5-2

Third round: Thorne beat Reardon 5-3; Thorburn beat Wilson 5-3; E. Hughes beat Griffiths 5-2; Johnson beat Charlton 5-0; Stevens beat Wildman 5-0; Campbell beat Martin 5-0; Knowles beat S. Francisco 5-0; Meo beat Hallett 5-3

Quarter-finals: Johnson beat Thorburn 5-1; Thorne beat E. Hughes 5-1; Meo beat Stevens 5-3; Knowles beat Campbell 5-3

Semi-finals: Knowles beat Thorne 9-7; Johnson beat Meo 9-6

Final: Knowles beat Johnson 9-8

1984

Qualifying: I. Williamson beat P. Thornley 5-2; J. Donnelly beat J. Hargreaves 5-4; B. Demarco *wo* P. Fagan *scr*; V. Harris beat F. Davis 5-1; J. Dunning beat D. Hughes 5-0; D. O'Kane beat B. Kelly 5-4; M. Gauvreau beat R. Foldvari 5-2; E. McLaughlin beat S. Longworth 5-2; M. Morra beat G. Cripsey 5-3; S. Duggan beat P. Browne 5-2; D. Sheehan *wo* L. Condo *scr*; Sheehan beat B. Mikkelsen 5-3; P. Burke beat M. Darrington 5-3; D. Chalmers beat R. Andrewartha 5-2; W. King beat D. Greaves 5-0; P. Medati beat L. Dodd 5-4; R. Chaperon beat A. Kearney 5-1; Chaperon beat M. Gibson 5-4; P. Francisco beat I. Black 5-4; G. Rigitano beat R. Edmonds 5-3; M. Bradley beat F. Jonik 5-1; W. Jones beat M. Watterson 5-3; John Rea beat J. Fitzmaurice 5-2; R. Bales *wo* J. Wych *scr*; S. Newbury beat M. Fisher 5-0; W. Oliver beat B. Bennett 5-3; C. Everton beat P. Houlihan 5-3; J. McLaughlin beat J. Meadowcroft 5-1; T. Chappel beat G. Scott 5-1; T. Murphy beat G. Foulds 5-1; T. Jones beat E. Sinclair 5-4; C. Roscoe beat D. French 5-0; P. Watchorn *wo* P. Morgan *scr*; D. Fowler *wo* P. Mifsud *scr*

First round: A. Knowles beat V. Harris 5-1; Dunning beat P. Mans 5-4; Williamson beat B. Werbeniuk 5-2; J. Johnson beat Medati 5-1; W. Thorne beat Newbury 5-2; M. Macleod beat King 5-4; N. Foulds beat Demarco 5-2; T. Jones beat T. Griffiths 5-3; R. Reardon beat Roscoe 5-1; C. Wilson beat Donnelly 5-2; Dennis Taylor beat Watchorn 5-1; J. Virgo beat Bradley 5-0; A. Higgins beat Bales 5-1; M. Hallett beat Sheehan 5-1; R. Williams beat Chalmers 5-0; K. Stevens beat Chappel 5-3; C. Thorburn beat Rigitano 5-4; J. Campbell beat W. Jones 5-4; T. Meo beat Burke 5-1; D. Martin beat Chaperon 5-4; D. Mountjoy beat E. McLaughlin 5-4; M. Wildman beat J. McLaughlin 5-3; J. Parrott beat Gauvreau 5-3; E. Charlton beat Everton 5-1; J. White beat Oliver 5-1; S. Francisco beat Duggan 5-3; P. Francisco beat J. Spencer 5-2; D. Reynolds beat Fowler 5-2; David Taylor beat O'Kane 5-1; John Rea beat E. Hughes 5-4; G. Miles beat Murphy 5-3; S. Davis beat Morra 5-2

Second round: Knowles beat Dunning 5-1; Williamson beat Johnson 5-4; Thorne beat Macleod 5-3; N. Foulds beat T. Jones 5-0; Reardon beat Wilson 5-4; Dennis Taylor beat Virgo 5-3; Hallett beat Higgins 5-3; Stevens beat Williams 5-3; Thorburn beat Campbell 5-1; Meo beat Martin 5-4; Mountjoy beat Wildman 5-0; Charlton beat Parrott 5-1; S. Francisco beat White 5-1; David Taylor beat John Rea 5-1; S. Davis beat Miles 5-0; Reynolds beat P. Francisco 5-4

Third round: Knowles beat Williamson 5-2; N. Foulds beat Thorne 5-1; Dennis Taylor beat Reardon 5-3; Stevens beat Hallett 5-3; Thorburn beat Meo 5-4; Mountjoy beat Charlton 5-4; Reynolds beat S. Francisco 5-1; S. Davis beat David Taylor 5-1

Quarter-finals: N. Foulds beat Knowles 5-2; Dennis Taylor beat Stevens 5-2; Thorburn beat Mountjoy 5-3; S. Davis beat Reynolds 5-0

Semi-finals: Dennis Taylor beat N. Foulds 9-3; Thorburn beat S. Davis 9-7

Final: Dennis Taylor beat Thorburn 10-2

CORAL UK OPEN

Coral, the bookmakers, have sponsored this tournament since 1978 after Super Crystalate had instigated a UK Championship the previous year. Over the years, the qualifications for entry to the event have varied from UK passport holders only to anyone resident in this country but, for the first time in 1984, it became a ranking tournament when it was thrown open to all professionals. It is, strictly, the UK Open not the UK Championship.

Under Coral's banner it has been held every year at Preston Guild Hall although the 1977 event evoked memories of past world finals when it was staged at the Tower Circus, Blackpool.

Because of its long term initial contract, the event does not carry the wealth in prize-money of more recently sponsored ranking tournaments but gains prestige through its seniority and through being the only event, apart from the World Championship, in which no match is played over fewer than the best of 17 frames.

1977 (*Super Crystalate UK Championship*)
First round: J. Virgo *wo* J. Barrie *scr*; C. Ross beat J. Karnehm 5-4; P. Fagan beat Jack Rea 5-1; J. Meadowcroft beat P. Houlihan 5-1; D. Mountjoy beat R. Andrewartha 5-2; W. Thorne beat B. Bennett 5-1; J. Dunning beat M. Parkin 5-4; David Taylor beat D. Greaves 5-4

Second round: Virgo beat Dennis Taylor 5-2; G. Miles beat Ross 5-1; Fagan beat F. Davis 5-0; Meadowcroft beat R. Reardon 5-4; Mountjoy beat J. Spencer 5-3; Thorne beat R. Williams 5-4; Dunning *wo* J. Pulman *scr*; A. Higgins beat David Taylor 5-4

Quarter-finals: Virgo beat Miles 5-2; Fagan beat Meadowcroft 5-4; Mountjoy beat Thorne 5-4; Higgins beat Dunning 5-0

Semi-finals: Fagan beat Virgo 9-8; Mountjoy beat Higgins 9-2

Final: Fagan beat Mountjoy 12-9

1978
Qualifying: W. Thorne beat B. Bennett 9-4; R. Andrewartha beat P. Houlihan 9-3; D. Mountjoy beat J. Barrie 9-5; R. Williams beat T. Griffiths 9-8; J. Dunning beat D. Greaves 9-3; J. Virgo beat R. Edmonds 9-4; David Taylor beat M. Parkin 9-2; J. Meadowcroft beat Jack Rea 9-5

First round: David Taylor beat Fagan 9-7; Virgo beat J. Pulman 9-3; F. Davis beat Dunning 9-2; A. Higgins beat Meadowcroft 9-6; Thorne beat R. Reardon 9-6; G. Miles beat Williams 9-8; Mountjoy beat Dennis Taylor 9-4; Andrewartha beat J. Spencer 9-8

Quarter-finals: David Taylor beat Virgo 9-2; Higgins beat F. Davis 9-4; Miles beat Thorne 9-1; Mountjoy beat Andrewartha 9-4

Semi-finals: David Taylor beat Higgins 9-5; Mountjoy beat Miles 9-1

Final: Mountjoy beat David Taylor 15-9

1979
Qualifying: Jack Rea beat B. Bennett 9-8; M. Hallett beat M. Parkin 9-1; J. Dunning beat D. Greaves 9-8

First round: W. Thorne beat R. Andrewartha 9-4; P. Houlihan beat Jack Rea 9-3; S. Davis beat Dunning 9-3; P. Fagan beat Hallett 9-4; B. Werbeniuk beat J. Johnson 9-3; R. Edmonds beat J. Meadowcroft 9-3; T. Meo beat David Taylor 9-7; C. Wilson beat J. Pulman 9-7

Second round: S. Davis beat D. Mountjoy 9-5; T. Griffiths beat Wilson 9-4; A. Higgins beat Houlihan 9-3; Fagan beat G. Miles 9-5; Werbeniuk beat J. Spencer 9-8; Dennis Taylor beat Thorne 9-8; J. Virgo beat Meo 9-6; Edmonds beat F. Davis 9-6

Quarter-finals: Werbeniuk beat Edmonds 9-8; Dennis Taylor beat Fagan 9-6; Virgo beat S. Davis 9-7; Griffiths beat Higgins 9-7

Semi-finals: Virgo beat Dennis Taylor 9-4; Griffiths beat Werbeniuk 9-3

Final: Virgo beat Griffiths 14-13

1980
Preliminary round: M. Hallett beat B. Bennett 9-4; S. Hood beat C. Ross 9-3

Qualifying: Hallett beat R. Edmonds 9-8; E. Sinclair beat K. Kennerley 9-1; M. Wildman beat C. Wilson 9-8; J. Meadowcroft beat D. Greaves 9-1; R. Andrewartha beat A. Knowles 9-8; R. Williams beat J. Barrie 9-1; J. Johnson beat J. Dunning 9-6; T. Meo beat Hood 9-5

First round: Meo beat P. Houlihan 9-1; S. Davis beat Hallett 9-1; P. Fagan beat Johnson 9-4; Sinclair beat G. Miles 9-5; Thorne beat Meadowcroft 9-1; Wildman beat J. Spencer 9-7; Williams beat D. Mountjoy 9-8; Andrewartha beat J. Pulman 9-6

Second round: Meo beat J. Virgo 9-1; S. Davis beat B. Werbeniuk 9-3; Dennis Taylor beat Sinclair 9-6; T. Griffiths beat Fagan 9-8; A. Higgins beat Thorne 9-7; F. Davis beat Wildman 9-6; R. Reardon beat Andrewartha 9-3; Williams beat David Taylor 9-7

Quarter-finals: S. Davis beat Meo 9-5; Griffiths beat Dennis Taylor 9-2; Higgins beat F. Davis 9-6; Reardon beat Williams 9-4

Semi-finals: S. Davis beat Griffiths 9-0; Higgins beat Reardon 9-7

Final: S. Davis beat Higgins 16-6

1981
Qualifying groups
1   P. Medati beat E. McLaughlin 9-5; Medati beat J. Donnelly 9-7;
    W. Thorne beat Medati 9-6
2   M. Hallett beat V. Harris 9-4; Hallett beat D. Hughes 9-6; Hallett beat
    P. Fagan 9-5
3   M. Gibson beat J. Fitzmaurice 9-6; C. Everton beat Gibson 9-7; J. White
    beat Everton 9-4
4   J. Johnson beat T. Murphy 9-1; M. Watterson beat B. Bennett 9-4;
    Johnson beat Watterson 9-3; Johnson beat C. Wilson 9-5
5   P. Houlihan beat K. Kennerley 9-1; Houlihan beat I. Black 9-4; Houlihan
    beat J. Meadowcroft 9-4
6   G. Foulds beat B. Kelly 9-7; A. Knowles beat Foulds 9-1
7   E. Sinclair beat M. Wildman 9-8; Sinclair beat S. Hood 9-0; D. Martin beat
    Sinclair 9-7
8   R. Williams beat D. French 9-3; C. Roscoe beat M. Macleod 9-7; Williams
    beat Roscoe 9-4; Williams beat J. Dunning 9-4

First round: Thorne beat R. Edmonds 9-4; K. Stevens beat Hallett 9-4; White
beat J. Virgo 9-6; Johnson beat J. Spencer 9-5; G. Miles beat Houlihan 9-5;
Knowles beat F. Davis 9-6; A. Higgins beat Martin 9-7; T. Meo beat Williams
9-8

Second round: S. Davis beat Thorne 9-2; B. Werbeniuk beat Stevens 9-7; White
beat Dennis Taylor 9-5; R. Reardon beat Johnson 9-7; T. Griffiths beat Miles
9-4; Knowles beat D. Mountjoy 9-6; Higgins beat David Taylor 9-5; Meo beat
C. Thorburn 9-6

Quarter-finals: S. Davis beat Werbeniuk 9-5; White beat Reardon 9-8; Griffiths
beat Knowles 9-5; Meo beat Higgins 9-4

Semi-finals: S. Davis beat White 9-0; Griffiths beat Meo 9-3

Final: S. Davis beat Griffiths 16-3

1982
Qualifying groups
1   T. Meo beat G. Scott 9-5
2   C. Wilson beat E. McLaughlin 9-6
3   D. Martin beat M. Macleod 9-6
4   J. Meadowcroft beat D. Hughes 9-8
5   J. Donnelly beat C. Ross 9-5
6   P. Houlihan *wo* J. Dunning *scr*
7   M. Hallett beat B. Demarco 9-1
8   B. Kelly beat J. Fitzmaurice 9-0
9   G. Foulds beat M. Gibson 9-2; R. Williams beat Foulds 9-7
10   V. Harris beat M. Owen 9-4; J. Johnson beat Harris 9-8
11   T. Murphy beat C. Everton 9-4; E. Sinclair beat Murphy 9-5
12   B. Harris beat G. Cripsey 9-6; Harris beat M. Watterson 9-3
13   M. Fisher beat I. Black 9-3; Fisher beat R. Edmonds 9-8

14   L. Dodd beat I. Williamson 9-1; Dodd beat D. French 9-7
15   B. Bennett *wo* J. Phillips *scr*; P. Medati beat Bennett 9-1
16   C. Roscoe beat Jack Rea 9-6; M. Wildman beat Roscoe 9-4

First round: S. Davis beat Williams 9-6; P. Fagan beat B. Harris 9-6;
T. Griffiths beat Johnson 9-1; Dennis Taylor beat Meadowcroft 9-7; David
Taylor beat Dodd 9-7; Meo beat G. Miles 9-4; J. Virgo beat Kelly 9-2; D.
Mountjoy beat Houlihan 9-3; R. Reardon beat Wildman 9-5; Hallett beat
F. Davis 9-7; Wilson beat W. Thorne 9-7; J. White beat Medati 9-7; J. Spencer
beat Sinclair 9-8; A. Knowles beat Donnelly 9-6; D. Reynolds beat Fisher 9-6;
A. Higgins beat Martin 9-7

Second round: S. Davis beat Fagan 9-3; Griffiths beat Dennis Taylor 9-7; Meo
beat David Taylor 9-6; Virgo beat Mountjoy 9-5; Reardon beat Hallett 9-8;
White beat Wilson 9-5; Spencer beat Knowles 9-6; Higgins beat Reynolds 9-8

Quarter-finals: Griffiths beat S. Davis 9-6; Meo beat Virgo 9-6; Reardon beat
White 9-8; Higgins beat Spencer 9-5

Semi-finals: Griffiths beat Meo 9-7; Higgins beat Reardon 9-6

Final: Griffiths beat Higgins 16-15

1983
Qualifying groups
1   J. Johnson beat M. Gibson 9-6
2   T. Jones beat E. Sinclair 9-3
3   M. Wildman beat D. Greaves 9-5
4   M. Macleod beat B. Bennett 9-0
5   M. Watterson beat C. Everton 9-6; Watterson beat F. Davis 9-6
6   M. Darrington beat G. Cripsey 9-3; M. Hallett beat Darrington 9-1
7   N. Foulds beat C. Roscoe 9-2; Foulds beat J. Meadowcroft 9-2
8   V. Harris beat P. Houlihan 9-6; R. Williams beat Harris 9-6
9   D. French beat Jack Rea 9-5; D. Martin beat French 9-3
10   G. Foulds beat S. Duggan 9-8; Foulds beat L. Dodd 9-7
11   J. Parrott beat G. Scott 9-7; Parrott beat M. Fisher 9-0
12   R. Andrewartha beat W. Oliver 9-1; J. Dunning beat Andrewartha 9-2
13   T. Murphy beat B. Demarco 9-4; Murphy beat Donnelly 9-4
14   P. Medati beat D. Hughes 9-3; Medati beat R. Edmonds 9-7
15   B. Harris beat E. McLaughlin 9-8; Harris beat J. Fitzmaurice 9-3
16   I. Williamson beat J. Hargreaves 9-4; I. Black beat Williamson 9-6

First round: T. Griffiths beat Martin 9-4; Hallett beat G. Miles 9-4; Johnson
beat J. Virgo 9-6; David Taylor beat N. Foulds 9-4; A. Knowles beat J. Jones
9-5; D. Mountjoy beat Watterson 9-2; A. Higgins beat Macleod 9-6; Medati
beat D. Reynolds 9-3; C. Wilson beat Williams 9-4; R. Reardon beat B. Harris
9-7; Dennis Taylor beat Murphy 9-6; J. White beat Black 9-1; J. Spencer beat
Dunning 9-7; T. Meo beat Parrott 9-7; W. Thorne beat Wildman 9-5; S. Davis
beat G. Foulds 9-1

Second round: Griffiths beat Hallett 9-5; Johnson beat David Taylor 9-3; Knowles beat Mountjoy 9-5; Higgins beat Medati 9-1; Reardon beat Wilson 9-4; White beat Dennis Taylor 9-4; Meo beat Spencer 9-5; S. Davis beat Thorne 9-3

Quarter-finals: White beat Reardon 9-4; Griffiths beat Johnson 9-2; Higgins beat Knowles 9-5; S. Davis beat Meo 9-4

Semi-finals: Higgins beat Griffiths 9-4; S. Davis beat White 9-4

Final: Higgins beat S. Davis 16-15

1984
Qualifying groups
 1   T. Jones beat R. Chaperon 9-1; Jones beat P. Fagan 9-2; Jones beat M. Wildman 9-2
 2   P. Watchorn beat B. Harris 9-7; Watchorn beat C. Everton 9-6; M. Fisher beat Watchorn 9-5; R. Williams beat Fisher 9-8
 3   R. Foldvari beat D. Greaves 9-5; G. Cripsey beat Foldvari 9-7; J. Fitzmaurice beat Cripsey 9-8; J. Parrott beat Fitzmaurice 9-6
 4   P. Francisco beat D. Sheehan 9-5; P. Francisco beat I. Williamson 9-2; E. Sinclair beat P. Francisco 9-8; S. Francisco beat Sinclair 9-4
 5   D. Fowler beat B. Demarco 9-3; Fowler beat W. Oliver 9-3; Fowler beat F. Davis 9-4; Fowler beat N. Foulds 9-6
 6   D. O'Kane beat W. Jones 9-7; O'Kane beat S. Duggan 9-6; G. Scott beat O'Kane 9-7; M. Macleod beat Scott 9-5
 7   S. Newbury beat G. Rigitano 9-6; Newbury beat F. Jonik 9-3; L. Dodd beat Newbury 9-6; C. Wilson beat Dodd 9-8
 8   J. McLaughlin beat D. French 9-3; McLaughlin *wo* P. Morgan *scr*; McLaughlin beat C. Roscoe 9-8; McLaughlin beat G. Miles 9-8
 9   R. Bales beat D. Chalmers 9-2; Bales beat E. McLaughlin 9-4; M. Gauvreau beat Bales 9-8; Gauvreau beat P. Mans 9-6
10   G. Foulds beat D. Hughes 9-7; P. Browne beat Foulds 9-5; W. King beat Browne 9-5; King beat J. Virgo 9-4
11   John Rea beat B. Bennett 9-5; Rea beat F. Dunning 9-3; Rea beat R. Edmonds 9-6; J. Johnson beat Rea 9-6
12   T. Chappel beat P. Houlihan 9-3; Chappel beat I. Black 9-3; Chappel *wo* R. Andrewartha *scr*; Chappel beat D. Reynolds 9-6
13   J. Hargreaves beat P. Medati 9-6; M. Gibson beat Hargreaves 9-8; J. Donnelly beat Gibson 9-6; J. Campbell beat Donnelly 9-6
14   M. Bradley beat V. Harris 9-8; Bradley beat B. Kelly 9-6; Bradley beat J. Meadowcroft 9-7; M. Hallett beat Bradley 9-8
15   S. Longworth beat M. Darrington 9-5; Longworth beat P. Burke 9-4; M. Morra beat Longworth 9-1; E. Hughes beat Morra 9-8
16   T. Murphy beat A. Kearney 9-2; Murphy beat M. Watterson 9-4; Murphy beat D. Martin 9-8

First round: A. Higgins beat T. Jones 9-7; S. Davis beat Murphy 9-1; J. White beat Campbell 9-7; Williams beat B. Werbeniuk 9-1; W. Thorne beat Parrott 9-7; E. Charlton beat S. Francisco 9-4; D. Mountjoy beat Hallett 9-2; T. Meo

beat E. Hughes 9-4; R. Reardon beat Fowler 9-2; K. Stevens beat Chappel 9-7;
Dennis Taylor beat King 9-5; Wilson beat T. Griffiths 9-6; Johnson beat
J. Spencer 9-6; David Taylor beat Macleod 9-6; A. Knowles beat Gauvreau 9-5;
C. Thorburn beat J. McLaughlin 9-4

Second round: Thorne beat Charlton 9-7; White beat Mountjoy 9-2; Higgins
beat Williams 9-7; Stevens beat Johnson 9-2; Reardon beat David Taylor 9-4;
Thorburn beat Wilson 9-3; Knowles beat Dennis Taylor 9-2; S. Davis beat Meo
9-7

Quarter-finals: Higgins beat Thorne 9-5; S. Davis beat White 9-4; Thorburn
beat Reardon 9-8; Stevens beat Knowles 9-7

Semi-finals: Higgins beat Thorburn 9-7; S. Davis beat Stevens 9-2

Final: S. Davis beat Higgins 16-8

HOFMEISTER WORLD DOUBLES CHAMPIONSHIP

Though pairs snooker had long been popular at grass roots amateur
level, it was not until 1982 that professional snooker gained a World
Doubles Championship when Hofmeister sponsored the inaugural
event at Crystal Palace.

The venue was completely inappropriate to Snooker's intimate, cosy
ambience but the Championship proved popular with television
audiences. The following season it moved to the better suited Derngate
Centre in Northampton, which is still its home, although the same two
players took the title – Steve Davis and Tony Meo. Last season they
were beaten in the semi-finals by Alex Higgins and Jimmy White.

One of the Championship's fascinations is who is playing with
whom. Players are free to choose any professional as their partner and
while some duos like Davis and Meo have been together for three
years, some find they are unsuited to each other and split up after just
one attempt.

The event is televised by ITV.

1982
Qualifying groups
1   J. Johnson & C. Wilson *wo* M. Morra & F. Jonik *scr*; Johnson & Wilson
    beat R. Edmonds & J. Meadowcroft 6-4; R. Reardon & J. Spencer beat
    Johnson & Wilson 6-2
2   D. Martin & Dennis Taylor beat L. Dodd & D. French 6-2; T. Griffiths &
    D. Mountjoy beat Martin & Taylor 6-0
3   F. Davis & P. Medati beat J. Dunning & B. Demarco 6-0; A. Higgins &
    E. Charlton beat Davis & Medati 6-3

4   P. Houlihan & B. Bennett beat E. Sinclair & I. Black 6-2; D. Reynolds &
     M. Watterson beat Houlihan & Bennett 6-3; S. Davis & T. Meo beat
     Reynolds & Watterson 6-3
5   M. Hallett & G. Cripsey beat M. Macleod & E. McLaughlin 6-3; Hallett &
     Cripsey beat P. Fagan & G. Foulds 6-2; K. Stevens & J. Wych beat Hallett
     & Cripsey 6-4
6   V. Harris & I. Williamson beat T. Murphy & E. Hughes 6-1; R. Williams
     & J. Fitzmaurice beat Harris & Williamson 6-1; G. Miles & B. Werbeniuk
     beat Williams & Fitzmaurice 6-5
7   J. White & A. Knowles beat G. Scott & D. Hughes 6-2; White & Knowles
     beat David Taylor & W. Thorne 6-1
8   M. Fisher & M. Wildman beat C. Everton & C. Roscoe 6-3; Fisher &
     Wildman beat J. Donnelly & M. Gibson 6-5; C. Thorburn & J. Virgo beat
     Fisher & Wildman 6-2

First round: Griffiths & Mountjoy beat Stevens & Wych 6-1; S. Davis & Meo
beat Thorburn & Virgo 6-2; White & Knowles beat Reardon & Spencer 6-2;
Higgins & Charlton beat Miles & Werbeniuk 6-3

Semi-finals: Griffiths & Mountjoy beat Charlton & Higgins 10-7; S. Davis &
Meo beat White & Knowles 10-5

Final: S. Davis & Meo beat Griffiths & Mountjoy 13-2

1983
Preliminary round: B. Bennett & P. Houlihan beat M. Gibson & M. Macleod
5-2; S. Duggan & J. Hargreaves beat W. Oliver & P. Browne 5-1; G. Scott &
J. Parrott beat G. Foulds & N. Foulds 5-4; B. Harris & M. Morra beat
D. Sheehan & E. McLaughlin 5-2

Qualifying: T. Murphy & P. Morgan beat P. Burke & D. Martin 5-4;
J. Fitzmaurice & V. Harris beat Bennett & Houlihan 5-4; J. Donnelly &
C. Roscoe beat W. King & J. Campbell 5-3; Duggan & Hargreaves beat
D. Hughes & B. Kelly 5-0; J. Dunning & B. Demarco beat M. Hallett & G.
Cripsey 5-4; R. Edmonds & J. Meadowcroft beat D. French & C. Everton 5-2;
E. Hughes & L. Dodd beat Scott & Parrott 5-2; B. Harris & Morra beat
M. Darrington & I. Williamson 5-1

First round: Murphy & Morgan beat I. Black & E. Sinclair 5-1; Dennis Taylor
& R. Williams beat Fitzmaurice & V. Harris 5-1; T. Jones & S. Francisco beat
Donnelly & Roscoe 5-2; G. Miles & G. Ganim beat Duggan & Hargreaves 5-3;
F. Davis & M. Watterson beat Dunning & Demarco 5-3; D. Reynolds and
P. Fagan beat Edmonds & Meadowcroft 5-0; E. Hughes & Dodd beat
C. Wilson & J. Johnson 5-1; B. Harris & Morra beat M. Fisher and
M. Wildman 5-2

Second round: S. Davis & T. Meo beat Murphy & Morgan 5-2; David Taylor &
W. Thorne beat Dennis Taylor & Williams 5-4; E. Charlton & B. Werbeniuk
beat T. Jones & S. Francisco 5-3; A. Higgins & K. Stevens *wo* Miles & Ganim
scr; R. Reardon & J. Spencer beat F. Davis & Watterson 5-2; J. Virgo &
C. Thorburn beat Reynolds & Fagan 5-2; T. Griffiths & D. Mountjoy beat E.
Hughes & Dodd 5-3; A. Knowles & J. White beat B. Harris & Morra 5-4

Quarter-finals: S. Davis & Meo beat David Taylor & Thorne 5-3; Charlton & Werbeniuk beat Higgins & Stevens 5-1; Thorburn & Virgo beat Reardon & Spencer 5-0; Knowles & White beat Griffiths & Mountjoy 5-0

Semi-finals: S. Davis & Meo beat Charlton & Werbeniuk 9-1; Knowles & White beat Thorburn & Virgo 9-7

Final: S. Davis & Meo beat Knowles & White 10-2

1984

Qualifying: J. Donnelly & C. Roscoe beat S. Longworth & D. French 5-3; D. Chalmers & J. McLaughlin beat P. Fagan & B. Harris 5-0; M. Morra & M. Bradley beat I. Williamson & M. Darrington 5-1; G. Miles & P. Francisco beat J. Hargreaves & S. Duggan 5-1; T. Chappel & S. Newbury beat G. Rigitano & G. Scott 5-0; M. Gauvreau & D. Fowler beat B. Bennett & P. Houlihan 5-1; R. Bales & W. Oliver beat John Rea & E. McLaughlin 5-2; J. Meadowcroft & R. Edmonds beat F. Jonik and R. Chaperon 5-4; V. Harris & J. Fitzmaurice beat P. Burke and B. Kelly 5-2; D. Sheehan & P. Watchorn beat M. Macleod & M. Gibson 5-0; F. Davis & M. Watterson beat C. Everton & R. Foldvari 5-3; P. Medati & P. Browne beat I. Black & E. Sinclair 5-1; D. Hughes & A. Kearney *wo* J. Dunning & B. Demarco *scr*

First round: D. Mountjoy & W. Jones beat Chappel & Newbury 5-1; S. Francisco & T. Jones beat J. Campbell and W. King 5-4; A. Higgins & J. White beat D. Martin & G. Cripsey 5-2; David Taylor & M. Hallett beat E. Hughes & L. Dodd 5-3; P. Francisco & Miles beat C. Wilson & J. Johnson 5-4; D. Reynolds & D. O'Kane beat Gauvreau & Fowler 5-4; Dennis Taylor & R. Williams beat Medati & Browne 5-0; Bales & Oliver beat G. Foulds and N. Foulds 5-2; S. Davis & T. Meo beat D. Hughes & Kearney 5-2; R. Reardon & T. Murphy beat F. Davis & Watterson 5-2; M. Fisher & M. Wildman beat Edmonds & Meadowcroft 5-3; E. Charlton & B. Werbeniuk beat Sheehan & Watchorn 5-2; T. Griffiths & J. Parrott beat Chalmers & J. McLaughlin 5-0; J. Virgo & K. Stevens beat Morra & Bradley 5-1; A. Knowles & J. Spencer beat V. Harris & Fitzmaurice 5-2

Second round: S. Davis & Meo beat Miles & P. Francisco 5-2; Virgo & Stevens beat Dennis Taylor & Williams 5-3; Higgins & White beat Reynolds & O'Kane 5-4; Thorburn & Thorne beat Mountjoy & W. Jones 5-3; Reardon & Murphy beat S. Francisco & T. Jones 5-3; Griffiths & Parrot beat Bales & Oliver 5-4; David Taylor & Hallett beat Charlton & Werbeniuk 5-4; Knowles & Spencer beat Fisher & Wildman 5-4

Quarter-finals: Knowles & Spencer beat Reardon & Murphy 5-4; Higgins & White beat Griffiths & Parrott 5-2; Thorburn & Thorne beat Virgo & Stevens 5-3; S. Davis & Meo beat Hallett & David Taylor 5-1

Semi-finals: Thorburn & Thorne beat Knowles & Spencer 9-1; Higgins & White beat S. Davis & Meo 9-6

Final: Higgins & White beat Thorburn & Thorne 10-2

MERCANTILE CREDIT CLASSIC

The nature, status and sponsorship of this event has changed several times since 1980 when it was born as the Wilsons Classic, an invitation tournament recorded by Granada Television for later showing.

When the event was networked for the first time in 1982, it was still by invitation but it had a new sponsor, the Russian car company, Lada. Stepping in at the last moment, Lada by chance achieved an enormous bonus when, during his first round match at Oldham Civic Centre, Steve Davis compiled the first televised maximum break.

The event moved to its present home, the Spectrum Arena, Warrington, in 1983 and a year later earned the status of a world ranking tournament when it was thrown open to all professionals. 1984, though, was to be Lada's last year and in 1985 the city finance house, Mercantile Credit, stepped in with a total prize fund of £200,000.

Willie Thorne won his first major title and £40,000 by beating Steve Davis and Cliff Thorburn in the last two rounds.

1980 (Jan) (*Wilsons Classic*)
Final: J. Spencer beat A. Higgins 4-3

1980 (Dec) (*Wilsons Classic*)
Final: S. Davis beat Dennis Taylor 4-1

1982 (*Lada Classic*)
First round: T. Griffiths beat C. Thorburn 5-1; A. Higgins beat Dennis Taylor 5-1; R. Reardon beat David Taylor 5-1; S. Davis beat J. Spencer 5-2

Semi-finals: Griffiths beat Higgins 5-1; S. Davis beat Reardon 5-4

Final: Griffiths beat S. Davis 9-8

1983 (*Lada Classic*)
First round: E. Charlton beat J. Virgo 5-2; J. Spencer beat R. Reardon 5-3; C. Thorburn beat C. Wilson 5-3; D. Mountjoy beat T. Griffiths 5-1; David Taylor beat J. White 5-3; B. Werbeniuk beat A. Higgins 5-4; K. Stevens beat A. Knowles 5-0; S. Davis beat Dennis Taylor 5-2

Quarter-finals: Spencer beat David Taylor 5-2; Werbeniuk beat Mountjoy 5-2; Stevens beat Thorburn 5-3; S. Davis beat Charlton 5-4

Semi-finals: S. Davis beat Spencer 5-4; Werbeniuk beat Stevens 5-2

Final: S. Davis beat Werbeniuk 9-5

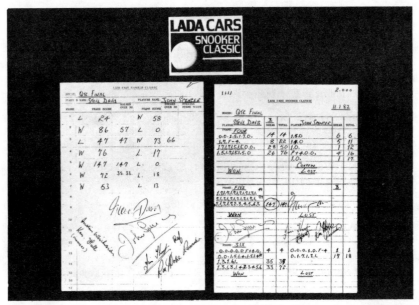

The recorder's sheet showing Steve Davis's break of 147, the first maximum made in a tournament on television.

1984 *(Lada Classic)*

First qualifying round: G. Foulds beat M. Gauvreau 5-2; B. Demarco beat M. Gibson 5-2; N. Foulds beat P. Houlihan 5-3; M. Morra beat P. Burke 5-2; G. Ganim beat D. Hughes 5-2; I. Williamson beat D. French 5-1; J. Hargreaves beat W. King 5-3; W. Oliver beat D. Sheehan 5-3; T. Jones beat P. Mifsud 5-3; P. Morgan beat M. Darrington 5-3; G. Cripsey beat V. Harris 5-4; J. Parrott beat B. Bennett 5-0; P. Browne beat D. Greaves 5-2; P. Watchorn beat R. Andrewartha 5-2; S. Duggan beat B. Harris 5-2; P. Medati beat T. Murphy 5-4

Second qualifying round: E. McLaughlin beat G. Foulds 5-1; G. Scott beat Demarco 5-2; N. Foulds beat Jack Rea 5-1; Morra beat C. Everton 5-0; C. Roscoe beat Ganim 5-3; F. Jonik beat Williamson 5-1; Hargreaves beat B. Kelly 5-4; Oliver beat J. Donnelly 5-4; Morgan beat M. Watterson 5-3; T. Jones beat I. Black 5-0; J. Campbell beat Cripsey 5-3; Parrott beat J. Fitzmaurice 5-2; R. Edmonds beat Browne 5-1; M. Fisher beat Watchorn 5-4; L. Dodd beat Duggan 5-2; E. Hughes beat Medati 5-1

Third qualifying round: E. McLaughlin beat W. Thorne 5-3; D. Reynolds beat Scott 5-3; C. Wilson beat N. Foulds 5-4; S. Francisco beat Morra 5-1; Roscoe beat G. Miles 5-2; J. Johnson beat Jonik 5-2; M. Wildman beat Hargreaves 5-1; P. Fagan beat Oliver 5-1; E. Sinclair beat Morgan 5-2; M. Macleod beat T. Jones 5-2; Campbell beat F. Davis 5-0; Parrott beat D. Martin 5-1; R. Williams beat Edmonds 5-1; J. Meadowcroft beat Fisher 5-0; M. Hallett beat Dodd 5-1; E. Hughes beat J. Dunning 5-4

First round: K. Stevens beat E. McLaughlin 5-4; T. Griffiths beat Reynolds 5-2; E. Charlton beat Wilson 5-0; S. Francisco beat C. Thorburn 5-1; Roscoe beat B. Werbeniuk 5-4; J. Spencer beat Johnson 5-4; Wildman beat J. Virgo 5-2; A. Higgins beat Fagan 5-3; S. Davis beat Sinclair 5-2; Macleod beat David Taylor 5-4; J. White beat Campbell 5-1; Parrott beat D. Mountjoy 5-4; Williams beat R. Reardon 5-4; T. Meo beat Meadowcroft 5-1; Hallett beat Dennis Taylor 5-4; A. Knowles beat E. Hughes 5-1

Second round: S. Davis beat Spencer 5-1; Charlton beat White 5-2; Wildman beat S. Francisco 5-1; Knowles beat Hallett 5-3; Stevens beat Macleod 5-1; Griffiths beat Roscoe 5-2; Meo beat Williams 5-3; Parrot beat Higgins 5-2

Quarter-finals: Wildman beat Charlton 5-4; S. Davis beat Griffiths 5-4; Meo beat Stevens 5-2; Parrott beat Knowles 5-1

Semi-finals: Meo beat Wildman 5-3; S. Davis beat Parrott 5-4

Final: S. Davis beat Meo 9-8

1985
Preliminary round: P. Watchorn beat D. Hughes 5-0; B. Mikkelsen beat D. Chalmers 5-1

First qualifying round: T. Jones beat D. Greaves 5-2; J. Giannaros beat T. Chappel 5-2; S. Newbury beat V. Harris 5-3; G. Foulds beat R. Chaperon 5-3; D. Sheehan beat John Rea 5-2; R. Bales beat B. Bennett 5-1; R. Foldvari beat P. Houlihan 5-1; P. Medati beat G. Cripsey 5-4; J. McLaughlin beat B. Demarco 5-1; S. Longworth beat P. Francisco 5-4; A. Kearney beat D. French 5-1; P. Browne beat M. Bradley 5-3; W. Jones beat D. O'Kane 5-0; D. Fowler beat Rigitano 5-0; J. Hargreaves beat Darrington 5-2

Second qualifying round: T. Jones beat M. Gibson 5-0; Newbury beat P. Burke 5-1; G. Foulds beat F. Jonik 5-2; E. McLaughlin beat Sheehan 5-2; Bales beat B. Kelly 5-3; Foldvari beat Jack Rea 5-4; J. McLaughlin beat I. Black 5-0; Longworth beat B. Oliver 5-1; Watchorn beat Mikkelsen 5-1; I. Williamson beat Kearney 5-3; Browne beat C. Everton 5-0; S. Duggan beat W. Jones 5-0; Fowler beat T. Murphy 5-0; R. Edmonds beat Hargreaves 5-2

Third qualifying round: T. Jones beat L. Dodd 5-1; M. Gauvreau beat Giannaros 5-3; Newbury beat M. Morra 5-2; G. Foulds beat J. Fitzmaurice 5-1; E. McLaughlin beat F. Davis 5-1; Medati beat C. Roscoe 5-4; G. Scott beat J. McLaughlin 5-4; Longworth beat M. Fisher 5-1; J. Donnelly beat Watchorn 5-1; P. Fagan beat Williamson 5-1; W. King beat Duggan 5-4; Fowler beat J. Meadowcroft 5-2; Edmonds beat M. Watterson 5-2

Fourth qualifying round: S. Francisco beat T. Jones 5-1; Fagan beat M. Wildman 5-3; M. Hallett beat G. Foulds 5-4; M. Macleod beat E. McLaughlin 5-4; Medati beat J. Parrott 5-3; C. Wilson beat Fowler 5-4; Gauvreau beat E. Sinclair 5-1; J. Johnson beat Edmonds 5-4; Scott beat J. Campbell 5-4; E. Hughes beat Newbury 5-3; King beat D. Reynolds 5-2; R. Williams beat Donnelly 5-3; J. Virgo beat Bales 5-1; Longworth beat N. Foulds 5-3; Foldvari beat D. Martin 5-2; Browne beat G. Miles 5-3

First round: Longworth beat David Taylor 5-4; Johnson beat A. Knowles 5-1; C. Thorburn beat Scott 5-1; King beat J. Spencer 5-2; T. Griffiths beat Fagan 5-0; J. White beat Browne 5-2; E. Hughes beat T. Meo 5-4; Macleod beat Charlton 5-1; A. Higgins beat Gauvreau 5-3; Virgo beat B. Werbeniuk 5-2; Wilson beat D. Mountjoy 5-4; Williams beat Dennis Taylor 5-3; R. Reardon beat Hallett 5-3; S. Davis beat S. Francisco 5-0; W. Thorne beat Foldvari 5-2; K. Stevens beat Medati 5-4

Second round: Reardon beat E. Hughes 5-1; S. Davis beat Higgins 5-2; Virgo beat Macleod 5-0; Thorne beat Stevens 5-1; Thorburn beat Longworth 5-3; Griffiths beat Williams 5-3; Johnson beat Wilson 5-0; King beat White 5-2

Quarter-finals: S. Davis beat Reardon 5-1; Thorburn beat Griffiths 5-4; Johnson beat King 5-3; Thorne beat Virgo 5-1

Semi-finals: Thorne beat S. Davis 9-8; Thorburn beat Johnson 9-2

Final: Thorne beat Thorburn 13-8

BENSON AND HEDGES MASTERS

Inaugurated in 1975, the Benson and Hedges Masters is the oldest tournament on the circuit to have been continuously sponsored by the same company.

After only one year at the West Centre Hotel, it moved to the New London Theatre in Drury Lane thus establishing a link between snooker and theatre in the round. The event moved to its present home, Wembley Conference Centre, in 1979.

Initially, only the final was televised and only ten players were invited to compete. Now it is restricted to the top 16 players in the world rankings and is televised by the BBC for its full eight days.

Snooker's only London tournament, its prize fund has risen from £5,000 in 1975 to £150,000 in 1985.

In 1984, Kirk Stevens set a new break record when he compiled a 147 maximum in the semi-finals against Jimmy White.

1975
First round: J. Pulman beat C. Thorburn 5-3; A. Higgins beat B. Werbeniuk 5-0

Quarter-finals: E. Charlton beat F. Davis 5-3; J. Spencer beat Pulman 5-3; R. Reardon beat G. Miles 5-3; R. Williams beat Higgins 5-3

Semi-finals: Spencer beat Charlton 5-2; Reardon beat Williams 5-4

Final: Spencer beat Reardon 9-8

1976
First round: F. Davis beat C. Thorburn 4-2; J. Pulman beat Dennis Taylor 4-2

Quarter-finals: G. Miles beat A. Higgins 4-1; R. Reardon beat Pulman 4-1; J. Spencer beat F. Davis 4-0; E. Charlton beat R. Williams 4-1

Semi-finals: Miles beat Spencer 5-4; Reardon beat Charlton 5-4

Final: Reardon beat Miles 7-3

1977
First round: D. Mountjoy beat J. Pulman 4-2; J. Spencer beat Dennis Taylor 4-2

Quarter-finals: R. Reardon beat R. Williams 4-1; G. Miles beat Spencer 4-1; A. Higgins beat P. Mans 4-2; Mountjoy beat F. Davis 4-2

Semi-finals: Mountjoy beat Higgins 5-3; Reardon beat Miles 5-2

Final: Mountjoy beat Reardon 7-6

1978
First round: J. Pulman beat P. Fagan 4-2; G. Miles beat F. Davis 4-3

Quarter-finals: J. Spencer beat Pulman 4-2; A. Higgins beat Dennis Taylor 4-3; C. Thorburn beat D. Mountjoy 4-2; R. Reardon beat Miles 4-1

Semi-finals: Higgins beat Reardon 5-1; Thorburn beat Spencer 5-3

Final: Higgins beat Thorburn 7-5

1979
First round: D. Mountjoy beat F. Davis 5-2; David Taylor beat P. Fagan 5-4

Quarter-finals: A. Higgins beat E. Charlton 5-2; P. Mans beat C. Thorburn 5-4; Mountjoy beat Spencer 5-0; R. Reardon beat Taylor 5-2

Semi-finals: Higgins beat Mountjoy 5-1; Mans beat Reardon 5-3

Final: Mans beat Higgins 8-4

1980
First round: C. Thorburn beat J. Virgo 5-3; A. Higgins beat F. Davis 5-1

Quarter-finals: R. Reardon beat Dennis Taylor 5-3; T. Griffiths beat Thorburn 5-3; J. Spencer beat E. Charlton 5-2; Higgins beat P. Mans 5-1

Semi-finals: Griffiths beat Spencer 5-0; Higgins beat Reardon 5-2

Final: Griffiths beat Higgins 9-5

Cliff Thorburn with the Benson and Hedges Masters trophy in 1983.

1981
First round: P. Mans beat S. Davis 5-3; D. Mountjoy beat E. Charlton 5-0; F. Davis beat K. Stevens 5-4; J. Spencer beat Dennis Taylor 5-2

Quarter-finals: A. Higgins beat Mountjoy 5-1; C. Thorburn beat Mans 5-4; Spencer beat R. Reardon 5-1; T. Griffiths beat F. Davis 5-2

Semi-finals: Higgins beat Thorburn 6-5; Griffiths beat Spencer 6-5

Final: Higgins beat Griffiths 9-6

1982
First round: R. Reardon beat Dennis Taylor 5-3; D. Mountjoy beat J. Spencer 5-4; T. Meo beat David Taylor 5-2; E. Charlton beat J. White 5-4

Quarter-finals: Meo beat C. Thorburn 5-0; S. Davis beat Mountjoy 5-2; A. Higgins beat Charlton 5-1; T. Griffiths beat Reardon 5-3

Semi-finals: S. Davis beat Meo 6-4; Griffiths beat Higgins 6-5

Final: S. Davis beat Griffiths 9-5

1983
First round: B. Werbeniuk beat A. Higgins 5-4; E. Charlton beat T. Meo 5-3; T. Griffiths beat K. Stevens 5-3; C. Thorburn beat J. Johnson 5-2; R. Reardon beat D. Reynolds 5-1; D. Mountjoy beat J. Virgo 5-1; S. Davis beat M. Wildman 5-2; J. White beat David Taylor 5-2

Quarter-finals: Charlton beat Werbeniuk 5-3; Thorburn beat Griffiths 5-3; Reardon beat White 5-2; Mountjoy beat S. Davis 5-4

Semi-finals: Thorburn beat Charlton 6-5; Reardon beat Mountjoy 6-3

Final: Thorburn beat Reardon 9-7

1984
First round: A. Knowles beat Dennis Taylor 5-2; R. Reardon beat J. Virgo 5-3; J. Spencer beat C. Thorburn 5-4; T. Griffiths beat B. Werbeniuk 5-1; J. White beat E. Charlton 5-2; A. Higgins beat D. Mountjoy 5-2; K. Stevens beat David Taylor 5-1; S. Davis beat T. Meo 5-0

Quarter-finals: Griffiths beat Spencer 5-4; Knowles beat Higgins 5-1; White beat Reardon 5-3; Stevens beat S. Davis 5-3

Semi-finals: Griffiths beat Knowles 6-4; White beat Stevens 6-4

Final: White beat Griffiths 9-5

1985
First round: J. White beat W. Thorne 5-2; J. Spencer beat E. Charlton 5-3;
R. Reardon beat David Taylor 5-1; C. Thorburn beat Dennis Taylor 5-3;
D. Mountjoy beat Knowles 5-3; T. Meo beat K. Stevens 5-2; T. Griffiths beat
B. Werbeniuk 5-2; A. Higgins beat S. Davis 5-4

Quarter-finals: White beat Spencer 5-2; Thorburn beat Reardon 5-0; Mountjoy
beat Meo 5-4; Griffiths beat Higgins 5-1

Semi-finals: Thorburn beat White 6-4; Mountjoy beat Griffiths 6-2

Final: Thorburn beat Mountjoy 9-6

DULUX BRITISH OPEN

When Yamaha withdrew from sponsorship of a televised non-ranking
tournament, the WPBSA had the opportunity to stage another ranking
event and the Dulux British Open was created to fill the late
February/early March slot in the circuit.

To make the event different from both the Jameson International and
the Mercantile Credit Classic (ITV's other two ranking tournaments) it
was originally decided that matches up to and including the
quarter-finals would be over the best of 11 frames – the other events
being two frames shorter – and the early rounds followed this
arrangement.

But ITV were nervous of the overtime implications of such long
matches for the televised stage and so the format was consequently
reduced to the more usual best of nine.

At the time, the event was the richest in the sport's history, carrying
prize-money of £250,000. Silvino Francisco took a record cheque for
£50,000 after beating Kirk Stevens in the final, which was the first in a
major tournament not to feature a British player.

1985
Qualifying: T. Chappel beat I. Williamson 6-5; D. Chalmers beat P. Burke 6-5;
John Rea beat M. Fisher 6-0; W. King beat P. Medati 6-4; D. Fowler beat
C. Everton 6-1; T. Murphy beat D. Sheehan 6-3; R. Foldvari beat S. Duggan
6-4; V. Harris beat L. Dodd 6-1; T. Jones beat G. Foulds 6-0; P. Francisco beat
B. Kelly 6-3; D. O'Kane beat G. Cripsey 6-4; S. Newbury beat P. Browne 6-0;
M. Bradley beat M. Morra 6-2; A. Kearney beat M. Watterson 6-4; D. French
beat E. McLaughlin 6-0; R. Chaperon beat P. Fagan 6-5; B. Harris beat
J. Meadowcroft 6-1; S. Longworth beat F. Davis 6-1; B. Mikkelsen beat
D. Hughes 6-0; G. Scott beat M. Darrington 6-3; J. Giannaros beat C. Roscoe
6-1; F. Jonik beat J. McLaughlin 6-2; W. Jones beat J. Donnelly 6-1;
P. Watchorn beat J. Fitzmaurice 6-1; R. Bales beat I. Black 6-4; M. Gauvreau
beat D. Greaves 6-3; M. Gibson beat B. Demarco 6-1; R. Edmonds beat
D. Mienie 6-1

First round: D. Reynolds beat Giannaros 6-3; M. Macleod beat Murphy 6-5; E. Hughes beat Watchorn 6-4; Longworth beat C. Wilson 6-3; W. Jones beat J. Johnson 6-5; M. Hallett *wo* Mikkelsen *scr*; C. Thorburn beat G. Rigitano 6-3; A. Higgins beat Bales 6-3; Chaperon beat B. Werbeniuk 6-1; S. Francisco beat Kearney 6-4; T. Meo beat Foldvari 6-0; W. Thorne beat W. Oliver 6-3; B. Harris beat E. Charlton 6-3; J. White beat T. Jones 6-5; A. Knowles beat French 6-2; N. Foulds beat J. Hargreaves 6-1; Newbury beat E. Sinclair 6-3; M. Wildman beat Gibson 6-1; J. Spencer beat Jonik 6-0; V. Harris beat D. Mountjoy 6-5; O'Kane beat J. Campbell 6-4; G. Miles beat Edmonds 6-1; T. Griffiths beat Chalmers 6-0; R. Reardon beat King 6-5; J. Parrott beat John Rea 6-4; Bradley beat David Taylor 6-3; K. Stevens beat Gauvreau 6-3; J. Virgo beat P. Francisco 6-2; Fowler beat R. Williams 6-4; D. Martin beat B. Bennett 6-0; S. Davis beat Chappel 6-5; Dennis Taylor beat Scott 6-2

Second round: Newbury beat Griffiths 5-3; Bradley beat Fowler 5-4; S. Davis beat Virgo 5-2; Knowles beat Longworth 5-2; O'Kane beat V. Harris 5-3; Thorburn beat Reynolds 5-3; Higgins beat N. Foulds 5-1; Dennis Taylor beat Parrott 5-2; Macleod beat Thorne 5-0; Martin beat Reardon 5-4; Miles beat Spencer 5-3; S. Francisco beat White 5-4; Meo beat Hallett 5-4; E. Hughes beat B. Harris 5-4; Stevens beat Wildman 5-2; Chaperon beat W. Jones 5-2

Third round: Meo beat Knowles 5-2; S. Davis beat Bradley 5-2; O'Kane beat Martin 5-4; S. Francisco beat Chaperon 5-2; Dennis Taylor beat Newbury 5-3; E. Hughes beat Macleod 5-2; Stevens beat Miles 5-2; Higgins beat Thorburn 5-2

1985 Dulux British Open winner Silvino Francisco and runner-up Kirk Stevens. (David Muscroft)

Quarter-finals: Stevens beat Dennis Taylor 5-2; S. Davis beat O'Kane 5-1; S. Francisco beat Meo 5-4; Higgins beat E. Hughes 5-2

Semi-finals: Stevens beat S. Davis 9-7; S. Francisco beat Higgins 9-6

Final: S. Francisco beat Stevens 12-9

GUINNESS WORLD CUP

When State Express withdrew from their five-year sponsorship of the team championship, their slot in the television schedules was taken over by the Rothmans Grand Prix, as was their venue, The Hexagon, Reading.

However, a new sponsor, venue, format and date were found and the Guinness World Cup was played on a knock-out basis at the Conference Centre, Bournemouth in March with all four days' play being televised by the BBC.

1979 (*State Express World Team Classic*)
Group A
England (F. Davis, G. Miles, J. Spencer) beat Rest of World (P. Mans, J. van Rensberg, P. Fagan) 8-7; England beat Northern Ireland (Jack Rea, A. Higgins, Dennis Taylor) 8-7; Northern Ireland beat Rest of World 8-7

Group B
Wales (R. Reardon, T. Griffiths, D. Mountjoy) beat Canada (C. Thorburn, K. Stevens, B. Werbeniuk) 9-6; Australia (E. Charlton, G. Owen, P. Morgan) beat Canada 8-7; Wales beat Australia 9-6

Final: Wales beat England 14-3

1980 (*State Express World Team Classic*)
Group A
Wales (R. Reardon, T. Griffiths, D. Mountjoy) beat Canada (C. Thorburn, K. Stevens, B. Werbeniuk) 10-5; Canada beat Rest of World (J. Rempe, E. Sinclair, P. Mans) 9-6; Wales beat Rest of World 13-2

Group B
England (F. Davis, J. Virgo, David Taylor) beat Ireland (A. Higgins, Dennis Taylor, P. Fagan) 11-4; Australia (E. Charlton, I. Anderson, P. Morgan) beat England 8-7; Ireland beat Australia 10-5

Semi-finals: Wales beat Ireland 8-7; Canada beat England 8-5

Final: Wales beat Canada 8-5

1981 (*State Express World Team Classic*)
Preliminary match: Republic of Ireland (E. Hughes, P. Fagan, D. Sheehan)
beat Scotland (I. Black, M. Macleod, E. Sinclair) 4-2

Group A
England (S. Davis, J. Spencer, David Taylor) beat Australia (I. Anderson,
E. Charlton, P. Morgan) 4-3; Northern Ireland (T. Murphy, Dennis Taylor,
A. Higgins) beat Australia 4-1; England beat Northern Ireland 4-3

Group B
Wales (R. Reardon, D. Mountjoy, T. Griffiths) beat Canada (K. Stevens,
C. Thorburn, B. Werbeniuk) 4-2; Wales beat Republic of Ireland 4-0; Canada
beat Republic of Ireland 4-2

Semi-finals: England beat Canada 4-2; Wales beat Northern Ireland 4-3

Final: England beat Wales 4-3

1982 (*State Express World Team Classic*)
Preliminary match: Scotland (E. Sinclair, J. Donnelly, I. Black) beat Republic
of Ireland (E. Hughes, P. Fagan, D. Sheehan) 4-2

Group A
England (A. Knowles, S. Davis, J. White) beat Northern Ireland (A. Higgins,
T. Murphy, Dennis Taylor) 4-3; Scotland beat Northern Ireland 4-1; England
beat Scotland 4-1

Group B
Canada (C. Thorburn, B. Werbeniuk, K. Stevens) beat Wales (T. Griffiths,
D. Mountjoy, R. Reardon) 4-3; Canada beat Australia (E. Charlton, P. Morgan,
I. Anderson) 4-0; Wales beat Australia 4-1

Semi-finals: England beat Wales 4-2; Canada beat Scotland 4-0

Final: Canada beat England 4-2

1983 (*State Express World Team Classic*)
Preliminary match: Scotland (E. Sinclair, M. Macleod, I. Black) beat Republic
of Ireland (B. Kelly, E. Hughes, P. Fagan) 4-2

Group A
Wales (D. Mountjoy, R. Reardon, T. Griffiths) beat Canada (C. Thorburn,
B. Werbeniuk, K. Stevens) 4-3; Canada beat Australia (E. Charlton, W. King,
J. Campbell) 4-2; Wales beat Australia 4-0

Group B
England (S. Davis, A. Knowles, T. Meo) beat Northern Ireland (A. Higgins,
T. Murphy, Dennis Taylor) 4-1; Northern Ireland beat Scotland (E. Sinclair,
I. Black, M. Macleod) 4-3; England beat Scotland 4-0

Eugene Hughes holds the Guinness World Cup while his team-mates in 1985, Alex Higgins and Dennis Taylor, hold the cheque.

Semi-finals: Wales beat Northern Ireland 4-1; England beat Canada 4-2

Final: England beat Wales 4-2

1985
First round: Wales beat Australia 5-4 (T. Griffiths drew with E. Charlton 1-1; D. Mountjoy beat J. Campbell 2-0; R. Reardon lost to W. King 0-2; Mountjoy drew with Charlton 1-1; Griffiths beat King 1-0); England A beat Scotland 5-4 (S. Davis lost to E. Sinclair 0-2; A. Knowles drew with M. Macleod 1-1; T. Meo beat J. Donnelly 2-0; S. Davis drew with Sinclair 1-1; Knowles beat Macleod 1-0); England B beat Rest of World 5-2 (J. White beat S. Francisco 2-0; W. Thorne drew with J. Rempe 1-1; J. Spencer drew with D. O'Kane 1-1; White beat Francisco 1-0); Ireland beat Canada 5-2 (Dennis Taylor beat K. Stevens 2-0; E. Hughes drew with C. Thorburn 1-1; A. Higgins drew with B. Werbeniuk 1-1; Higgins beat Thorburn 1-0)

Semi-finals: Ireland beat Wales 5-3 (Dennis Taylor drew with Mountjoy 1-1; E. Hughes lost to Griffiths 0-2; Higgins beat Reardon 2-0; Higgins beat Mountjoy 2-0); England A beat England B 5-2 (S. Davis beat Spencer 2-0; Knowles drew with Thorne 1-1; Meo drew with White 1-1; S. Davis beat White 1-0)

Final: Ireland beat England A 9-7 (Dennis Taylor drew with Knowles 1-1; E. Hughes lost to S. Davis 0-2; Higgins drew with Meo 1-1; Dennis Taylor drew with Knowles 1-1; Dennis Taylor drew with S. Davis 1-1; E. Hughes drew with Knowles 1-1; Higgins beat Meo 2-0; Higgins beat S. Davis 2-0)

BENSON AND HEDGES IRISH MASTERS

In 1978 the Benson and Hedges Irish Masters began as a low-key tournament with round robin groups and play-off semi-finals and final. It was not until 1981, when it changed to a straight knock-out formula, that it became established as a major event.

Although restricted to 12 players, its importance on the circuit really lies in its timing – it is the last tournament before the World Championship. Its mixture of serious competitiveness and Irish hospitality makes this tournament the ideal pre-championship warm-up for the leading players.

1978
Final: J. Spencer beat D. Mountjoy 5-3

1979
Final: D. Mountjoy beat R. Reardon 6-5

1980
Final: T. Griffiths beat D. Mountjoy 9-8

1981
First round: Dennis Taylor beat J. Spencer 4-2; S. Davis beat J. Virgo 4-3

Quarter-finals: T. Griffiths beat K. Stevens 4-0; C. Thorburn beat D. Mountjoy 4-0; R. Reardon beat S. Davis 4-2; A. Higgins beat Dennis Taylor 4-2

Semi-finals: Griffiths beat Thorburn 6-5; Reardon beat Higgins 6-5

Final: Griffiths beat Reardon 9-7

1982
First round: Dennis Taylor beat D. Sheehan 5-3; T. Meo beat J. Spencer 5-3; A. Higgins beat J. Wych 5-3; D. Mountjoy beat E. Hughes 5-4

Quarter-finals: T. Griffiths beat Meo 5-3; R. Reardon beat Dennis Taylor 5-4; S. Davis beat Mountjoy 5-2; Higgins beat C. Thorburn 5-4

Semi-finals: Griffiths beat Reardon 6-3; S. Davis beat Higgins 6-2

Final: Griffiths beat S. Davis 9-5

1983
First round: J. White beat Dennis Taylor 5-4; T. Meo beat P. Burke 5-0; D. Mountjoy beat A. Knowles 5-1; E. Charlton beat David Taylor 5-4

Quarter-finals: R. Reardon beat Meo 5-4; A. Higgins beat White 5-2; S. Davis beat Charlton 5-1; T. Griffiths beat Mountjoy 5-4

Semi-finals: Reardon beat Higgins 6-3; S. Davis beat Griffiths 6-2

Final: S. Davis beat Reardon 9-2

1984
First round: T. Griffiths beat B. Werbeniuk 5-2; Dennis Taylor beat E. Hughes 5-1; T. Meo beat J. White 5-4; A. Higgins beat E. Charlton 5-2

Quarter-finals: Dennis Taylor beat C. Thorburn 5-2; Griffiths beat A. Knowles 5-0; Higgins beat R. Reardon 5-2; S. Davis beat Meo 5-4

Semi-finals: Griffiths beat Dennis Taylor 6-5; S. Davis beat Higgins 6-4

Final: S. Davis beat Griffiths 9-1

1985
First round: E. Charlton beat Dennis Taylor 5-4; J. White beat T. Meo 5-1; E. Hughes beat R. Reardon 5-0; A. Higgins beat T. Griffiths 5-2

Quarter-finals: A. Knowles beat Charlton 5-3; White beat C. Thorburn 5-3; S. Davis beat Hughes 5-4; Higgins beat K. Stevens 5-3

Semi-finals: White beat Knowles 6-4; Higgins beat S. Davis 6-2

Final: White beat Higgins 9-5

EMBASSY WORLD PROFESSIONAL CHAMPIONSHIP

The World Professional Championship was first organised by – and won by – Joe Davis in 1927 when Joe and a Birmingham billiard trader, Bill Camkin, persuaded the then governing body, the Billiards Association and Control Council, to sanction a world championship. That first final was played, inauspiciously, in one of Camkin's billiard halls in John Bright Street, Birmingham, and it wasn't until the mid-1930s that the Championship began to parallel and then overtake billiards as the main attraction at the game's 'holy of holies', Thurstons in Leicester Square.

Davis dominated all the Championships before the war and won it again in 1946 – his 14th title – before retiring from championship play. The Championship, still played over the entire season with the final often scheduled to last a fortnight, was dominated for the next decade by Joe's younger brother, Fred with eight wins, and a dour Scot, Walter Donaldson, with two.

But the cumbersome nature of the format and the advent of other forms of entertainment – especially television – caused the popularity of the event to decline and Fred did not enter the 1957 Championship (won for the first time by John Pulman). With apathy now reigning, there was no Championship at all for the next six years. Through the efforts of Rex Williams it was revived in 1964 on a challenge basis, a system which continued until 1968 by which time Pulman had successfully countered seven challenges.

Commercial sponsorship was forthcoming for the first time in the 1968–69 season, so ending the era of the challenged match, and Players No. 6 also sponsored the 1970 event. In late 1970, the tournament was staged in Australia for the first time – without a sponsor. There was no sponsorship in 1972 either, although another tobacco company, Park Drive, filled the breach in 1973 and 1974.

Those two years saw the end of the Championship being staged throughout the season at a variety of venues. Eight tables were installed in one venue and the Championship was compressed into a fortnight. Although the set-up was found to be unwieldy with so many tables the pattern of the modern tournament format began to emerge.

After another sojourn in Australia in 1975, the event came back to Britain the following year and acquired its present sponsors, Embassy. A year later, it found its present-day home, the Crucible Theatre, Sheffield.

Now, the top 16 players on the world ranking list are exempted until the last 32 at Sheffield and the other players come through a qualifying section which in 1985 was played over eight days at Preston Guild Hall on six tables. Until the semi-finals two tables are used at Sheffield with a screen being lowered before play to separate them.

The Crucible Theatre and the Embassy World Championship have now attained such a special relationship that it is difficult to imagine the world champion being crowned anywhere else.

1927
First round: M. Inman beat T. Newman 8-5; T. Carpenter beat N. Butler 8-3

Second round: T. A. Dennis beat F. Lawrence 8-7; A. Cope beat A. Mann 8-6; J. Davis beat J. Brady 10-5; Carpenter beat Inman 8-3

Semi-finals: J. Davis beat Cope 16-7; Dennis beat Carpenter 12-10

Final: J. Davis beat Dennis 20-11

1928
First round: T. Newman beat F. Smith 12-6; A. Mann beat A. Cope 14-9

Second round: Newman beat T. A. Dennis 12-5; F. Lawrence beat Mann 12-11

Third round: Lawrence beat Newman 12-7

Final: J. Davis beat Lawrence 16-13

1929
First round: F. Lawrence beat A. Mann 13-12

Semi-finals: J. Davis beat Lawrence 13-10; T. A. Dennis beat K. Prince 14-6

Final: J. Davis beat Dennis 19-14

1930
First round: F. Lawrence beat A. Mann 13-11; N. Butler beat T. Newman 13-11

Semi-finals: J. Davis beat Lawrence 13-2; T. A. Dennis beat Butler 13-11

Final: J. Davis beat Dennis 25-12

1931
Final: J. Davis beat T. A. Dennis 25-21

1932
First round: C. McConachy beat T. A. Dennis 13-11

Final: J. Davis beat McConachy 30-19

1933
First round: W. Donaldson beat W. Leigh 13-11

Semi-finals: J. Davis beat Donaldson 13-1; W. Smith beat T. A. Dennis 16-9

Final: J. Davis beat Smith 25-18

1934
Final: J. Davis beat T. Newman 25-23

1935
First round: W. Smith beat C. Stanbury 13-12

Semi-finals: Smith beat A. Mann 13-4; J. Davis beat T. Newman 15-10

Final: J. Davis beat Smith 25-20

1936
First round: C. O'Donnell beat S. Lee 16-15; H. Lindrum beat H. Terry 20-11; J. Davis beat T. Newman 29-2; W. Smith beat S. Smith 16-15; C. Stanbury beat A. Mann 22-9

Second round: Alec Brown beat Stanbury 16-15; Lindrum beat O'Donnell 19-6 (*retd*); J. Davis beat W. Smith 22-9; S. Newman *wo*

Semi-finals: J. Davis beat Alec Brown 21-10; Lindrum beat S. Newman 29-2

Final: J. Davis beat Lindrum 34-27

1937
First round: W. A. Withers beat F. Davis 17-14

Second round: J. Davis beat Withers 30-1; H. Lindrum beat S. Lee 20-11; W. Smith beat T. Newman 16-15; S. Smith beat Alec Brown 18-13

Semi-finals: Lindrum beat W. Smith 20-11; J. Davis beat S. Smith 18-13

Final: J. Davis beat Lindrum 32-29

1938
First qualifying round: H. Holt beat C. W. Read 21-10

Second qualifying round: F. Davis beat Holt 23-8

First round: F. Davis beat Alec Brown 14-6 (*retd ill*); S. Smith beat C. Stanbury 27-4; J. Davis beat S. Lee 24-7; W. Smith beat T. Newman 16-15

Semi-finals: J. Davis beat W. Smith (*nrs*); S. Smith beat F. Davis (*nrs*)

Final: J. Davis beat S. Smith 37-24

1939
First qualifying round: W. Donaldson beat H. Holt 18-13; H. W. Laws beat
S. Newman 19-12

Second qualifying round: Donaldson beat Laws 18-13

First round: S. Smith beat S. Lee 21-10; W. Donaldson beat C. Falkiner 21-10;
T. Newman beat A. Mann 19-12; F. Davis beat C. Stanbury 19-12

Second round: J. Davis beat W. Smith 19-12; F. Davis beat T. Newman 20-11;
Alec Brown beat H. Lindrum 17-14; S. Smith beat Donaldson 16-15

Semi-finals: J. Davis beat F. Davis 17-14; S. Smith beat Alec Brown 20-11

Final: J. Davis beat S. Smith 43-30

1940
Qualifying round: H. Holt beat C. Stanbury 18-13

First round: W. Donaldson beat Holt 24-7; J. Davis beat Alec Brown 20-11;
F. Davis beat S. Lee 20-11; S. Smith beat T. Newman 22-9

Semi-finals: J. Davis beat Donaldson 22-9; F. Davis beat S. Smith 17-14

Final: J. Davis beat F. Davis 37-36

1946
First qualifying round: K. Kennerley beat F. Lawrence 22-9; C. Stanbury beat
J. Barrie 18-13; S. Newman beat W. Leigh 16-15

Second qualifying round: Kennerley beat T. Reece 8-2 (*retd*); S. Newman beat
Stanbury 17-14

Third qualifying round: S. Newman beat Kennerley 21-10

First round: J. Davis beat W. Donaldson 21-10; S. Newman beat S. Lee 19-12;
F. Davis beat Alec Brown 24-7; H. Lindrum beat H. Holt 17-14

Semi-finals: J. Davis beat S. Newman 21-10; Lindrum beat F. Davis 16-12

Final: J. Davis beat Lindrum 78-67

1947
First qualifying round: Albert Brown beat J. Pulman 21-14; W. Leigh beat
H. F. Francis 19-16; S. Lee beat J. Lees 19-16; K. Kennerley beat C. Stanbury
23-12; E. Newman *wo* H. Holt *scr*

Second qualifying round: J. Barrie beat F. Lawrence 25-10; Albert Brown beat
Newman 28-7; Kennerley beat A. Mann 23-12; Leigh beat Lee 25-10

Third qualifying round: Albert Brown beat Barrie 24-11; Kennerley beat Leigh 21-14

Fourth qualifying round: Albert Brown beat Kennerley 21-14

First round: H. Lindrum beat Albert Brown 39-34; S. Smith beat Alec Brown 43-28; W. Donaldson beat S. Newman 46-25; F. Davis beat C. McConachy 53-20

Semi-finals: Donaldson beat Lindrum 39-32; F. Davis beat Smith 39-32

Final: Donaldson beat F. Davis 82-63

1948
First qualifying round: C. Stanbury beat E. Newman 26-9; W. Leigh beat H. Holt 18-17; J. Barrie beat H. F. Francis 19-16; J. Pulman *wo* S. Lee *scr*

Second qualifying round: Leigh beat Barrie 21-14; Pulman beat Stanbury 19-16

Third qualifying round: Pulman beat Leigh 18-17

First round: F. Davis beat Alec Brown 43-28; C. McConachy beat J. Pulman 42-29; Albert Brown beat S. Smith 36-35; W. Donaldson beat K. Kennerley 46-25

Semi-finals: F. Davis beat McConachy 43-28; Donaldson beat Alec Brown 40-31

Final: F. Davis beat Donaldson 84-61

1949
First qualifying round: C. Stanbury beat H. F. Francis 18-17

Second qualifying round: Stanbury beat J. Rea 18-17

Third qualifying round: Stanbury beat H. Holt 18-17

First round: W. Donaldson beat Stanbury 58-13; J. Pulman beat Albert Brown 42-29; S. Smith beat Alec Brown 41-30; F. Davis beat K. Kennerley 50-21

Semi-finals: Donaldson beat Pulman 49-22; F. Davis beat Smith 42-29

Final: F. Davis beat Donaldson 80-65

1950
First qualifying round: W. Smith beat W. A. Withers 28-7; H. Holt beat H. W. Laws 26-9; S. Lee beat C. Stanbury 20-15; K. Kennerley beat J. Barrie 21-14

Second qualifying round: Kennerley beat Smith 22-13; Lee beat Holt 16-8 (*retd ill*)

Third qualifying round: Kennerley beat Lee 21-14

First round: Albert Brown beat J. Pulman 37-34; W. Donaldson beat K. Kennerley 42-29; G. Chenier beat P. Mans 37-34; F. Davis beat Alec Brown 44-27

Semi-finals: Donaldson beat Albert Brown 37-34; F. Davis beat Chenier 43-28

Final: Donaldson beat F. Davis 51-46

1951
First qualifying round: J. Barrie beat S. Lee 23-12

Second qualifying round: Barrie beat H. W. Laws 28-7

First round: F. Davis beat Barrie 42-29; H. Lindrum beat Albert Brown 43-28; W. Donaldson beat K. Kennerley 41-30; J. Pulman beat S. Smith 38-33

Semi-finals: Donaldson beat Lindrum 41-30; F. Davis beat Pulman 22-14 (*retd ill*)

Final: F. Davis beat Donaldson 58-39

1952
First round: Alec Brown beat R. Williams 39-22; J. Rea beat J. Lees 38-32; Albert Brown beat J. Pulman 32-27 (*records incomplete*)

Semi-finals: W. Donaldson beat Albert Brown 31-30

Final: F. Davis beat Donaldson 38-35

1953
First qualifying round: W. Smith beat J. Lees 21-14; K. Kennerley beat R. Williams 25-12

Second qualifying round: Kennerley beat Smith 42-29

First round: Albert Brown beat Alec Brown 35-26; J. Pulman beat J. Rea 36-25; W. Donaldson beat Kennerley 42-19; F. Davis beat J. Barrie 32-29

Semi-finals: Donaldson beat Brown (*nrs*); F. Davis beat Pulman 36-25

Final: F. Davis beat Donaldson 37-34

1954
First round: J. Pulman beat J. Rea 31-30

Semi-finals: W. Donaldson beat Alec Brown 36-25; F. Davis beat Pulman 32-29

Final: F. Davis beat Donaldson 39-21

1955

First round: J. Pulman beat R. Williams 22-15; J. Rea beat H. Stokes (*nrs*)

Semi-finals: F. Davis beat Rea 36-25; Pulman beat Alec Brown (*nrs*)

Final: F. Davis beat Pulman 37-34

1956

Semi-finals: J. Pulman beat J. Rea 36-25; F. Davis beat R. Williams 35-26

Final: F. Davis beat Pulman 38-35

1957

Semi-finals: J. Pulman beat R. Williams 21-16; J. Rea beat K. Kennerley 25-12

Final: Pulman beat Rea 39-34

Through lack of public support no Championship was organised between 1957 and 1964. After a truce with the BA and CC a new system was adopted whereby the champion defended his title against a series of single challengers. These matches resulted as follows:

1964

J. Pulman beat F. Davis 19-16; J. Pulman beat R. Williams 40-33

1965

J. Pulman beat F. Davis 37-36; J. Pulman beat R. Williams 25-22 (*matches*); J. Pulman beat F. van Rensburg 39-12

1966

J. Pulman beat F. Davis 5-2 (*matches*)

1968

J. Pulman beat E. Charlton 39-34

1969 (*Players No. 6*)

First round: J. Spencer beat J. Pulman 25-18; R. Williams beat B. Bennett 25-4; G. Owen beat J. Rea 25-17; F. Davis beat R. Reardon 25-24

Semi-finals: Spencer beat Williams 37-12; G. Owen beat Davis 37-24

Final: Spencer beat Owen 37-24

1970 (April) (*Players No. 6*)

First round: David Taylor beat B. Bennett 11-8

Quarter-finals: J. Pulman beat David Taylor 31-20; G. Owen beat R. Williams 31-11; R. Reardon beat F. Davis 31-26; J. Spencer beat Jack Rea 31-15

Semi-finals: Pulman beat G. Owen 37-12; Reardon beat Spencer 37-33

Final: Reardon beat Pulman 37-33

1970 (November)
Round robin
J. Spencer beat P. Mans 20-17; beat N. Squire 27-10; beat J. Pulman 23-14
R. Reardon beat Mans 22-15; beat E. Charlton 21-16; beat Spencer 21-16
W. Simpson beat G. Owen 19-18; beat Pulman 21-16; beat Mans 19-18
Charlton beat Squire 27-10; beat Mans 26-11; beat Owen 23-14
Owen beat P. Morgan 26-11; beat Squire 26-11; Morgan beat Simpson 21-16

Semi-finals: Spencer beat Reardon 34-15; Simpson beat Charlton 27-22

Final: Spencer beat Simpson 37-29

1972
First qualifying round: A. Higgins beat R. Gross 15-6; M. Parkin beat
G. Thompson 11-10; G. Miles beat B. Bennett 15-6; J. Dunning beat
P. Houlihan 11-10

Second qualifying round: Higgins beat Parkin 11-3; Dunning beat Miles 11-5

First round: J. Pulman beat Dunning 19-7; Higgins beat Jack Rea 19-11

Quarter-finals: J. Spencer beat F. Davis 31-21; E. Charlton beat David Taylor
31-25; Higgins beat Pulman 31-23; R. Williams beat R. Reardon 25-23

Semi-finals: Higgins beat Williams 31-30; Spencer beat Charlton 37-32

Final: Higgins beat Spencer 37-32

1973 (*Park Drive*)
First round: P. Houlihan beat Jack Rea 9-2; D. Greaves beat B. Bennett 9-8;
G. Miles beat G. Thompson 9-5; P. Mans beat R. Gross 9-2; W. Simpson beat
M. Parkin 9-3; C. Thorburn beat Dennis Taylor 9-8; David Taylor beat
J. Dunning 9-4; J. Meadowcroft *wo* K. Kennerley *scr*

Second round: F. Davis beat Greaves 16-1; Miles beat J. Pulman 16-10;
E. Charlton beat Mans 16-8; G. Owen beat Simpson 16-14; R. Reardon beat
Meadowcroft 16-10; R. Williams beat Thorburn 16-15; J. Spencer beat David
Taylor 16-5; A. Higgins beat Houlihan 16-3

Quarter-finals: Higgins beat F. Davis 16-14; Spencer beat Williams 16-7;
Charlton beat Miles 16-6; Reardon beat G. Owen 16-6

Semi-finals: Charlton beat Higgins 23-9; Reardon beat Spencer 23-22

Final: Reardon beat Charlton 38-32

1974 (*Park Drive*)
Qualifying: J. Dunning beat D. Greaves 8-2; W. Simpson beat Jack Rea 8-3;
J. Meadowcroft beat P. Houlihan 8-5; C. Thorburn beat A. McDonald 8-3;

J. Pulman beat J. Karnehm 8-0; David Taylor beat R. Gross 8-7; M. Owen beat Dennis Taylor 8-1

First round: B. Bennett beat Simpson 8-2; B. Werbeniuk beat G. Thompson 8-3; Meadowcroft beat K. Kennerley 8-5; M. Owen beat M. Parkin 8-5; P. Mans beat I. Anderson 8-1; Pulman beat S. Lee 8-0; Dunning beat David Taylor 8-6; P. Morgan beat Thorburn 8-4

Second round: Mans beat J. Spencer 15-13; Dunning beat E. Charlton 15-13; M. Owen beat G. Owen 15-8; A. Higgins beat Bennett 15-4; G. Miles beat Morgan 15-7; R. Williams beat Pulman 15-12; F. Davis beat Werbeniuk 15-5; R. Reardon beat Meadowcroft 15-3

Quarter-finals: Williams beat Mans 15-4; Reardon beat M. Owen 15-11; Miles beat Dunning 15-13; F. Davis beat Higgins 15-14

Semi-finals: Miles beat Williams 15-7; Reardon beat F. Davis 15-3

Final: Reardon beat Miles 22-12

1975
Qualifying: P. Tarrant beat B. Bennett 15-8; L. Condo beat M. Parkin 15-8; D. Greaves beat J. Charlton 15-14

First round: W. Simpson beat R. Mares 15-5; J. Pulman beat Tarrant 15-5; David Taylor beat R. King 15-8; I. Anderson beat Condo 15-8; Dennis Taylor beat P. Mans 15-12; G. Owen beat Greaves 15-3; B. Werbeniuk beat J. Meadowcroft 15-9; C. Thorburn beat P. Morgan 15-6

Second round: R. Reardon beat Simpson 15-11; J. Spencer beat Pulman 15-10; A. Higgins beat David Taylor 15-2; R. Williams beat Anderson 15-4; Dennis Taylor beat F. Davis 15-14; G. Owen beat J. Dunning 15-8; E. Charlton beat Werbeniuk 15-11; Thorburn beat G. Miles 15-2

Quarter-finals: Reardon beat Spencer 19-17; Higgins beat Williams 19-12; Dennis Taylor beat G. Owen 19-9; Charlton beat Thorburn 19-12

Semi-finals: Charlton beat Dennis Taylor 19-12; Reardon beat Higgins 19-14

Final: Reardon beat Charlton 31-30

1976
First qualifying round: Jack Rea beat I. Anderson 8-5; D. Greaves beat J. Charlton 8-5; J. Meadowcroft beat D. Wheelwright 8-1; R. Gross beat M. Parkin 8-5; L. Condo beat M. Owen 8-6

Second qualifying round: Jack Rea beat B. Bennett 8-5; David Taylor beat Greaves 8-1; Meadowcroft beat Gross 8-4; W. Thorne beat Condo 8-3

First round: R. Reardon beat J. Dunning 15-7; Dennis Taylor beat G. Owen 15-9; P. Mans beat G. Miles 15-10; Meadowcroft beat R. Williams 15-7;

E. Charlton beat J. Pulman 15-9; F. Davis beat B. Werbeniuk 15-12; A. Higgins beat C. Thorburn 15-14; J. Spencer beat David Taylor 15-5

Quarter-finals: Reardon beat Dennis Taylor 15-2; Mans beat Meadowcroft 15-8; Charlton beat F. Davis 15-13; Higgins beat Spencer 15-14

Semi-finals: Reardon beat Mans 20-10; Higgins beat Charlton 20-18

Final: Reardon beat Higgins 27-16

1977
First qualifying round: J. Virgo beat R. Andrewartha 11-1

Second qualifying round: P. Fagan beat J. Meadowcroft 11-9; Virgo beat J. Dunning 11-6; W. Thorne beat B. Bennett 11-4; J. Pulman *wo*; David Taylor beat D. Greaves 11-0; C. Thorburn beat C. Ross 11-0; Dennis Taylor beat J. Karnehm 11-0; D. Mountjoy beat Jack Rea 11-9

First round: R. Reardon beat Fagan 13-7; J. Spencer beat Virgo 13-9; G. Miles beat Thorne 13-4; Pulman beat F. Davis 13-12; E. Charlton beat David Taylor 13-5; Thorburn beat R. Williams 13-6; Dennis Taylor beat P. Mans 13-11; Mountjoy beat A. Higgins 13-12

Quarter-finals: Spencer beat Reardon 13-6; Pulman beat Miles 13-10; Thorburn beat Charlton 13-12; Dennis Taylor beat Mountjoy 13-11

Semi-finals: Spencer beat Pulman 18-16; Thorburn beat Dennis Taylor 18-16

Final: Spencer beat Thorburn 25-21

1978
First qualifying round: M. Parkin beat B. Bennett 9-4; R. Andrewartha beat J. Karnehm 9-0; J. Barrie beat D. Greaves 9-3; P. Houlihan beat C. Ross 9-1

Second qualifying round: D. Mountjoy beat Andrewartha 9-3; P. Fagan beat J. Dunning 9-5; W. Thorne beat R. Williams 9-3; B. Werbeniuk beat M. Parkin 9-2; P. Mans beat Barrie 9-6; David Taylor beat P. Morgan 9-7; Houlihan beat J. Meadowcroft 9-6; F. Davis beat J. Virgo 9-8

First round: Mans beat J. Spencer 13-8; G. Miles beat David Taylor 13-10; Fagan beat A. Higgins 13-12; F. Davis beat Dennis Taylor 13-9; E. Charlton beat Thorne 13-12; C. Thorburn beat Houlihan 13-8; Werbeniuk beat J. Pulman 13-4; R. Reardon beat Mountjoy 13-9

Quarter-finals: Mans beat Miles 13-7; F. Davis beat Fagan 13-10; Charlton beat Thorburn 13-12; Reardon beat Werbeniuk 13-6

Semi-finals: Mans beat F. Davis 18-16; Reardon beat Charlton 18-14

Final: Reardon beat Mans 25-18

1979
First qualifying round: D. Mountjoy beat D. Mienie 9-1; T. Griffiths beat
B. Bennett 9-2; P. Houlihan beat J. Barrie 9-5; W. Thorne beat J. Charlton 9-3;
J. Virgo beat M. Parkin 9-0; J. Dunning beat Jack Rea 9-5; R. Williams beat
D. Greaves 9-2; J. Meadowcroft beat J. van Rensberg 9-7; R. Andrewartha
beat R. Edmonds 9-8; S. Davis beat I. Anderson 9-1; K. Stevens beat
R. Amdor 9-1

Second qualifying round: Virgo beat Thorne 9-8; B. Werbeniuk beat
Andrewartha 9-2; David Taylor beat Dunning 9-8; Mountjoy beat Houlihan 9-6;
S. Davis beat P. Fagan 9-2; Griffiths beat Meadowcroft 9-6; Stevens beat
J. Pulman 9-0; G. Miles beat Williams 9-5

First round: E. Charlton beat Mountjoy 13-6; Werbeniuk beat J. Spencer 13-11;
Virgo beat C. Thorburn 13-10; F. Davis beat Stevens 13-8; Dennis Taylor beat
S. Davis 13-11; A. Higgins beat David Taylor 13-5; Griffiths beat P. Mans 13-8;
R. Reardon beat Miles 13-8

Quarter-finals: Charlton beat F. Davis 13-4; Dennis Taylor beat Reardon 13-8;
Virgo beat Werbeniuk 13-9; Griffiths beat Higgins 13-12

Semi-finals: Griffiths beat Charlton 19-17; Dennis Taylor beat Virgo 19-12

Final: Griffiths beat Dennis Taylor 24-16

1980
Qualifying groups
1   Jack Rea beat B. Bennett 9-1; W. Thorne beat K. Robitaille 9-4; Thorne
    beat Rea 9-1
2   S. Davis beat C. Ross 9-3; P. Morgan beat P. Thornely 9-4; Davis beat
    Morgan 9-0
3   M. Hallett beat K. Kennerley 9-2; K. Stevens beat D. Greaves 9-3; Stevens
    beat Hallett 9-3
4   J. Johnson beat R. Andrewartha 9-5; P. Houlihan beat Johnson 9-6; T. Meo
    beat J. van Rensberg 9-1; Meo beat Houlihan 9-1
5   R. Amdor beat B. Mikkelsen 9-7; R. Williams beat Amdor 9-4; J. Wych beat
    J. Bear 9-5; Wych beat Williams 9-7
6   F. Jonik beat M. Wildman 9-7; C. Wilson beat Jonik 9-6
7   R. Edmonds beat M. Parkin 9-2; S. Hood beat J. Dunning 16-7; Edmonds
    beat Hood 9-6
8   E. Sinclair beat M. Morra 9-5; Sinclair beat D. Mienie 9-7; J. Meadowcroft
    beat Sinclair 9-1

First round: S. Davis beat P. Fagan 10-6; A. Higgins beat Meo 10-9;
D. Mountjoy beat Wilson 10-6; Wych beat J. Pulman 10-5; J. Virgo beat
Meadowcroft 10-2; Stevens beat G. Miles 10-3; David Taylor beat Edmonds
10-3; B. Werbeniuk beat Thorne 10-9

Second round: S. Davis beat T. Griffiths 13-10; Higgins beat P. Mans 13-6;
Stevens beat J. Spencer 13-8; E. Charlton beat Virgo 13-12; C. Thorburn beat
Mountjoy 13-10; Wych beat Dennis Taylor 13-10; R. Reardon beat Werbeniuk
13-6; David Taylor beat F. Davis 13-5

Quarter-finals: David Taylor beat Reardon 13-11; Thorburn beat Wych 13-6; Stevens beat Charlton 13-7; Higgins beat S. Davis 13-9

Semi-finals: Thorburn beat David Taylor 16-7; Higgins beat Stevens 16-13

Final: Thorburn beat Higgins 18-16

1981
Qualifying groups
1   W. Thorne beat M. Morra 9-5; D. Greaves beat M. Parkin 9-5; Thorne beat Greaves 9-3
2   J. White beat B. Mikkelsen 9-4; White beat J. Meadowcroft 9-8
3   R. Edmonds beat M. Wildman 9-3; R. Williams beat S. Hood 9-4; Edmonds beat Williams 9-7
4   T. Meo beat J. Johnson 9-8; M. Hallett beat F. Jonik 9-1; Meo beat Hallett 9-4
5   J. Dunning beat B. Bennett 9-6; Dunning beat P. Fagan 9-7
6   D. Martin beat I. Anderson 9-3; Martin beat J. Pulman 9-2
7   C. Wilson beat R. Andrewartha 9-4; E. Sinclair beat P. Morgan 9-8; Wilson beat Sinclair 9-4
8   A. Knowles beat C. Ross 7-0 (*retd*); Knowles beat J. Wych 9-3

First round: G. Miles beat Knowles 10-8; David Taylor beat Wilson 10-6; D. Mountjoy beat Thorne 10-6; K. Stevens beat Dunning 10-4; Meo beat J. Virgo 10-6; S. Davis beat White 10-8; B. Werbeniuk beat Martin 10-4; J. Spencer beat Edmonds 10-9

Second round: C. Thorburn beat Miles 13-2; David Taylor beat F. Davis 13-3; T. Griffiths beat Meo 13-6; S. Davis beat Alex Higgins 13-8; Mountjoy beat E. Charlton 13-7; Dennis Taylor beat Stevens 13-11; Werbeniuk beat P. Mans 13-5; R. Reardon beat Spencer 13-11

Quarter-finals: Thorburn beat David Taylor 13-6; S. Davis beat Griffiths 13-9; Mountjoy beat Dennis Taylor 13-8; Reardon beat Werbeniuk 13-10

Semi-finals: S. Davis beat Thorburn 16-10; Mountjoy beat Reardon 16-10

Final: S. Davis beat Mountjoy 18-12

1982
Qualifying groups
1   J. Bear beat F. Jonik 9-4; Bear beat J. Wych 9-4
2   D. Hughes beat C. Everton 9-4; T. Meo beat Hughes 9-4
3   D. Reynolds beat D. Sheehan 9-5; Reynolds beat R. Edmonds 9-6
4   E. Hughes *wo* D. Mienie *scr*; A. Knowles beat Hughes 9-7
5   M. Wildman beat G. Foulds 9-8; J. White beat Wildman 9-4
6   C. Roscoe beat B. Mikkelsen 9-6; W. Thorne beat Roscoe 9-1
7   P. Medati beat J. Phillips 9-3; C. Wilson beat Medati 9-5
8   P. Houlihan beat I. Anderson 9-5; D. Martin beat Houlihan 9-3
9   M. Macleod beat E. McLaughlin 9-8; J. Dunning beat Macleod 9-4
10 M. Watterson beat B. Demarco 9-6; J. Meadowcroft beat Watterson 9-7

11   D. French beat B. Bennett 9-3; P. Fagan beat French 9-6
12   I. Black beat M. Parkin 9-6; R. Williams beat Black 9-2
13   J. Johnson beat V. Harris 9-4; M. Hallett beat Johnson 9-8
14   J. Donnelly beat M. Gibson 9-8; E. Sinclair beat B. Kelly 9-8; Donnelly
     beat Sinclair 9-8
15   P. Morgan beat D. Greaves 9-2; S. Francisco beat C. Ross 9-0; Francisco
     beat Morgan 9-1
16   M. Morra beat T. Murphy 9-5; J. Fitzmaurice *wo* J. Pulman *scr*;
     Fitzmaurice beat Morra 9-7

First round: Knowles beat S. Davis 10-1; G. Miles beat Martin 10-5;
B. Werbeniuk beat Bear 10-7; E. Charlton beat Wilson 10-5; S. Francisco beat
Dennis Taylor 10-7; Reynolds beat F. Davis 10-7; J. Virgo beat Hallett 10-4;
R. Reardon beat Donnelly 10-5; A. Higgins beat Meadowcroft 10-5;
D. Mountjoy beat Williams 10-3; Fagan beat David Taylor 10-9; K. Stevens
beat Fitzmaurice 10-4; P. Mans beat Meo 10-8; White beat C. Thorburn 10-4

Second round: Knowles beat Miles 13-7; Charlton beat Werbeniuk 13-5;
S. Francisco beat Reynolds 13-8; Reardon beat Virgo 13-8; Thorne beat
Spencer 13-5; Higgins beat Mountjoy 13-12; Stevens beat Fagan 13-7; White
beat Mans 13-6

Quarter-finals: Charlton beat Knowles 13-11; Reardon beat S. Francisco 13-8;
Higgins beat Thorne 13-10; White beat Stevens 13-9

*Alex Higgins with wife Lynn and daughter Lauren after his capture of the Embassy
World Professional Championship in 1982. (David Muscroft)*

Semi-finals: Reardon beat Charlton 16-11; Higgins beat White 16-15

Final: Higgins beat Reardon 18-15

1983
Qualifying groups
 1 B. Kelly beat B. Demarco 10-4; S. Francisco beat Kelly 10-5
 2 P. Morgan beat P. Burke 10-9; G. Miles beat Morgan 10-6
 3 T. Murphy beat P. Houlihan 10-9; J. Virgo beat Murphy 10-8
 4 R. Williams beat M. Darrington 10-0; Williams beat F. Davis 10-1
 5 M. Wildman beat B. Harris 10-7; Wildman *wo* J. Wych *scr*
 6 R. Edmonds beat F. Jonik 10-4; D. Reynolds beat Edmonds 10-6
 7 M. Fisher beat P. Fagan 10-8; E. McLaughlin beat D. Greaves 10-7; Fisher
     beat McLaughlin 10-9
 8 T. Meo beat V. Harris 10-0; G. Foulds beat M. Gibson 10-6; Meo beat
     Foulds 10-4
 9 I. Black beat M. Morra 10-9; P. Medati beat J. Bear 10-7; Black beat
     Medati 10-4
10 C. Wilson beat C. Everton 10-1; J. Johnson beat P. Watchorn 10-0; Wilson
     beat Johnson 10-8
11 M. Macleod beat M. Owen 10-5; D. Martin beat M. Parkin 10-1; Martin
     beat Macleod 10-7
12 J. Meadowcroft beat B. Bennett 10-3; G. Cripsey beat D. Hughes 10-2;
     Meadowcroft beat Cripsey 10-6
13 J. Donnelly beat D. Sheehan 10-6; J. Campbell beat M. Watterson 10-6;
     Campbell beat Donnelly 10-2
14 L. Dodd *wo* J. Dunning *scr*; I. Williamson beat D. French 10-8; Dodd beat
     Williamson 10-9
15 M. Hallett beat R. Andrewartha 10-7; W. King beat I. Anderson 10-6;
     Hallett beat King 10-6
16 E. Hughes beat J. Fitzmaurice 10-7; E. Sinclair beat C. Roscoe 10-2;
     Hughes beat Sinclair 10-8

First round: A. Higgins beat Reynolds 10-4; W. Thorne beat Virgo 10-3;
B. Werbeniuk beat Martin 10-4; David Taylor beat Meadowcroft 10-2;
E. Charlton beat Dodd 10-7; J. Spencer beat Hallett 10-7; Dennis Taylor beat
S. Francisco 10-9; S. Davis beat Williams 10-4; C. Thorburn beat Campbell
10-5; T. Griffiths beat Wildman 10-8; P. Mans beat Black 10-3; K. Stevens beat
Fisher 10-2; D. Mountjoy beat Wilson 10-2; Meo beat J. White 10-8;
A. Knowles beat Miles 10-3; R. Reardon beat E. Hughes 10-7

Second round: Higgins beat Thorne 13-8; Werbeniuk beat David Taylor 13-10;
Charlton beat Spencer 13-11; S. Davis beat Dennis Taylor 13-11; Thorburn
beat Griffiths 13-12; Meo beat Mountjoy 13-11; Knowles beat Reardon 13-12;
Stevens beat Mans 13-3

Quarter-finals: Higgins beat Werbeniuk 13-11; S. Davis beat Charlton 13-5;
Thorburn beat Stevens 13-12; Knowles beat Meo 13-9

Semi-finals: Thorburn beat Knowles 16-15; S. Davis beat Higgins 16-5

Final: S. Davis beat Thorburn 18-6

1984

Qualifying groups

1   J. Parrott beat D. Hughes 10-3; Parrott beat C. Everton 10-2; Parrott beat P. Mans 10-0

2   B. Mikkelsen beat P. Medati 10-8; Mikkelsen beat F. Jonik 10-9; W. Thorne beat Mikkelsen 10-3

3   M. Morra beat G. Foulds 10-2; T. Murphy beat J. Fitzmaurice 10-8; Morra beat Murphy 10-5; Morra beat D. Reynolds 10-7

4   W. Sanderson beat P. Morgan 10-8; P. Mifsud beat E. Hughes 10-5; Mifsud beat Sanderson 10-5; Mifsud beat C. Wilson 10-8

5   J. van Rensberg beat V. Harris 10-7; R. Edmonds beat D. Greaves 10-0; van Rensberg beat Edmonds 10-9; S. Francisco beat van Rensberg 10-3

6   I. Williamson beat P. Houlihan 10-5; M. Hines beat I. Black 10-5; Williamson beat Hines 10-6; G. Miles beat Williamson 10-6

7   M. Gibson beat G. Rigitano 10-7; M. Fisher beat P. Thornley 10-8; Gibson beat Fisher 10-7; J. Johnson beat Gibson 10-3

8   E. McLaughlin beat J. Hargreaves 10-5; R. Andrewartha *wo* J. Bear *scr*; Andrewartha beat McLaughlin 10-8; Andrewartha beat M. Wildman 10-9

9   J. Wych beat G. Ganim Jr 10-1; G. Scott beat L. Heywood 10-7; Wych beat Scott 10-6; Wych beat P. Fagan 10-3

10   P. Browne beat S. Duggan 10-9; C. Roscoe beat B. Demarco 10-7; Browne beat Roscoe 10-4; E. Sinclair beat Browne 10-1

11   M. Gauvreau beat J. Campbell 10-7; G. Cripsey beat M. Parkin 10-4; Gauvreau beat Cripsey 10-1; Gauvreau beat M. Macleod 10-6

12   I. Anderson beat G. Watson 10-4; J. Donnelly beat P. Watchorn 10-7; Donnelly beat Anderson 10-6; F. Davis beat Donnelly 10-5

13   W. King beat T. Jones 10-9; M. Watterson beat B. Bennett 10-5; King beat Watterson 10-8; King beat Dave Martin 10-8

14   J. Caggianello beat M. Darrington 10-7; W. Oliver beat J. Dunning 10-3; Oliver beat Caggianello 10-7; R. Williams beat Oliver 10-8

15   N. Foulds beat D. French 10-5; L. Dodd beat J. Giannaros 10-1; Foulds beat Dodd 10-4; Foulds beat J. Meadowcroft 10-2

16   B. Harris beat D. Sheehan 10-3; P. Burke beat B. Kelly 10-7; Burke beat Harris 10-4; M. Hallett beat Burke 10-5

First round: S. Davis beat King 10-3; J. Spencer beat Miles 10-3; T. Griffiths beat Mifsud 10-2; B. Werbeniuk beat F. Davis 10-4; N. Foulds beat A. Higgins 10-9; D. Mountjoy beat Hallett 10-4; Dennis Taylor beat Johnson 10-1; Parrott beat A. Knowles 10-7; C. Thorburn beat Morra 10-3; Thorne beat J. Virgo 10-9; J. White beat Williams 10-6; E. Charlton beat Andrewartha 10-4; K. Stevens beat Sinclair 10-1; David Taylor beat Gauvreau 10-5; S. Francisco beat T. Meo 10-5; R. Reardon beat Wych 10-7

Second round: S. Davis beat Spencer 13-5; Griffiths beat Werbeniuk 13-5; Mountjoy beat N. Foulds 13-6; Dennis Taylor beat Parrott 13-11; Thorburn beat Thorne 13-11; White beat Charlton 13-7; Stevens beat David Tyalor 13-10; Reardon beat S. Francisco 13-8

Quarter-finals: S. Davis beat Griffiths 13-10; Dennis Taylor beat Mountjoy 13-8; White beat Thorburn 13-8; Stevens beat Reardon 13-2

The Crucible Theatre, Sheffield, just before the start of play. A screen will be lowered to separate the two tables. (David Muscroft)

Semi-finals: S. Davis beat Dennis Taylor 16-9; White beat Stevens 16-14

Final: S. Davis beat White 18-16

1985
Qualifying groups
1 G. Rigitano beat D. Sheehan 10-9; Rigitano beat B. Harris 10-4; Rigitano beat B. Kelly 10-6; Rigitano beat M. Fisher 10-2; N. Foulds beat Rigitano 10-8

2 D. O'Kane *wo* J. McLaughlin *scr*; O'Kane beat V. Harris 10-5; O'Kane beat F. Jonik 10-5; O'Kane beat L. Dodd 10-7; O'Kane beat D. Martin 10-8

3 S. Longworth beat J. Giannaros 10-1; Longworth beat G. Cripsey 10-8; J. van Rensberg beat Longworth 10-7; M. Gauvreau beat van Rensberg 10-9; D. Reynolds beat Gauvreau 10-1

4 R. Chaperon beat R. Bales 10-7; Chaperon beat L. Heywood 10-1; Chaperon beat P. Morgan 10-3; F. Davis beat Chaperon 10-9; R. Williams beat F. Davis 10-6

5 D. Hughes beat D. French 10-5; S. Newbury beat Hughes 10-9; Newbury beat P. Burke 10-3; Newbury beat G. Scott 10-2; E. Hughes beat Newbury 10-6

6 M. Hines beat T. Chappel 10-8; Hines beat P. Watchorn 10-4; M. Gibson beat Hines 10-7; P. Fagan beat Gibson 10-8; Fagan beat C. Wilson 10-9

7 D. Fowler beat J. Hargreaves 10-0; Fowler *wo* G. Watson *scr*; Fowler *wo*

J. Caggianello *scr*; Fowler beat J. Donnelly 10-0; J. Parrott beat Fowler 10-2

8   R. Foldvari *wo* P. Thornley *scr*; Foldvari beat B. Oliver 10-3; R. Edmonds beat Foldvari 10-3; Edmonds beat M. Wildman 10-7

9   D. Chalmers beat D. Greaves 10-3; Chalmers beat E. McLaughlin 10-9; Chalmers beat I. Black 10-4; M. Hallett beat Chalmers 10-1

10   G. Foulds beat M. Parkin 10-6; Foulds beat C. Everton 10-2; Foulds beat C. Roscoe 10-7; J. Johnson beat Foulds 10-6

11   P. Medati beat B. Bennett 10-4; Medati beat I. Williamson 10-8; Medati beat W. King 10-9; S. Francisco beat Medati 10-7

12   I. Anderson beat A. Kearney 10-8; P. Browne beat Anderson 10-5; M. Morra beat Browne 10-6; J. Campbell beat Morra 10-9

13   W. Jones beat John Rea 10-3; Jones beat J. Dunning 10-6; Jones beat M. Watterson 10-5; Jones beat G. Miles 10-8

14   M. Bradley beat D. Mienie 10-4; Bradley beat B. Mikkelsen 10-9; J. Wych beat Bradley 10-7; J. Virgo beat Wych 10-4

15   P. Francisco beat B. Demarco 10-4; Francisco beat T. Murphy 10-4; Francisco beat J. Meadowcroft 10-5; M. Macleod beat Francisco 10-7

16   T. Jones beat M. Darrington 10-2; Jones beat S. Duggan 10-8; Jones beat J. Fitzmaurice 10-4; Jones beat E. Sinclair 10-2

First round: S. Davis beat N. Foulds 10-8; David Taylor beat O'Kane 10-4; A. Higgins beat Reynolds 10-4; T. Griffiths beat Williams 10-3; R. Reardon beat E. Hughes 10-9; Fagan beat W. Thorne 10-6; Parrott beat J. Spencer 10-3; K. Stevens beat Edmonds 10-8; C. Thorburn beat Hallett 10-8; B. Werbeniuk beat Johnson 10-8; Dennis Taylor beat S. Francisco 10-2; E. Charlton beat Campbell 10-3; J. White beat W. Jones 10-4; T. Meo beat Virgo 10-6; D. Mountjoy beat Macleod 10-5; A. Knowles beat T. Jones 10-8

Second round: S. Davis beat David Taylor 13-4; Griffiths beat Higgins 13-7; Reardon beat Fagan 13-9; Parrott beat Stevens 13-6; Thorburn beat Werbeniuk 13-3; Dennis Taylor beat Charlton 13-6; White beat Meo 13-11; Knowles beat Mountjoy 13-6

Quarter-finals: S. Davis beat Griffiths 13-6; Reardon beat Parrott 13-12; Dennis Taylor beat Thorburn 13-5; Knowles beat White 13-10

Semi-finals: S. Davis beat Reardon 16-5; Dennis Taylor beat Knowles 16-5

Final: Dennis Taylor beat S. Davis 18-17

NATIONAL PROFESSIONAL CHAMPIONSHIPS

ENGLISH PROFESSIONAL CHAMPIONSHIP

John Courage sponsored the first English Professional Championship in 1981 but the event was not held again until 1985 when Tolly

Cobbold, another brewer, switched its support from an invitation tournament. The Tolly Cobbold Classic (see discontinued tournaments) had been recorded by Anglia Television for showing later in the year and their coverage too was switched to the Championship.

From the 1984–85 season, the staging of all the national professional championships became easier when the WPBSA decided to inject cash to the tune of £1,000 per entrant into both domestic and other national championships. The Welsh Professional Championship is the only other event to be televised.

1981 (*John Courage*)
Qualifying: R. Edmonds beat M. Hallett 9-3; J. Johnson beat A. Knowles 9-2; M. Wildman beat B. Bennett 9-3; J. Dunning beat D. Greaves 9-4; J. Meadowcroft beat J. Barrie 9-3

First round: Edmonds beat F. Davis 9-6; T. Meo beat J. Virgo 9-6; G. Miles beat S. Hood 9-1; S. Davis beat Meadowcroft 9-2; J. Spencer beat P. Houlihan 9-1; W. Thorne beat Wildman 9-2; Johnson *wo*; Dunning beat David Taylor 9-8

Quarter-finals: S. Davis beat Spencer 9-7; Meo beat Miles 9-7; Thorne beat Dunning 9-0; Edmonds beat Johnson 9-5

Semi-finals: S. Davis beat Edmonds 9-0; Meo beat Thorne 9-8

Final: S. Davis beat Meo 9-3

1985 (*Tolly Cobbold*)
Qualifying: D. Fowler beat W. Oliver 9-7; M. Bradley beat I. Williamson 9-8; T. Jones beat P. Houlihan 9-1; L. Dodd beat R. Bales 9-5; J. Fitzmaurice beat D. Greaves 9-3; M. Fisher beat D. French 9-8; S. Duggan beat B. Harris 9-8; D. Hughes beat M. Watterson 9-5; D. Chalmers beat J. Meadowcroft 9-3; S. Longworth beat R. Edmonds 9-4; P. Medati beat J. Hargreaves 9-8; G. Foulds beat F. Davis 9-2; G. Cripsey beat B. Bennett 9-0; G. Scott beat V. Harris 9-7

First round: S. Davis beat Fowler 9-3; M. Hallett beat Duggan 9-4; J. Johnson beat Scott 9-1; T. Meo beat Fisher 9-3; J. Virgo beat M. Darrington 9-0; D. Reynolds beat Fitzmaurice 9-2; R. Williams beat T. Jones 9-6; W. Thorne beat Dodd 9-1; Longworth beat M. Wildman 9-3; J. White beat Chalmers 9-5; Medati beat J. Spencer 9-4; N. Foulds beat D. Hughes 9-3; David Taylor beat Cripsey 9-5; J. Parrott beat G. Foulds 9-4; D. Martin beat G. Miles 9-7; A. Knowles beat Bradley 9-8

Second round: Virgo beat Johnson 9-4; Reynolds beat Thorne 9-6; S. Davis beat Williams 9-2; Meo beat Hallett 9-4; Knowles beat Martin 9-3; David Taylor beat Parrott 9-7; White beat N. Foulds 9-7; Longworth beat Medati 9-7

Quarter-finals: Meo beat Reynolds 9-4; Longworth beat White 9-5; Knowles beat David Taylor 9-2; S. Davis beat Virgo 9-2

Semi-finals: Knowles beat Longworth 9-6; S. Davis beat Meo 9-8

Final: S. Davis beat Knowles 9-2

IRISH PROFESSIONAL CHAMPIONSHIP

1972
Challenge: A. Higgins beat Jack Rea 28-12

1978
Challenge: A. Higgins beat Dennis Taylor 21-7

1979
Challenge: A. Higgins beat P. Fagan 21-13

1980
Challenge: Dennis Taylor beat A. Higgins 21-15

1981
Challenge: Dennis Taylor beat P. Fagan 22-21

1982
First round: E. Hughes beat D. Sheehan 6-1

Quarter-finals: E. Hughes beat Jack Rea 6-0; T. Murphy beat P. Fagan 6-2

Semi-finals: Dennis Taylor beat Murphy 6-0; A. Higgins beat E. Hughes 6-2

Final: Taylor beat Higgins 16-13

1983
First round: Dennis Taylor beat B. Kelly 6-0; P. Fagan beat T. Murphy 6-4; A. Higgins beat Jack Rea 6-3; E. Hughes beat P. Burke 6-2

Semi-finals: Higgins beat E. Hughes 6-2; Taylor beat Fagan 6-1

Final: Higgins beat Taylor 16-11

1985 (*Strongbow*)
Preliminary: J. McLaughlin beat D. Sheehan 6-3

Qualifying: P. Burke beat A. Kearney 6-4; T. Murphy beat P. Browne 6-3; B. Kelly beat P. Watchorn 6-2; Jack Rea beat McLaughlin 6-5

Quarter-finals: P. Fagan beat Murphy 6-2; Dennis Taylor beat Jack Rea 6-0; A. Higgins beat Burke 6-0; E. Hughes beat Kelly 6-2

Semi-finals: Dennis Taylor beat Hughes 6-5; Higgins beat Fagan 6-3

Final: Dennis Taylor beat Higgins 10-5

SCOTTISH PROFESSIONAL CHAMPIONSHIP

1980
Challenge: E. Sinclair beat C. Ross 11-6

1981
First round: M. Gibson beat B. Demarco 5-3; J. Donnelly beat E. Sinclair 5-0; E. McLaughlin beat Č. Ross 5-3; I. Black beat M. Macleod 5-4

Semi-finals: Gibson beat Donnelly 6-4; Black beat E. McLaughlin 6-3

Final: Black beat Gibson 11-7

1982
First round: M. Macleod beat J. Donnelly 6-5

Quarter-finals: C. Ross beat B. Demarco 6-5; M. Gibson beat E. McLaughlin 6-3; I. Black beat Macleod 6-0; E. Sinclair beat J. Phillips 6-3

Semi-finals: Black beat Ross 6-4; Sinclair beat Gibson 6-2

Final: Sinclair beat Black 11-7

1983
First round: J. Donnelly beat B. Demarco 6-4; I. Black beat E. McLaughlin 6-4; M. Macleod beat M. Gibson 6-5

Semi-finals: E. Sinclair beat Donnelly 6-5; Macleod beat Black 6-2

Final: Macleod beat Sinclair 11-9

1985
First round: M. Macleod beat E. McLaughlin 6-4; M. Gibson beat I. Black 6-2; John Rea beat J. Donnelly 6-2; E. Sinclair beat B. Demarco 6-3

Semi-final: Macleod beat Gibson 6-4; Sinclair beat John Rea 6-2

Final: Macleod beat Sinclair 10-2

WELSH PROFESSIONAL CHAMPIONSHIP

1977 (*William Hill*)
Challenge: R. Reardon beat D. Mountjoy 12-8

1980 (*Woodpecker*)
First round: D. Mountjoy beat T. Griffiths 9-6; R. Reardon beat C. Wilson 9-3

Final: Mountjoy beat Reardon 9-6

1981 (*Woodpecker*)
Qualifying: C. Wilson beat R. Andrewartha 6-5

First round: Wilson beat D. Mountjoy 9-6; R. Reardon beat T. Griffiths 9-6

Final: Reardon beat Wilson 9-6

1982 (*Woodpecker*)
First round: C. Wilson beat M. Owen 6-0; T. Griffiths beat C. Roscoe 6-2; R. Reardon beat C. Everton 6-1; D. Mountjoy beat R. Andrewartha 6-3

Semi-finals: Griffiths beat Wilson 9-6; Mountjoy beat Reardon 9-7

Final: Mountjoy beat Griffiths 9-8

1983 (*Woodpecker*)
First round: T. Griffiths beat C. Everton 6-1; R. Reardon beat R. Andrewartha 6-2; C. Wilson beat C. Roscoe 6-4; D. Mountjoy beat M. Owen 6-0

Semi-finals: Reardon beat Griffiths 9-4; Mountjoy beat Wilson 9-3

Final: Reardon beat Mountjoy 9-1

1984 (*Strongbow*)
First round: D. Mountjoy beat C. Everton 6-1; T. Griffiths beat R. Andrewartha 6-1; R. Reardon beat M. Owen 6-1; C. Wilson beat C. Roscoe 6-2

Semi-finals: Mountjoy beat Griffiths 9-5; Wilson beat Reardon 9-4

Final: Mountjoy beat Wilson 9-3

1985 (*BCE*)
First round: S. Newbury beat W. Jones 6-2; T. Chappel beat M. Owen 6-0

Quarter-finals: R. Reardon beat C. Everton 6-2; D. Mountjoy beat Newbury 6-5; C. Wilson beat C. Roscoe 6-3; T. Griffiths beat Chappel 6-0

Semi-finals: Griffiths beat Reardon 9-3; Mountjoy beat Wilson 9-2

Final: Griffiths beat Mountjoy 9-4

DISCONTINUED TOURNAMENTS

TOLLY COBBOLD CLASSIC

After a pilot four-man tournament proved successful at the Corn Exchange, Ipswich in 1978, both Tolly Cobbold and Anglia Television became involved. For the next three years, the event consisted of a four-man round robin with the top two finishers contesting the final.

However, in 1982 the event was expanded to encompass eight professionals and changed to a knockout format.

1979
Final: A. Higgins beat R. Reardon 5-4

1980
Final: A. Higgins beat Dennis Taylor 5-4

1981
Final: G. Miles beat C. Thorburn 5-1

1982
First round: G. Miles beat T. Meo 3-0; A. Knowles beat David Taylor 3-0; Dennis Taylor beat J. White 3-1; S. Davis beat W. Thorne 3-0

Semi-finals: S. Davis beat Miles 5-2; Dennis Taylor beat Knowles 5-2

Final: S. Davis beat Dennis Taylor 8-3

1983
First round: B. Werbeniuk beat D. Mountjoy 4-2; T. Griffiths beat R. Reardon 4-2; S. Davis beat White 4-3; Dennis Taylor beat A. Higgins 4-2

Semi-finals: Griffiths beat Werbeniuk 5-3; S. Davis beat Dennis Taylor 5-1

Final: S. Davis beat Griffiths 7-5

1984
First round: C. Thorburn beat T. Meo 5-4; A. Knowles beat White 5-1; K. Stevens beat E. Charlton 5-3; S. Davis beat W. Thorne 5-2

Semi-finals: Knowles beat Thorburn 5-3; Davis beat Stevens 5-4

Final: S. Davis beat Knowles 8-2

YAMAHA

As a variant to straight matchplay, the experimental, untelevised British Gold Cup was staged in 1980 and proved popular with the public if not with the players. Yamaha stepped forward to sponsor the event the following year and continued to do so for four years. During the event's lifetime, the format underwent several changes but remained round robin with matches of no more than three frames.

The slot and the venue, the Assembly Rooms, Derby are now occupied by the Dulux British Open.

1980 (*British Gold Cup*)
Group 1: A. Higgins beat P. Fagan 2-1; beat Griffiths 3-0; T. Griffiths beat David Taylor 3-0; beat Fagan 2-1; David Taylor beat Higgins 2-1; beat Fagan 2-1

Group 2: Dennis Taylor beat Virgo 3-0; beat Thorne 3-0; beat Pulman 3-0; W. Thorne beat Pulman 2-1; beat Virgo 3-0; J. Virgo beat Pulman 3-0

Group 3: T. Meo beat Mountjoy 2-1; beat Spencer 3-0; G. Miles beat Spencer 3-0; beat Meo 2-1; D. Mountjoy beat Miles 2-1; J. Spencer beat Mountjoy 2-1

Group 4: R. Reardon beat F. Davis 3-0; beat Houlihan 3-0; beat Werbeniuk 2-1; B. Werbeniuk beat F. Davis 2-1; beat Houlihan 3-0; F. Davis beat Houlihan 2-1

Semi-finals: Higgins beat Meo 4-0; Reardon beat Dennis Taylor 4-3

Final: Higgins beat Reardon 5-1

1981
Qualifying group 1: P. Houlihan beat J. Pulman 2-1; J. White beat Pulman 2-1; Houlihan beat P. Fagan 2-1; White beat Fagan 2-1; Pulman beat Fagan 3-0

Qualifying group 2: A. Knowles beat J. Johnson 3-0; M. Hallett beat Johnson 3-0; Hallett beat W. Thorne 2-1; Hallett beat Knowles 2-1; Thorne beat Knowles 2-1; Thorne beat Johnson 2-1

Qualifying group 3: J. Spencer beat J. Meadowcroft 3-0; R. Edmonds beat Meadowcroft 2-1; Meadowcroft beat D. Martin 2-1; Spencer beat Martin 2-1; Edmonds beat Spencer 2-1

Qualifying group 4: C. Wilson beat M. Wildman 3-0; G. Miles beat Wildman 2-1; Miles beat T. Meo 3-0; Miles beat Wilson 2-1; Meo beat Wilson 2-1; Meo beat Wildman 3-0

Group 1: D. Mountjoy beat R. Reardon 3-0; David Taylor beat Mountjoy 3-0; David Taylor beat Miles 2-1; Mountjoy beat Miles 3-0; Reardon beat Miles 3-0; Reardon beat David Taylor 2-1; *play-off*: David Taylor beat Mountjoy 1-0

Group 2: T. Griffiths beat B. Werbeniuk 3-0; K. Stevens beat Werbeniuk 2-1; Hallett beat Stevens 2-1; Hallett beat Werbeniuk 2-1; Griffiths beat Hallett 2-1; Stevens beat Griffiths 3-0

Group 3: Dennis Taylor beat A. Higgins 3-0; Higgins beat F. Davis 3-0; Edmonds beat F. Davis 2-1; Higgins beat Edmonds 2-1; Dennis Taylor beat Edmonds 2-1; F. Davis beat Dennis Taylor 2-1

Group 4: S. Davis beat C. Thorburn 2-1; S. Davis beat J. Virgo 3-0; White beat Virgo 2-1; S. Davis beat White 3-0; White beat Thorburn 3-0; Thorburn beat Virgo 2-1

Semi-finals: David Taylor beat Stevens 5-3; S. Davis beat Dennis Taylor 5-2

Final: S. Davis beat David Taylor 9-6

1982
Preliminary match: D. Reynolds beat T. Murphy 3-0

Preliminary groups

M   C. Wilson beat G. Foulds 2-0; Foulds beat J. Dunning 2-1; Wilson beat Dunning 2-0

L   P. Medati beat E. Sinclair 2-0; Medati beat E. Hughes 2-0; Sinclair beat Hughes 2-0

K   J. Meadowcroft beat M. Watterson 2-1; Watterson beat C. Everton 2-0; Meadowcroft beat Everton 2-1

J   E. McLaughlin beat P. Fagan 2-0; Reynolds beat McLaughlin 2-1; Reynolds beat Fagan 2-0

H   D. Martin beat J. Johnson 2-1; Martin beat C. Wilson 2-1; Wilson beat G. Foulds 2-0; Martin beat Foulds 2-1; Johnson beat Foulds 2-0; Johnson beat Wilson 2-0

G   W. Thorne beat J. White 2-0; White beat P. Medati 2-0; E. Sinclair beat Medati 2-0; White beat Sinclair 2-1; Thorne beat Sinclair 2-0; Medati beat Thorne 2-1

F   P. Houlihan beat M. Hallett 2-1; J. Meadowcroft beat Houlihan 2-0; M. Watterson beat Meadowcroft 2-0; Watterson beat Houlihan 2-1; Hallett beat Watterson 2-1; Meadowcroft beat Hallett 2-1

E   R. Williams beat A. Knowles 2-1; D. Reynolds beat Williams 2-1; Reynolds beat E. McLaughlin 2-0; Williams beat E. McLaughlin 2-1; Knowles beat E. McLaughlin 2-0; Knowles beat Reynolds 2-1

Qualifying groups

D   J. Virgo beat J. Spencer 2-0; Spencer beat Martin 2-1; Johnson beat Martin 2-1; Johnson beat Spencer 2-1; Virgo beat Johnson 2-1; Virgo beat Martin 2-1

C   G. Miles beat F. Davis 2-0; Miles beat Thorne 2-1; White beat Thorne 2-0; White beat Miles 2-0; White beat Davis 2-0; Thorne beat Davis 2-1

B   A. Higgins beat T. Meo 2-1; Meo beat Meadowcroft 2-0; Meadowcroft beat Watterson 2-1; Meo beat Watterson 2-0; Higgins beat Watterson 2-1; Higgins beat Meadowcroft 2-0

A   K. Stevens beat R. Edmonds 2-0; Edmonds beat Reynolds 2-0; Reynolds beat Knowles 2-1; Knowles beat Edmonds 2-1; Stevens beat Knowles 2-1; Stevens beat Reynolds 2-1

Group 1: S. Davis beat B. Werbeniuk 2-0; Stevens beat Werbeniuk 2-1; Stevens beat Edmonds 2-1; Edmonds beat Werbeniuk 2-0; Edmonds beat Davis 2-1; Davis beat Stevens 2-0

Group 2: David Taylor beat C. Thorburn 2-1; David Taylor beat Higgins 2-1; Meo beat Higgins 2-0; David Taylor beat Meo 2-1; Thorburn beat Meo 2-0; Higgins beat Thorburn 2-1

Group 3: T. Griffiths beat D. Mountjoy 2-1; Mountjoy beat White 2-0; Miles beat White 2-1; Miles beat Mountjoy 2-0; Griffiths beat Miles 2-1; Griffiths beat White 2-1

Group 4: Dennis Taylor beat R. Reardon 2-1; Virgo beat Dennis Taylor 2-1; Johnson beat Virgo 2-1; Dennis Taylor beat Johnson 2-0; Reardon beat Johnson 2-0; Virgo beat Reardon 2-0

Semi-final (Group A): S. Davis beat Virgo 2-0; Virgo beat Edmonds 2-0; Edmonds beat Dennis Taylor 2-1; Davis beat Taylor 2-1; Davis beat Edmonds 2-0

Semi-final (Group B): Griffiths beat David Taylor 2-0; Griffiths beat Thorburn 2-1; Thorburn beat Miles 2-1; Griffiths beat Miles 2-0; Miles beat Taylor 2-0; Thorburn beat Taylor 2-1

Final: S. Davis beat Griffiths 9-7

1983
Preliminary groups

1   J. Virgo beat J. Donnelly 2-1; Donnelly beat E. Hughes 2-0; R. Edmonds beat Hughes 2-1; Edmonds beat Donnelly 2-0; Virgo beat Edmonds 2-1; Virgo beat Hughes 2-0

2   F. Davis beat G. Foulds 2-0; Foulds beat R. Williams 2-0; Williams beat B. Kelly 2-1; Foulds beat Kelly 2-1; Kelly beat Davis 2-1; Davis beat Williams 2-0

3   J. Johnson beat M. Macleod 2-0; M. Morra beat Macleod 2-1; Johnson beat Morra 2-0

4   D. Reynolds beat P. Houlihan 2-0; Houlihan beat E. McLaughlin 2-0; Reynolds beat I. Black 2-1; McLaughlin beat Reynolds 2-0; Black beat McLaughlin 2-1; Black beat Houlihan 2-0

5   P. Fagan beat J. Fitzmaurice 2-0; Gibson beat Fitzmaurice 2-0; Gibson beat D. Hughes 2-0; Fitzmaurice beat Hughes 2-0; Hughes beat Fagan 2-1; Fagan beat Gibson 2-0

6   T. Meo beat P. Medati 2-1; M. Hallett beat Medati 2-0; Hallett beat J. Meadowcroft 2-1; Meadowcroft beat Medati 2-1; Meo beat Meadowcroft 2-1; Meo beat Hallett 2-0

7   C. Wilson beat J. Dunning 2-1; E. Sinclair beat Dunning 2-0; Sinclair beat M. Watterson 2-1; Watterson beat Dunning 2-0; Wilson beat Watterson 2-0; Wilson beat Sinclair 2-0

8   M. Wildman beat D. Martin 2-0; C. Roscoe beat Wildman 2-0; D. French beat Roscoe 2-1; French beat Wildman 2-1; French beat Martin 2-1 (*last match not played*)

Qualifying groups

A   J. White beat G. Miles 2-0; Miles beat Virgo 2-1; French beat Virgo 2-0; French beat Miles 2-1; White beat French 2-0; Virgo beat White 2-1

B   Wilson beat F. Davis 2-1; Wilson beat J. Spencer 2-1; Spencer beat F. Davis 2-0

C   W. Thorne beat Dennis Taylor 2-0; Thorne beat Johnson 2-0; T. Meo beat Johnson 2-0; Thorne beat Meo 2-0; Meo beat Taylor 2-0

D   T. Griffiths beat A. Knowles 2-0; Knowles beat Black 2-0; P. Fagan beat Black 2-1; Knowles beat Fagan 2-0; Griffiths beat Fagan 2-1; Griffiths beat Black 2-1

Group 1: S. Davis beat B. Werbeniuk 2-0; White beat Werbeniuk 2-0; White beat Knowles 2-0; Werbeniuk beat Knowles 2-0; Knowles beat Davis 2-1; White beat Davis 2-0

Group 2: R. Reardon beat David Taylor 2-0; Taylor beat Wilson 2-1; Meo beat Wilson 2-1; Taylor beat Meo 2-0; Meo beat Reardon 2-0; Reardon beat Wilson 2-0

Group 3: D. Mountjoy beat A. Higgins 2-1; Thorne beat Mountjoy 2-0; Thorne beat Spencer 2-0; Mountjoy beat Spencer 2-0; Spencer beat Higgins 2-0; Higgins beat Thorne 2-1

Group 4: E. Charlton beat K. Stevens 2-1; Griffiths beat Stevens 2-0; Griffiths beat French 2-1; French beat Stevens 2-0; Charlton beat French 2-0; Griffiths beat Charlton 2-0

Semi-final (Group A): Griffiths beat White 2-0; Griffiths beat David Taylor 2-1; Taylor beat Mountjoy 2-0; Mountjoy beat Griffiths 2-0; White beat Mountjoy 2-0; White beat Taylor 2-0

Semi-final (Group B): Thorne beat Reardon 2-1; S. Davis beat Thorne 2-0; Davis beat Charlton 2-1; Thorne beat Charlton 2-1; Reardon beat Charlton 2-0; Reardon beat Davis 2-1

Final: Reardon beat White 9-6

1984
Preliminary Groups

1   N. Foulds beat J. Parrott 2-1; Parrott beat G. Ganim Jr 2-0; T. Jones beat Ganim 2-0; Jones beat Parrott 2-0; Foulds beat Jones 2-1; N. Foulds beat Ganim 2-0 *Qualifiers*: N. Foulds, T. Jones.

2   W. King beat B. Demarco 2-0; G. Foulds beat B. Bennett 2-0; King beat
    Bennett 2-1; Bennett beat Demarco 2-0; Demarco beat Foulds 2-0
    Qualifiers: G. Foulds, W. King
3   M. Morra beat P. Morgan 2-1; Morra beat D. Greaves 2-1; P. Browne beat
    Greaves 2-1; Morgan beat Greaves 2-0; Morgan beat Browne 2-1; Morra
    beat Browne 2-0 *Qualifiers*: M. Morra, P. Morgan
4   M. Gauvreau beat M. Gibson 2-0; Gibson beat P. Houlihan 2-0; Houlihan
    beat J. Hargreaves 2-0; Hargreaves beat Gibson 2-0; Hargreaves beat
    Gauvreau 2-0; Houlihan beat Gauvreau 2-0 *Qualifiers*: P. Houlihan,
    J. Hargreaves
5   M. Darrington beat R. Andrewartha 2-0; B. Harris beat Andrewartha 2-1;
    Harris beat S. Duggan 2-1; Darrington beat Harris 2-1; Darrington beat
    Duggan 2-1; Andrewartha beat Duggan 2-1 *Qualifiers*: M. Darrington,
    B. Harris
6   D. French beat P. Watchorn 2-0; L. Heywood and J. Giannaros *scr*
    Qualifiers: D. French, P. Watchorn
7   G. Rigitano beat W. Oliver 2-1; Rigitano beat D. Hughes 2-0; P. Medati
    beat Hughes 2-1; Hughes beat Oliver 2-1; Medati beat Oliver 2-1; Rigitano
    beat Medati 2-0 *Qualifiers*: G. Rigitano, P. Medati
8   V. Harris beat P. Burke 2-0; Burke beat D. Sheehan 2-0; Harris beat
    Sheehan 2-1 *Qualifier*: V. Harris

Qualifying rounds
10   J. White beat F. Jonik 2-0; Jonik beat Rigitano 2-0; White beat Rigitano 2-0
     Qualifier: J. White
11   D. Mountjoy beat T. Murphy 2-1; J. Bear *scr Qualifier*: D. Mountjoy
12   G. Scott beat Dennis Taylor 2-1; N. Foulds beat Taylor 2-0; Foulds beat
     Scott 2-0 *Qualifier*: N. Foulds
13   J. Virgo beat I. Black 2-0; G. Cripsey beat Black 2-0; Virgo beat Cripsey
     2-1 *Qualifier*: J. Virgo
14   T. Meo beat C. Everton 2-0; Everton beat P. Morgan 2-0; Morgan beat
     Meo 2-0; *Tie break*: Morgan potted 30 balls, Meo 29, Everton 3 *Qualifier*:
     P. Morgan
15   J. Fitzmaurice beat J. Spencer 2-1; Spencer beat V. Harris 2-1;
     Fitzmaurice beat Harris 2-0 *Qualifier*: J. Fitzmaurice
16   W. Thorne beat E. Hughes 2-0; T. Jones beat Hughes 2-0; Thorne beat
     Jones 2-0 *Qualifier*: W. Thorne
17   J. Dunning beat D. Reynolds 2-1; P. Watchorn beat Reynolds 2-1; Dunning
     beat Watchorn 2-1 *Qualifier*: J. Dunning
18   C. Wilson beat M. Hallett 2-1; Hallett beat M. Darrington 2-1; Darrington
     beat Wilson 2-0 *Qualifier*: M. Darrington
19   Medati beat G. Miles 2-1; J. Campbell *scr Qualifier*: P. Medati
20   C. Roscoe beat J. Johnson 2-0; D. French beat Johnson 2-0; French beat
     Roscoe 2-0 *Qualifier*: D. French
21   M. Wildman beat J. Donnelly 2-0; M. Morra beat Donnelly 2-0; Morra beat
     Wildman 2-0 *Qualifier*: M. Morra
22   E. McLaughlin beat P. Fagan 2-1; Fagan beat W. King 2-1; King beat
     McLaughlin 2-0 *Qualifier*: W. King
23   E. Sinclair beat R. Edmonds 2-0; Edmonds beat J. Hargreaves 2-1;
     Sinclair beat Hargreaves 2-0 *Qualifier*: E. Sinclair

24 M. Watterson beat M. Macleod 2-1; Macleod beat G. Foulds 2-0;
    Watterson beat Foulds 2-0 *Qualifier*: M. Watterson
25 D. Martin beat M. Fisher 2-1; Fisher beat B. Harris 2-0; Martin beat Harris
    2-1 *Qualifier*: D. Martin
26 R. Williams beat L. Dodd 2-1; Dodd beat P. Houlihan 2-0; Houlihan beat
    Williams 2-0 *Qualifier*: L. Dodd
27 B. Kelly beat J. Meadowcroft 2-1; I. Williamson beat Meadowcroft 2-1;
    Kelly beat Williamson 2-0 *Qualifier*: B. Kelly

First round
 1 R. Reardon beat M. Darrington 2-0; M. Morra beat Darrington 2-1;
    Reardon beat Morra 2-0 *Qualifier*: R. Reardon
 2 S. Davis beat D. Mountjoy 2-0; Mountjoy beat B. Kelly 2-0; Davis beat
    Kelly 2-0 *Qualifier*: S. Davis
 3 J. Dunning beat A. Knowles 2-1; Knowles beat L. Dodd 2-0; Dunning beat
    Dodd 2-0 *Qualifier*: J. Dunning
 4 A. Higgins beat J. Fitzmaurice 2-0; W. King beat Fitzmaurice 2-1; King
    beat Higgins 2-1 *Qualifier*: W. King
 5 E. Charlton beat J. Virgo 2-0; Virgo beat P. Medati 2-0; Medati beat
    Charlton 2-1 *Qualifier*: E. Charlton
 6 W. Thorne beat K. Stevens 2-1; Stevens beat M. Watterson 2-1; Thorne
    beat Watterson 2-1 *Qualifier*: W. Thorne
 7 B. Werbeniuk beat N. Foulds 2-0; Foulds beat D. French 2-1; French beat
    Werbeniuk 2-0 *Qualifier*: D. French
 8 T. Griffiths beat J. White 2-1; White beat E. Sinclair 2-0; Griffiths beat
    Sinclair 2-0 *Qualifier*: T. Griffiths
 9 David Taylor beat P. Morgan 2-0; D. Martin beat Morgan 2-0; Martin beat
    Taylor 2-0 *Qualifier*: D. Martin

Semi-finals
Group 1: King beat Dunning 2-1; Dunning beat Griffiths 2-0; Griffiths beat King
2-1 *Qualifier*: J. Dunning

Group 2: Charlton beat Reardon 2-0; Martin beat Reardon 2-0; Martin beat
Charlton 2-1 *Qualifier*: D. Martin

Group 3: S. Davis beat Thorne 2-1; Thorne beat French 2-0; Davis beat French
2-0 *Qualifier*: S. Davis

Final: Martin beat Dunning 3-2; S. Davis beat Dunning 4-1; Davis beat Martin
3-0 *Winner*: S. Davis

NORWICH UNION OPEN

For two years, an attempt was made to establish a major tournament
open to both professionals and amateurs. It was staged in London and
televised by London Weekend but proved to be dominated by the
professionals.

1973 (* *denotes amateur*)
First round: *S. Hood beat Jack Rea 4-0; *C. Ross beat *M. Owen 4-3; *A. Savur beat D. Greaves 4-1; David Taylor beat J. Karnehm 4-2; Dennis Taylor beat *A. Lloyd 4-1; *J. Barron beat R. Gross 4-2; J. Dunning beat J. Meadowcroft 4-2; P. Houlihan beat *J. Virgo 4-3

Second round: G. Miles beat *Savur 4-1; *R. Edmonds beat *Barron 4-3; *Hood beat *M. Francisco 4-3; E. Charlton beat *Ross 4-0; C. Thorburn beat Houlihan 4-0; A. Higgins beat Dennis Taylor 4-3; J. Spencer beat Dunning 4-3; Pulman beat Miles 4-3

Quarter-finals: Spencer beat *Edmonds 4-0; Charlton beat *Hood 4-0; Higgins beat Thorburn 4-2; Pulman beat Miles 4-3

Semi-finals: Spencer beat Higgins 8-2; Pulman beat Charlton 8-3

Final: Spencer beat Pulman 8-7

1974 (* *denotes amateur*)
First round: C. Thorburn beat F. Davis 5-4; B. Werbeniuk beat J. Dunning 5-1; J. Spencer beat *R. Edmonds 5-0; J. Pulman beat *G. Thomas 5-0; G. Miles beat *E. Sinclair 5-0; R. Williams beat M. Owen 5-3; A. Higgins beat Dennis Taylor 5-1; R. Reardon beat *P. Burke 5-2

Quarter-finals: Higgins beat Werbeniuk 5-4; Thorburn beat Pulman 5-3; Spencer beat Miles 5-2; Reardon beat Williams 5-2

Semi-finals: Reardon beat Higgins 9-8; Spencer beat Thorburn 9-7

Final: Spencer beat Reardon 10-9

*Joe Davis and Walter Lindrum, two of the 'Big Four' billiards players, shake hands in 1932.
(Central Press Photos Ltd)*

PROFESSIONAL BILLIARDS

PROFESSIONAL BILLIARDS

THE WORLD PROFESSIONAL BILLIARDS CHAMPIONSHIP

Founded in 1870, the World Professional Billiards Championship is the oldest of all the game's events but since snooker has become by far the most popular of the billiard table games it has declined steadily in public appeal.

The problems started in the 1930s when the four best players in the world, Walter Lindrum, Joe Davis, Tom Newman and Clark McConachy, mastered all aspects of the game so completely that they effectively killed it as a public entertainment. They did such a thorough job that there was only one Championship between 1934 and 1968 that they did not claim – when Rex Williams travelled to New Zealand and beat McConachy, then 73 and suffering from Parkinson's disease.

Williams successfully defended the title three times against various challengers but lost it in June 1980 to Joe's younger brother Fred, who thus became only the second player to have held world titles at both billiards and snooker – the first, of course, was Joe.

In November 1980, the event reverted to a tournament format and a variety of playing systems was tried: time-limit games, points-up games and, for the first time last season, the best of five games of 400-up. This formula gave frequent climaxes, as in frames of snooker, and also eliminated the possibility of very large breaks.

1985 also saw Channel 4 attempt a 'Pot Black'-style billiards event, the Blue Arrow Masters. The viewing figures for this were encouraging and it is hoped that, together with the new format for the World Championship, it may signal a marked improvement in billiards' fortunes.

World Professional Billiards Championship (1870–1920)

1870 (Feb)	W. Cook	J. Roberts Sr	1,200-1,083	
(Apr)	J. Roberts Jr	W. Cook	1,000- 522	
(June)	J. Roberts Jr	A. Bowles	1,000- 759	
(Nov)	J. Bennett	J. Roberts Jr	1,000- 905	
1871 (Jan)	J. Roberts Jr	J. Bennett	1,000- 637	
(May)	W. Cook	J. Roberts Jr	1,000- 985	
(Nov)	W. Cook	J. Bennett	1,000- 942	
1872 (Mar)	W. Cook	J. Roberts Jr	1,000- 799	
1874 (Feb)	W. Cook	J. Roberts Jr	1,000- 784	
1875 (May)	J. Roberts Jr	W. Cook	1,000- 837	
(Dec)	J. Roberts Jr	W. Cook	1,000- 865	

1877 (May)	J. Roberts Jr	W. Cook	1,000- 779
1880 (Nov)	J. Bennett	W. Cook	1,000- 949
1881 (Jan)	J. Bennett	T. Taylor	1,000- 910
1885 (Apr)	J. Roberts Jr	W. Cook	3,000-2,908
(June)	J. Roberts Jr	J. Bennett	3,000-1,360
1899	C. Dawson	J. North	9,000-4,715
1900	C. Dawson	H. W. Stevenson	9,000-6,775
1901	H. W. Stevenson	C. Dawson	9,000-6,406
	C. Dawson	H. W. Stevenson	9,000-5,796
	H. W. Stevenson (*declared champion – no contest*)		
1903	C. Dawson	H. W. Stevenson	9,000-8,700
1908	M. Inman (*declared champion – no contest*)		
1909	M. Inman	A. Williams	9,000-7,662
Under Billiards Control Club Rules			
1909	H. W. Stevenson (*declared champion – no contest*)		
1910	H. W. Stevenson	M. Inman	13,370-13,212
		(*match abandoned*)	
	H. W. Stevenson	M. Inman	18,000-16,907
1911	H. W. Stevenson	M. Inman	18,000-16,914
1912	M. Inman	T. Reece	18,000- 9,675
1913	M. Inman	T. Reece	18,000-16,627
1914	M. Inman	T. Reece	18,000-12,826
1919	M. Inman	H. W. Stevenson	16,000- 9,468
1920	W. Smith	C. Falkiner	16,000-14,500

World Professional Billiards Championship (1921–85)

Winner (breaks)	Score (average)	Loser (breaks)	Score (average)
1921			
First round			
C. Falkiner 560	7,334 (35.3)	H. W. Stevenson	5,084 (24.3)
T. Newman 467	8,000 (54.0)	T. Tothill	3,267 (22.0)
Semi-finals			
Newman 627, 531	8,000 (56.7)	Falkiner 587	6,627 (47.3)
T. Reece	*nr*	F. Lawrence	*nr*
Final			
Newman	16,000 (*nr*)	Reece	10,744 (*nr*)
1922			
First round			
T. Reece	8,000 (35.2)	C. McConachy	6,767 (29.9)
Semi-finals			
T. Newman 561, 512	8,000 (52.6)	J. Davis	5,181 (34.1)
C. Falkiner 391	8,000 (41.9)	Reece 455	7,289 (38.2)
Final			
Newman	16,000 (56.4)	Falkiner	15,167 (52.7)

Winner (breaks)	Score (average)	Loser (breaks)	Score (average)
1923			
First round			
M. Inman	16,000 (*nr*)	A. Peall	11,758 (*nr*)
C. Falkiner	16,000 (*nr*)	T. Reece	14,952 (*nr*)
Semi-finals			
T. Newman	16,000 (56.3)	Inman	14,506 (51.1)
850, 705, 500 × 4		701	
W. Smith	16,000 (71.7)	Falkiner	8,695 (29.2)
688		782, 620	
Final			
Smith	16,000 (46.4)	Newman	15,180 (44.0)
451, 446		638, 629, 575	
1924			
First round			
T. Newman	16,000 (71.4)	C. McConachy	8,703 (38.9)
875		349	
Final			
Newman	16,000 (43.5)	T. Reece	14,845 (40.3)
1,021			
1925			
T. Newman	16,000 (68.4)	T. Reece	10,092 (43.1)
957, 672		512	
1926			
T. Newman	16,000 (82.0)	J. Davis	9,505 (49.0)
637, 574, 588		414	
1927			
First round			
M. Inman	8,000 (*nr*)	T. Reece	5,527 (*nr*)
459		1,151	
Second round			
J. Davis	8,000 (*nr*)	Inman	6,895
504, 588			
Challenge round			
T. Newman	16,000 (73.0)	Davis	14,763 (68.0)
787, 1,073, 1,012, 891		2,501, 727	
1928			
First round			
T. Carpenter	8,000 (22.4)	T. Reece	7,283 (20.5)
Second round			
J. Davis	8,000 (66.4)	Carpenter	5,602 (41.8)
Challenge round			
Davis	16,000 (74.4)	T. Newman	14,874 (69.5)
529, 525, 501, 425, 408,		564, 489, 467, 455,	
404, 403, 400		451, 427	
1929			
First round			
T. Newman	8,000 (74.1)	T. Carpenter	5,984 (55.4)
553		453	

Winner (breaks)	Score (average)	Loser (breaks)	Score (average)
Final			
J. Davis	18,000 (100.0)	Newman	17,219 (96.2)
838, 609, 599		723, 691, 672, 647, 576	
1930			
First round			
T. Newman	24,001 (85.1)	M. Inman	10,104 (35.8)
1,567, 1,047			
J. Davis	21,975 (82.0)	C. Falkiner	19,815 (74.0)
Final			
Davis	20,918 (113.1)	Newman	20,117 (109.9)
2,052, 500 × 9		500 × 12	
1932			
J. Davis	25,161 (112.0)	C. McConachy	19,259 (98.0)
1,058, 844, 774		1,432, 916, 889	
1933			
First round			
W. Lindrum	21,470 (*nr*)	T. Newman	20,252 (*nr*)
1,578, 984		877, 805	
J. Davis	20,136 (*nr*)	C. McConachy	16,110 (*nr*)
995		675	
Final			
Lindrum	21,815 (92.0)	Davis	21,121 (89.0)
1,492, 1,272, 1,013		792	
1934			
First round			
W. Lindrum	21,903 (*nr*)	C. McConachy	20,795 (*nr*)
1,065, 807		892, 829	
Final			
Lindrum	23,533 (*nr*)	J. Davis	22,678 (*nr*)
1,474, 1,353		824, 728	
1951			
C. McConachy	6,681 (60.0)	J. Barrie	5,057 (44.8)
481, 438, 425, 397, 376		367, 336	
1968			
R. Williams	5,499 (*nr*)	C. McConachy	5,234 (*nr*)
293		236, 200	
1971			
R. Williams	9,250 (*nr*)	B. Bennett	4,058 (*nr*)
480, 372, 353, 325, 302		132	
1973			
R. Williams	8,360 (50.7)	J. Karnehm	4,336 (26.1)
528, 363, 309		215	
1974			
R. Williams	7,017 (43.6)	E. Charlton	4,916 (30.4)
506, 365, 308, 307		488, 401	
1976			
R. Williams	9,105 (42.1)	E. Charlton	5,149 (23.9)
532, 349, 382, 306		333	

Winner (breaks)	Score (average)	Loser (breaks)	Score (average)
1980 (May)			
Challenge round			
F. Davis	5,978 (39.9)	R. Williams	4,452 (29.9)
403, 225, 234, 239, 275, 583		226, 202, 439, 229	
1980 (Nov)			
Qualifying			
P. Morgan	1,655 (21.5)	J. Dunning	1,107 (12.9)
M. Wildman	1,968 (26.2)	B. Bennett	678 (9.0)
S. Davis	1,809 (16.9)	K. Kennerley	965 (9.1)
Quarter-finals			
J. Barrie	2,186 (53.3)	S. Davis	870 (21.8)
335			
F. Davis	1,907 (43.3)	Morgan	978 (22.2)
309			
R. Edmonds	1,513 (19.4)	J. Karnehm	1,306 (17.0)
Wildman	1,476 (25.9)	R. Williams	1,415 (24.8)
Semi-finals			
F. Davis	1,253 (34.8)	Barrie	1,153 (32.0)
501			
Wildman	1,629 (21.4)	Edmonds	955 (12.6)
204			
Final			
F. Davis	3,037 (30.4)	Wildman	2,064 (20.6)
200, 361			
1982			
First round			
C. Everton	1,500 (23.4)	B. Bennett	556 (8.6)
Quarter-finals			
F. Davis	1,500 (30.6)	Everton	652 (13.6)
R. Williams	1,500 (31.9)	J. Karnehm	569 (11.9)
R. Edmonds	1,500 (16.5)	K. Kennerley	753 (8.2)
M. Wildman	1,500 (21.7)	J. Fitzmaurice	721 (10.5)
Semi-finals			
Williams	1,500 (20.3)	Davis	1,494 (19.9)
Wildman	1,500 (24.2)	Edmonds	765 (12.1)
203			
Final			
Williams	3,000 (26.1)	Wildman	1,785 (15.5)
207, 259, 217			
1983			
Qualifying			
I. Williamson	1,000 (12.5)	D. Martin	710 (8.8)
63, 79, 72, 81		52	
B. Bennett	1,000 (11.2)	G. Cripsey	683 (6.3)
63, 55, 58, 75		50	
First round			
J. Karnehm		M. Darrington	
I 122, 117, 53	752 (15.0)	54, 86, 67	679 (13.3)

Winner (breaks)	Score (average)	Loser (breaks)	Score (average)
II 59, 79	748 (12.1)	63	520 (8.4)
	1,500 (13.4)		1,199 (10.6)
B. Bennett		J. Fitzmaurice	
I 58	751 (10.0)		666 (8.8)
II 70, 80, 81, 50	749 (10.3)	61, 54	730 (10.1)
	1,500 (10.1)		1,396 (9.4)
C. Everton		I. Williamson	
I 153, 72, 84	752 (15.0)	60, 67, 52	591 (11.6)
II 105, 61, 59, 81	748 (17.8)	56, 68	494 (12.0)
	1,500 (16.3)		1,085 (11.8)
E. Charlton		T. Murphy	
I 85, 61, 53	751 (11.7)	61, 54, 51, 112	694 (10.8)
II 55, 102, 92	749 (18.3)	64, 56	411 (10.0)
	1,500 (14.3)		1,105 (10.5)
Quarter-finals			
R. Williams		Bennett	
I 87, 69, 63, 147, 107,			
100 (*unf*)	751 (30.0)		225 (8.7)
II 105 (*full*), 233, 228,			
50 (*unf*)	749 (30.6)		218 (9.5)
	1,500 (31.3)		443 (9.0)
F. Davis		Everton	
I 169, 113, 51, 147,			
83 (*unf*)	751 (37.6)	51	236 (11.2)
II 121 (*full*), 66, 71, 427	749 (39.4)	94, 51	241 (12.7)
	1,500 (38.5)		477 (11.9)
R. Edmonds		Karnehm	
I 60, 75, 135, 61	559 (13.0)	83, 59, 71, 84	
		68, 153	750 (17.4)
II 61, 358, 84, 64,			
138, 92	941 (29.4)	91, 62	325 (9.8)
	1,500 (20.0)		1,075 (14.1)
Charlton		M. Wildman	
I 58, 116, 96, 59	750 (15.6)		408 (8.5)
II 53, 93, 65, 53, 81 (*unf*)	750 (15.0)	51, 58	370 (7.6)
	1,500 (15.3)		778 (8.0)
Semi-finals			
F. Davis		Charlton	
I 92, 88, 214, 93	750 (25.9)	86, 75	410 (14.1)
II 228, 166, 52, 125	750 (30.0)	80, 102, 76	546 (21.8)
	1,500 (27.8)		956 (17.7)
Williams		Edmonds	
I 56, 54, 194, 84, 161,			
85 (*unf*)	750 (57.7)	50, 79	288 (22.2)
II 127 (*full*), 53, 316, 83			
194 (*unf*)	750 (62.5)	70, 60, 100	383 (31.9)
	1,500 (60.0)		671 (26.8)

Winner (breaks)	Score (average)	Loser (breaks)	Score (average)
Final			
Williams		F. Davis	
I 50, 170, 54, 235,			
132 (unf)	751 (32.7)	102	227 (9.5)
II 212 (full), 64, 192, 120,			
67, 71	749 (46.8)	63, 103, 137	378 (23.6)
	1,500 (38.4)		605 (15.1)
1984			
Preliminary round			
T. Murphy		M. Darrington	
I 76	400 (12.5)		505 (15.8)
II 75	621 (17.7)	66	356 (10.2)
	1,021 (15.0)		861 (12.9)
First round			
P. Morgan		B. Bennett	
I 148, 54	508 (13.0)		306 (8.1)
II 79, 63	513 (17.7)	79, 65	333 (11.5)
	1,021 (15.0)		639 (9.5)
I. Williamson		C. Everton	
I 55, 112, 50	373 (12.4)		189 (6.5)
II 65	373 (14.3)		307 (11.4)
	746 (13.3)		496 (8.9)
J. Karnehm		G. Ganim Jr	
I 56, 62, 127, 52, 61	600 (23.1)	75, 91, 92	383 (14.2)
II 89, 106, 148	670 (23.1)	112 (unf)	350 (12.5)
	1,270 (23.1)		733 (13.3)
Murphy		J. Fitzmaurice	
I 52, 94 (unf)	425 (12.1)	53, 61	497 (14.2)
II 94 (full), 57, 138	625 (15.6)		371 (9.3)
	1,050 (14.2)		868 (11.6)
Quarter-finals			
F. Davis		Murphy	
I 66, 82, 61, 73	550 (21.1)	84, 61, 50	453 (17.4)
II 101, 114, 111, 110, 71	692 (26.6)	89, 81, 58	399 (16.0)
	1,242 (23.9)		852 (16.7)
E. Charlton		Karnehm	
I 130	343 (16.3)	75, 73, 93, 193	623 (28.5)
II 319, 64, 92 (unf)	601 (35.4)	62	308 (19.3)
	944 (24.8)		931 (24.5)
Williamson		R. Edmonds	
I 81, 96, 54	407 (22.6)	58, 65, 112, 65	432 (22.7)
II 124, 60, 72, 175	511 (31.9)	85, 57, 127	373 (23.3)
	918 (27.0)		805 (23.0)
M. Wildman		Morgan	
I 168, 97, 178, 107	749 (37.4)	65, 85	299 (14.2)
II 87 (full), 58, 50, 62,			
71, 106	598 (15.8)	53, 53, 70, 50	460 (17.6)
	1,347 (28.7)		759 (15.8)

Winner (breaks)	Score (average)	Loser (breaks)	Score (average)
Semi-finals			
Charlton		F. Davis	
I 114, 94, 50, 81, 98,			
121 (*unf*)	795 (29.4)	56, 55	268 (9.2)
II 144 (*full*), 61, 60, 65,			
71, 62, 63	641 (27.9)	62, 135, 143, 124	561 (25.5)
	1,436 (28.7)		829 (16.6)
Wildman		Williamson	
I 226, 61	610 (23.5)	70	468 (17.3)
II 125, 188, 58, 91, 205	891 (35.6)	74, 103	381 (15.2)
	1,501 (29.4)		849 (16.4)
Final			
Wildman		Charlton	
I 111, 121, 241	599 (27.2)	100, 68, 50, 56	508 (23.1)
II 97, 115	446 (14.4)	101, 98, 54 (*unf*)	504 (16.3)
	1,045 (19.7)		1,012 (19.1)
1985			
First round			
P. Francisco 3		M. Darrington 0	
I 75, 125 (*unf*)	400 (22.2)	54	166 (9.2)
II 65	400 (12.6)		249 (7.5)
III 63, 55, 56	400 (16.1)		161 (6.7)
I. Williamson 3		B. Bennett 0	
I 96, 107	400 (17.0)	90	200 (8.6)
II 50, 164	400 (30.9)		89 (6.4)
III 50, 53, 65, 52	400 (15.4)	82	331 (12.7)
J. Karnehm 3		E. Charlton 0	
I 57, 56, 103, 89	400 (22.2)	154, 90	308 (16.2)
II 54, 184	400 (21.1)	77	217 (11.4)
III 98, 85	400 (14.8)	106	354 (12.6)
R. Edmonds 3		A. Higgins 0	
I 55, 68, 63, 111	400 (25.0)	69	188 (11.0)
II 51, 74, 147 (*unf*)	400 (26.7)	51, 89	221 (14.7)
III 81, 72, 121	400 (25.0)		110 (6.9)
M. Wildman 3		T. Jones 0	
I	400 (20.0)		237 (11.3)
II 188, 53, 55	400 (30.9)		144 (11.0)
III 98, 105, 103	400 (44.4)		125 (12.5)
N. Dagley 3		J. Fitzmaurice 0	
I 60, 63, 75 (*unf*)	400 (16.7)	60, 96	325 (13.5)
II 83, 94, 59, 67	400 (44.4)	103, 78	284 (28.4)
III 253	400 (33.5)		80 (6.7)
R. Foldvari *wo*		B. Oliver *scr*	
F. Davis 3		C. Everton 1	
I 84, 74, 82, 80	400 (16.2)	80	275 (11.4)
II 75, 78, 87	400 (28.6)		206 (13.7)
III 73, 100	293 (20.9)	70, 132 (*unf*)	400 (30.8)
IV 167, 150	400 (30.8)	54	156 (11.1)

Winner (breaks)	Score (average)	Loser (breaks)	Score (average)
Quarter-finals			
Dagley 3		Karnehm 0	
I 88, 270 (*unf*)	400 (80.0)		24 (4.8)
II 155, 56, 96, 60	400 (21.1)	102, 79	294 (14.7)
III 90, 104, 182 (*unf*)	400 (44.4)		59 (6.6)
Foldvari 3		F. Davis 0	
I 98, 80, 50 (*unf*)	400 (15.4)		130 (4.8)
II 107, 54, 114	400 (33.3)	84, 73, 50	316 (26.3)
III 161, 65, 88	400 (20.0)	71	342 (16.3)
Wildman 3		Francisco 0	
I 162, 102, 84 (*unf*)	400 (28.6)	55	186 (12.4)
II 184, 126 (*unf*)	400 (28.6)		106 (7.6)
III 245, 62, 50 (*unf*)	400 (66.7)		70 (10.0)
Edmonds 3		Williamson 1	
I 117	378 (15.0)	84, 73, 126 (*unf*)	400 (16.0)
II 159	400 (25.0)	65, 68	246 (15.4)
III 252, 102	400 (28.6)	79	212 (14.1)
IV 56, 54, 118	400 (23.5)	101, 67	248 (14.6)
Semi-finals			
Edmonds 3		Wildman 0	
I 69, 76, 97 (*unf*)	400 (28.6)	131	313 (22.3)
II 78, 73, 91	400 (22.3)	89	196 (10.3)
III 141, 60 (*unf*)	400 (22.3)	227	298 (16.6)
Dagley 3		Foldvari 0	
I 53, 52, 164	400 (22.2)	64, 146	352 (19.6)
II 104, 115	400 (25.0)	64, 88, 56	248 (14.6)
III 140	400 (15.4)	58, 50, 60	282 (11.0)
Final			
Edmonds 3		Dagley 1	
I 107, 150, 60	400 (33.3)	58, 201	395 (30.4)
II 159, 77	307 (28.0)	125, 126, 95	400 (40.0)
III 60, 140 (*unf*)	400 (26.6)	52, 106, 75	315 (19.6)
IV 188	400 (20.0)	60, 119, 52, 110	386 (19.3)

United Kingdom Professional Billiards Championship (1934–51)

1934

J. Davis	18,745	T. Newman	18,301
537, 504		809, 693, 603, 547	

1935

J. Davis	21,733	T. Newman	19,919
609, 1,264, 548, 564,		848, 677, 749, 732,	
638, 1,002, 545		598	

1936

First round

W. Smith	10,373 (60.0)	S. Lee	7,212 (42.0)

Semi-finals

T. Newman	9,561 (75.0)	S. Smith	7,792 (60.0)
J. Davis	10,965 (93.0)	W. Smith	9,566 (80.0)

Winner (breaks)	Score (average)	Loser (breaks)	Score (average)
Final			
J. Davis	21,710 (125.0)	T. Newman	19,790 (114.0)
1937			
First round			
S. Smith	8,135	S. Lee	4,209
(match abandoned after nine sessions)			
Semi-finals			
T. Newman	*wo*	W. Smith	*scr*
J. Davis	12,046	S. Smith	8,516
Final			
J. Davis	22,601 (146.0)	T. Newman	18,321 (118.0)
1,191, 1,179, 1,000,		782, 774, 720, 671,	
997, 793, 592, 587, 580,		670, 603, 593, 588,	
556, 550, 500		547	
1938			
Semi-finals			
T. Newman	8,959	S. Smith	7,227
556, 771, 602, 599		740	
J. Davis	15,238	S. Lee	6,048
1,013, 840, 988, 666			
Final			
J. Davis	20,933	T. Newman	19,542
1939–45 *No contests*			
1946			
J. Barrie	8,972	W. Leigh	6,782
1947			
S. Smith	7,002	J. Barrie	6,428
1948–49 *No contests*			
1950			
First round			
J. Barrie	7,645 (34.8)	S. Lee	5,593 (25.4)
Semi-finals			
J. Barrie	7,009 (46.7)	W. Smith	5,941 (39.6)
K. Kennerley	*wo*		
Final			
J. Barrie	9,046 (48.9)	K. Kennerley	5,069 (27.4)
1951			
F. Davis	8,120	K. Kennerley	6,011

United Kingdom Professional Billiards Championships (1979–83)

1979 (*Super Crystalate*)

Quarter-finals			
J. Karnehm	2,041 (35.8)	J. Dunning	760 (13.1)
281, 286			
R. Williams	1,557 (31.8)	R. Edmonds	1,350 (27.0)
259, 309			
J. Barrie	2,292 (46.8)	S. Davis	629 (12.6)
238, 404, 206 (*unf*)			

Winner (breaks)	Score (average)	Loser (breaks)	Score (average)
F. Davis	1,953 (34.9)	B. Bennett	679 (12.1)
Semi-finals			
Williams	1,539 (32.7)	Karnehm	1,182 (24.6)
224, 372			
Barrie	1,548 (43.0)	F. Davis	1,031 (28.6)
227, 444		245	
Final			
Williams	2,952 (44.4)	Barrie	2,116 (32.0)
228, 388, 253		379	
1980			
First round			
S. Davis	1,670 (21.7)	S. Hood	1,029 (13.4)
B. Bennett	1,093 (12.0)	C. Ross	933 (10.1)
Quarter-finals			
J. Barrie	2,001 (32.8)	M. Wildman	815 (13.1)
J. Karnehm	1,990 (28.0)	K. Kennerley	842 (11.9)
322			
R. Edmonds	1,380 (17.7)	Bennett	914 (11.6)
R. Williams	1,871 (33.4)	S. Davis	862 (15.4)
205			
Semi-finals			
Karnehm	1,755 (35.1)	Barrie	1,085 (21.3)
225, 230		229	
Williams	2,159 (41.5)	Edmonds	789 (15.2)
230, 234 (*unf*)			
Final			
Karnehm	2,518 (28.0)	Williams	2,423 (26.6)
205, 208		256, 423	
1981			
Qualifying			
S. Davis	980	B. Bennett	770
R. Edmonds	1,881	G. Miles	473
206			
J. Pulman	1,078	K. Kennerley	879
Quarter-finals			
J. Karnehm	1,307 (22.2)	Edmonds	935 (15.8)
207			
J. Barrie	1,743 (41.5)	Pulman	509 (12.1)
381			
R. Williams	1,575 (50.8)	S. Davis	579 (18.1)
265, 385, 290			
F. Davis	1,304 (29.0)	M. Wildman	805 (17.9)
217			
Semi-finals			
Karnehm	1,338 (23.1)	Barrie	1,074 (18.5)
390			
Williams	2,003 (74.2)	F. Davis	999 (37.0)
217, 505, 231			
Final			
Williams	1,592 (45.5)	Karnehm	1,112 (31.8)
393, 385			

Winner (breaks)	Score (average)	Loser (breaks)	Score (average)
1983			
First round			
B. Bennett	750 (10.4)	D. Greaves	280 (3.7)
C. Everton	750 (28.9)	M. Darrington	177 (6.5)
I. Williamson	750 (14.4)	T. Murphy	625 (11.8)
R. Edmonds	750 (19.7)	J. Fitzmaurice	505 (13.3)
Quarter-finals			
Edmonds	1,500 (30.0)	J. Karnehm	1,194 (23.4)
M. Wildman 285, 217	1,500 (41.7)	Everton 393	1,170 (33.4)
F. Davis 292	1,500 (42.9)	Williamson	604 (17.3)
R. Williams 246, 461 (*unf*)	1,500 (46.9)	Bennett	230 (7.0)
Semi-finals			
Wildman 495	1,500 (45.5)	Williams 225, 307	1,272 (38.5)
F. Davis 208, 201	1,500 (36.6)	Edmonds	936 (22.8)
Final			
Wildman	1,500 (21.4)	Davis	1,032 (14.5)

BILLIARDS PROFESSIONALS

NORMAN DAGLEY
Norman Dagley, from Earl Shilton, Leicestershire, won the World Amateur Billiards Championship twice, in 1971 and 1975, and the English Amateur Championship a record 15 times.

Prompted by the upturn in professional billiards, he turned professional comparatively late in his career and reached the final of the World Professional Championship at his first attempt in 1985 where he lost 3-1 to Ray Edmonds.

JACK KARNEHM
Although he has played snooker professionally, Jack Karnehm is predominantly a billiards player. He won the English Amateur Championship in 1969 and later that year also captured the World Amateur title when the event was staged in his home city, London.

He became a member of the World Professional Billiards and Snooker Association in 1971 and unsuccessfully challenged Rex Williams for the World Professional title in 1973. He did, however, beat Williams in the final of the Super Crystalate United Kingdom Championship in 1980.

Bob Close, three times English Amateur champion, was accepted as a billiards only professional in January 1985 and is expected to compete in the 1985-86 season.

THE AMATEUR GAME

THE WORLD AMATEUR SNOOKER CHAMPIONSHIP

The English Amateur Billiards Championship is the oldest domestic amateur title. It was started in 1888 and was followed in 1916 by the English Amateur Snooker Championship. It was not until 1926 that the first World Amateur Billiards Championship, then called the British Empire Championship, was staged, and in 1963, the inaugural World Amateur Snooker Championship was held in Calcutta.

The two events then took place in alternate years until it was decided that from 1985 the snooker would become an annual event. For that first Championship in 1963 there were only five entries from four countries – England, Australia, India and Ceylon (now Sri Lanka). The 1984 Championship in Dublin boasted 41 players representing 22 countries – an indication of just how fast the game is developing all over the world.

Before India's Omprakash Agrawal captured the title in Dublin, the event had been dominated by British players. Gary Owen (England) won it in 1963 and 1966 and another Englishman, David Taylor, in 1968. Jonathan Barron gave England their fourth title in 1970 and Ray Edmonds made it six in a row when he won both in 1972 and 1974.

Welshman Doug Mountjoy broke the stranglehold by taking the 1976 title and his fellow countryman Cliff Wilson won it in 1978 before England gave the Championship its youngest ever titleholder when Jimmy White won in 1980 at the age of 18. The title went back to Wales with Terry Parsons in 1982 and Parsons again reached the final in 1984 only to lose to Agrawal.

Each country affiliated to the International Billiards and Snooker Federation is entitled to send two competitors who are initially split into round robin groups with the quarter-finals onwards being knockout.

The biggest innovation in amateur snooker came in 1972 when the then world governing body, the Billiards and Snooker Control Council (now effectively the English body), lifted all restrictions on amateurs accepting prize-money or fees for exhibitions. This brought about a new breed of full-time amateur players who capitalise fully on a variety of privately organised tournaments which carry thousands of pounds in prize-money.

However, the money available in the 'amateur' game pales into insignificance when compared to the prosperity at the top of the professional game. Consequently, there is a high turnover of top amateurs who, as soon as they become eligible, join the professional ranks.

World Amateur Snooker Championships

	Wins	For	Agst	Highest break
1963 (*Calcutta*)				
G. Owen (England)	4	23	7	71
F. Harris (Australia)	3	21	17	52
M. J. M. Lafir (Ceylon)	2	19	18	67
T. Monteiro (India)	1	14	19	56
W. Jones (India)	0	7	24	36
1966 (*Karachi*)				
G. Owen (England)	5	30	7	118
J. Spencer (England)	4	26	14	101
W. Barrie (Australia)	3	23	22	73
M. J. M. Lafir (Ceylon)	2	22	20	45
L. U. Demarco (Scotland)	1	14	28	36
H. Karim (Pakistan)	0	6	30	60
1968 (*Sydney*)				
Group A				
David Taylor (England)	4	24	13	96
J. van Rensburg (S. Africa)	3	22	14	–
H. Andrews (Australia)	2	17	16	–
T. Monteiro (India)	1	17	22	–
L. Napper (N. Zealand)	0	9	24	–
Group B				
M. Williams (Australia)	3	22	14	–
P. Morgan (Ireland)	3	19	14	88
M. J. M. Lafir (Ceylon)	2	19	16	–
S. Shroff (India)	2	20	19	–
R. Flutey (N. Zealand)	0	7	24	–

Play-offs
Semi-finals: Williams beat van Rensburg 8-7; David Taylor beat Morgan 8-3
Final: David Taylor beat Williams 8-7

	Wins	For	Agst	Highest break
1970 (*Edinburgh*)				
Group A				
S. Hood (England)	5	20	9	50
P. Mifsud (Malta)	4	22	11	61
M. J. M. Lafir (Sri Lanka)	4	20	16	50
J. Phillips (Scotland)	4	19	18	62
D. Sneddon (Scotland)	2	17	17	38
L. Glozier (N. Zealand)	2	10	21	34
J. Clint (N. Ireland)	0	8	24	46
Group B				
J. Barron (England)	5	21	13	51
D. May (Wales)	4	22	18	64
S. Shroff (India)	3	18	14	47
E. Sinclair (Scotland)	3	16	16	49
J. Rogers (Ireland)	3	16	19	65
L. U. Demarco (Scotland)	2	15	19	32
H. Andrews (Australia)	1	13	22	35

Final: Barron beat Hood 11-7

1972 (Cardiff)	Wins	For	Agst	Highest break
Group A				
J. van Rensburg (S. Africa)	3	12	6	45
K. Tristram (N. Zealand)	1	8	8	50
G. Thomas (Wales)	1	6	8	32
L. U. Demarco (Scotland)	1	6	10	41
Group B				
M. Francisco (S. Africa)	3	15	5	47
J. Barron (England)	3	15	10	50
A. Borg (Malta)	2	12	11	59
A. Lloyd (Wales)	2	11	14	41
T. Monteiro (India)	0	3	16	46
Group C				
P. Mifsud (Malta)	4	16	5	61
R. Edmonds (England)	3	14	7	101
J. Rogers (Ireland)	2	8	8	36
M. Berni (Wales)	1	7	12	47
B. Bennett (N. Zealand)	0	3	16	30
Group D				
A. Savur (India)	2	10	6	38
M. Williams (Australia)	2	9	7	48
D. Sneddon (Scotland)	2	9	9	34
D. May (Wales)	0	6	12	42
Semi-final groups				
Group A				
Barron	3	12	4	35
Savur	2	10	8	68
Tristram	1	6	8	29
Mifsud	0	6	12	50
Group B				
M. Francisco	2	11	9	70
Edmonds	2	11	9	39
van Rensburg	1	8	10	51
Williams	1	9	11	78

Semi-finals: Edmonds beat Barron 8-6; M. Francisco beat Savur 8-7 (51, 72)
Final: Edmonds beat M. Francisco 11-10

1974 (Dublin)				
Group A				
R. Edmonds (England)	7	31	11	66
M. J. M. Lafir (Sri Lanka)	6	30	19	77
E. Sinclair (Scotland)	6	28	21	67
G. Thomas (Wales)	4	24	22	43
D. Sheehan (Ireland)	4	25	24	43
P. Donnelly (N. Ireland)	3	21	28	42
S. Shroff (India)	3	16	26	44
N. Stockman (N. Zealand)	2	18	29	51
J. Sklazeski (Canada)	1	18	31	79
Group B				
A. Lloyd (Wales)	8	32	14	104

	Wins	For	Agst	Highest break
W. Hill (N. Zealand)	5	26	21	58
P. Burke (Ireland)	4	26	20	71
L. Condo (Australia)	4	26	21	53
A. Borg (Malta)	4	27	23	37
D. Sneddon (Scotland)	4	23	21	54
A. Savur (India)	4	24	23	50
R. Cowley (Isle of Man)	3	16	27	50
N. J. Rahim (Sri Lanka)	0	2	32	25

Quarter-finals: Edmonds beat Condo 4(60)-3; Sinclair beat Hill 4-2; Burke beat Lafir 4-3; Thomas beat Lloyd 4-2
Semi-finals: Edmonds beat Sinclair 8(54)-4(79); Thomas beat Burke 8-2
Final: Edmonds beat Thomas 11-9
1976 (*Johannesburg*)
Group A

	Wins	For	Agst	Highest break
D. Mountjoy (Wales)	7	28	9	107
J. van Rensburg (S. Africa)	5	24	16	72
R. Edmonds (England)	4	20	18	77
N. Stockman (N. Zealand)	4	21	19	45
E. Sinclair (Scotland)	4	21	21	51
P. Burke (Ireland)	2	17	25	48
J. van Niekerk (S. Africa)	1	17	27	35
P. Reynolds (Isle of Man)	1	14	27	46

Group B

	Wins	For	Agst	Highest break
P. Mifsud (Malta)	6	25	9	47
S. Francisco (S. Africa)	6	27	12	68
T. Griffiths (Wales)	5	23	14	69
C. Ross (England)	4	19	17	58
R. Paquette (Canada)	4	22	22	72
E. Swaffield (N. Ireland)	1	16	26	59
L. Heywood (Australia)	1	13	27	46
L. Watson (Ireland)	1	9	27	45

Group C

	Wins	For	Agst	Highest break
M. Francisco (S. Africa)	6	27	12	62
R. Atkins (Australia)	6	25	12	45
R. Andrewartha (England)	5	25	14	100
J. Clint (N. Ireland)	4	17	18	33
L. U. Demarco (Scotland)	3	21	21	75
B. Mikkelsen (Canada)	3	19	22	60
K. Tristram (N. Zealand)	1	9	27	46
R. Cowley (Isle of Man)	0	11	28	41

Elimination match: Griffiths beat Andrewartha 4(51)-0
Quarter-finals: Mountjoy beat Atkins 5(80)-1; van Rensburg beat Griffiths 5-3(52); S. Francisco beat M. Francisco 5-1; Mifsud beat Edmonds 5-1
Semi-finals: Mountjoy beat S. Francisco 8(51)-2; Mifsud beat van Rensburg 8(50)-4
Final: Mountjoy beat Mifsud 11(62,79)-1
1978 (*Malta*)
Group A

	Wins	For	Agst	Highest break
K. Burles (Australia)	6	26	10	69

	Wins	For	Agst	Highest break
P. Mifsud (Malta)	6	26	10	62
J. Johnson (England)	5	23	9	101
J. Donnelly (Scotland)	5	20	13	78
D. McVeigh (N. Ireland)	2	15	20	56
P. Reynolds (Isle of Man)	2	10	22	45
V. Cremona (Malta)	2	9	25	–
M. Mohideen (Sri Lanka)	0	8	28	–
Group B				
A. Lloyd (Wales)	6	26	12	65
K. Stevens (Canada)	5	23	16	94
J. Grech (Malta)	4	23	16	63
E. Hughes (Ireland)	4	23	21	56
M. J. M. Lafir (Sri Lanka)	3	19	20	50
D. Meredith (N. Zealand)	3	18	20	81
S. Shroff (India)	2	14	23	39
L. McCann (N. Ireland)	1	10	27	40
Group C				
C. Wilson (Wales)	8	32	10	66
R. Paquette (Canada)	5	24	14	81
D. Kwok (N. Zealand)	5	23	20	49
A. Savur (India)	5	26	22	56
I. Williamson (England)	3	22	24	52
R. Atkins (Australia)	3	21	24	49
R. Miller (Scotland)	3	18	24	48
A. Borg (Malta)	2	15	27	44
C. Cooper (Isle of Man)	2	13	29	33

Elimination match: Grech beat Kwok 4-0

Quarter-finals: Burles beat Paquette 5-4; Stevens beat Mifsud 5-0; Johnson beat Lloyd 5(72)-0; Wilson beat Grech 5-4

Semi-finals: Johnson beat Burles 8(85)-4; Wilson beat Stevens 8(64)-2(81)

Final: Wilson beat Johnson 11(87)-5(66)

1980 (*Launceston*)

Group A

	Wins	For	Agst	Highest break
J. White (England)	6	24	9	99
A. Savur (India)	4	20	11	67
E. Hughes (Ireland)	4	21	13	127
J. Grech (Malta)	3	19	18	80
L. Adams (N. Zealand)	3	15	18	54
Loo Yap Long (Singapore)	1	6	23	57
R. Burke (N. Ireland)	0	11	24	50
Group B				
J. Giannaros (Australia)	6	24	11	54
S. Newbury (Wales)	4	20	14	100
R. Paquette (Canada)	4	20	15	90
D. Meredith (N. Zealand)	4	20	16	67
G. Parikh (India)	2	17	18	46
S. Clarke (N. Ireland)	1	10	22	44
Lau Weng Yew (Singapore)	0	8	24	36

	Wins	For	Agst	Highest break
Group C				
P. Mifsud (Malta)	6	24	3	77
R. Atkins (Australia)	4	19	15	67
J. Bonner (Australia)	4	17	17	53
W. King (Australia)	3	19	15	57
E. McLaughlin (Scotland)	3	16	16	67
J. O'Boye (England)	1	14	21	98
S. Padayachi (Fiji)	0	2	24	40
Group D				
A. Lloyd (Wales)	6	24	4	47
J. Campbell (Australia)	5	22	8	84
D. Sheehan (Ireland)	4	17	14	69
M. Gibson (Scotland)	3	16	20	80
H. Boteju (Sri Lanka)	2	16	20	45
P. Reynolds (Isle of Man)	1	11	23	35
W. Barrie (Australia)	0	7	24	39

Quarter-finals: Savur beat Lloyd 5(54)-3; Atkins beat Giannaros 5(53)-3(82); Mifsud beat Campbell 5(63)-3; White beat Newbury 5(70)-4
Semi-finals: Atkins beat Savur 8-6; White beat Mifsud 8(100)-6(83)
Final: White beat Atkins 11(80, 101)-2(60)

1982 (*Calgary*)

	Wins	For	Agst	Highest break
Group A				
J. Grech (Malta)	6	28	13	68
A. Kearney (Ireland)	6	26	15	57
D. O'Kane (N. Zealand)	6	28	18	68
B. McConnell (Canada)	5	26	19	43
P. Kippie (Scotland)	5	23	16	68
S. Habib (India)	4	22	21	52
V. Saengthong (Thailand)	3	20	28	73
Lui Yew Keong (Singapore)	1	13	30	60
J. A. Wahid (Sri Lanka)	0	6	32	26
Group B				
T. Parsons (Wales)	7	31	7	63
P. Browne (Ireland)	7	31	12	65
G. Kwok Kwan Shing (Hong Kong)	7	28	12	56
G. Parikh (India)	5	27	21	72
A. Thomson (Zimbabwe)	4	17	23	36
G. Kwok (N. Zealand)	3	17	26	62
H. Boteju (Sri Lanka)	2	15	28	31
W. Craig (Isle of Man)	1	14	29	35
T. Dada (Pakistan)	0	10	32	39
Group C				
J. Bear (Canada)	7	30	12	71
M. Bradley (England)	7	30	12	68
J. Jorgensen (Canada)	6	25	17	46
W. Mills (N. Ireland)	5	26	17	89
J. Giannaros (Australia)	5	25	21	68
P. Reynolds (Isle of Man)	3	23	23	36

	Wins	For	Agst	Highest break
Cheung Che-Ming (Hong Kong)	2	17	25	40
E. Amro (Egypt)	1	11	31	40
V. Yassa (Sudan)	0	3	32	22
Group D				
W. Jones (Wales)	6	27	13	70
P. Mifsud (Malta)	6	29	15	80
W. King (Australia)	6	29	17	83
R. Chaperon (Canada)	5	24	18	56
D. Chalmers (England)	5	25	24	57
R. Lane (Scotland)	3	23	23	44
S. Pavis (N. Ireland)	3	19	27	82
Lau Weng Yew (Singapore)	2	15	29	53
S. Sherif (Egypt)	0	7	32	27

Quarter-finals: W. Jones beat Kearney 5-1; Parons beat Bradley 5(69, 54)-0; Grech beat Browne 5(55)-3; Bear beat Mifsud 5-2
Semi-finals: Parsons beat Jones 8(103, 87)-5(54); Bear beat Grech 8-7
Final: Parsons beat Bear 11(61, 58, 58)-8(57, 69)

1984 (*Dublin*)
Group A

	Wins	For	Agst	Highest break
A. Micallef (Malta)	9	38	16	75
T. Parsons (Wales)	8	37	11	102
P. Ennis (Ireland)	8	34	28	110
V. Saengthong (Thailand)	7	34	19	86
J. Sigurossonn (Iceland)	6	29	29	70
T. Finstad (Canada)	4	28	28	85
B. Bjorkman (Sweden)	4	26	27	52
A. Thomson (Zimbabwe)	3	24	34	36
D. Feeney (U.S.A.)	3	21	35	42
K. Sirisoma (Sri Lanka)	3	16	33	40
L. Talman (Belgium)	0	11	40	37
Group B				
D. John (Wales)	9	37	10	72
T. Drago (Malta)	8	35	15	132
A. Robidou (Canada)	8	36	20	107
S. Sim-Ngarm (Thailand)	7	33	20	70
J. Long (Ireland)	6	30	24	62
M. G. Jayaram (India)	5	30	23	84
A. Campbell (Australia)	4	25	29	96
J. McIntyre (N. Ireland)	4	21	30	91
R. Cowley (Isle of Man)	3	20	30	52
M. Sedupathi (Sri Lanka)	1	6	36	37
C. D'Avoine (Mauritius)	0	3	40	38
Group C				
G. Wilkinson (Australia)	8	30	13	68
J. Wright (England)	7	27	14	68
H. Haenga (N. Zealand)	7	26	14	66
H. Bakahati (Egypt)	6	26	21	73
M. Colquitt (Isle of Man)	5	24	20	57

	Wins	For	Agst	Highest break
S. Hendry (Scotland)	5	23	22	118
T. Kollins (U.S.A.)	3	16	27	92
K. Friopjofssonn (Iceland)	3	15	28	28
H. Thwaites (Belgium)	1	3	32	21
Lui Yew Keong (Singapore)	scr			
Group D				
C. Archer (England)	9	32	15	80
O. B. Agrawal (India)	7	33	16	68
D. Kwok (New Zealand)	5	27	21	64
G. Kwok Kwan Shing (Hong Kong)	5	26	23	129
H. Morgan (N. Ireland)	5	27	27	78
J. Selby (Wales)	4	24	23	72
L. Yew (Singapore)	3	25	28	55
G. Carnegie (Scotland)	3	22	32	69
M. Hallgren (Sweden)	2	17	32	43
M. Sadek (Egypt)	2	15	31	59

Quarter-finals: Agrawal beat John 5-4; Wright beat A. Micallef 5(69, 70)-1; Archer beat Drago 5-4; Parsons beat Wilkinson 5(66)-2
Semi-finals: Agrawal beat Wright 8(75)-5; Parsons beat Archer 8(58, 78, 52)-3
Final: Agrawal beat Parsons 11(69, 74, 62, 54)-7

World Amateur Billiards Championships

	Won	Score (average)	Highest break	No of centuries
1926 (*London*)				
J. Earlham (England)	4	8,000 (25.6)	282	18
G. Shailer (Australia)	3	7,394 (16.8)	203	13
M. Smith (Scotland)	2	6,569 (12.7)	130	4
P. Rutledge (S. Africa)	1	5,902 (12.5)	142	2
T. McCluney (N. Ireland)	0	5,617 (11.9)	144	4
1927 (*London*)				
A. Prior (S. Africa)	3	6,000 (16.6)	184	9
H. F. Coles (Wales)	2	5,533 (12.2)	164	2
L. Steeples (England)	1	5,506 (14.8)	236	9
M. Smith (Scotland)	0	4,499 (12.6)	158	1
1929 (*Johannesburg*)				
L. Hayes (Australia)	3	6,000 (15.5)	136	6
A. Prior (S. Africa)	2	5,512 (16.0)	226	7
H. F. Coles (England)	1	5,592 (14.7)	170	7
P. Rutledge (S. Africa)	0	2,882 (10.9)	164	1
1931 (*Sydney*)				
L. Steeples (England)	4	8,000 (37.3)	461	24
S. Lee (England)	3	7,126 (22.1)	433	18
L. Hayes (Australia)	2	6,113 (15.3)	167	6
H. Goldsmith (Australia)	1	4,995 (13.0)	179	4
W. Hackett (N. Zealand)	0	3,549 (7.7)	97	0
1933 (*London*)				
S. Lee (England)	4	12,402 (28.0)	394	31

	Won	Score (average)	Highest break	No of centuries
T. Jones (Wales)	3	9,883 (18.7)	144	8
A. Prior (S. Africa)	2	9,113 (18.3)	235	13
M. Smith (Scotland)	1	8,292 (17.5)	166	5
J. Blackburn (N. Ireland)	0	6,362 (12.5)	94	0
1935 (*London*)				
H. F. Coles (England)	4	13,665 (28.4)	267	33
J. McGhie (Scotland)	3	9,359 (19.4)	207	11
I. Edwards (Wales)	2	9,814 (18.1)	196	11
S. Fenning (Ireland)	1	9,068 (17.4)	161	6
P. Deb (India)	0	7,461 (13.1)	123	5
1936 (*Johannesburg*)				
R. Marshall (Australia)	3	8,526 (22.0)	248	24
A. Prior (S. Africa)	2	7,014 (17.7)	197	11
J. Thompson (England)	1	7,705 (21.2)	245	15
A. Bowlly (S. Africa)	0	4,548 (9.0)	93	0
Three 2½ hour sessions				
1938 (*Melbourne*)				
R. Marshall (Australia)	6	17,626 (39.0)	427	59
K. Kennerley (England)	5	14,528 (30.1)	472	45
T. Cleary (Australia)	4	8,535 (19.7)	322	17
S. Moses (N. Zealand)	2	6,727 (13.1)	129	4
M. M. Begg (India)	2	6,685 (13.4)	111	2
A. Burke (S. Africa)	1	5,993 (12.0)	119	1
A. Albertson (N. Zealand)	1	5,805 (12.4)	107	1
1951 (*London*)				
R. Marshall (Australia)	6	14,735 (38.1)	423	42
F. Edwards (England)	5	13,459 (26.7)	345	36
T. Cleary (Australia)	4	12,373 (25.5)	330	31
W. Ramage (Scotland)	3	7,638 (19.1)	151	8
W. Pierce (Wales)	2	6,029 (13.6)	225	3
W. Jones (India)	1	7,202 (16.6)	138	10
E. Haslem (N. Ireland)	0	5,896 (14.1)	125	3
1952 (*Calcutta*)				
L. Driffield (England)	5	8,529 (34.5)	278	31
R. Marshall (Australia)	3	9,237 (37.3)	351	27
C. Hirjee (India)	3	7,701 (22.7)	230	14
W. Ramage (Scotland)	3	6,525 (20.8)	211	10
W. Jones (India)	1	6,731 (23.3)	253	6
A. Yunoos (Burma)	0	3,768 (11.0)	79	0
1954 (*Sydney*)				
T. Cleary (Australia)	4	11,496 (33.5)	682	35
R. Marshall (Australia)	3	11,488 (36.0)	407	35
F. Edwards (England)	2	9,053 (24.7)	328	26
W. Jones (India)	1	8,523 (20.5)	209	17
T. G. Rees (S. Africa)	0	6,271 (16.9)	207	6
1958 (*Calcutta*)				
W. Jones (India)	5	16,493	501	56
L. Driffield (England)	4	14,370	499	48

	Won	Score (average)	Highest break	No of centuries
T. Cleary (Australia)	3	13,626	431	52
C. Hirjee (India)	2	12,853	226	38
W. Asciak (Malta)	1	6,329	154	7
M. Hman (Burma)	0	5,633	215	8
1960 (*Edinburgh*)				
J. H. Beetham (England)	7	9,351	277	29
J. Long (Australia)	6	10,634	353	26
W. Jones (India)	5	12,397	589	30
M. Francisco (S. Africa)	4	7,773	148	11
W. Ramage (Scotland)	3	7,938	283	12
W. Asciak (Malta)	2	8,408	194	11
W. Dennison (N. Ireland)	1	6,231	155	4
A. Ramage (Scotland)	0	5,706	101	2
1962 (*Perth*)				
R. Marshall (Australia)	5	12,367 (35.6)	348	57
W. Jones (India)	5	10,805 (26.9)	489	34
T. Cleary (Australia)	4	9,808 (27.0)	315	27
J. H. Beetham (England)	3	7,626 (22.9)	283	18
S. Benajee (India)	3	8,332 (17.2)	219	9
R. A. Karim (Pakistan)	1	5,657 (11.9)	130	3
W. Harcourt (N. Zealand)	0	5,623 (14.3)	123	5
Play-off: Marshall beat Jones 3,623-2,891				
1964 (*Pukekohe*)				
W. Jones (India)	9	16,628 (24.5)	294	49
J. Karnehm (England)	8	12,953 (21.8)	390	28
M. Ferreira (India)	7	13,345 (19.0)	182	29
M. Francisco (S. Africa)	6	12,957 (22.0)	518	38
A. Nolan (England)	5	12,126 (19.9)	259	26
T. Cleary (Australia)	4	10,781 (13.9)	241	19
H. Robinson (N. Zealand)	3	7,643 (10.5)	85	0
T. Yesberg (N. Zealand)	2	7,528 (10.4)	80	0
M. Mavalwala (Pakistan)	1	8,404 (11.3)	174	1
A. E. Redmond (N. Zealand)	0	6,914 (9.0)	107	1
1967 (*Colombo*)				
L. Driffield (England)	8	13,556 (30.5)	421	53
M. J. M. Lafir (Ceylon)	7	12,562 (18.4)	218	31
M. Francisco (S. Africa)	6	12,477 (20.4)	301	32
M. Ferreira (India)	5	11,140 (19.5)	507	22
J. Long (Australia)	4	11,068 (17.5)	261	27
T. Cleary (Australia)	3	9,252 (11.6)	322	15
N. J. Rahim (Ceylon)	2	6,895 (8.8)	116	3
M. S. M. Marzuq (Ceylon)	1	7,153 (7.9)	88	0
F. Holz (N. Zealand)	0	5,350 (7.1)	68	0
1969 (*London*)				
J. Karnehm (England)	9	12,902	232	27
M. Ferreira (India)	7	14,115	629	34
M. Francisco (S. Africa)	7	13,760	335	35
M. J. M. Lafir (Ceylon)	7	12,934	296	28

	Won	Score (average)	Highest break	No of centuries
R. Marshall (Australia)	6	13,033	216	33
M. Wildman (England)	6	11,739	274	22
R. Oriel (Wales)	5	13,306	297	30
S. Mohan (India)	5	13,407	219	24
P. Mifsud (Malta)	2	10,410	173	8
A. Twohill (N. Zealand)	1	10,016	146	12
F. Holz (N. Zealand)	0	6,061	65	0
1971 (*Malta*)				
Group A				
M. Francisco (S. Africa)	4	6,450	321	15
M. J. M. Lafir (Ceylon)	3	4,757	233	4
P. Mifsud (Malta)	2	4,142	134	2
D. Sneddon (Scotland)	1	3,160	121	2
L. Napper (N. Zealand)	0	3,798	87	0
Group B				
S. Mohan (India)	4	5,839	188	11
N. Dagley (England)	3	5,454	330	11
M. Ferreira (India)	2	4,423	227	4
C. Everton (Wales)	1	3,893	205	5
W. Asciak (Malta)	0	4,511	188	7
Play-offs:				
Dagley	3	6,041	348	17
M. Francisco	2	3,981	353	11
Mohan	1	3,822	327	11
Lafir	0	2,514	211	5
1973 (*Bombay*)				
M. J. M. Lafir (Sri Lanka)	9	16,956 (34.1)	859	43
S. Mohan (India)	7	17.016 (30.8)	468	53
M. Ferreira (India)	7	15,639 (25.4)	421	41
P. Tarrant (Australia)	6	13,200 (24.4)	373	36
C. Everton (Wales)	5	9,921 (18.2)	240	17
A. Nolan (England)	4	12,709 (20.8)	265	31
P. Mifsud (Malta)	4	12,253 (18.8)	203	23
E. Simons (N. Zealand)	2	8,521 (12.4)	94	0
B. Kirkness (N. Zealand)	1	8,464 (13.5)	195	7
L. U. Demarco (Scotland)	0	7,488 (10.4)	87	0
1975 (*Auckland*)				
Group A				
N. Dagley (England)	5	9,257	477	24
D. Sneddon (Scotland)	4	6,272	124	4
G. Parikh (India)	3	6,471	197	16
J. Reece (Australia)	2	4,058	125	4
H. Robinson (N. Zealand)	1	4,529	123	2
M. Shaharwardi (Sri Lanka)	0	4,032	121	1
Group B				
M. Ferreira (India)	5	9.022	411	26
C. Everton (Wales)	4	6,043	272	13
R. Close (England)	3	5,449	164	10
T. Yesberg (N. Zealand)	2	4,373	131	3

	Won	Score (average)	Highest break	No of centuries
J. Long (Australia)	1	4,598	157	5
B. Bennett (N. Zealand)	0	3,684	95	0

Play-offs
Semi-finals: Dagley beat Everton 1,293(222)-755; Ferreira beat Sneddon 2,470(211)-681
Final: Dagley beat Ferreira 3,385(200, 228, 202, 314)-2,268(281)

1977 (*Melbourne*)
Group A

	Won	Score (average)	Highest break	No of centuries
N. Dagley (England)	5	7,546	272	16
C. Everton (Wales)	4	4,962	170	7
S. Aleem (India)	3	7,028	263	11
G. Ganim Sr (Australia)	2	6,322	231	6
H. Robinson (N. Zealand)	1	4,133	93	0
J. Nugent (Scotland)	0	4,131	68	0

Group B

	Won	Score (average)	Highest break	No of centuries
M. Ferreira (India)	5	12,554	519	33
R. Close (England)	4	7,252	207	15
G. Ganim Jr (Australia)	3	6,424	192	9
T. Yesberg (N. Zealand)	2	4,349	109	1
W. Weerasinghe (Sri Lanka)	1	4,364	97	0
D. Pratt (Scotland)	0	4,316	108	1

Play-offs
Semi-finals: Ferreira beat Everton 2,155-1,310; Close beat Dagley 1,912(234)-1,781(236)
Final: Ferreira beat Close 2,683-2,564(231)

1979 (*Colombo*)
Group A

	Won	Score (average)	Highest break	No of centuries
M. Ferreira (India)	7	14,695	467	40
M. J. M. Lafir (Sri Lanka)	5	12,456	370	30
K. Shirley (England)	5	10,656	195	13
W. Barrie (Australia)	4	8,255	128	2
B. Kirkness (N. Zealand)	4	7,283	214	8
H. Nimmo (Scotland)	2	7,022	105	2
M. S. U. Mohideen (Sri Lanka)	1	6,408	76	0
R. Lim Sin Foo (Singapore)	0	6,433	97	0

Group B

	Won	Score (average)	Highest break	No of centuries
N. Dagley (England)	6	12,539	466	39
P. Mifsud (Malta)	6	12,193	325	31
S. Agrawal (India)	6	11,924	355	30
G. Ganim Jr (Australia)	3	8,486	267	15
C. Everton (Wales)	3	6,905	211	11
W. A. J. Weerasinghe (Sri Lanka)	3	7,883	202	7
B. Bennett (N. Zealand)	1	6,083	101	1
E. Fisher (Canada)	0	4,198	88	0

Play-offs
Semi-finals: Mifsud beat Ferreira 2,489(338, 285)-1,856; Dagley beat
Lafir 2,694(266, 444, 289)-1,692(240)
Final: Mifsud beat Dagley 2,943(361)-2,152

1981 (*New Delhi*)
Group A

	Won	Score (average)	Highest break	No of centuries
N. Dagley (England)	6	11,982	416	42

	Won	Score (average)	Highest break	No of centuries
S. Agrawal (India)	5	12,967	384	39
G. Ganim Jr (Australia)	4	7,934	178	13
A. K. B. Giles (N. Zealand)	3	6,895	162	5
D. Sneddon (Scotland)	2	7,071	123	6
J. W. H. Boteju (Sri Lanka)	1	6,312	107	1
A. A. Essam (Egypt)	0	3,948	59	–
Group B				
M. Ferreira (India)	6	13,862	630	58
L. A. Bux (Pakistan)	5	8,712	257	21
R. Close (England)	3	7,161	217	15
J. Grech (Malta)	3	7,388	402	9
D. Meredith (N. Zealand)	3	6,507	154	7
H. Roberts-Thomson (Australia)	2	6,535	151	5
S. M. Shahawardi (Sri Lanka)	0	5,111	77	–

Semi-finals: Dagley beat Bux 2,890(229, 277, 218)-1,505(257); Ferreira beat Agrawal 3,272(213, 532, 327, 527, 630)-1,964(233, 253)
Final: Ferreira beat Dagley 2,725(208, 349, 245, 244)-2,631(223, 296, 281)

Guinness World Amateur Billiards

	Wins	Highest break	No of centuries
1983 (*Malta*)			
Group A			
M. Ferreira (India)	6	463	31
R. Foldvari (Australia)	5	302	30
L. A. Bux (Pakistan)	4	177	9
H. Nimmo (Scotland)	3	224	6
D. Meredith (N. Zealand)	2	157	7
H. Griffiths (Wales)	1	112	1
A. Micallef (Malta)	0	122	6
Group B			
S. Agrawal (India)	5	635	42
N. Dagley (England)	5	368	30
J. Grech (Malta)	5	286	31
V. Ellul (Malta)	2	145	2
R. Lim (Singapore)	2	96	–
W. Loughan (N. Ireland)	2	198	5
H. Boteju (Sri Lanka)	0	120	2

Semi-finals: Agrawal beat Foldvari 2,047(240, 503)-1,900(302, 225, 231); Ferreira beat Dagley 1,983(463)-1,919(258)
Final: Ferreira beat Agrawal 3,933(353, 398, 201, 254)-2,744(242, 212)

World Amateur Championship Records

Snooker
E. Hughes (Ireland)   127   1980

Billiards
T. Cleary (Australia)   682 (2 pots)   1954
M. J. M. Lafir (Sri Lanka) 859 (5 pots)   1973
M. Ferreira (India)   467 (3 pots)   1979

NATIONAL AMATEUR CHAMPIONSHIPS

ENGLAND
Snooker

1916	C. N. Jacques	1938	P. H. Matthews	1964	R. Reardon
1917	C. N. Jacques	1939	P. Bendon	1965	P. Houlihan
1918	T. N. Palmer	1940	K. Kennerley	1966	J. Spencer
1919	S. H. Fry	*1941–45*	*No contests*	1967	M. Owen
1920	A. R. Wisdom	1946	H. J. Pulman	1968	David Taylor
1921	M. J. Vaughan	1947	H. Morris	1969	R. Edmonds
1922	J. McGlynn	1948	S. Battye	1970	J. Barron
1923	W. Coupe	1949	T. C. Gordon	1971	J. Barron
1924	W. Coupe	1950	A. Nolan	1972	J. Barron
1925	J. McGlynn	1951	R. Williams	1973	M. Owen
1926	W. Nash	1952	C. Downey	1974	R. Edmonds
1927	O. T. Jackson	1953	T. C. Gordon	1975	S. Hood
1928	P. H. Matthews	1954	G. Thompson	1976	C. Ross
1929	L. Steeples	1955	M. Parkin	1977	T. Griffiths
1930	L. Steeples	1956	T. C. Gordon	1978	T. Griffiths
1931	P. H. Matthews	1957	R. Gross	1979	J. White
1932	W. E. Bach	1958	M. Owen	1980	J. O'Boye
1933	E. Bedford	1959	M. Owen	1981	V. Harris
1934	C. H. Beavis	1960	R. Gross	1982	D. Chalmers
1935	C. H. Beavis	1961	A. Barnett	1983	T. Jones
1936	P. H. Matthews	1962	R. Gross	1984	S. Longworth
1937	K. Kennerley	1963	G. Owen	1985	T. Whitthread

Billiards

1888	H. A. O. Lonsdale	1913	H. C. Virr	1952	A. L. Driffield
	A. P. Gaskell	1914	H. C. Virr	1953	A. L. Driffield
1889	A. P. Gaskell	1915	A. W. T. Good	1954	A. L. Driffield
	A. P. Gaskell	1916	S. H. Fry	1955	F. Edwards
	A. P. Gaskell	1917	J. Graham-Symes	1956	F. Edwards
1890	A. P. Gaskell	1918	J. Graham-Symes	1957	A. L. Driffield
	W. D. Courtney	1919	S. H. Fry	1958	A. L. Driffield
1891	W. D. Courtney	1920	S. H. Fry	1959	A. L. Driffield
	A. P. Gaskell	1921	S. H. Fry	1960	J. H. Beetham
1892	A. R. Wisdom	1922	J. Graham-Symes	1961	J. H. Beetham
	S. S. Christey	1923	W. P. McLeod	1962	A. L. Driffield
	A. R. Wisdom	1924	W. P. McLeod	1963	J. H. Beetham
1893	S. H. Fry	1925	S. H. Fry	1964	A. Nolan
	A. H. Vahid	1926	J. Earlam	1965	N. Dagley
1894	H. Mitchell	1927	L. Steeples	1966	N. Dagley
	W. T. Maughan	1928	A. Wardle	1967	A. L. Driffield
1895	*No contests*	1929	H. F. E. Coles	1968	M. Wildman
1896	S. H. Fry	1930	L. Steeples	1969	J. Karnehm
1897–98	*No contests*	1931	S. Lee	1970	N. Dagley
1899	A. R. Wisdom	1932	S. Lee	1971	N. Dagley
1900	S. H. Fry	1933	S. Lee	1972	N. Dagley
1901	S. S. Christey	1934	S. Lee	1973	N. Dagley
1902	A. W. T. Good	1935	H. F. E. Coles	1974	N. Dagley
	A. W. T. Good	1936	J. Thompson	1975	N. Dagley
1903	A. R. Wisdom	1937	K. Kennerley	1976	R. Close
	S. S. Christey	1938	K. Kennerley	1977	R. Close
1904	W. A. Lovejoy	1939	K. Kennerley	1978	N. Dagley
1905	A. W. T. Good	1940	K. Kennerley	1979	N. Dagley
1906	E. C. Breed	*1941–45*	*No contests*	1980	N. Dagley
1907	H. C. Virr	1946	M. Showman	1981	N. Dagley
1908	H. C. Virr	1947	J. Thompson	1982	N. Dagley
1909	Major Fleming	1948	J. Thompson	1983	N. Dagley
1910	H. A. O. Lonsdale	1949	F. Edwards	1984	N. Dagley
1911	H. C. Virr	1950	F. Edwards	1985	R. Close
1912	H. C. Virr	1951	F. Edwards		

NORTHERN IRELAND
Snooker

1927	G. Barron	1948	J. Bates	1967	D. Anderson
1928	J. Perry	1949	J. Bates	1968	A. Higgins
1929	W. Lyttle	1950	J. Bates	1969	D. Anderson
1930	J. Luney	1951	J. Stevenson	1970	J. Clint
1931	J. McNally	1952	J. Stevenson	1971	S. Crothers
1932	Capt. J. Ross	1953	J. Stevenson	1972	P. Donnelly
1933	J. French	1954	W. Seeds	1973	J. Clint
1934	Capt. J. Ross	1955	J. Stevenson	1974	P. Donnelly
1935	W. Agnew	1956	S. Brooks	1975	J. Clint
1936	W. Lowe	1957	M. Gill	1976	E. Swaffield
1937	J. Chambers	1958	W. Agnew	1977	D. McVeigh
1938	J. McNally	1959	W. Hanna	1978	D. McVeigh
1939	J. McNally	1960	M. Gill	1979	R. Burke
1940	*No contest*	1961	D. Anderson	1980	S. Clarke
1941	J. McNally	1962	S. McMahon	1981	T. Murphy
1942–44	*No contests*	1963	D. Anderson	1982	S. Pavis
1945	J. McNally	1964	P. Morgan	1983	J. McLaughlin Jr
1946	J. McNally	1965	M. Gill	1984	J. McLaughlin Jr
1947	J. Rea	1966	S. Crothers	1985	S. Pavis

Billiards

1925	T. McCluney	1947	J. Bates	1965	W. Ashe
1926	T. McCluney	1948	J. Bates	1966	D. Anderson
1927	J. Sloan	1949	J. Bates	1967	W. Loughan
1928	A. Davison	1950	J. Bates	1968	D. Anderson
1929	J. Blackburn	1951	E. Haslem	1969	W. Loughan
1930	J. Blackburn	1952	R. Taylor	1970	S. Crothers
1931	J. Blackburn	1953	W. Scanlon	1971	J. Bates
1932	W. Lowe	1954	W. Scanlon	*1972–73*	*No contests*
1933	W. Mills	1955	D. Turley	1974	P. Donnelly
1934	W. Lowe	1956	J. Stevenson	1975	P. Donnelly
1935	W. Morrison	1957	W. Scanlon	1976	P. Donnelly
1936	J. Blackburn	1958	W. Hanna	1977	T. Taylor
1937	J. Blackburn	1959	W. Hanna	1978	W. Loughan
1938	W. Lowe	1960	W. Dennison	1979	J. Bates
1939	W. Lowe	1961	R. Hanna	1980	S. Clarke
1940	*No contest*	1962	N. McQuay	1981	W. Loughan
1941	E. Haslem	1963	W. Hanna	1982	P. Donnelly
1942–44	*No contests*	1964	{ D. Anderson / D. Turley }	1985	F. Clarke
1945	E. Haslem				
1946	J. Holness				

REPUBLIC OF IRELAND
Snooker

1931	J. Ayres	*1950–51*	*No contests*	1969	D. Dally
1932	*No contest*	1952	W. Brown	1970	D. Sheehan
1933	S. Fenning	1953	S. Brooks	1971	D. Sheehan
1934	*No contest*	1954	S. Fenning	1972	J. Rogers
1935	S. Fenning	1955	S. Fenning	1973	F. Murphy
1936	*No contest*	1956	W. Brown	1974	P. Burke
1937	P. J. O'Connor	1957	J. Connolly	1975	F. Nathan
1938–39	*No contests*	1958	G. Gibson	1976	P. Burke
1940	P. Merrigan	*1959–60*	*No contests*	1977	J. Clusker
1941	*No contest*	1961	W. Brown	1978	E. Hughes
1942	P. J. O'Connor	1962	J. Weber	1979	E. Hughes
1943	*No contest*	1963	J. Rogers	1980	D. Sheehan
1944	S. Fenning	1964	J. Rogers	1981	A. Kearney
1945–46	*No contests*	1965	W. Fields	1982	P. Browne
1947	C. Downey	1966	G. Hanway	1983	J. Long
1948	P. Merrigan	1967	P. Morgan	1984	P. Ennis
1949	S. Fenning	1968	G. Hanway	1985	G. Burns

Billiards

1931	J. Ayres	1953	D. Turley	1970	L. Drennan		
1932	No contest	1954	M. Nolan	1971	L. Codd		
1933	J. Ayres	1955	M. Nolan	1972	L. Codd		
1934	S. Fenning	1956	M. Nolan	1973	T. Martin		
1935	S. Fenning	1957	M. Nolan	1974	T. Doyle		
1936	S. Fenning	1958	W. Dennison	1975	P. Fenelon		
1937	T. O'Brien	1959–60	No contests	1976	J. Rogers		
1938–41	No contests	1961	K. Smyth	1977	E. Hughes		
1942	S. Fenning	1962	K. Smyth	1978	E. Hughes		
1943	No contest	1963	J. Bates	1979	L. Drennan		
1944	S. Fenning	1964	J. Bates	1980	P. Burke		
1945–47	No contests	1965	L. Codd	1981	P. Burke		
1948	W. Brown	1966	L. Codd	1982	D. Elliott		
1949	S. Fenning	1967	P. Morgan	1984	A. Murphy		
1950–51	No contests	1968	P. Morgan	1985	A. Roche		
1952	M. Nolan	1969	J. Rogers				

SCOTLAND
Snooker

1931	G. Brown	1958	J. Phillips	1972	D. Sneddon
1932–45	No contests	1959	J. Phillips	1973	E. Sinclair
1946	J. Levey	1960	E. Sinclair	1974	D. Sneddon
1947	J. Levey	1961	J. Phillips	1975	E. Sinclair
1948	I. Wexelstein	1962	A. Kennedy	1976	E. Sinclair
1949	W. Ramage	1963	E. Sinclair	1977	R. Miller
1950	W. Ramage	1964	J. Phillips	1978	J. Donnelly
1951	A. Wilson	1965	L. U. Demarco	1979	S. Nivison
1952	D. Emerson	1966	L. U. Demarco	1980	M. Gibson
1953	P. Spence	1967	E. Sinclair	1981	R. Lane
1954	D. Edmond	1968	E. Sinclair	1982	P. Kippie
1955	L. U. Demarco	1969	A. Kennedy	1983	G. Carnegie
1956	W. Barrie	1970	D. Sneddon	1984	S. Hendry
1957	T. Paul	1971	J. Phillips		

Billiards

1913	Captain Croneen	1946	J. Levey	1966	W. Ramage
1914–21	No contests	1947	A. Ramage	1967	W. Ramage
1922	H. L. Fleming	1948	W. Ramage	1968	A. Kennedy
1923	M. Smith	1949	W. Ramage	1969	A. Kennedy
1924	No contest	1950	A. Ramage	1970	D. Sneddon
1925	W. D. Greenlees	1951	W. Ramage	1971	D. Sneddon
1926	M. Smith	1952	J. Murray	1972	L. U. Demarco
1927	M. Smith	1953	J. Bates	1973	D. Sneddon
1928	M. Smith	1954	J. Bates	1974	D. Sneddon
1929	J. McGhee	1955	W. Ramage	1975	D. Sneddon
1930	M. Smith	1956	W. Ramage	1976	D. Sneddon
1933	A. Ramage	1957	W. Ramage	1977	J. Nugent
1934	N. Canney	1958	W. Ramage	1978	D. Sneddon
1935	H. King	1959	W. Ramage	1979	H. Nimmo
1936	N. Canney	1960	A. Ramage	1980	D. Sneddon
1937	J. McGhee	1961	P. Spence	1981	D. Sneddon
1938	J. McGhee	1962	W. Ramage	1982	W. Kelly
1939	No contest	1963	W. Ramage	1983	H. Nimmo
1940	W. McCann	1964	W. Ramage		
1941–45	No contests	1965	W. Ramage		

WALES
Snooker

1930	T. Jones	1932	T. Jones	1934	T. Jones
1931	T. Jones	1933	T. Jones	1935	T. Jones

1936	T. Jones	1957	R. D. Meredith	1972	G. Thomas
1937	G. Howells	1958	A. Kemp	1973	A. Lloyd
1938	B. Gravenor	1959	J. R. Price	1974	A. Lloyd
1939	W. E. James	1960	L. Luker	1975	T. Griffiths
1940-46	No contests	1961	T. Parsons	1976	D. Mountjoy
1947	T. Jones	1962	A. J. Ford	1977	C. Wilson
1948	R. Smith	1963	R. D. Meredith	1978	A. Lloyd
1949	A. J. Ford	1964	M. L. Berni	1979	C. Wilson
1950	R. Reardon	1965	T. Parsons	1980	S. Newbury
1951	R. Reardon	1966	L. L. O'Neill	1981	C. Roscoe
1952	R. Reardon	1967	L. L. O'Neill	1982	T. Parsons
1953	R. Reardon	1968	D. Mountjoy	1983	W. Jones
1954	R. Reardon	1969	T. Parsons	1984	T. Parsons
1955	R. Reardon	1970	D. T. May		
1956	C. Wilson	1971	D. T. May		

Billiards

1920	H. F. E. Coles	1939	B. Gravenor	1963	R. W. Oriel
1921	H. F. E. Coles	1940-46	No contests	1964	R. W. Oriel
1922	H. F. E. Coles	1946	T. G. Rees	1965	R. W. Oriel
1923	H. F. E. Coles	1947	T. C. Morse	1966	R. W. Oriel
1924	H. F. E. Coles	1948	J. Tregoning	1967	R. W. Oriel
1925	Unknown	1949	I. Edwards	1968	D. E. Edwards
1926	Unknown	1950	W. Pierce	1969	R. W. Oriel
1927	Unknown	1951	W. Pierce	1970	R. W. Oriel
1928	G. Moore	1952	J. Tregoning	1971	R. W. Oriel
1929	J. Tregoning	1953	B. Sainsbury	1972	C. Everton
1930	Unknown	1954	R. Smith	1973	C. Everton
1931	L. Prosser	1955	J. Tregoning	1974	R. W. Oriel
1932	T. Jones	1956	A. J. Ford	1975	R. W. Oriel
1933	T. Jones	1957	R. Smith	1976	C. Everton
1934	Unknown	1958	R. W. Oriel	1977	C. Everton
1935	I. Edwards	1959	A. J. Ford	1978	R. W. Oriel
1936	J. Tregoning	1960	C. Everton	1979	R. W. Oriel
1937	B. Gravenor	1961	R. W. Oriel		No further contests
1938	J. Tregoning	1962	R. W. Oriel		

AUSTRALIA
Snooker

1953	W. Simpson	1964	W. Barrie	1975	R. Atkins
1954	W. Simpson	1965	W. Barrie	1976	R. Atkins
1955	E. Pickett	1966	M. Williams	1977	R. Atkins
1956	R. Marshall	1967	M. Williams	1978	K. Burles
1957	W. Simpson	1968	M. Williams	1979	J. Campbell
1958	F. Harris	1969	W. Barrie	1980	W. King
1959	K. Burles	1970	M. Williams	1981	W. King
1960	K. Burles	1971	M. Williams	1982	J. Giannaros
1961	M. Williams	1972	M. Williams	1983	G. Lackenby
1962	W. Barrie	1973	M. Williams	1984	G. Wilkinson
1963	F. Harris	1974	L. Condo		

Billiards

1913	G. B. Shailer	1931	H. L. Goldsmith	1949	R. Marshall
1914-19	No contests	1932	A. Sakzewski	1950	T. Cleary
1920	J. R. Hooper	1933	L. W. Hayes	1951	R. Marshall
1921	G. B. Shailer	1934	L. W. Hayes	1952	R. Marshall
1922	G. B. Shailer	1935	L. W. Hayes	1953	R. Marshall
1923	G. B. Shailer	1936	R. Marshall	1954	R. Marshall
1924	E. Eccles	1937	R. Marshall	1955	R. Marshall
1925	G. B. Shailer	1938	R. Marshall	1956	J. Long
1926	L. W. Hayes	1939	R. Marshall	1957	R. Marshall
1927	L. W. Hayes	1940-45	No contests	1958	T. Cleary
1928	L. W. Hayes	1946	R. Marshall	1959	R. Marshall
1929	A. H. Hearndon	1947	T. Cleary	1960	J. Long
1930	S. Ryan	1948	R. Marshall	1961	R. Marshall

1962	R. Marshall	1970	R. Marshall	1978	G. Ganim Jr
1963	R. Marshall	1971	M. Williams	1979	G. Ganim Jr
1964	J. Long	1972	P. Tarrant	1980	G. Ganim Jr
1965	T. Cleary	1973	P. Tarrant	1981	G. Ganim Jr
1966	T. Cleary	1974	J. Reece	1982	R. Foldvari
1967	J. Long	1975	J. Long	1983	R. Foldvari
1968	J. Long	1976	G. Ganim Jr	1984	F. Humphreys
1969	R. Marshall	1977	G. Ganim Jr	1985	R. Marshall

CANADA
Snooker

1979	J. Wych	1981	R. Chaperon	1984	T. Finstad
1980	Jim Bear	1983	A. Robidoux		

Billiards

1979	E. Fisher	1981	R. Chaperon
1980	S. Holden	1982	R. Chaperon

INDIA
Snooker

1939	P. K. Deb	1956	M. J. M. Lafir	1971	T. Monteiro
1940	P. K. Deb	1957	M. J. M. Lafir	1972	S. Shroff
1941	V. R. Freer	1958	W. Jones	1973	S. Shroff
1942	P. K. Deb	1959	M. J. M. Lafir	1974	M. J. M. Lafir
1943–45	No contests	1960	W. Jones	1974	M. J. M. Lafir
1946	T. A. Selvaraj	1961	M. J. M. Lafir	1975	M. J. M. Lafir
1947	T. Sadler	1962	R. Marshall (Aust)	1976	A. Savur
1948	W. Jones	1963	M. J. M. Lafir	1977	M. J. M. Lafir
1949	T. A. Selvaraj	1964	S. Shroff	1978	A. Savur
1950	F. Edwards (Eng)	1965	S. Shroff	1979	A. Savur
1951	T. A. Selvaraj	1966	T. Monteiro	1980	J. White (Eng)
1952	W. Jones	1967	S. Shroff	1981	G. Parikh
1953	A. L. Driffield (Eng)	1968	S. Mohan	1984	M. G. Jayaran
1954	W. Jones	1969	S. Shroff		
1955	T. A. Selvaraj	1970	S. Shroff		

Billiards

1931	M. M. Begg	1949	T. A. Selvaraj	1965	W. Jones
1932	P. K. Deb	1950	W. Jones	1966	W. Jones
1933	Major Meade	1951	W. Jones	1967	A. Savur
1934	Mg Ba Sin	1952	W. Jones	1968	S. Mohan
1935	P. K. Deb	1953	L. Driffield (Eng)	1969	M. Ferreira
1936	P. K. Deb	1954	W. Jones	1970	S. Mohan
1937	M. M. Begg	1955	W. Jones	1971	S. Mohan
1938	P. K. Deb	1956	C. Hirjee	1972	S. Mohan
1939	P. K. Deb	1957	W. Jones	1973	S. Mohan
1940	S. H. Lyth	1958	C. Hirjee	1974	M. Ferreira
1941	V. R. Freer	1959	T. Cleary (Aust)	1975	G. C. Parikh
1942	V. R. Freer	1960	W. Jones	1976	M. Ferreira
1943–45	No contests	1961	W. Jones	1977	M. J. M. Lafir
1946	C. Hirjee	1962	R. Marshall (Aust)	1978	M. Ferreira
1947	C. Hirjee	1963	W. Jones	1979	M. Ferreira
1948	V. R. Freer	1964	W. Jones	1980	M. Ferreira
				1981	G. Sethi

MALTA
Snooker

1947	L. Galea	1949	L. Galea	1951	W. Asciak
1948	T. B. Oliver	1950	W. Asciak	1952	A. Borg

1953	A. Borg	1964	A. Borg	1975	P. Mifsud
1954	W. Asciak	1965	A. Borg	1976	P. Mifsud
1955	A. Borg	1966	A. Borg	1977	A. Borg
1956	W. Asciak	1967	A. Borg	1978	P. Mifsud
1957	W. Asciak	1968	P. Mifsud	1979	P. Mifsud
1958	W. Asciak	1969	P. Mifsud	1980	J. Grech
1959	A. Borg	1970	P. Mifsud	1981	J. Grech
1960	A. Borg	1971	P. Mifsud	1982	P. Mifsud
1961	A. Borg	1972	P. Mifsud	1983	P. Mifsud
1962	A. Borg	1973	A. Borg	1984	T. Drago
1963	M. Tonna	1974	A. Borg	1985	P. Mifsud

Billiards

1947	V. Micallef	1959	A. Asciak	1972	W. Asciak
1948	*No contest*	1960	A. Asciak	1973	P. Mifsud
1949	E. Bartolo	1961	A. Borg	1974	P. Mifsud
1950	W. Asciak	1962	J. Bartolo	1975	P. Mifsud
1951	W. Asciak	1963	J. Bartolo	1976	P. Mifsud
1952	W. Asciak	1964	W. Asciak	1977	P. Mifsud
1953	W. Asciak	1965	A. Asciak	1978	J. Grech
1954	W. Asciak	1966	A. Asciak	1979	P. Mifsud
1955	W. Asciak	1967	A. Asciak	1980	J. Grech
1956	W. Asciak	1969	P. Mifsud	*1981*	*No contest*
1957	A. Asciak	1970	W. Asciak	1982	V. Ellul
1958	A. Asciak	1971	P. Mifsud	1983	J. Grech

NEW ZEALAND
Snooker

1945	S. Moses	1959	W. Thomas	1973	W. Hill
1946	J. Munro	1960	T. Yesberg	1974	K. Tristram
1947	W. Thompson	1961	F. Franks	1975	K. Tristram
1948	L. Stout	1962	K. Murphy	1976	D. Kwok
1949	L. Stout	1963	W. Harcourt	1977	D. Meredith
1950	L. Stout	1964	T. Yesberg	1978	D. Meredith
1951	N. Lewis	1965	L. Napper	1979	D. Meredith
1952	L. Stout	1966	L. Napper	1980	D. O'Kane
1953	L. Stout	1967	R. Flutey	1981	G. Kwok
1954	R. Franks	1968	L. Napper	1982	D. Kwok
1955	L. Stout	1969	L. Glozier	1983	D. Kwok
1956	L. Stout	1970	K. Tristram	1984	D. Kwok
1957	W. Harcourt	1971	B. J. Bennett		
1958	W. Harcourt	1972	N. Stockman		

Billiards

1908	J. Ryan	1932	C. Mason	1956	A. Twohill
1909	*No contest*	1933	A. Albertson	1957	A. Twohill
1910	F. Lovelock	1934	H. McLean	1958	A. Albertson
1911	F. Lovelock	1935	L. Holdsworth	1959	A. Twohill
1912	H. Valentine	1936	S. Moses	1960	W. Harcourt
1913	H. Valentine	1937	S. Moses	1961	A. Albertson
1914	N. Lynch	1938	L. Holdsworth	1962	W. Harcourt
1915	W. E. Warren	1939	R. Carrick	1963	H. C. Robinson
1916	H. Siedeberg	1940	S. Moses	1964	T. Yesberg
1917	H. Siedeberg	1941	R. Carrick	1965	L. Napper
1918	W. E. Warren	1942	R. Carrick	1966	A. Twohill
1919	H. Siedeberg	1943	A. Albertson	1967	A. Twohill
1920	W. E. Warren	1944	S. Moses	1968	A. Twohill
1921	H. Siedeberg	1945	J. Shepherd	1969	E. Simmons
1922	E. V. Roberts	1946	R. Carrick	1970	L. Napper
1923	E. V. Roberts	1947	C. Peek	1971	W. Harcourt
1924	R. Fredotovich	1948	R. Carrick	1972	B. Kirkness
1925	C. Mason	1949	R. Carrick	1973	H. C. Robinson
1926	E. V. Roberts	1950	R. Carrick	1974	H. C. Robinson
1927	E. V. Roberts	1951	R. Carrick	1975	T. Yesberg
1928	A. Bowie	1952	L. Stout	1976	H. C. Robinson
1929	L. Stout	1953	A. Twohill	1977	B. Kirkness
1930	W. E. Hackett	1954	A. Twohill	1978	B. Kirkness
1931	A. Duncan	1955	A. Twohill	1979	R. Adams

1980	D. Meredith	**1982**	D. Meredith	**1984**	D. Meredith
1981	D. Meredith	**1983**	D. Meredith		

SOUTH AFRICA

Snooker

1937	A. Prior	**1956**	F. Walker	**1970**	J. van Rensburg
1938	A. H. Ashby	**1957**	J. van Rensburg	**1971**	M. Francisco
1939	A. Prior	**1958**	R. Walker	**1972**	J. van Rensburg
1940–45	*No contests*	**1959**	M. Francisco	**1973**	J. van Rensburg
1946	F. Walker	**1960**	P. Mans Jr	**1974**	S. Francisco
1947	*No contest*	**1961**	J. van Rensburg	**1975**	M. Francisco
1948	F. Walker	**1962**	J. van Rensburg	*1976*	*No contest*
1949	E. Kerr	**1963**	J. van Rensburg	**1977**	S. Francisco
1950	T. G. Rees	**1964**	M. Francisco	**1978**	J. van Niekerk
1951	T. G. Rees	**1965**	M. Francisco	**1979**	F. Ellis
1952	T. G. Rees	**1966**	M. Francisco	**1980**	F. Ellis
1953	J. van Rensburg	**1967**	J. van Rensburg	**1981**	P. Francisco
1954	J. van Rensburg	**1968**	S. Francisco	**1982**	P. Francisco
1955	J. van Rensburg	**1969**	S. Francisco	**1983**	P. Francisco

Billiards

1920	Sgt Bruyns	**1948**	P. G. Kempen	**1966**	M. Francisco
1921	A. Prior	**1949**	T. G. Rees	**1967**	J. van Rensburg
1922	A. Prior	**1950**	T. G. Rees	**1968**	M. Francisco
1923	*No contest*	**1951**	I. Drapin	**1969**	M. Francisco
1924	A. Prior	**1952**	T. G. Rees	**1970**	M. Francisco
1925	P. Rutledge	**1953**	T. G. Rees	**1971**	M. Francisco
1926	A. Prior	**1954**	F. Walker	**1972**	S. Francisco
1927	A. Percival	**1955**	F. Walker	**1973**	S. Francisco
1928	P. Rutledge	**1956**	G. Povall	**1974**	M. Francisco
1929–30	*No contests*	**1957**	F. Walker	**1975**	S. Francisco
1931	A. Prior	**1958**	F. Walker	*1976*	*No contest*
1932–36	*No contests*	**1959**	M. Francisco	**1977**	M. Francisco
1937	A. M. Burke	**1960**	R. Walker	**1978**	C. van Dijk
1938	A. Prior	**1961**	M. Francisco	**1979**	C. van Dijk
1939	A. Prior	**1962**	M. Francisco	**1980**	C. van Dijk
1940–45	*No contests*	**1963**	M. Francisco	**1981**	P. Spence
1946	P. G. Kempen	**1964**	M. Francisco	**1983**	P. Francisco
1947	*No contest*	**1965**	M. Francisco		

SRI LANKA

Snooker

1948	M. J. M. Lafir	**1959**	M. J. M. Lafir	**1970**	N. J. Rahim
1949	M. M. Faiz	**1960**	M. J. M. Lafir	*1971*	*No contest*
1950	M. J. M. Lafir	**1961**	M. J. M. Lafir	**1972**	N. J. Rahim
1951	M. S. A. Hassan	**1962**	M. J. M. Lafir	**1973**	M. J. M. Lafir
1952	M. J. M. Lafir	**1963**	M. J. M. Izzath	**1974**	*Abandoned*
1953	M. J. M. Lafir	**1964**	M. J. M. Lafir	**1975**	N. A. Rahim
1954	M. J. M. Lafir	**1965**	M. J. M. Lafir	**1976**	M. S. U. Mohideen
1955	M. J. M. Lafir	**1966**	M. J. M. Lafir	**1977**	M. S. U. Mohideen
1956	M. J. M. Lafir	**1967**	N. J. Rahim	**1978**	N. A. Rahim
1957	M. J. M. Lafir	*1968*	*No contest*	**1981**	J. W. H. Boteju
1958	M. J. M. Lafir	**1969**	M. J. M. Lafir	**1982**	J. A. Wahid

Billiards

1948	A. C. Cambal	**1959**	M. J. M. Lafir	**1972**	M. J. M. Lafir
1949	M. J. M. Lafir	**1960**	M. J. M. Lafir	**1973**	M. J. M. Lafir
1950	M. J. M. Lafir	**1961**	M. J. M. Lafir	**1974**	S. Shaharwardi
1951	M. J. M. Lafir	**1962**	M. J. M. Lafir	**1975**	M. S. U. Mohideen
1952	M. J. M. Lafir	**1963**	M. H. M. Mujahid	**1976**	W. Weerasinghe
1953	M. J. M. Lafir	**1964**	M. J. M. Lafir	**1977**	W. Weerasinghe
1954	A. C. Cambal	**1966**	M. J. M. Lafir	**1978**	J. W. H. Boteju
1955	T. A. Selvaraj	**1967**	J. K. Bakshani	**1979**	W. Weerasinghe
1956	T. A. Selvaraj	**1969**	M. J. M. Lafir	**1981**	J. W. H. Boteju
1957	M. J. M. Lafir	**1970**	M. J. M. Lafir		

ZIMBABWE
Snooker

1981	A. Thomson	1982	A. Thomson	1983	J. Daly

NB *No billiards records*

BRITISH JUNIOR CHAMPIONSHIP
Under-16 Snooker

1944	G. Owen	1957	P. Shelley	1971	J. Mills
1945	R. Baker	1958	D. Bend	1972	J. Mills
1946	D. Thomas	1959	J. Doyle	1973	P. Bardsley
1947	M. Knapp	1960	N. Cripps	1974	S. Holroyd
1948	R. Williams	*1961*	*No contest*	1975	M. Hallett
1949	R. Williams	1962	J. Virgo	1976	W. Jones
	D. Lewis	1963	J. Hollis	1977	J. White
1950	M. Owen	1964	D. Clinton	1978	D. Adds
1951	M. Owen	*1965*	*No contest*	1979	A. Pyle
1952	M. Wildman	1966	J. Terry	1980	T. Whitthread
1953	J. Board	*1967*	*No contest*	1981	C. Hamson
1954	D. Bond	1968	E. Stone	1982	S. Ventham
1955	P. Shelley	1969	P. Hughes	1983	S. Hendry
1956	A. Hart	1970	W. Thorne	1984	B. Morgan
				1985	B. Bunn

Under-19 Snooker

1949	A. Kemp	1961	I. Rees	1973	W. Thorne
1950	J. Carney	1962	A. Matthews	1974	A. Knowles
1951	R. Williams	1963	A. Matthews	1975	E. Hughes
1952	C. Wilson	1964	J. Fisher	1976	I. Williamson
1953	C. Wilson	1965	J. Virgo	1977	I. Williamson
1954	M. Wildman	1966	J. Hollis	1978	T. Meo
1955	W. McGivern	*1967*	*No contest*	1979	J. O'Boye
1956	E. Sinclair	1968	J. Maughan	1980	T. Murphy
1957	H. Burns	1969	J. Terry	1981	D. Reynolds
1958	W. West	1970	J. Terry	1982	N. Foulds
1959	D. Root	1971	J. Johnson	1983	M. Thompson
1960	D. Bend	1972	A. Knowles	1984	M. Clark
				1985	W. Rendle

Under-16 Billiards

1922	W. Donaldson	1940	B. Smith	1969	P. Bardsley
1923	W. Leigh	*1941-47*	*No contests*	1970	W. Thorne
1924	L. Steeples	1948	R. Williams	1971	P. Bardsley
1925	S. Lee	1949	R. Williams	1972	P. Bardsley
1926	R. Gartland	1950	M. Owen	1973	T. Wells
1927	R. Gartland	1951	E. Parry	1974	P. Allan
1928	R. L. Bennett	1952	M. Wildman	1975	S. McNamara
1929	F. Davis	1953	C. Everton	1976	D. Bonney
1930	H. J. Bennett	1954	H. Burns	1977	D. Bonney
1931	C. Desbottes	1955	D. Deakes	1978	K. Walsh
1932	D. Hawkes	1956	C. Dean	1979	A. Pyle
1933	Unknown	1957	P. Shelley	1980	K. Walsh
1934	W. Swinhoe	1958	P. Morgan	1981	D. Presgrave
1935	D. Cruikshank	1959	P. Morgan	1982	S. Naisby
1936	D. Cruikshank	1960	A. Matthews	1983	P. Gilchrist
1937	D. Curson	1961	B. Whitehead	1984	C. Rowntree
1938	J. Hamilton	*1962-67*	*No contests*	1985	M. Russell
1939	R. Smith	1968	C. Williamson		

Under-19 Billiards

1949	G. Toner	1960	D. Bend	1974	T. Wells
1950	R. Williams	1961	P. Morgan	1975	E. Hughes
1951	R. Williams	1962	A. Matthews	1976	S. Davis
1952	J. Sinclair	1963	A. Matthews	1977	I. Williamson
1953	M. Wildman	*1964-67*	*No contests*	1978	I. Williamson
1954	M. Wildman	1968	D. Taylor	1979	M. Garvey
1955	D. Scott	1969	D. Burgess	1980	G. Charville
1956	C. Everton	1970	J. Terry	1981	S. Hawkins
1957	C. Myers	1971	W. Thorne	1982	R. Marshall
1958	C. Marks	1972	W. Thorne	1983	S. Naisby
1959	P. Morgan	1973	W. Thorne	1984	S. Naisby
				1985	S. Naisby

HOME INTERNATIONAL CHAMPIONSHIP

1969
England beat Wales 10-8

1970–71
England beat Wales 14-4; England beat Ireland 14-4; Wales beat Ireland 17-1

	W	D	L	For	Agst	Pts
England	2	0	0	28	8	4
Wales	1	0	1	21	15	2
Ireland	0	0	2	5	31	0

1971–72
England beat Scotland 10-8; England beat Ireland 14-4; England drew with Wales 9-9; Scotland drew with Wales 9-9; Scotland beat Ireland 12-6; Wales beat Ireland 13-5

	W	D	L	For	Agst	Pts
England	2	1	0	33	21	5
Wales	1	2	0	31	23	4
Scotland	1	1	1	29	25	3
Ireland	0	0	3	15	39	0

1972–73
England beat Scotland 16-2; England beat Ireland 13-5; England drew with Wales 9-9; Wales beat Ireland 15-3; Wales beat Scotland 10-8; Scotland beat Ireland 13-5

	W	D	L	For	Agst	Pts
England	2	1	0	38	16	5
Wales	2	1	0	32	22	5
Scotland	1	0	2	23	31	2
Ireland	0	0	3	15	41	0

1973–74
England beat Wales 14-4; England beat Scotland 11-7; England drew with Ireland 9-9; Wales beat Ireland 11-7; Wales beat Scotland 14-4; Ireland drew with Scotland 9-9

	W	D	L	For	Agst	Pts
England	2	1	0	34	20	5
Wales	2	0	1	29	25	4
Ireland	0	2	1	25	29	2
Scotland	0	1	2	20	34	1

1974–75
Wales beat Ireland 12-6; Wales beat Scotland 14-4; Wales beat England 10-8; England beat Scotland 12-6; England beat Ireland 11-7; Scotland beat Ireland 12-6

	W	D	L	For	Agst	Pts
Wales	3	0	0	36	18	6
England	2	0	1	31	23	4
Scotland	1	0	2	22	32	2
Ireland	0	0	3	19	35	0

1975–76
Wales beat Ireland 13-5; Wales beat Scotland 11-7; Wales beat England 11-7; England beat Ireland 13-5; England beat Scotland 12-6; Scotland beat Ireland 12-6

	W	D	L	For	Agst	Pts
Wales	3	0	0	35	19	6
England	2	0	1	32	22	4
Scotland	1	0	2	25	29	2
Ireland	0	0	3	16	38	0

1976–77
England beat Ireland 13-5; England beat Wales 12-6; England beat Scotland 11-7; Wales beat Scotland 14-4; Wales beat Ireland 13-5; Scotland beat Ireland 12-6

	W	D	L	For	Agst	Pts
England	3	0	0	36	18	6
Wales	2	0	1	33	21	4
Scotland	1	0	2	23	31	2
Ireland	0	0	3	16	38	0

1977–78
Wales beat England 10-8; Wales beat Scotland 12-6; Wales beat Ireland 15-3; England beat Scotland 10-8; England beat Ireland 11-7; Scotland beat Ireland 12-6

	W	D	L	For	Agst	Pts
Wales	3	0	0	37	17	6
England	2	0	1	29	25	4
Scotland	1	0	2	26	28	2
Ireland	0	0	3	16	38	0

1978–79
England beat Isle of Man 15-3; England beat Rep. of Ireland 14-4; England beat Scotland 16-2; England beat Wales 10-7; Wales beat Isle of Man 16-2; Wales beat Rep. of Ireland 11-7; Wales drew with Scotland 9-9; Scotland beat Isle of Man 15-3; Scotland drew with Rep. of Ireland 9-9; Rep. of Ireland beat Isle of Man 15-3

	W	D	L	For	Agst	Pts
England	4	0	0	55	16	8
Wales	2	1	1	43	28	5
Scotland	1	2	1	35	37	4
Rep. of Ireland	1	1	2	34	38	3
Isle of Man	0	0	4	11	61	0

1979–80
England beat N. Ireland 16-2; England beat Isle of Man 16-2; England beat Rep. of Ireland 11-7; England beat Scotland 10-8; England beat Wales 10-7; Wales beat N. Ireland 12-6; Wales beat Isle of Man 16-2; Wales beat Scotland 11-7; Wales drew with Rep. of Ireland 9-9; Rep. of Ireland beat Scotland 10-8; Rep. of Ireland drew with Northern Ireland 9-9; Rep. of Ireland beat Isle of Man 12-6; Scotland beat Isle of Man 13-5; Scotland beat N. Ireland 10-8; N. Ireland beat Isle of Man 14-4

	W	D	L	For	Agst	Pts
England	5	0	0	63	26	10
Wales	3	1	1	55	34	7
Rep. of Ireland	2	2	1	47	43	6
Scotland	2	0	3	46	44	4
N. Ireland	1	1	3	39	51	3
Isle of Man	0	0	5	19	71	0

1980-81

England beat N. Ireland 15-3; Scotland beat Isle of Man 14-4; Wales beat N. Ireland 10-8; England beat Isle of Man 15-3; Wales beat Scotland 12-6; Rep. of Ireland beat N. Ireland 11-7; N. Ireland beat Isle of Man 12-6; Wales beat Rep. of Ireland 14-4; Rep. of Ireland drew with Scotland 9-9; Wales beat Isle of Man 15-3; England beat Rep. of Ireland 12-6; Scotland drew with N. Ireland 9-9; Rep. of Ireland beat Isle of Man 13-5; England beat Scotland 14-4; Wales beat England 10-7

	W	D	L	For	Agst	Pts
Wales	5	0	0	61	28	10
England	4	0	1	63	26	8
Rep. of Ireland	2	1	2	43	47	5
Scotland	1	2	2	42	48	4
N. Ireland	1	1	3	39	51	3
Isle of Man	0	0	5	21	69	0

1981-82

N. Ireland drew with Rep. of Ireland 9-9; Scotland beat Isle of Man 13-5; England beat Isle of Man 17-1; Wales beat N. Ireland 11-7; England beat Rep. of Ireland 11-7; Wales beat Scotland 13-5; Wales beat Rep. of Ireland 12-6; England beat N. Ireland 10-8; Rep. of Ireland drew with Isle of Man 9-9; Scotland beat N. Ireland 10-8; Wales beat Isle of Man 15-3; Rep. of Ireland beat Scotland 10-8; Scotland beat England 10-8; N. Ireland beat Isle of Man 10-8; England beat Wales 8-7

	W	D	L	For	Agst
*Wales	4	0	0	58	29
*England	3	0	1	54	33
Scotland	3	0	2	46	44
Rep. of Ireland	1	2	2	41	49
N. Ireland	1	1	3	42	48
Isle of Man	0	1	4	26	64

Not including the Wales v England match, which was abandoned at the point where Wales were assured of retaining the championship

1982-83

Wales beat Isle of Man 16-2; England beat Isle of Man 12-6; England drew with Scotland 9-9; Wales beat N. Ireland 10-8; Rep. of Ireland drew with N. Ireland 9-9; Wales beat Scotland 12-6; Isle of Man drew with Scotland 9-9; England beat Rep. of Ireland 11-7; Rep. of Ireland beat Isle of Man 15-3; England beat N. Ireland 14-4; N. Ireland beat Scotland 12-6; Wales beat Rep. of Ireland 11-7; Scotland beat Rep. of Ireland 11-7; *Wales beat England 9-8; N. Ireland beat Isle of Man 15-3

	W	D	L	For	Agst
*Wales	4	0	0	49	23
*England	3	1	0	46	26
N. Ireland	2	1	2	53	37
Scotland	1	2	2	41	49
Rep. of Ireland	1	1	3	44	46
Isle of Man	0	1	4	26	66

Not including Wales v England match which was curtailed when Wales led 9-8, at which point they could not be overtaken

1983-84

Wales beat Scotland 13-5; Isle of Man beat Rep. of Ireland 11-7; England beat Rep. of Ireland 13-5; Scotland drew with N. Ireland 9-9; Wales beat N. Ireland 13-5; Rep. of Ireland beat N. Ireland 10-8; Scotland beat Isle of Man 11-7; England beat Isle of Man 14-4; England beat N. Ireland 13-5; Wales beat Rep. of Ireland 14-4; Wales beat Isle of Man 10-8; England beat Scotland 11-7; N. Ireland beat Isle of Man 13-5; Wales beat England 10-7; Scotland beat Rep. of Ireland 10-8

	W	D	L	For	Agst
Wales	5	0	0	60	29
England	4	0	1	58	31
Scotland	2	1	2	42	48
N. Ireland	1	1	3	40	50
Isle of Man	1	0	4	35	55
Rep. of Ireland	1	0	4	34	56

1984-85

Rep. of Ireland drew with Scotland 9-9; England beat N. Ireland 13-5; Wales beat Isle of Man 15-3; England drew with Scotland 9-9; N. Ireland beat Rep. of Ireland 12-6; Scotland drew with Wales 9-9; N. Ireland beat Isle of Man 11-7; England beat Isle of Man 12-6; England beat Rep. of Ireland 11-7; Scotland beat Isle of Man 15-3; Wales beat N. Ireland 11-7; Wales beat England 10-8; Rep. of Ireland beat Isle of Man 12-6; Scotland beat N. Ireland 10-8; Wales beat Rep. of Ireland 14-4

	W	D	L	For	Agst
Wales	4	0	1	59	31
England	3	1	1	53	37
Scotland	2	0	3	52	38
N. Ireland	2	3	0	37	67
Rep. of Ireland	1	3	1	38	52
Isle of Man	0	5	0	25	53

PONTINS

Pontins instigated a week-long snooker extravaganza at their Prestatyn holiday village in 1974. Entry was open to anyone on the camp and, with a substantial points start, the amateurs competed against the invited professionals in a big-money Open. So successful was it that other holiday camp companies – Warners is one – have also staged snooker weeks but Pontins Spring Festival of Snooker holds a unique place in the calendar.

Conditions of play vary enormously between the set-piece arenas in the ballroom and the hurly-burly of the camp's billiard room but the Open and its various side events like the women's and junior attract a thousand entries. Pontins are also hosts, in the autumn, to the Home International Championship, alongside which they run an amateurs only tournament.

	Professional	Open		Professional	Open
1974	R. Reardon	D. Mountjoy*	1980	J. Virgo	W. Thorne
1975	R. Reardon	R. Reardon	1980**	A. Higgins	Dennis Taylor
1976	R. Reardon	D. Mountjoy*	1981	T. Griffiths	J. Hargreaves*
1977	J. Spencer	A. Higgins	1982	S. Davis	J. Parrott*
1978	R. Reardon	S. Davis*	1983	D. Mountjoy	T. Griffiths
1979	D. Mountjoy	S. Davis	1984	W. Thorne	N. Foulds
			1985	T. Griffiths	J. Chambers

**held at Camber Sands*
Amateur

FIXTURES 1985-86

19-22 September　　　LANGS SCOTTISH MASTERS
at Hospitality Inn, Glasgow
Box office: 041 332 3311

23 September-6 October　GOYA MATCHROOM TROPHY
at Trentham Hall, Stoke
Box office: 0782 657341

19-27 October　　　ROTHMANS GRAND PRIX
at the Hexagon, Reading
Box office: 0734 591591

16 November-1 December CORAL UK OPEN
at Preston Guild Hall
Box office: 0772 21721

6-15 December　　　HOFMEISTER WORLD DOUBLES
CHAMPIONSHIP
at Derngate Centre, Northampton
Box office: 0604 24811

3-12 January　　　MERCANTILE CREDIT CLASSIC
at Spectrum Arena, Warrington
Box office: 0925 813700

26 January-2 February　BENSON AND HEDGES MASTERS
at Wembley Conference Centre
Box office: 01 902 1234

16 February-2 March　DULUX BRITISH OPEN
at Assembly Rooms, Derby
Box office: 0332 369311

8-13 April　　　BENSON AND HEDGES IRISH
MASTERS
at Goffs, Kill, Co. Kildare
Box office: by post to venue

19 April-5 May　　EMBASSY WORLD PROFESSIONAL
CHAMPIONSHIP
at Crucible Theatre, Sheffield
Box office: by post to Box Office,
Crucible Theatre, 55 Norfolk Street,
Sheffield S1 1DA

*Although correct at time of going to press, all dates are subject to
alteration.*